BETWEEN RACE AND EMPIRE

African-Americans and Cubans
before the Cuban Revolution

BETWEEN RACE AND EMPIRE

African-Americans and Cubans before the Cuban Revolution

Edited by
Lisa Brock and Digna Castañeda Fuertes

Temple University Press

Philadelphia

TEMPLE UNIVERSITY PRESS, PHILADELPHIA 19122
Copyright © 1998 by Temple University. All rights reserved
Printed in the United States of America

⊗ The paper used in this book meets the requirements of the American
National Standard for Information Sciences—Permanence of Paper for
Printed Library Materials, ANSI Z39.48–1984

Text design by Gary Gore

Library of Congress Cataloging-in-Publication Data

Between race and empire : African-Americans and Cubans before the
  Cuban Revolution / edited by Lisa Brock and Digna Castañeda Fuertes.
      p.   cm.
    Includes bibliographical references and index.
    ISBN 1–56639–586–0 (cloth : alk. paper). — ISBN 1-56639-587-9
  (pbk. : alk. paper)
    1. Afro-Americans—Relations with Cubans. 2. United States—Race
  relations. 3. Cuba—Race relations. 4. Afro-Americans—Civil
  rights—History. 5. Blacks—Civil rights—Cuba—History. 6. Cuba—
  Civilization—American influences.   I. Brock, Lisa.   II. Castañeda
  Fuertes, Digna.
  E185.61.F49   1998
  972.9106'4—dc21   97–20278

In memory of
Carmen Montejo Arrechea,
Chizuru Brock,
and
Terrence Gaston Johnson

CONTENTS

Photographs follow page 128

ACKNOWLEDGMENTS

Imagining this book was not easy. There remain formidable barriers between Cuba and the United States, and crosscultural and transnational histories are still in their infancy. Because of such issues, many of our colleagues thought us crazy for daring to envision such an anthology; "dreamin' too much of the impossible can make you mental," as one of our grandmothers used to say. Yet there were those who, from the beginning, did not think us "mental." They believed in the project and gave it their unconditional support. Foremost among the faithful was Otis Cunningham, who not only helped develop the paradigms that ultimately shaped the book but saw it as his job all along the way to be our intellectual buoy and troubleshooter and to chase away momentary doubts and anxiety. It is to him that we owe our deepest gratitude.

Two others shared early confidence in the collection. We owe a heartfelt thanks to Cuban scholar Louis Pérez Jr. and senior acquisitions editor Doris Braendel of Temple University Press. It was Lou, upon reading the first prospectus, who went out of his way to introduce it and us to Doris. We are very appreciative for Lou's initial support (we needed it) and for Doris's belief in the importance of nonelite international history and her bottomless reservoir of patience.

Others offered a tangible support that only those with special knowledge and skills can. Most prominent among them is our friend Francine Cronshaw, who as a Latin American historian and founder of East Mountain Editing Services in Tijeras, New Mexico, spent untold hours translating all of the Cuban contributions. She made them read as well in English as they did in Spanish and never really charged us what she could have for her time. She also undertook the painstaking but absorbing endeavor of researching and translating the Cuban poetry in Carmen Gómez García's chapter. To her we owe a singular and personal debt. (All other translations were done by the authors themselves.) A special thanks is also owed to Elizabeth Johns, our copy editor, who worked wonders with our manuscript.

We are also obliged to Raúl Rodrígues, an instructor of U.S. culture at the University of Havana, and Eduardo Lourenzo, a teacher at Cuba's Pedagogical Institute. Along with Reynaldo Verrie, they are, by far, the best damn simultaneous interpreters in the Americas. Raúl, especially, was always willing to work gatherings between us and our Cuban contributors. Moreover, during two summers, scholars from the United States attended conferences sponsored by the Radical Philosophy Association (RPA) at the University of Havana and participated on panels focused on themes in this book. It was Raúl, Eddie, and Reynaldo who translated for us in what sometimes were very complex and heated discussions on race and history. The density of their understanding of current issues in the United States and Cuba as well as black discourse cannot be overstated. In addition, Clif Durand of the RPA and past deans of faculty at the University of Havana, Antonio Toledo Garela and Teresa Muñoz, deserve a warm thank you for providing Raúl, Eddie, and Reynaldo and the forums for such dialogue to take place.

Kudos to photographer Esther Parada, who gave freely of her time and expertise to digitize the images included in this volume; we took many of the photos ourselves, and they needed more than a bit of touching up. We also express our sincere appreciation to Sonia Baez Hernandes, our research assistant; her multilingual and organizational abilities were crucial in the final stages of this book.

Because few people had written before about black American and Cuban relations, we depended on colleagues (many of whom we did not yet know) to recommend persons they thought able and possibly willing to develop essays for this anthology. Many writers, historians, sociologists, anthropologists, artists, musicologists, and ministers, all of them very busy, offered their time, their contacts, and their encouragement. We could not have completed this project without them. They are Robin D. G. Kelley, Gerald Poyo, Danny Duncan Collum, Aline Helg, Jean Stubbs, Pedro Pérez Sarduy, Felix Masud-Piloto, Adrianne Andrews, John Holway, Marta Moreno Vega, Rev. Jeremiah Wright Jr., Mark Solomon, Barbara Ransby, Samuel Floyd, Rosemari Mealy, Nancy Morejón, Geraldo Mosquera, Janet Bruce Campbell, Willard Gatewood, Johnetta Cole, Bruce Dixon, Donn Rogosin, Dominique René de Lerma, David Roediger, Max Salazar, and Robert Heuer. Probably there are others whose deeds, while important, have escaped us; to them we offer our apologies. To all we extend our thanks.

We are also beholden to the numerous friends and organizations who made our staying in contact possible, often when communication was extremely restricted between the two countries. Their support was indispensable. Some put their e-mail addresses and fax numbers at our disposal, and others served as postal couriers. To Karen Wald, Walter Turner, Assata Shakur, Gayle Reed, Debra Evenson, Maxine Orris, Milagros Martínez, Joy James, Marguerite Horberg, Harry Targ, and to Orlaida Cabrera, director of the North American section of the Instituto Cubano de Amistad con los Pueblos (a Cuban nongovernmental organization) and the Cuban Interests Section in Washington, D.C.: words cannot adequately express our appreciation. In this regard, an extra special thanks is due the household of María Josefa Díaz and María Josefina Vigil, in Lawton, Ciudad de la Habana, who permitted us to use their telephone as regularly as if it were our own.

Both of our deans of faculty and our academic institutions were very supportive of our project, which made all the difference in the world. They gave us release time from teaching and access to financial resources for travel and research. They are Dean Rubén Zardoya of the University of Havana, Dean Carol Becker of the School of the Art Institute of Chicago (SAIC), and members of the Faculty Enrichment Grant team at SAIC. We hope we have made them proud.

Many institutions and individuals graciously made available their collections, their know-how, and their stories. We are eternally grateful. The New York Public Library's Schomburg Center for Research in Black Culture in Harlem; the University of New Mexico Library in Albuquerque; the Cincinnati Public Library in Cincinnati, Ohio; the José Martí National Library, the Instituto de Literaturas y Lingüísticas, and the Archivo Nacional de Cuba in Havana; Northwestern University Library in Evanston, Illinois; SAIC's John M. Flaxman Library; the Carter G. Woodson, George Pullman, Martin Luther King, and Humbolt Park public libraries in Chicago—all, at one time or another, served as sites of research. Specifically, the Vivian G. Harsh Collection of the Carter G. Woodson Chicago Public Library was particularly rich in resources and its staff especially helpful. In addition, some very special people who trusted in the project went out of their way to locate and share sources and useful images. They are Sheila Scott of the *Baltimore Afro-American;* Larry Lester, affiliated with the Negro Leagues Baseball Museum; Robert Chrisman of *Black Scholar;* retired photographer Gordon Anderson; Afro-Cuban music scholar Max Salazar; Sandra Levinson of the Center for Cuban Studies; Jim Huffman of the Photo and Prints Division at the Schomburg Center; and Susan Greenbaum and Paul Camp

of the University of South Florida. A very warm and special thanks to retired baseball player Minnie Minoso for sharing the story of his life in baseball with us, and to the anonymous readers for their very helpful comments
on the manuscript for this book.

Many family members, friends, and students nurtured us with large
and small acts of kindness. It is, in fact, difficult to isolate the multiple and
complex ways that associates, extended family, and support staff buttress
and promote the evolution of a book. From photocopying and typing, to
driving us to a library, to sharing borrowing privileges, to showing us the
site of an old baseball field, to teaching one of our classes, to child care, to
feeding us, to housing us, to making sure our car ran in Havana, to cleaning our homes, to listening to our woes—in myriad large and small ways
they made our lives manageable and kept us sane. To Toussaint Brock Cunningham; Lucille Graham; James E. Brock; Marc Chery; Zeinabu Davis;
Schyler Cunningham; Mildred, Willie, and Camille Williamson; Susan
Avila; Charlene Mitchell; Willie Mae Williams; Adjoa Aiyetoro; Kelechi,
Sharon, and Josina Cunningham; Ruby Pattillo; Lorene, Michele, and
Loren Johnson; Melina Pappademos; Alexander Pantalion; Jim and
Michele Patton; Cheryl Howard; Burton Flemming; Kevin Thompson;
Shanna Linn; and the liberal arts staff at the School of the Art Institute of
Chicago, and to our students, thank you!

Our final and surely fullest gratitude is for our contributors, who are
the young and old, male and female, Cuban and North American scholars
who responded to our call. We want to applaud them for their hard work,
and their perseverance and faith in the connectedness of the Cuban and
African-American stories. This book took years to complete, and we are
very grateful that they stuck it out with us. All of the essays are superb. We
hope they are as pleased as we are.

BETWEEN RACE AND EMPIRE

African-Americans and Cubans
before the Cuban Revolution

Introduction

Between Race and Empire

LISA BROCK ·

Calculating Revelations

When I was young my grandmother played the numbers. She consulted dream books to enumerate her night visions and counting books to calculate their odds. She would work up sequences of numbers and list them in long single columns. With the concentration of a statistician and using a math that was clearly beyond my reach, she would add, subtract, and formulate new combinations of figures. At the moment in which it was right, the number would reveal itself to her and she would quietly say, "That's it; that's the number that is surely going to hit." And it often did.

I wish I had my grandmother's ability to divine what was hidden in the future. I might have foreseen the academic and ideological challenges that preparing an anthology on Cuba and African-Americans would entail. I might have realized that the centering of two peoples not in state power *across* nation-state boundaries would come to feel like a mountain-moving task, that gathering the contributors to unravel the threads of this connected historical saga would be difficult. Layers of racism and imperialism have marginalized both sets of peoples, not only in their own societies and in the region but also within their academies. In addition, conventional Western scholarship has been bound by the questions and contexts of nation-states. It was difficult, then, to locate Cuban and North American intellectuals willing and able to break away from their traditional national moorings.

Yet, we—the editors of and contributors to this collection—knew there existed a rich and diverse history of unrecognized linkages between African-Americans and Cubans. Inklings of them appear in the biographical footnotes of Langston Hughes, in the liner notes of Dizzy Gillespie records, in the political proclamations of Frederick Douglass, and in bold Havana headlines condemning the treatment of performer Josephine Baker. It became increasingly clear to us that these black, mulatto, Latin American, West Indian, and Latino peasants, sharecroppers, ministers, immigrants, artists, workers, and socialists had in fact centered themselves; these men and women had consistently subverted the agendas of their nations' elites and created a universe in which they cohabited. Within the dual but overlapping struggles against racism and imperialism, a common space had been created. A body of nonelite pan-African *and* pan-American political, social, and cultural relations evolved. Our task was to explore how and where these occurred and to wager, like my grandmother, that revelations would be forthcoming.

Thirty-eight years of the U.S. bloackade against Cuba and a general hostility toward the island have raised the odds, however. Easy communication between Digna Castañeda and me was nearly impossible during most of the time we were developing this book. Exchanging telephone calls, faxes, and e-mail messages was extremely difficult, so much so that we were forced to book calls and send faxes through third countries. Things seemed to get worse after February 1996, when Cuba shot down a plane belonging to a Cuban-American group called Brothers to the Rescue. According to the Havana government, this Miami-based anti-Castro organization had persistently violated Cuban airspace to engage in provocative activities (dropping leaflets, encouraging people to defect), and had been warned repeatedly to stop. Cuba had also petitioned the U.S. government to halt this illegal activity, but Washington evidently took no action. While the United Nations International Civil Aviation Organization (ICAO) condemned Cuba's downing of the ostensibly civilian airplane, it also instructed the United States to warn its citizens against using civilian aircraft for noncivilian purposes (international espionage, for example). The U.S. government, on the other hand, responded with talk of retribution.

By mid 1996, however, the United States relaxed a policy that had denied U.S. telephone companies full access to Cuba, and new cables were laid between Cuba and the mainland. Finally, after nearly thirty years, placing a call became less difficult; e-mail linkages were established for the first time. But perversely, the U.S. government at the same time took steps that made travel to Cuba more complicated. Beginning in October 1995, every U.S. citizen desiring to travel to Cuba had to apply for a license directly from the U.S. Treasury Department. Sometimes one would receive a license, sometimes one would not; sometimes there would be no response at all until after the projected departure date. This obstacle obviously hindered Digna Castañeda's and my ability to meet face to face. Before this, researchers, educators, journalists, and family members had not been required to apply for a license. They fell within categories established under a policy initiated by President Jimmy Carter, which allowed for family visits and the free exchange of ideas and information. While Cuba was still off limits for American tourists, and business relations were prohibited, family visits and scholarly and journalistic exchanges were possible without going through an official licensing process. Under the new policy, however, one cannot purchase a ticket without a license in hand. In fact, travel agents, under the threat of fine or imprisonment, cannot issue a ticket without proof of a license.

To these complications was added the Helms-Burton bill, which was initiated by North Carolina Senator Jesse Helms and signed by President Bill Clinton in early 1996. It penalizes businesses conducting trade in Cuba and allows Cuban-Americans to sue foreign companies for engaging in business relations with the Cuban government. The law states that the Cuban government is operating on property "stolen" from certain Cuban-Americans and that they are entitled to compensation. The law has been denounced by most nations and regional trade bodies because it violates customary laws of national sovereignty; nations have generally had the unfettered right to choose their trading partners. In fact, the European Union, Mexico, and Canada all vigorously opposed the law before its enactment and have repeatedly informed the Clinton administration of their objections. The European Union in February 1997, angry at the United States's "illegal attempt to impose U.S. law in other jurisdictions," made a formal complaint to the World Trade Organization. The WTO appointed an international panel to decide the case. The recalcitrant U.S. trade representatives at the WTO immediately announced that they would not be bound by any WTO decision.[1] There is no doubt that the passage of Helms-Burton has created a hostile climate for scholarly collaboration.

Nonetheless, we did beat the odds. The essays came in and they are revelatory. Interestingly, though, what became apparent about past relations proved problematic for some in today's climate. Such was the case for *Jet* magazine, which refused to let us reprint their February 19, 1959, cover photo of a beautiful young black Cuban woman. Upon receipt of my request, a *Jet* staff member telephoned to say that the picture was "quite old" and of a "political nature," and they would not grant permission to use it. Although I was not totally surprised, I was hurt. After all, I had grown up on *Jet;* scores of editions must have been lifted from their perch on my family's coffee table and flipped through and read over the last thirty years. Yet the staffer was correct: this striking photograph, which accompanies a human-interest story on the life of this woman, *is* political. It reveals that a *Jet* correspondent was assigned to cover the Cuban revolution. Moreover, the article treats with sympathy the woman's support for the revolution. This woman now felt, the writer explained, that she could go to school; before the revolution, economic and racial impediments had made such a dream impossible. *Jet*, like most of the black press in 1959, applauded the revolution; and it is this that they apparently do not want known today. Thankfully, the *Baltimore Afro-American* and New York's *Amsterdam News* were not concerned to distance themselves from photographs that reflect their recent past.

Not Just Black

My grandmother passed away before I could apprentice myself to study her wondrous ability to calculate revelations. But in a poignant way, pursuing this project brought back many memories of her. In fact, bits and pieces of those hot summer days when school was out and I spent extra time with her only made sense as I researched African-American and Cuban relations. Let me explain. Often, my grandmother had the radio on, especially when she was working up her numbers. The radio was one of those big square black ones with a silver tuner knob on the side and a pull-up aerial, a precursor to today's boom boxes. It was a gift to my grandfather upon his retirement, after forty years, from the Stearns and Foster mattress factory. My grandmother cursed it each time she turned it on because by that time my grandfather had been diagnosed with brown-lung disease (emphysema) after years of inhaling cotton and synthetic fibers on the job. Nonetheless, she used it to listen to two things and two things only: Cincinnati Reds baseball games and River Downs horse racing. Two days clearly stand out in my mind. One day she was working up her numbers, listening to baseball, and baking hundreds of fresh homemade rolls—she catered "rich white folks'" parties to make her living. All of a sudden, she leaped up from her chair, saying, "Uh huh, that Tony Pérez is a real slugger. He from Cuba, but he's really just black." Being a preteen in the small town of Glendale, Ohio, on the outskirts of Cincinnati, I didn't know where Cuba was, but the name Tony Pérez caused me to envision a big handsome black man from some far-off place. The second incident occurred when she was listening to horse racing. She told me she had bet on a horse named Darling Lisa, and if Darling Lisa placed as my grandmother predicted, she would use the money to start my college fund. I agreed but asked her why baseball and horse racing excited her so much. She told me it was because black people invented horse racing and they were so good at baseball that white folks had shut them out for fear of getting whupped. And then she laughed. Darling Lisa did place that day, and my college fund got started with the eighteen dollars my grandmother won.

It took me years of academic research to discover what my grandmother, who had little formal schooling, knew well—that blacks had been central to the evolution of professional horse racing, and that they were shut out of baseball even though black players often showed themselves to be more talented than their white counterparts. Interestingly, the contests between white and black teams often took place in Cuba, where racial segregation in baseball was rare. Blacks keenly followed these off-season competitions and were overjoyed when mixed teams of blacks and Cubans defeated such contenders as the Detroit Tigers and outhit stars such as Ty Cobb. Moreover, my grandmother's numbers playing linked her to baseball and Cuba in ways that I had yet to understand. It was, in fact, numbers bankers, as the only sector in the black community with large capital resources, who underwrote successful Negro-league teams. A pivotal "underground entrepreneur"[2] involved in black baseball turned out to be Alessandro (Alex) Pómpez, a black Cuban from Tampa who worked in the Harlem rackets. He was the agent of most black Cuban ballplayers who came to the United States before the 1950s and was the owner-manager of the Harlem-based Cuban Stars and the New York Cubans.

My grandmother's comment about Cubans being really "just black" was equally telling. All of the essays included in this collection reveal a mutable black context in which African-Americans and Cubans met. For instance, the chapter that Bijan Bayne and I wrote, "Not Just Black: African-Americans, Cubans, and Baseball," illustrates that not only did Cuban baseball players of obvious African descent live in a black context when in the United States but even those few "white" Cubans who played in the white majors found themselves largely constructed as black. The one-drop rule and U.S. images of a racially mixed Latin America meant that many black Americans identified with all Cubans while many white Americans called all Cubans "nigger." More importantly, Cubans were perceived as black because some Cubans were black, Cuban culture as a whole was strongly influenced by Africa, and all Cubans were colonial subjects of a sort. Could Africanized colonial subjects in the world of Jim Crow really be perceived as "white"?

Nancy Mirabal's essay, "Telling Silences and Making Community: Afro-

Cubans and African-Americans in Ybor City and Tampa, 1899–1915," explores the painful dimensions of this question in a Cuban immigrant community in Florida. After the Cuban-Spanish-American War ended in 1898, and the U.S. gained hegemony over the island, some Cubans living in Florida remained in the United States. Clubs that had once been integrated, and whose members had worked together toward Cuban independence, began to divide along racial lines. The only way that "white" Cubans could expect to partake in the privileges that went with white skin, especially in the South, was to dissociate themselves from their fellow compatriots of color; and so they did. But to do so meant a certain distancing from their Cubanness as well. Most Cubans had by 1902 accepted (if not always practiced) a broad ethos of nonracialism. This had been strongly encouraged by Cuba's major intellectual and political leader of the late nineteenth century, José Martí. Martí had argued that Cubans were more than white, more than black, and that to be Cuban went beyond race. He also pushed for socioeconomic equality: "our goal is not so much a mere political change as a good, sound, and just and equitable social system without demagogic fawning or arrogance."[3] It was necessary, Martí argued, "to make common cause with the oppressed to secure the system opposed to the interest and habits of the oppressors."[4] This message had great appeal to exploited Cuban cigar workers in Tampa and Ybor City, both black and white. But Martí was killed in 1895, and the war had not brought the much-sought-after *Cuba libre.* "White" Cubans acquiesced to racism in the hope of achieving racial privilege in the United States. Strikingly, though, while they were divided by job category and in their social lives, Cubans remained physically integrated in the Cuban-founded cigar factories and community of Ybor City. Mirabal points out that because of the obvious incongruity between the racial unity promoted by Martí and de facto segregation, neither white nor black clubs openly articulated the reason behind the separate organizations in 1902. And Cubans in Tampa and Ybor City remain uncomfortable today about remembering the ouster of blacks from the community's social clubs. In any case, members of the new Afro-Cuban society, La Unión Martí-Maceo, found themselves living along the borders of that black American context. They tried to hold on to Cuban culture in the Jim Crow South as they struggled with an "in-between" status. They did ultimately build community and a relationship across language and culture with indigenous African-Americans.

It is clear that Cubans were never "just black," as my grandmother had concluded; but neither were African-Americans. Each carried with them discrete notions of color that framed the way they negotiated racism(s) and their relations with one another. Moreover, distinct histories of racism had created specific sets of race relations. This difference influenced African-Americans and Cubans in Tampa and proved a persistent thread running through all relations. In fact, contrasting the experiences of racism and weighing the contradictions of each shaped much of the written discourse discussed in this book. Rosalie Schwartz, in her essay "Cuba's Roaring Twenties: Race Consciousness and the Column 'Ideales de una Raza,'" found that Cuban contributors to this column employed the North American experience to reflect upon Cuban racism and potential solutions to Cuba's racial problems: what was similar, what was different, and how did what they observed affect the struggle against racism in Cuba? More provocatively, writers in the column at times evoked U.S.-style segregation and the threat of black anger as a warning to white Cubans. Cubans generally were becoming restive in the 1930s. After twenty years of unrestrained U.S. penetration, there was a revolutionary call once again for national sovereignty and unity. Black Cubans, given demography and history, knew that their participation was essential to any revolutionary future. If racism continued, they subtly implied, black Cubans might be forced to seek solutions different from those articulated by Martí.

Carmen Gómez García's essay, "Cuban Social Poetry and the Struggle against Two Racisms," illustrates that Cuban social poets such as Regino Pedroso and Nicolás Guillén thrust the viciousness of U.S. racism into their poetry, partly in solidarity with blacks in the United States and partly to express anti-imperialist sentiment. They lyricized their anger on the issues of lynching, the Ku Klux Klan, and legally sanctioned injustice in the United States. Specifically, the Scottsboro case and the murder of Emmett Till caused great consternation and drew many a pen to paper. How could a young boy's flirtations lead to murder, Guillén lamented? Ignorance and Wall Street, he charged! The poet Pedroso, who often challenged black Cubans to fight racism, urged them in his 1930s poem "Hermano negro" (Black Brother) to "silence your maracas a while. And learn here, and watch there, and listen yonder in Scottsboro, in Scottsboro, among the lamentation of slave distress, longings of man, rage of man."

A key aspect of the 1930s revolutionary culture was the Afrocubanismo arts movement. Emerging in the 1920s as part of a broad Western interest in things black, Afrocubanismo, while centering black life and therefore providing a forum in which black artists might be heard, also tended to exoticize black culture and reduce it to stereotype. Pedroso seems to be specifically criticizing this movement and the black entertainers who too willingly fit themselves into it while ignoring the crucial antiracist struggle. Pedroso, known for his strong proletarian and left sentiments, might also be warning black Cubans to be alert, for Scottsboro might happen in Cuba if U.S. domination continued.

To most Afro-Cubans, Cuban racism was indeed a disgrace, especially after their stellar contributions to Cuba's wars of independence. But most Afro-Cubans and African-Americans seemed to agree that the racism in Cuba was less violent and less pervasive than that which manifested itself in the United States. But was that a good thing or bad? Not surprisingly, most African-Americans, given their own tragic history, thought it could only be a good thing. David Hellwig in his essay "The African-American Press and United States Involvement in Cuba, 1902–1917," uses the term "racial paradise" to describe the African-American press's perception of Cuba at the turn of the century. His chapter shows that even as black editors acknowledged that racism was increasing on the island after 1902, they rarely blamed white Cubans for it. Instead, they attributed it to the penetration of "the Anglo-Saxon" style. In May 1912, when Afro-Cubans led a massive revolt in Oriente province against U.S. and Spanish land grabbing and hunger, and Cuban troops massacred nearly five thousand, the press continued to denounce only the United States. While the U.S. presence did deepen racism in Cuba, it found and worked with a racist Cuban constituency. The so-called Race War of 1912 is evidence of that.

But the notion that black Cubans held a status unattainable for black Americans was deeply rooted in African-American historical memory, making it difficult to dislodge. It dated at least to the Ten Years War (1868–78), when American blacks became aware that Cuba's anti-Spanish army was integrated, that its leading general, Antonio Maceo, was black, and it was simultaneously fighting against slavery and for independence. Given that U.S. nationhood came with slavery intact and blacks were only belatedly permitted to fight in the war to end slavery—in despised and segregated units at that—African-Americans immediately rose in solidarity with the Cuban war. Frederick Douglass, in fact, proclaimed that "the first gleam of the sword of freedom and independence in Cuba secured my sympathy with the revolutionary cause," and he encouraged "Afro-American youth to surrender their citizenship to join their fortunes with those of their suffering brethren in Cuba."[5] Abolitionists Henry Highland Garnet and Samuel R. Scottron formed a Cuban Anti-Slavery Society, held a meeting at Cooper Union in New York

City in 1872, and collected over five thousand signatures on a petition, which they presented to President Ulysses S. Grant, demanding that he support the Cuban belligerents. Moreover, that José Martí was white and spent much of his time in exile in New York must also have had an impact. Men like Douglass and Garnet knew few white men who were as ideologically grounded and politically committed as was Martí. During the 1880s Martí published literally hundreds of essays in newspapers as wide ranging as the *New York Times* and *La Nación* of Buenos Aires. In addition to writing about Cuba, he indicted antiblack racism and America's genocidal practices against Native Americans, and attempted to frame a pan-American consciousness. In fact, when Garnet died, Martí's eulogy to him appeared in the *New York Times*.

No country in the nineteenth century, other than Haiti, so stirred the African-American imagination as Cuba did. In fact, the very first African-American professional baseball team, established in the 1880s, was called the Cuban Giants. Because other teams were named the Toussaint L'Ouvertures, the Hannibals, and the P.B.S. Pinchbacks, this name was likely chosen because it too evoked pride for African-Americans. Similarly, Martin Delaney, often called the father of black nationalism, named one of his children Plácido, the popular name of the Cuban poet Gabriel de la Concepción, who was murdered in the 1845 Spanish anti-abolitionist tirade known as La Escalera. Plácido also figured heavily in Delaney's book *Blake, or the Huts of America: A Tale of the Mississippi Valley, the Southern United States and Cuba*. Serialized in 1859, it is often hailed as African-America's first novel.[6] Blake, the central character, travels throughout North America and Cuba organizing a general slave insurrection; in Havana he receives instruction and inspiration from Plácido.

Given this history, it was impossible to dislodge totally the image of Cuba as a racial paradise in African-American lore, even though the internal reality of Cuba was quite different. For instance, while it is true that Maceo and his integrated army, known as the *mambises,* predominated in both wars, it is also true that the Ten Years War imploded because of internal racism, elitism, and a civil-military conflict that pitted the largely white Creole political leadership against the largely black generalship. In fact, white Creoles feared a *mambí* victory more than they did continued Spanish rule. They wanted to maintain their privilege in any republican political configuration and trembled at the social-reform agenda of the black general Antonio Maceo. Because of this, Creoles ended the war without a decisive Spanish victory and signed the Treaty of Zanjón with Spain in 1878.

Nonetheless, race relations in Cuba did differ from those in the United

States. There was no random racist terror to speak of, and although the elite
in Cuba remained separate and white, race-based segregation among the
lower classes was rare. Interracial dating, while not encouraged by whites,
did happen, and it was almost never the cause for murder. African-
American soldiers, baseball players, artists, and activists visited Cuba and
maintained that blacks were better off there. Van Gosse in his essay, "The
African-American Press Greets the Cuban Revolution," found this impression confirmed by the revolution. The press at that time saw the revolution's overwhelming black support and its radical social policies as the culmination of a century's vision of racial equality.

But there were before 1959, and still are today, Afro-Cubans who, while
recognizing U.S racism to be blunt and brutish, find the island's more subtle
forms of racism equally if not more distressing. For these Cubans, the assertiveness of American blacks, provoked by an overt and unabashed U.S.
racism, is preferable to the undermined sense of self created by the more hidden Cuban racism. Such was the analysis of Cuban intellectual Bernardo Ruiz
Suárez in his 1920s book *The Colour Question in Two Americas;* Cuban musician Mario Bauza said something similar while on a visit to Cuba in the 1940s.
Asked if he would remain there, Bauza said, "I only got one plan. I want to be
with people like me, [in the United States, to] know what it is to be a black
man in a black [country]. My roots have got to be there. [There, in Harlem,]
was a big black race, they had shows, they had good orchestras, good artists."[7]
Geoffrey Jacques, in his chapter "CuBop! Afro-Cuban Music and Mid-
Twentieth-Century American Culture," notes that Bauza and the Tampa
Cuban musician Frank "Machito" Grillo did find a solid place in black
Harlem. They played the Savoy and the Apollo to adoring black fans and
influenced the music of Charlie Parker and Dizzy Gillespie.

Tomás Fernández Robaina in his essay "Marcus Garvey in Cuba: Urrutia, Cubans, and Black Nationalism," develops an analysis of Cuban racism
that reinforces the perspectives of Bauza and Ruiz Suárez. While Garvey attracted huge followings in the United States and among Jamaicans in Cuba,
he enjoyed minimal support from indigenous Afro-Cubans. According to Fernández Robaina, the visions of José Martí and Antonio Maceo actually served
as a bulwark against Garvey's black nationalism. Cuban blacks chose to make
their demands for rights not as blacks but as Cubans; thus, when Gustavo Urrutia challenged racism, he did so from within the framework of nation. In
fact, one might argue that he relied on a "metalanguage of nation" to raise
questions of race, just as Carmen Montejo Arrechea has shown in her essay

"*Minerva:* A Magazine for Women (and Men) of Color," that black women in Cuba often depended on "a metalanguage of race" to raise questions of gender. In both cases, though, there were consequences. Fernández Robaina provocatively argues that because Cuban blacks sought no special treatment "as blacks," they obtained nothing "as blacks" as well. He implies that the discourse on race in Cuba was impeded by the otherwise positive visions of Martí and Maceo.

But blacks could at least achieve recognition "as Cubans," a national distinction that was denied to blacks in the United States. This difference becomes apparent as Keith Ellis in his essay "Nicolás Guillén and Langston Hughes: Convergences and Divergences" deftly sketches the starkly divergent lives of Langston Hughes and Nicolás Guillén, two remarkably similar poets. Both were born in 1902 and both came of age in the 1920s. They drew inspiration equally from the musical rhythms of their own black communities, and both situated themselves as social poets. Each emerged as a leading voice in his culture's black renaissance (Harlem and Afro-Cubanism), and both were loved by their communities. As if fated, they met in 1930 and became colleagues and friends, a relationship that, while tested at times, lasted throughout their lives. Hughes lived in Harlem, the teeming black capital of the United States, where he spent much of his life struggling against poverty and racism. He was supported by white patrons who, more often than not, wanted to dictate the timing and content of his artistic production and urged him to socialize with people whose ideas he rejected. Hughes would periodically get fed up and quit them, only to be faced with the necessity of paying the bills. According to Ellis, Hughes often felt frustrated and isolated.

Nicolás Guillén, on the other hand, while equally impoverished, "threw in his lot with his comrades and subsisted or suffered with them," as Ellis puts it. Although he lived under dictators in conditions of repression and frequent U.S. intervention, he thrived as a social poet; he was in the company of his Cuban (black, mulatto, and white) compatriots and psychically he thrived. He had no white patrons; most white Cubans, like black Cubans, were themselves struggling to survive. In fact, from the 1930s onward, Cubans grew increasingly outraged at U.S. domination and their *cubanidad* (Cuban national spirit) deepened. Thus, while the vision of Martí was limited, it did offer a space within which black Cubans could influence the very definition of Cuban nationhood. In fact, black culture became accepted (albeit with contradictions) as a central element in what it meant to be Cuban. Guillén, therefore, found his Cuban homeland a much more hospitable place than Hughes ever did the United States.

No point is more telling of this than what happened to both men toward the end of their lives. While Hughes was brought before the House Un-American Activities Committee during the anticommunist McCarthy era of the 1950s for attacking racism and expressing socialist ideas, Guillén was heralded as a national treasure and made the premier *national* poet for doing exactly the same thing. Hughes was forced publicly to renounce many of his ideals, and he died unexpectedly at the age of sixty-five, while Guillén survived as a beloved senior mentor to young poets in revolutionary Cuba until the age of eighty-seven.

The Beast Has Many Bellies

My grandmother never told me why Cubans were so much a part of American baseball. The relaxed way in which she spoke of them, though, indicated that their presence was a comfortable one, a part of her historical memory. What my grandmother may not have been able to explain, many of her Cuban contemporaries could have. Cubans were part of African-American life because of racism and a historical set of imperial arrangements. As the United States occupied the island militarily (1898–1902) and forced the Platt Amendment into the Cuban Constitution (1902),[8] a classic imperial bridge, both structural and ideological, was built between colonizer and colony. Regular rapid transportation, fluid communication, and a level of mutual cultural awareness emerged to facilitate U.S. economic exploitation of the island. Openly racist and paternalistic colonial discourse arose to justify it as well. Cubans visited and settled in the United States in search of a better life, while North Americans went to Cuba in search of business opportunities and religious converts. Strikingly, many white Americans drew upon the same pool of stereotypes for the foreign Cuban "other" that served for the domestic African-American one. For Kansas editor William Allen White, Cubans were "yellow-legged, garlic eating, dagger sticking treacherous vermin,"[9] a characterization strikingly like the turn-of-the-century *Encyclopedia Britannica*'s description of the Negro people as a goat smelling, developmentally arrested, miniature-brained race with no history.[10] There developed a congruence in racism and imperialism that was impossible for Cubans and African-Americans to ignore.

Following the tradition of Frederick Douglass, African-Americans generally weighed in against U.S. imperialism in Cuba. They did this partly out of pan-African and antiracist solidarity and partly out of anti-imperialist sentiment. Because of the undeniable confluence of U.S. imperialism and racism, they, like their Cuban counterparts, found it easy to be against both at the same time. In fact, the early African-American press, according to David Hellwig, was keenly concerned with the extension of racism via imperialism into Cuba. While they may have been naive on the nuances of Cuban racism, they were quite clear on the "mission of the Anglo-Saxon." They consistently criticized the U.S. military and U.S. businessmen for introducing American-style racism to the island. When a U.S.-owned Havana hotel refused to serve two Afro-Cuban congressmen in January 1910, and large protests turned into a riot, most of the twenty papers surveyed by Hellwig were outraged. The riot was the natural result of "American greed and damphool color prejudice," wrote the African Methodist Episcopal Church's *Star of Zion.* The press reached a similar conclusion with respect to a 1906 uprising and the so-called "Race War" of 1912. In general, most of the editorials praised the unwillingness of Afro-Cubans to let U.S. racism and imperialism penetrate unchallenged.

But issues of empire, like race, were not without contradiction. For while the African-American press supported Cuba's right to self-determination, a view of imperialism seen largely through the lens of race had its limitations. For instance, when the United States first intervened in Cuba in 1898, four black American units were recruited for the conflict. Because this was the first international conflict in which black soldiers would be allowed to fight since slavery (discounting the Indian Wars), the black press overwhelmingly applauded black involvement. Their support was bolstered by the argument that U.S. troops were there to assist the Cuban *independistas* and by the fact that 40 percent of the Cuban officers were black. Also, black troops suffered such racism from white fellow soldiers that the press felt obligated to rally the community behind them. But even as U.S. intervention turned to occupation, the black press continued to express broad support for the troops; this was an experiment in race relations that the African-American community wanted to watch closely. That all might be guilty of supporting imperialism rarely came up.

Tension over this apparent contradiction was sharper in the Philippines, where an indigenous force openly combated U.S. troops. This was especially so for such newspapers as the *Richmond Planet,* which had consistently challenged U.S. expansion. That Cubans generally did not mount an armed resistance to the United States may have been a factor in the absence of self-criticism over black involvement in Cuba. Some Afro-Cuban soldiers did fight U.S. troops, but their actions were not broadly supported. Maceo's death in 1896 left the old Creole elites in the top positions of leadership, and they, along with Spanish-born Cubans, positioned themselves to become the beneficiaries of U.S. intervention. Indeed, their class orientation and their European racial heritage led them naturally into the U.S. transition team. It appears as if an African-American contradiction engaged a Cuban one.

One might argue that the press, black or white, is still the press. While the black press was clearly more anti-imperialistic than the white press, it too tended to be middle class and business oriented. Yet the black press of the time did seem to reflect a fairly broad range of middle-class views on U.S. involvement in Cuba. For instance, while Booker T. Washington argued that blacks should join U.S. soldiers in Cuba to show white Americans how patriotic they could be, others argued for their inclusion for less accommodationist reasons. T. Thomas Fortune of the *New York Age,* for example, cheekily called for a black artillery unit so that blacks might get guns and "show whites how to soldier."[11] Interestingly, even those who argued against black American involvement did so more in protest of domestic racial issues than they did for reasons having to do with Cuba. One young Midwesterner is quoted in the press as saying, "I will not go to war. I have no country to fight for. [As a black] I have not been given my rights."[12] George Dudley, of the *American Citizen* of Kansas, suggested that the United States should get out of Cuba; its resources and so-called humanitarianism would be better utilized in the protection of black American rights.[13]

Prominent black Americans thus opposed U.S. penetration into Cuba largely out of racial solidarity, a problematical stance that enabled most to support black involvement and oppose a racist U.S. imperialism at exactly the same time. In fact, when perceived domestic race gains were weighed against anti-imperialism, which was rare, the domestic concerns generally won out. Yet to say that African-Americans commonly framed the issue in such terms would be inaccurate; most assumed that what was good for them was ultimately good for all blacks. After all, that had largely been the case during the abolitionist era. But issues of nation and empire complicated identities and alliances in the African diaspora. What relationships should newly freed slaves promote? What position should second-class black citizens take vis-à-vis empire? How should blacks respond to colonialism in Africa, Latin America, and Asia?[14] These were important questions for all peoples of African descent, but they were critical ones for African-Americans, who lived in the epicenter of one of the world's most powerful nations and emerging empires. While race allied them to all peoples of color struggling against racism and empire, their desire for inclusion in what it meant to be a U.S. citizen threatened to put them at odds with those very same people.

That U.S. penetration into Cuba occurred at the turn of the century, then, is important. African-Americans had had nearly two generations since slavery to grapple with what it meant to be both black and "free" in the United States. What W.E.B. Du Bois discovered is that blacks had by then developed a deep yearning to be part of the nation of their birth, but as descendants of black slaves they continued to suffer a virulent, abusive, persistent, and endemic racism. The twinning of these two experiences generated a psychic conflict that Du Bois theorized in 1907 as a "double consciousness."[15] Blacks, he argued, struggled against racism and for racial pride but also sought acceptance and inclusion into the white society that despised them. The evolution of this contradictory consciousness then played itself out in African-American responses to U.S. penetration of Cuba. On one hand, they supported Cubans, especially Cubans of color, against a racist imperialism; on the other, they wished at all costs to be part of American endeavors. But Du Bois also suggested that while this consciousness was in conflict with itself, African-Americans were in fact both black and North American and had been for many years. While they carried with them a specific history of racial oppression, they also bore much of the cultural and ideological baggage of the nation as a whole. This was especially so for the small black middle class, who were literate and positioned broadly enough for their voices to be heard on international issues.

African-Americans' double sensibility, of course, unfolded in different ways with respect to Cuba. Their "North Americanness" emerged in 1898, when Cuba's close proximity and its reputation as a racial paradise led some to see it as prospective site for large-scale emigration, along with Africa and Haiti. Promoters argued that blacks could escape racist violence in the United States and make money by taking their "North American" ingenuity and skills to help develop a largely poor and black Cuba. Because black Americans and Cubans as a whole did not support them, most of the schemes never came to fruition. But the fact that an Afro-American Cuban Emigration Committee was established and a Reverend W. L. Grant of Topeka, Kansas, petitioned the U.S. Congress to underwrite it, is telling. It shows that some African-Americans could ally themselves as race brothers while possessing both North American chauvinism and a belief in capitalism at the same time. It is striking that they, with no capital and no status in their own land, believed they might have something other than solidarity to offer Cubans. Even more astonishing were those who thought Congress might support them, for they showed themselves to be willing to work with racists eager to get rid of them.[16]

Not surprisingly, Afro-Cubans opposed such schemes while welcoming individual black Americans. African-Americans seemed surprised at the Cubans' lack of enthusiasm, yet they failed to understand the new challenges Afro-Cubans faced. During the first two years after the Spanish defeat and while Cuba remained under U.S. occupation, immigration to the island had skyrocketed. Between 1898 and 1901 some seventy thousand immigrants arrived in Cuba; most were European and unskilled, and they displaced Cuban peasants. The United States, working with Cuban elites, finally sped up the island's long attempted (because of fear of a black majority) "whitening up" policy.[17] Further, North American capital had begun pouring into Cuba at a dizzying rate, making peasants out of Afro-Cuban landowners and paupers out of peasants. Afro-Cubans had no idea how black Americans might fit themselves into Cuban society—as another pool of laborers with whom they would have to compete, or as hungry capitalists who would take their land. Black promoters of such schemes never seriously reckoned with the fact that any mass emigration had the potential to be colonialistic, especially if it had the backing of the United States government. Questions concerning whose land would be taken, whose culture would be hegemonic, and who would dominate economically were woefully lacking in discussions of proposed resettlement.

A less problematic though probably more complex working of race and nation emerges in Jualynne Dodson's essay "Encounters in the African Atlantic World: The African Methodist Episcopal Church in Cuba." Utilizing church documents, Dodson analyzes nearly fifty years of AME attempts to establish a solid base in Cuba. She argues that, unlike the emigrationists mentioned above, it was the AME's deep opposition to white clergy and their racial consciousness that propelled their efforts in Cuba. In fact, under the radical leadership of the early twentieth-century bishop Henry McNeal Turner, the church became more internationalist and a steadfast critic of U.S. and European colonialism. The AME Church did not go to Cuba to make money, and while it could have used financial support from the U.S. companies who generously gave to white Protestant efforts in Cuba, church leaders never expected

to receive it. Nonetheless, they were Christians who believed in missionary activity abroad. Their desire was to convert Afro-Cubans to African Methodism
by awakening their racial awareness. But despite numerous efforts, few Afro-
Cubans became believers. The church was always under terrible financial con-
straints, and AME officials in Cuba were neither Cuban nationals nor speakers of Spanish. More importantly, the church never found a workable strategy
for arousing racial consciousness without stepping on the toes of Cuba nationalism. Cognizant of the deepening racism brought by the U.S. presence,
church representatives expected more race awareness among Afro-Cubans;
but they underestimated the impact of empire. Cubans' rising anti-imperialist
fervor revisited and then evoked the national vision of Martí. Thus, as with
the call of Marcus Garvey, it was the English-speaking Jamaican immigrants
in Cuba who were most attracted to the AME's message.

One of the most striking points that Dodson makes is that the AME
Church paid little heed to the existing indigenous belief systems of black
Cubans. Dodson, in fact, states early on that there is nothing in the documents
she examined to show the church recognized the African-derived religions
then practiced in Cuba. While scholars have long known that European missionaries in Africa disregarded indigenous religions, viewing them as no religion at all, one wishes better of AME Church officials. Were they as chauvin-
istic as white Christians in their approach to so-called nonbelievers? Maybe.
But while their very proselytizing presumed an embrace of monotheistic
Christianity, it is also true that they appeared more interested in forging a international black institution than in producing Christian converts. Yet they
were like other blacks of the period in their inability to transcend their own
nationally constructed notions of race. They carried cultural baggage that limited their ability to reflect on the complexities of what it meant to be black or
African in a truly international way. While the nearly four hundred thousand
members (in 1886) of the AME Church in the United States saw themselves
as *African* Methodist and surely had within their practices African styles and
rhythms passed down through the generations, their "being African" had become little more than a racial category disconnected from any discrete set of
African cultural or religious beliefs. Their racial identity was constructed and
reinvented over time from within their experiences in the United States, and
its center was very much in the tradition of western Christianity. This was very
different for Afro-Cubans, whose Regla de Ocha (Santeria) and Regla Congo
(Palo Monte), for example, were based on the gods and cosmological views of
specific African peoples. While influenced by Catholicism and surely dy-

namic, the essence of Afro-Cuban religion remained African. Because AME Church representatives did not deal seriously with African religions, they failed to consider not only Cuban nationalism but the fact that Afro-Cubans already had "black" religions.

The negation of Afro-Cuban religions in the documents of the AME Church may have been more calculated, though. During the first two decades of the century, church officials probably represented the contemporary ideals of an aspiring black middle class, if perhaps a segment that was more radical than the mainstream. As businessmen, ministers, lawyers, physicians, and skilled workers, small urban middle-class clusters tried to negotiate, in the words of Houston Baker, "a space of habitation"[18] between vicious racist violence and paternalistic Western values. To claim real "Africanness" in the prevailing social Darwinist ideology of the day would have linked them to a continent cast as primitive and backward while separating them from the dominant notions of civilization and progress; and it is to the latter that they aspired. Thus, they defended themselves against racial stereotypes by espousing an ethos of uplifting the race within which they became privileged class agents of European progress and civilization for the lower-class black majority. According to Kevin Gaines, "by claiming through uplift ideology the status of agents of civilizations, blacks hoped to topple racial barriers and regain citizenship rights."[19] Yet in so doing they completely devalued those African aspects of black culture evident in the rural South and in Africa, Latin America, and the Caribbean. Interestingly, a similar trend occurred in Cuba, where much of the discourse around race was similarly about "uplifting" peoples of African descent from *poca cultura* (little culture) or *baja cultura* (low culture) to the culture of Europeanized ways. This notion was often articulated from within the concept of *mestizaje,* which, while accepting what Fernando Ortiz had called a Cuban creole "stew" of the African, European, and Indian cultures, also maintained strong notions of white supremacy.

Popular Culture Transcends

My grandmother's comfort with Cuba can be multiplied many times over. Indeed, Cuba conjures up fond memories for many blacks who came of age between the 1930s and 1960. My mother-in-law, for example, excitedly remembers when she first heard the *son* sounds of the great Cuban balladeer Benny Moré. It was at a Westside Chicago nightclub, and she was with her girlfriends; they heard some of his songs, they closed their eyes, they swayed.

They asked a cluster of similarly enthralled Mexicans in the club who he was and were told. The next day they rushed out to buy as many wax discs as they could find. She still has those 78s. Similarly, in the 1990s, the Dominican community living in upper Manhattan, just north of Harlem, celebrated the history of Cuban baseball there. Thousands welcomed a Cuban team who were there to play a few innings with a local Dominican one. That a Cuban national team would be invited by local baseball enthusiasts surprised my friends who live in the neighborhood; I was not surprised. This very neighborhood had been the site of Alex Pómpez's Dykman Oval (stadium) at 204th and Nagel and the community base of his "mucho famous" New York Cubans. They were one of the best teams in the Negro Leagues, playing before thousands of black and Latino fans.

Michael Hanchard in his work on blacks in Brazil aptly argues that if you want to investigate racial politics in Brazil, you have to look beyond the formal institutional structures to the "samba schools, football soccer teams [and] dance halls." These, he suggests, are among the settings for community and resistance of marginalized peoples.[20] A similar argument can be made about African-American and Cuban relations. For it was in the nightclubs, dance halls, late night studios, baseball diamonds, record stores, barber shops, low-rent but clean hostels, and neighborhood eateries that the vast majority of Cubans and blacks engaged one another and expressed solidarity. While rarely articulated as overt political ideology or as a response to empire, these activities in fact were. Afro-Cubans and African-Americans spoke with their ears, their eyes, their entire bodies, their cheers, and most importantly their desires; they entered into each other's music and reveled in each other's athletic prowess. Even more so than racism and imperialism, the congruencies between African-American and Cuban art and style were too engaging to ignore.

This was especially so for rural and newly urbanized blacks and Cubans, whose cultural expressions shared similar African roots and served parallel counterhegemonic functions. In fact, until 1960, most Cubans and black Americans fit a similar profile; they were poor and agrarian yet on the move. Hundreds of thousands migrated to burgeoning urban areas with few material possessions, although they did carry bundles of psychic archives full of cultural memory and bound by oral tradition. Havana, Santiago de Cuba, New Orleans, and New York became key destinations, especially between the world wars. While the cultures of both peoples had blended to varying degrees with European elements, it was their shared cultural memories, causing a recognition of African aesthetic principles, and their similarly politicized cultural coordinates that most attracted one to the other. I speak of cultural memory here in the way that Samuel Floyd does in his *The Power of Black Music*. It is

> the nonfactual and nonreferential motivations, actions, and beliefs that members of a culture seem, without direct knowledge or deliberate training, to "know"—that feel unequivocally "true" and "right" when encountered, experienced, and executed. It may be defined as a repository of meanings that comprise the subjective knowledge of a people, its immanent thoughts, its structures, and its practices; these thoughts, structures and practices are transferred and understood unconsciously but become conscious and culturally objective in practice and perception.[21]

Evidence that Cubans and African-Americans pulled from the same or compatible cultural memory banks was everywhere. In fact, scholars make remarkably similar interpretations of Cuban (which is largely Afro-Cuban) and African-American approaches to art and sport in general, and movement and music in particular. For instance, Yvonne Daniel's account of the importance of rumba for Cubans could easily be applied, although not in precisely the same way, to many African-American dances. Rumba "embodies important elements of life: movement, spontaneity, sensuality, sexuality, love, tension, opposition, and both freedom and restraint."[22] Much the same could surely be said of dances as diverse as the slowdrag and grind to the jitterbug to the more recent butterfly. Likewise, Lou Pérez's comment that baseball gave "expression to Cuban nationality, both as a means to nationhood and as a metaphor for nation"[23] is very similar to Donn Rogosin's belief that baseball became a rallying point for community building, in fact, that "baseball was a unifying element for black communities in transition" and in the process of developing their identity.[24] Finally, because art and sport were, in the words of Rob Ruck, "forums for symbolic political assertion"[25] and sites of ideological contestation for both sets of peoples, conditions were ripe for positive cultural engagement. What I am arguing is this: although racism and empire thrust African-Americans and Cubans into each other's assigned physical spaces, it was who they were before and after segregation and exploitation that most influenced their cultural relations. Popular culture embodied the ways in which they overcame, resisted, and transcended these experiences.

Such conditions of overlapping communities and compatible aesthetic and political sensibilities were bound to lure African-Americans and

Cubans into each other's creative orbits. Each was especially drawn to elements of the other's aesthetics and style that are traceable to Africa's holistic approach to religion, life, and culture. Millions of West Africans came to the Americas with a worldview in which religion, art, and everyday life were inseparable. As Burton Peretti discusses, all had moved as one force in praising God and the gods and integrating spirit lore, possession rites, initiation processes, and funeral rituals; "communal gathering, singing, dancing and the playing of instruments [were] elements impossible to dissociate from each other."[26] Intricately carved and beautiful drums, made by skilled craftsmen, not only played music and communicated information but often housed specific spirits. Katrina Hazzard-Gordon notes that "dance served as a mediating force between people and the world of the gods . . . where specific dances and rhythms were appropriate for particular deities."[27] Dance also linked "one's personal identity to that of the group [and marked] events throughout the life cycle of the individual and the community."[28] Indeed, dance and movement, music, and art making are so much a part of the philosophy, customs, and sense of place that eliminating them would "radically alter the African view of the universe."[29]

But this African conception of the universe was shaken up when it encountered the division between the religious and the secular in the Americas, especially in the United States. But shaken up did not mean destroyed. Among blacks in the United States and Cuba, religious worship, while based on very different religions, continued to integrate music, movement, performance, and spirit possession into its practice. Additionally, secular musicians, dancers, and other sorts of artists and performers on both sides of the Caribbean often felt their craft to be infused with religious undercurrents. (Even today some members of Charlie Mingus's old band believe his spirit continues to influence their work).[30] Moreover, woven through and informing both religious and secular practices were key sets of African rhythmic patterns and improvisational sensibilities. Operating at both conscious and unconscious levels, these patterns and sensibilities were manipulated and refashioned in a multitude of ways and to varying degrees but continued to find complex expressions in black religion, art, sport, and everyday life.

Struggles against racism, imperialism, and other forms of oppression were incorporated as well. In fact, they worked reciprocally: African patterns and sensibilities informed struggle, and struggle often found expression through an African aesthetic. For instance, Hughes and Guillén integrated the musical cadences of their peoples into the rhythmically free style of their poetry. Each poet fused music and poetry, two components of what once made the African whole. Moreover, while the desire of Hughes, Guillén, and Pedroso to be social poets was surely counterhegemonic, it was also linked to the African practice in which art and social concerns are not made distinct.

Thus the African whole broke up in the Americas, but its parts continued to circulate. No component is more apparent than the art of improvisation; its expression in art and sport particularly thrilled African-American and Cuban audiences. At any moment during a ball game or on the dance floor, the performer might do the wonderfully unexpected—throw an "I don't believe he did that" kind of pitch, or suddenly alter the rhythmic pattern of the dance; he or she would improvise. In Africa such "change-ups" were often viewed as a sign of an unforeseen but desired spirit possession. Indeed, doing the unplanned within the context of structure and ritual was encouraged and taught in African aesthetics—in music, in dance, in performance. It was also instilled through African folk tales, which became trickster tales in the Americas. These tales, while varied and layered, often found Rabbit or Fox unexpectedly outwitting Lion or some other formidable foe. While tricksters were heroes because they "habitually overcame their more formidable opponents with guile and a certain amount of bravado," writes William Barlow,[31] the setting up of the story is also important. The reader or listener is lulled, through character construction and timing, into believing that Rabbit cannot possibly overcome the powerful Lion; and just when one least expects it, Rabbit does. This is the improvisational aspect of the story. Significantly, though, the listener trained in African sensibility does anticipate the unexpected, and therefore hopes for a "sneak attack,"[32] without knowing when, where, or how it will come. Improvisation in the black aesthetic, then, has always been tied to the hope, anticipation, and even the aching desire of the audience and the other performers that something magical will occur. In the words of one sports aficionado, one hoped that one might "affect the molecules in the surrounding air."[33] Black and Cuban athletes and artists hoped, as did their audiences, that in every game and performance someone might get possessed.

They were rarely disappointed, especially in baseball. Many black and Cuban Negro leaguers did indeed seem possessed. Baseball historians agree they employed a myriad of improvisational styles. David Wiggins describes them as "more daring, unpredictable, and [more] prone to improvise than [any of] their white counterparts."[34] Julius Tygiel adds that they offered their fans a more "freewheeling, and in many respects, more exciting brand of baseball than the major leagues."[35] They played in the "speed-dominated universe of tricky ball which emphasized the bunt, the stolen base, and the hit-and-run."[36] This is important, for the bunt seeks to catch the opposing team off-guard, while stealing a base requires the runner to match wits with the pitcher, the infielders, and the catcher. In fact, the base stealer, after watching and taunting and moving on and off the bag, makes a split-second decision and bolts. Significantly, when Jackie Robinson left the Negro leagues and took this style of play to the Brooklyn Dodgers, white America was in awe, having seen nothing like it since Ty Cobb. But had greater numbers of whites traversed the color line, they could have seen pitchers throw spitballs, emery balls, and shine balls. Ballplayers in the Negro leagues were encouraged to work with their creative impulses. In fact, Roy Campanella said of Negro league pitchers, "you never knew what the ball would do once it left the pitcher's hand."[37] This is because black ballplayers, according to David Wiggins, "viewed their sport . . . as a form of entertainment [where] a player could [both] express his individuality and . . . contribute to the team's overall effort."[38]

Two pitchers most exemplified the varied improvisational styles of the Negro leagues: the black North American Satchel Paige and the Cuban Luis Tiant Sr. Paige, "born in a [rundown] shotgun [house] with no plumbing in Mobile, Alabama, in 1906,"[39] is still considered one of the best all-around pitchers in the Negro leagues. He was flamboyant, and he became legendary for his skill and style. Tall and lanky, Paige moved with a slow gait. At times it seemed he could barely reach the mound; then he would joke with the batter, appearing comically bemused. (He got criticism for this.) Yet, like a trickster, once on the mound, he would slowly raise his arm and then, with a "double whammy, double pump," shoot a ninety-mile-an-hour fastball across the plate. His balls were so fast that some called them peaballs because that is what they supposedly resembled as they whizzed by. Paige also had a syncopation to his style, which was especially apparent in his hesitation pitch. What he would do was this: he would push off the mound as if for a regular windup, but as he raised his pitching arm, he would hesitate very slightly at the top of the delivery before completing the throw. The hitter, thinking the ball had left Paige's hand already, would stride forward and snap the bat to meet the nonexistent ball—soon to be coming over the plate, but a second too late. On one of the few occasions when the baseball did hit the bat (not the other way around), a sports commentator swore that friction almost caused the bat to catch fire. Finally, though Paige really only had a fastball, he boasted of having a wide repertoire of windups and pitches. Although he was called a "master of exaggeration" at the time, everyone had heard before Paige arrived in town for a game that he was prepared to whip his opponent with a combination of his Long Tom, trouble ball, Midnight Rider, bat dodger, blooper, looper, and jump ball. The opposing team never knew how much of this to believe. Paige exhibited a bravado and threat of the unexpected found in the aesthetics of most black athletics today.

Luis Tiant Sr. was a contemporary and at times a teammate of Paige. He was equally creative with his improvisational style even though that style was quite different. From a similar rural and poor background in Cuba, he played in the Negro leagues from 1930 to 1947. He was a small, quiet "lefty" whose pitches were not necessarily fast, and he was not one to brag or boast of his multitude of pitches; but in this case, he definitely had them! Whereas Paige struck out batters with his fastball, Tiant, also a trickster, struck batters out with an assortment of unpredictable, off-speed pitches. After twisting and turning on the mound with his herky-jerky motions, he might throw a devastating screwball, which would fly at one height and speed, only to drop and slow down just as it approached the plate. He also had his famous spitball, which might change direction and speed in flight, causing the batter to swing at either the wrong time or angle. He was also known for his fade-away move, where he would veer toward the third-base line, as if he were going to fall backward, before throwing a pitch. This would further confuse the batter, who had a difficult time gauging the angle and direction of the ball as it came toward home plate. However, he was best known for his pickoff, used to catch a player preparing to steal a base. What he would do was this: From the mound he would wind up as if to pitch the ball across the plate; but in a split-second decision, he would swing around and fire the ball to first base, allowing the baseman to tag the runner, who could not react fast enough to scramble back on base. All pitchers do this, but Tiant was so good at it that one incident, described by Peter Bjarkman, is fondly remembered in baseball lore. One day in the 1930s, while playing for Alex Pómpez's Cuban Stars, he wound up as usual, facing the Baltimore Elite Giants' Goose Curry at bat. Curry, watching Tiant, thought the ball was coming toward him, but in fact Tiant had "snapped his disguised pick-off throw toward first." The move was done "with such complete deception that a confused [Goose Curry] actually swung helplessly at the phantom pitch that never arrived in the catcher's mitt."[40] At once the home-plate umpire called a strike. A befuddled and angry Curry retorted, That can't be a strike because the ball never crossed the plate. The umpire yelled, If you were dumb enough to swing at the ball, then I am going to call it a strike!

That Cuban and African-American players and fans alike drew on their African-derived sensibilities to invigorate the game of baseball seems clear. I looked for distinctions linked to nationality and found none. In fact, according to Pettavino and Pye, Cuban baseball is still characterized by "tremendous speed, recklessness, superb defense and fascination with rules and strategy. . . . and this is as true for fans as of the players and managers. After all this nation worships [the] subtlety in its baseball."[41] Moreover, it was not just Jackie Robinson and North American blacks who brought speed, bunting, and a certain style to the majors. Jules Tygiel notes that between the 1947 integration of baseball and today, "a black or Latin player" has in all but two seasons "topped the National and American Leagues in stolen bases."[42]

Baseball players, then, both Cuban and African-American, were like their nations' social poets. They incorporated numerous aspects of the African cultural constellation into their game: improvisation, syncopation, performance, and call and response. They also incorporated, to paraphrase Toni Morrison, a symbolic fearlessness and comfort with that fearlessness[43] that has come to permeate the aesthetic of black athletes. Nelson George has, in fact, argued that black athletes actually "intimidate through improvisation."[44] By this he means that they make use of the unexpected to dominate their opponent psychologically and physically. Bayne and I show in our essay how this ability became truly counterhegemonic when black and Cuban players were pitted against all-white North American teams, which happened often "along the unpoliced boundaries of the national pastime."[45] As tricksters they would use "sneak attacks" to undermine the values of the dominant white and imperial culture, not only defeating the white teams but doing so with a style and aesthetic that was largely absent from white baseball. This was truly empowering for people like my grandmother.

Empowerment, though, must have happened on many levels, given cultural memory. That so many component parts, including the element of social and ideological struggle, could find their way into a single baseball game must have been truly magical and set the senses to tingling. One wonders if my grandmother, and those three million largely black and Latino fans who attended Negro league games in 1942,[46] felt the way that Nelson George did after a professional basketball game full of "improvisational flights." George recalls, "On the subway home, we laughed about those moves, compared them to past moments and savored [them] as intensely as any jazz aficionado might listening to a riff by Miles or Bird or Trane. Or a b-boy would be hyped by the rhymes of Rakim or Chuck Dee [*sic*] or L. L. Cool J. Or the righteously born again might shout 'Amen' at the rigorous rhetoric of Dr. Martin Luther King or Jesse Jackson. What links these baseball moves with rapping, sermonings, and soloing is that they all manifest a particular and shared African-American aesthetic."[47]

The unity and linkage of the senses that occur when one is engaged in an African-derived aesthetic have been noted by commentators as diverse as Arthur Ashe, John Edgar Wideman, August Wilson, Amiri Baraka, Toni Morrison, Gloria Rolando, and others. Strikingly, though, what most tingled the senses of leading African-American and Cuban musicians was to recognize this familiar linkage in one another's *distinctive* musical traditions. The discovery that Cubans and African-Americans had wrought different configurations from the same constellation of cultural elements was particularly intoxicating for artists such as Dizzy Gillespie and Frank Grillo, for underlying the uniqueness of the other's movements, patterns, styles, and instruments was a shared aesthetic. Geoffrey Jacques in his essay illustrates that a coming together between their two particular styles led to innovation and a radical change in African-American music.

Such was the case with bebop and Afro-Cuban jazz. Jacques carefully examines how Cuban music, while influencing American music via New Orleans from very early on, did not make a big impact on U.S. culture until the 1930s. Even then it was Xavier Cugat's Big Band, playing music that was highly arranged and lush with strings, and whose African rhythms were "discreet and unobtrusive, which appealed to a broad white American audience." That the original jazz of King Oliver and Louis Armstrong had in fact gone the way of the big band in the 1930s was of concern to a new breed of jazz musicians in the 1940s. Cubans Frank Grillo (Machito), his sister Graciella, and Mario Bauza began experimenting with a fusion between jazz and Afro-Cuban rhythms in 1943. Calling themselves Machito's Afro-Cubans, they began playing to large dance crowds at New York's Savoy and Apollo ballrooms, working and recording with emerging artists such as Charlie Parker and Dizzy Gillespie. Stan Wooley describes Machito as "a sensation, catching the imagination of jazz musicians, buffs and dancers alike."[48] However, it was only in the context of continued black disappointment in postwar culture that a group of consciously internationalist jazz revolutionaries moved to change the vocabulary of jazz with a style that would reflect their outrage. Chano Pozo, whose name as a talented (yet totally self-taught) composer had preceded him, arrived in New York in 1946, introduced his conga drum to jazz, and sparks began to fly!

Dizzy and Chano began the difficult and meticulous work of reworking and then merging their separate musical styles. They did this by fusing jazz horns and other North American orchestral instruments with the percussive conga, timbales, and bongos. Afro-Cuban or Latin jazz, also known as CuBop, became known to the world in 1947 with the release of *Manteca;* it was recorded by Dizzy's band and featured Pozo. Together they composed music for almost all of Dizzy's Latin jazz recordings.

The collaboration of Machito, Bauza, and Charlie Parker and then Dizzy and Chano is fascinating. Their own comments speak volumes. Machito in an interview in 1977 told Stan Wooley, "During my first year in the United States I spent practically every night at the Savoy Ballroom listening to everyone. In those days it was Benny Goodman . . . Duke Ellington and Count Basie . . . when I organized my own band I was . . . determined to marry Latin . . . and . . . American music." Of Charlie Parker and Dizzy he said, "those [guys] had such good taste . . . the harmonic sequences were so logical. You could follow the progression no matter how advanced it became. [Jazz] is like a painting—there is the main subject and there is the scenery. Their solos were the subjects and the harmony was the scenery." Of the differences between Cuban music and jazz he astutely noted, "In Cuban music, we never complicate the melody. It is the rhythm that is rich. But in jazz you have all the interest on top of the rhythm; everything is happening on top. Our music . . . occurs at the bottom, in the rhythm. [For example,] when there's a storm, then the thunder and lightning represents jazz . . . but when there's an earthquake, that's Cuban music. The rhythm moves you because it is where you're standing. You have to dance."[49]

Chano's and Dizzy's statements are equally rich. There is a famous comment attributed to Chano when someone asked how he and Dizzy collaborated given their language differences. Chano unequivocally responded, "He no speak Pani, me no speak Engli, but we both speak African!"[50] Yet Dizzy said it was Chano who was the real African: "Chano's concept came from Africa. When I heard it, it sounded on fire to me."[51] These comments reveal several things. One is that these musicians recognized the congruences as well as the differences between two African-derived aesthetic patterns. Yet they also knew that it was in the rhythmic structure of Cuban music that one found some of the most genuine African components. Interestingly, while Dizzy and other brass players surely blew "a little bit of Africa" into their European-derived instruments, African rhythmic patterns could probably be heard most clearly on the instruments that created them, carved all-wood drums with stretched goat skins meant to be played by hand. And this is what Dizzy understood.

The fact that Dizzy became familiar with these rhythms and arrangements through Chano was even more important. For Chano, life itself is representative of the Africa-based constellation discussed above. Born in 1915, he grew up in two working-class Havana barrios known as *solares*. *Solares* were the poorest of Havana's poor neighborhoods and were made up of old oblong dwellings that housed many families. They were known for having a common watering spout and few if any modern amenities, such as lighting and plumbing. Many had been constructed as slave quarters, possibly a hundred years before. It was in El Solar de Africa that Chano grew into manhood and joined Abakuá, an African-based religion largely derived from the Ibo religions of southern Nigeria. While Abakuá, like other Afro-Cuban religions, had many private rituals, it also, like other beliefs, had public ones. Chano publicly participated in Abakuá contingents in carnivals and street ceremonies and went on to become a musical performance legend in Cuba's Afro-Cuban religious celebrations. Over time this was as much for his lifestyle as for his musicianship. Even though he became famous and earned considerable sums of money during his life, he never moved out of El Solar de Africa. That he remained with his people made him into a folk hero. He parked his gold Cadillac in front of his building and wore his red silk robe to the common water spout to wash up every morning. According to neighbor Juan Alvarez, Chano "was a hero to us. He gave us a feeling of pride. . . . It made us feel good to see him change clothes a few times a day and own several cars. He gave us hope."[52]

Not surprisingly, lore about Chano's life abounded. For instance, after spending his teenage years in and out of reform school, Chano grew to be known as a ladies' man and a "fierce street battler."[53] According to Max Salazar, his charisma led women to fight over him, and Chano himself often threatened and brawled with those who wronged him. In fact, unscrupulous recording agents often felt Chano's wrath. In one case in 1940, Chano learned from a friend that many of his songs were hits in the United States. According to the friend, they were being played by a wide range of bands, including those led by Xavier Cugat, Machito, and the Quarteto La Playa. When Pozo realized how much profit was being made from his songs, he approached his agent, a Mr. Roca of Peer International. In the late 1930s Roca had given Chano a meager ten dollars for the publishing rights to his songs. When Roca denied that Chano's songs were money-making hits, Chano left his office, vowing to hospitalize Roca if he didn't get his money.

When Chano returned the following day, he found Roca in the company of a bodyguard, who had a pistol. He and Chano tussled, and Chano took two bullets to the stomach. While Chano survived, doctors were unable to remove one bullet lodged near his spine;[54] he carried it inside him for the rest of his life.

Chano's temper, as well as his extreme bravado, ultimately did cause his death, however. In 1948, less than two years after his arrival in New York, Chano was fatally shot by a fellow Cuban in El Rio Bar and Grill on 111th and Lenox Avenue. The Cuban, known only as Cabito, was a soft-spoken veteran who everyone said was depressed. After fighting in the U.S. armed forces in World War II, he had returned to New York with little money and no hope of a real job. He sustained himself on his small pension and by working in the numbers racket and in the exchange of contraband. On December 1, 1948, he and Chano had a dispute over a transaction in which Chano fought and beat Cabito in front of other people. Feeling betrayed and dishonored, Cabito walked into the bar and grill on December 2 and killed Chano in front of witnesses. Dizzy, Machito, Charlie Parker, and others held a service for him in New York and helped get his body back to Cuba. Max Salazar, in his research on Chano's life, interviewed Cuban friends of Chano and asked what they thought of his life and death. Interestingly, most saw his death in religious terms. Some said his death was the result of his having offended the gods of the Abakuá because he had given Dizzy sacred chants; others said he had neglected for too long his sacrifices to his personal god, Santa Barbara.

Chano Pozo's life does give us a window into all that was wonderful and rich in African-American and Cuban relations.[55] His membership in Abakuá illustrates that African culture, while fluid and dynamic, was nonetheless alive as Cubans entered into a relationship with African-Americans. Similarly, his working-class origins were shared by most African-Americans and Cubans before the civil rights movement and the Cuban revolution. Both were people who struggled to create a better life, to fight against systemic racism and imperialism, and to retain as much of their African heritage as they could. Toward this end, they played baseball, made music, played the numbers, created art, sold contraband, prayed to the gods, danced, wrote poetry, published newspapers, organized and mobilized and agitated and rebelled.

The following essays are our attempt to share at least part of the story with all of its beauty and its contradictions.

NOTES

1. "U.S.-Cuba: The Shriveling of Helms-Burton," *Cuba Update* 18, no. 1 (summer 1997): 2.

2. This is the title of a chapter on Caribbean numbers bankers in Irma Watkins-Owens, *Blood Relations: Caribbean Immigrants and the Harlem Community, 1900–1930* (Bloomington: Indiana University Press, 1996), 136–48.

3. Louis A. Pérez Jr., "Introduction," in *José Martí in the United States: The Florida Experience,* ed. Louis Pérez Jr. (Tempe: Arizona: Center for Latin American Studies, Arizona State University, 1995), 5–6.

4. Ibid., 6.

5. Quoted in Johnetta Cole, "Afro-American Solidarity with Cuba," *Black Scholar* 8, nos. 8–10 (1977): 74.

6. It was actually serialized twice—first in the *Anglo-African Magazine* in 1859, as it was being written, and again in 1861–62 in the new *Weekly Anglo-African.*

7. Quoted in Ruth Glasser, *My Music Is My Flag: Puerto Rican Musicians and Their New York Communities* (Berkeley and Los Angeles: University of California Press, 1995), 75.

8. Most Cubans, especially black Cubans, resisted the Platt Amendment of 1902. It guaranteed the United States the authority to intervene militarily to insure a "stable government," to determine Cuba's foreign relations, and to acquire land, set up naval stations, and conduct business. Even though the republic was technically independent, its national sovereignty was completed circumscribed.

9. White is quoted in Cathy Duke, "The Idea of Race: The Cultural Impact of American Intervention in Cuba, 1898–1912, in *Politics, Society and Culture in the Caribbean,* ed. Blanca G. Silvestrini (San Juan: University of Puerto Rico Press, 1983), 93.

10. *Encyclopedia Brittanica,* 1878, s.v. "Negro." This entry went substantially unrevised for nearly thirty years. All of these ideas were clearly stated within the discussion.

11. Quoted in Lisa Brock, "Back to the Future: African-American and Cuban Relations in the Time(s) of Race," *Contributions in Black Studies: A Journal of African and Afro-American Studies* 12 (1994): 20.

12. Ibid.

13. Ibid.

14. American black leaders such as W.E.B. Du Bois began working with blacks in Africa, the Caribbean, and Europe in an attempt to resolve these questions. While never without contradiction, between 1900 and 1945 there were five pan-African congresses and numerous meetings around these very issues.

15. See W.E.B. Du Bois, *The Souls of Black Folk* (1907; New York: Fawcett, 1961).

16. The one time such a thing was done was in the creation of Liberia. Freed blacks were recruited and settled there by the American Colonization Society between 1820 and 1840. They became a U.S.-controlled settler oligarchy who oppressed the majority population. One hundred years later, when the indigenous majority overturned the Americo-Liberians, the country as a whole was turned into turmoil.

17. Throughout the nineteenth century, Spanish authorities openly sought European immigrants with the hope of increasing the white presence on the island. Following the Haitian revolution, Spain and white Cubans feared a black majority and black uprising. Increasing the white population was a major topic in nineteenth-century colonial discourse.

18. Houston Baker, *Modernism and the Harlem Renaissance* (Chicago: University of Chicago Press, 1987), 20–21.

19. Kevin Gaines, "Black Americans' Racial Uplift Ideology as Civilizing Mission: Pauline Hopkins on Race and Imperialism," in *Cultures of United States Imperialism,* ed. Amy Kaplan and Donald E. Pease (Durham: Duke University Press, 1993), 437.

20. Michael Hanchard, *Orpheus and Power: The Movimento Negro of Rio de Janeiro and São Paulo, Brazil, 1945–1988* (Princeton: Princeton University Press, 1994), 28.

21. Samuel Floyd, *The Power of Black Music: Interpreting the History from Africa to the United States* (Oxford: Oxford University Press, 1995), 8.

22. Yvonne Daniel, *Rumba: Dance and Social Change in Contemporary Cuba* (Bloomington: Indiana University Press, 1995), 2.

23. Louis A. Pérez Jr., "Between Baseball and Bullfighting: The Quest for Nationality in Cuba, 1888–1898," *Journal of American History* 81 (Sept. 1994): 494.

24. Donn Rogosin, *Invisible Men: Life in Baseball's Negro Leagues* (New York: Kodansha International, 1995), 95.

25. Rob Ruck, *Sandlot Seasons: Sport in Black Pittsburgh* (Urbana: University of Illinois Press, 1993), 5.

26. Burton W. Peretti, *The Creation of Jazz, Music, Race and Culture in Urban America* (Urbana: University of Illinois Press, 1992), 12.

27. Katrina Hazzard-Gordon, *Jookin': The Rise of Social Dance Formations in African-American Culture* (Philadelphia: Temple University Press, 1990), 3.

28. Ibid., 3–4.

29. Ibid., 4.

30. "The Ghost of Charlie Mingus," presented on "Chicago Jazz Festival Preview," Richard Steel and Chris Hein, hosts, WBEZ-FM (National Public Radio), Chicago, August 27, 1997.

31. William Barlow, "*Looking Up at Down": The Emergence of Blues Culture* (Philadelphia: Temple University Press, 1989), 22.

32. Ibid.

33. Nelson George, *Elevating the Game: The History and Aesthetics of Black Men in Basketball* (New York: Fireside, Simon and Schuster), xvii.

34. David Wiggins, "The Notion of Double Consciousness and the Involvement of Black Athletes in American Sport," in *Ethnicity and Sport in North American History and Culture,* ed. George Eisen and David K. Wiggins (Westport, Conn.: Praeger, 1995), 139.

35. Julius Tygiel, "Black Ball," in *Total Baseball,* ed. John Thorn and Pete Palmer (New York: HarperPerennial, 1989), 492.

36. Ibid.

37. Campanella quoted in ibid.

38. Eisen and Wiggins, *Ethnicity and Sport,* 139–40.

39. Mark Ribowsky, *A Complete History of the Negro Leagues, 1884–1955* (New York: Birch Lane Press, 1995), 139.

40. Peter C. Bjarkman, *Baseball with a Latin Beat* (Jefferson, N.C.: McFarland Publishers, 1994), 181.

41. Paula J. Pettavino and Geralyn Pye, *Sport in Cuba: The Diamond in the Rough* (Pittsburgh: University of Pittsburgh Press, 1994), 185.

42. Tygiel, "Black Ball," 499.

43. Toni Morrison, *Black Women Writers at Work,* ed. Claudia Tate (New York: Continuum, 1983). Statement as epigraph in Nelson George, *Elevating the Game,* xiii.

44. George, *Elevating the Game,* xix.

45. Tygiel, "Black Ball," 493.

46. Ibid., 492.

47. George, *Elevating the Game,* xiv.

48. Stan Wooley, "Machito—Making Musical Earthquakes," *Jazz Journal International* 30, no. 11 (Nov. 1977): 36.

49. Ibid., 37. Most of this wonderful information on Chano Pozo was graciously shared with me by Max Salazar. See also Salazar, *Latin Beat Magazine,* April–June 1993, "Chano Pozo," Parts 1–3.

50. Dizzy Gillespie with Al Fraser, *To BE, or not . . . to BOP* (New York: Doubleday, 1979), 318.

51. Ibid., 324.

52. Salazar, "Chano Pozo," part 1, *Latin Beat Magazine,* April 1993, 10.

53. Ibid., 9.

54. While Chano did receive royalties from Roca for his songs, the monies he received never matched what he was actually owed. He was like hundreds of black songwriters and performers in the United States and Cuba of that day whose cultural properties were stolen.

55. Yet Chano is also representative of a bravado apparent in both black communities that, while counterhegemonic when posed to fight race and empire, can prove self-destructive if not skillfully and intentionally directed. That people today remember fondly the fact that women physically fought over Chano is indeed problematic and leads me to conclude this essay with a note. This anthology, while rich in presenting the myriad ways that race and empire were negotiated in the public sphere, does so largely through the voices of men in male-centered domains. We wished that this was not the case. But it is. Even though many of the chapters address gender issues to some extent, only one author centers women's voices and none deal explicitly with sexual orientation.

That these essays share hitherto unknown stories as well as deft analysis is telling. For if we can do this largely through the male eye, we can only imagine what African-American and Cuban relations might look like through the experiences and polemics of women as well.

Minerva

A Magazine for Women (and Men) of Color

CARMEN MONTEJO ARRECHEA

Despite the rough treatment of yesterday and the stupid opinions of today
unnerving our spirits, we prepare our defenses for the constant battle. We will do
so until we are accepted for who we are and not because some pirate artist has
agreed or decided that it meets his cowardly ends. You invite us to struggle? Well,
we'll fight. . . . Let us reflect, then, without distinction as to race on the judgment
that it has been women who have raised the majority of men and even some
slovenly servants, as well as raising us women.
Africa Céspedes, 1889

Africa Céspedes was an irregular contributor to the early (1880s) editions of
Minerva: Revista Quincenal Dedicada a la Mujer de Color (Minerva: The Biweekly Magazine for the Woman of Color), the first known magazine in Cuba
dedicated to black women. While few of the articles to be discussed in this
chapter were as powerful as Céspedes's irregular contributions, her opinions
reflect a bold current among black Cuban women, many of whom had just
attained freedom through the Spanish abolition proclamations of the 1880s.
Women fought for formal education and against the formidable double barriers of sexism and racism. An early twentieth-century sociologist, Blanche
Zacharie de Baralt, reflected the racial thinking common among elites in the
Western world (e.g., the positivist biological "science" of the French racist
Count Joseph-Arthur de Gobineau). Baralt described Cuba in a book, published in England in 1913, entitled *Sociología en impresiones de la República de
Cuba en el siglo XX.* Exemplifying the prejudices of that time, she accused
blacks of retarding the "social development" of Cuba. She wrote that, "race
mixture darkened the white element, contaminating it and staining it with the
stigma of inferiority. The curse of slavery weighing on the population con-

tributed to retarding its social evolution."[1] What she forgot to mention was that race mixture was largely the result of the desire for and power over black women's sexuality by male slave owners. The exoticization of black women then created terribly negative images that were used to devalue black "womanhood." A black woman was seen as a source of labor, an object of pleasure, or a commodity; she had little, if any, legal protection.

Newly freed black women in Cuba, then, struggled for respect for themselves and their race as a whole. *Minerva* magazine was created to advance such goals in the last quarter of the nineteenth century, during the twilight years of the Spanish colonial period in Cuba. Founded in 1888, it functioned not only as a voice of liberation for black women in Cuba but also as a pivotal vehicle through which Cuban women on the island could be linked to black Cuban women in the United States and in the Caribbean. Even though it only existed for a few years during its first run, it did reappear in the second decade of the twentieth century under the same name with the subtitle of "Illustrated Universal Magazine." Through their writings, black Cuban women called upon all of their sisters of color to cooperate in the effort "without fear of criticism and sarcasm from others."[2]

The Early Period

During the late nineteenth century, publications directed at women and at blacks already existed. In fact, there was a growth both in Afro-Cuban publications throughout the island and black women's writings in the United States. However, none focused specifically on black Cuban women. Under the editorship of Miguel Gualba, the first known edition of *Minerva* was published on October 15, 1888.[3] The guiding principle stated in the first issue was "that of offering a vehicle where our sisters who have studied literature can evolve a definite literary vocation [and] bring their efforts into the public eye and thus encourage our women to pursue further studies."[4] The fact that a man was the magazine's editor posed few problems at the time, given that such was expected. Literate Cuban women were, like their black North American sisters, "prepared to defend and celebrate black womanhood without disrupting the delicate balance of black male-female relations or challenging male authority."[5] They argued for the education of black women and for a defense of the virtue of black womanhood as important struggles for the race as whole, understanding quite clearly that "gender identity [in the Americas was] inextricably linked to and even determined by racial identity."[6] They therefore en-

gaged in a discourse about gender that used what Evelyn Brooks Higginbotham has termed the "metalanguage of race."[7] In so doing, they "invited
and received enthusiastic support of influential men"[8] and were able to reach
a wider audience of both women and men. Indication of this is seen in the
warm reception they received from the best-known black paper in Cuba at the
time, *La Fraternidad,* whose editors welcomed the publication of *Minerva* on
its first edition with the following comment:

> We have just received our first visit from *Minerva,* a biweekly maga-
> zine dated the fifteenth of this month and dedicated to women of
> color. The interesting magazine consists of eight pages, elegantly
> printed, with a cover in color in the form of a folder, where one finds
> the list of contributors who will enlighten the magazine with inter-
> esting literary, as well as musical pieces. Representative of the high
> quality contained in the magazine, there is a lovely composition from
> the inspired pen of señor Anselmo Font, entitled "Past and Present."
> To get a better idea of its contents, consider the following interesting
> table of contents: "Our Future"; "To the Press"; "Two Words," by
> Cecilia. Poetry Section: "Past and Present" by Anselmo Font; "Song"
> by Lucrecia González; "In a Fan" by Onatina; "*Minerva* Miscella-
> neous"; "Biweekly Notes" [by] E. T. Elvira.[9]

From the beginning *Minerva,* like many Cuban magazines of the time,
saw itself as linking the island with Cubans living abroad. Many black
women had fled the island as political exiles or economic or war refugees
during the Ten Years War (1868–78). They settled in Tampa, New York,
Key West, Jamaica, and other territories of the Americas. Most planned to
return to Cuba after Spain had been defeated, and they maintained strong
contacts with their homeland through the anticolonial struggle. When the
independence did not come about in 1878, many stayed abroad but continued to work in revolutionary clubs that raised money and support for
the final war of independence (1895–98). There was, in fact, an understood, actively articulated, and strongly nationalistic Cuban diaspora in the
latter nineteenth century. Black Cuban women who lived in cities such as
Tampa, Key West, New York, and New Orleans were part of that. *Minerva*
magazine, then, also explicitly saw itself as linking black Cuban women on
the island with those abroad and was circulated in many other areas. For
example, the magazine in 1888 listed the persons who were acting as its

agents abroad. There was Joaquín Granados in Key West, Primitivo Plumas in Tampa, Juan Bonillas in New York, and Isolina Regino in Kingston.

It is evident that Cuban émigrés abroad were primary financial supporters of the magazine in the early period. Inside the front cover there was always a listing by place, name, and country of origin of those women who supported the magazine. Interestingly, though, the lists always included women with anglicized names who were said to be black North Americans. For instance, Liboria Urrutia and Jennie Walters were said to be some of the magazine's most enthusiastic supporters and promoters in Key West; they worked together to gain a readership for *Minerva* there. Black Cuban women living abroad obviously made contacts and developed friendships with their black sisters in cities where the magazine circulated. The magazine, then, served to promote a little-known relationship between black Cuban and North American women that transcended language, nationality, and culture. One wonders if the flurry of black women's publications in the United States at exactly the same time had any influence on *Minerva* or vice versa.[10] For *Minerva's* editors seemed determined to echo all black women's concerns and to address women in general who identified with their struggles and who suffered similar kinds of affronts arising from the inferior status to which they were assigned. In addition, the magazine did provide a bridge between Cuban women on the island and some North American black women. Black women in various places supported the magazine not only by increasing its circulation but by sending it stories as well.

Originally, the editors had planned to illustrate the magazine's cover with portraits of the contributors, but due to financial difficulties only one known contributor, Ursula Coimbra de Valverde ("Cecilia"), ever appeared on a cover. The covers were painted gratis by a portrait artist named Torriente, who wanted, he explained, "to help the colored race." The editors also published the pen names of permanent contributors, which included Cecilia, Onatina, Lucrecia González, Cristina Ayala, América Font, Lino or Waal de Crees, Oscar de Ruzy, Natividad González, N. Lanita, and, as music editor, Raimundo Valenzuela. The publication was divided into several sections. In the first part appeared pieces submitted by contributors, female and male, from Cuba and elsewhere. The second section was devoted to poetry and the third to a biweekly news summary that focused primarily on events in Cuba and the United States. Some of the poems in the first editions were "Spring Morning" by Lucrecia González Consuegra, "Thought" by Cristina Ayala, "You and Me" by Rosa G. Nad, "To Onatina" by María Cleofa, and "To Cuba" by

América Céspedes. Some poems were sent from abroad, such as "The Ugly Woman," written by a woman in New York, and "The Dance" by Rafael Serra, the famous Cuban journalist living in Kingston.[11] Another important piece was "Winter Afternoons" by Joaquín Granados. *Minerva* also reprinted lectures that were important to women, such as that given by Martín Morúa Delgado, Cuban nationalist and journalist, to El Progreso Society of Key West entitled "Women and Their Rights." In it Morúa Delgado exhorted women to struggle to occupy their rightful place in society as well as to cooperate with men in the achievement of that task.

The writers, whether in Cuba or living abroad, consistently tried to inculcate in their readers a desire for self-improvement, learning, and for serving the black community as models of "virtue and abnegation." In fact, virtue, freedom, and education were interrelated in most of the aspirations expressed by *Minerva*'s contributors. América Font wrote that

> one of the gifts that every woman should treasure is her virtue, but this may be to some extent a kind of weakness if virtue is not accompanied and protected by the gifts of intellectual abilities and refinement. . . . Virtue and training are the factors which will produce the sum total of goods for women and I think the one is deficient without the other. . . . Women should aspire . . . to leave behind the slavery of ignorance. To be free, according to this thinking, women should be educated, since where there is no enlightenment there is no freedom.[12]

In a poem entitled "Ignorance" another writer, Natividad González, indicates that to fight ignorance, "You need to search with energy and tenacity, the best way to change yourself, and casting your gaze to the past, try in the present to raise yourself up."[13] In a letter sent to *Minerva* by María Storini, the author points to the importance of giving women an education. Storini stated that although she was born a slave, she was lucky enough to have owners who resided in the major capitals of the Western world. Her experiences showed her how inadequate education for Cuban women, especially black Cuban women, really was. She wrote: "It is well known how neglected it is, if indeed the woman of our race has ever received the attention she deserves . . . for many people educating females is a question of ornamentation, and thus not entirely essential."[14] She asserted that such neglect did not occur in other countries, such as the United States, where much attention was paid to women's education. Although this was not altogether true for poor or black women, clearly more women in the United States had access to education than was the case in Cuba. Storini asked as well that an association be founded for the instruction of black women in Cuba.[15]

Importantly, the magazine published articles on the significance of civil marriage. Like newly free black women throughout the Americas, many Cuban women understood that civil marriage was the only way to legalize common-law marriages. Even though some white feminists of the time opposed it, marriage had always been the primary way for women throughout the world to achieve a legally recognized adult status; for subordinated black slave women it was a natural first step toward achieving their humanity, which was gendered for all at the time. Storini, in her piece, emphasized this link between legal marriage, status, and humanity: "slavery has never produced wives but only concubines, and since bondage is over, degradation should end as well."[16] In an "open letter" addressed to Miss C. B., a woman identified simply as Amira warns women that "although one marries in the church today, Catholic marriages will not be valid without the civil procedure."[17] It was necessary that women be educated about marriage as free women and that they be aware that even if they got married in the church, in order to establish a family, the essential step was a civil marriage ceremony, since it entailed legal rights and some protections for women as well as for the children born to such unions.

Minerva advocated the glorification and preservation of the black family. An article published on December 30, 1888, under the title "Colored Race, Arise," encouraged the reader to consider that, "if the colored race wishes cordially to dignify itself and occupy its proper place in public functions, it should begin by establishing families according to the precepts dictated by morality and demanded by law. Keep in mind that without the family there is no possible psychological order [and] contemplate the fact that family is impossible to achieve without marriage."[18] The magazine also challenged all black men to seek wives among black women. "Honorable" women with the most education should be cherished and prized by black men; but no black Cuban woman, no matter how illiterate, should be rejected in favor a white woman; she too could be taught, and it was up to the man to work with black women to make sure that happened. The article went further to argue that the specific qualities of black women should be exalted, and elevation of the status of black women was all the more necessary given the extent of the degradation to which they and their sons, husbands, and fathers had been subjected for centuries. In a very sophisticated manner, black women appealed to race unity in their challenge to black men to marry black women: Do not abandon them for white women, they argued, or further devalue them by having sex with them outside of marriage.

Yet education, virtue, marriage, and family were not all that the writers of *Minerva* stressed. They linked these concerns with the overall struggle for social, racial, and gender equality and clearly sought to educate as they polemicized. Laura Clarence was one such author. In a piece printed in late 1888, she referred to an article in a Havana magazine called *El Eco de Galicia* concerning Emilia Pardo Bazán, a Galician writer initially denied entrance into the Royal Spanish Academy of Letters because she was a woman. Clarence, in an elegant and original fashion, examined the historical legacy of discrimination in education for blacks and women. She presented the case of Gertrudis Gómez de Avellaneda, a premier abolitionist and novelist whose mid-nineteenth-century works had been banned in Cuba, although they were well known in Spain. Gómez de Avellaneda had suffered the same fate many years before. Clarence lamented how little times had changed in that respect. She also explained that the denial of education for blacks had led to a fear of reading and writing that some blacks still possessed. Fear initially had been instilled during the long era of the Blood Code,[19] in effect until 1878, which did not allow free blacks education beyond the primary level. If colonial officials discovered that you could write, they assumed that you had earned an education; and if it could be shown that you had gotten it in Cuba, you could be arrested. Because of the Blood Code, free blacks would have to travel to Europe for an education, a luxury that few could afford. Denial of education was all the more prevalent for black women, many of whom were the daughters of artisans or had themselves been slaves. Clarence ended her very extensive piece by encouraging those who might not know how to read and write not to be afraid; rather, they should seek avenues to educate themselves. She also encouraged women who hesitated to write for the magazine for fear of criticism and persecution to do so, for only through exercising their new rights could they hope to make of new law new realities.

The call went out often in *Minerva* for women to make their voices heard by submitting a contribution. One woman who responded was a worker by the name of Margarita Gutiérrez, who wrote that she had never written an essay before. Her article was titled "Woman: Defense of Her Rights and Enlightenment," and it appeared in the issue of December 15, 1888. According to the magazine's directors, *Minerva* was important for encouraging writers like Gutiérrez, who were the precursors of a new age for black people in Cuba.

Africa Céspedes was probably the most prolific writer to take a bold and confrontational style in calling for black women to struggle against sexism and racism by any means necessary. Although we know little about her, the paragraph that introduced this chapter was published in the February 28, 1889, edition of the magazine, which included her article "Reflections." In it she denounces the situation of black women, who, while no longer slaves, were still viewed as such by their former masters. She indicates that many women are ready to defend themselves until their worth is finally recognized. She skillfully challenges both sexism and racism by arguing that all women, and not just black women, play a crucial role in raising children and thus should be more highly recognized and valued by society in general; but black women, not white women or black men, are "considered the last layers according to [the] disgraceful judgment."[20] They occupied the bottom of the socioeconomic ladder of Cuban society and therefore were the least valued and respected. One wonders why there are not more published articles that took the bold tone found in Céspedes's pieces. Were there other women who took such a position but whose essays were not published, or did most women simply use a style that was less confrontational?

It is clear from the number of writers identified with initials, single-word names, and pseudonyms that there was great concern about sanctions, penalties, and even arrest among women who used journalism to challenge the status quo. In addition, given that many of *Minerva*'s contributors were nationalist revolutionaries on the island or political exiles active in revolutionary clubs abroad, it was important both for them and for the magazine that they remain anonymous at least in the public realm to which Spanish authorities had access. For instance, a regular section of biweekly news and notes was written by someone using the pseudonym of E. T. Elvira. "Elvira" never wanted to reveal her or his true identity, even though the news that he or she wrote about tended to be more social than political. It was largely devoted to reports of black and mulatto social groups in Cuba and abroad, and included weddings, births, deaths, and social events. Yet because even this section encouraged race solidarity and revealed the importance of Cubans abroad in supporting the nationalist struggle, it could easily have been viewed as political and problematic. Similarly, there was Emilio Plana, who while writing for *El Sport* magazine in Tampa was also a regular translator for *Minerva* magazine under the name of Jonatás.

Given the nationalist background of many of the supporters, it makes sense that many of the writers would attempt to write in a nonthreatening tone. Some in fact went to painstaking effort to call for a reconciliation with whites, given that slavery had ended, as well as to challenge whites morally to rise above their own racism. For instance, an article by Natividad González emphasized the need to forgive those who had done so much harm to the poor and disinherited race. After all, blacks did not seek vengeance, according to González, but rather forgiveness as the way to attain unity and equality. Cristina Ayala in a piece entitled "I Agree" wrote that "a heart where noble aspirations reside cannot be deaf to the [black] voice[s] that [struggle for] the road to duty and virtue."[21]

On May 30, 1889, after nearly eight months of publication, *Minerva's* administrator, Enrique Cos,[22] announced the magazine might have to be suspended for financial reasons. He also indicated that the publication had always existed in an hostile climate and that Spanish authorities during its entire tenure had tried to shut it down. They did in fact shut down *La Fraternidad* and put its founder, Juan Gualberto Gómez, in jail. The last issue of the early period of *Minerva* appeared on July 19, 1889.

Minerva in the Republic

Following the Cuban-Spanish-American War (1895–1900) and a decade of regrouping, the black community again began to feel the need to express itself through journalism. Even though a kind of pseudo-independence had come, imperialism and racism continued. For a decade, officials were unresponsive to black veterans, who had made up the bulk of the nationalist army but received few of the civil-service or public-sector jobs, and others who pressed for black rights. Government indifference to continued discrimination provoked revolts and other serious disturbances; these in turn led to brutal suppression of all blacks by the authorities.[23]

Minerva reappeared on September 15, 1910, but under a different name and with a broader mission. From that point it would be called the *Minerva Illustrated Universal Magazine: Sciences, Art, Literature and Sport: The Expression of the Colored Race*. The new magazine announced that although it would have a section called "Feminist Pages" (and in fact it continued to have more women writers than any other black magazine at the time), it would emphasize issues of importance to the black race as a whole. Its content would focus exclusively on social, literary, artistic, and scientific matters. Its purpose was to "inculcate a love of beauty, utility and truth" without neglecting the struggle for social equality. It was important, again, not to be seen as too political.

But it was hard not to be political. Black Cubans had fought for years for a unified Cuban nation and now found themselves, although in possession of greater legal and national rights, economically, socially, and culturally marginalized—this time by some of the same Cuban leaders with whom they had worked to achieve independence. Moreover, if they raised their voices about racism, they themselves were accused of being racists. Thus from the beginning, this *Minerva* had few illusions that a conciliatory tone was likely to achieve much. In fact, its editors were continually forced to defend *Minerva's* right to exist. They were more open than they had been in the past about their determination to fight for social equality, and they expressed their outrage at the indignity of racism in forceful language. For example, in an strong editorial, the board of the magazine wrote:

> *Minerva,* the most authoritative expression of the colored race at this time, which accepts and seeks to bring black efforts to light by publishing [in the] literary, scientific, and social fields, finds itself incapable of stilling its indignation. Such rebellious indignation boils in the soul over the ominous act committed against the person of Julia Hernández Gutiérrez, who was rejected by the superintendency of the school of nursing at Reina Mercedes Hospital because she was black.

In another article entitled "Slanderous Accusations," the magazine refuted those in the press who published unfounded stories and offensive charges against members of the colored race who simply spoke out about the suffering of black people. The editors specifically defended Juan Gualberto Gómez, who had been under consistent attack in the press and in certain politicians' circles since 1902. Because he refused to accept second-class citizenship for blacks in the republic, just as he had declined to do during colonialism, he was accused of fomenting divisions between blacks and whites. According to *Minerva,* "to [attack Gómez] is to intentionally ignore the patriotic value of the prodigious body of work carried out by that incomparable man who dedicated the better part of his life to achieve the greatest fellowship between all the components of the Cuban population."[24]

The bolder approach of this *Minerva* is seen in its change of focus from education and racial uplift to promoting the contributions of blacks to human culture (so that "blacks are taken into account")[25] and instilling race pride in blacks themselves. For many writers, cases such as that of the nursing school applicant proved that even members of the race who had reached a high educational level were still forbidden from entering certain institutions. It was no longer "enough that a race, like an individual, [should] attain a great mental uplifting and [be] inclined toward mutual progress. Existing [black achievements in the social, economic, and cultural arenas] must be known about. . . . It is up to newspapers and magazines to assume such an obligation, in the context of a society only somewhat organized. *Minerva,* the exponent and voice for what culture means to us, has been carrying out precisely that mission."[26] Another issue explained that *Minerva* "features the history of our culture and its progress as well as providing a deft rhetorical device directed toward those who belittle our cultural beginnings."[27]

Toward this end the magazine had pieces on famous blacks in history, such as one on Alexander Pushkin, Russia's poet laureate, who was of African descent.[28] It also featured stories on black societies, black institutions, and successful individuals in contemporary Cuba whom blacks could be proud of. News such as the following appeared: "In Cienfuegos there has been much progress in a short time. We already have the following teachers [teaching in that region]: Eduviges Pérez de Rosa, Ursula Coimbra de Valverde, Dionisia de Wolf, Filomena Berravarza and others."[29] Another article mentioned the Society of Scientific and Literary Studies of Havana, which had among its members black writers, journalists, and teachers such as Regino Boti, José Manuel Pomeda, Rita Flores de Campo Marquetti, Inocencia Silveira, Graciela Serra, Cristina Ayala, and Digna de Lisle, and speakers and literary experts such as Camaño de Cárdenas. One writer followed up this story with a defense of *Minerva* by noting, "One could only characterize as highly laudable the initiative taken by the brilliant magazine from Havana, *Minerva,* which is dedicating special issues to the various societies of our ethnic ambiance."[30]

The magazine also expanded its call for support for black initiatives. Its editors made note of public establishments owned by black men, and exhorted the black community "to protect those places and show solidarity so their owners can get ahead." ("Protection" was a euphemism for financial support by community members.) The following announcement is a good example: "The telegraph [offices have] owners from our race. Your protection is requested for this establishment. The solidarity of mutual interests requires it."[31]

Interestingly, *Minerva* continued to serve as a link between Cubans on the island and Cubans resident in North America. The new discourse, however, employed a more sophisticated analysis, often of contrast and comparison, to highlight the specific ways that racism worked in both places. For instance, the publication frequently explained that the discrimination experienced by U.S. blacks was not all that different from discrimination in Cuba during the same period. Yet while the United States expressed its racism in violent terms, Cuba's expression was sly and underhanded. In the United States, blacks were isolated, insulted, and lynched, while in Cuba blacks were shortchanged on their economic and social rights. Thus, negrophobia existed in both places.

Another important article was written by Laura Clarence. In it, to make her points, Clarence reprinted parts of an essay titled "The White Smile" by the famous author Emilia Pardo Bazán. Pardo Bazán was a subject of great interest due to her hotly debated application for membership in the Spanish Royal Academy of Letters, which historically had accepted few women. Although white, she was also known for taking stands against both racism and sexism. Clarence focused on a comment Pardo Bazán had made about Dick Saunders, a world boxing prizefighter; Saunders had publicly stated that he did not believe that a white fighter should accept a boxing challenge from a black athlete. After talking about the famous black American fighter Jack Johnson, who went on to beat Sanders in a match, Pardo Bazán, in tongue-in-cheek fashion, lambasted Saunders and U.S. racism. Clarence quotes her:

> It could not be tolerated in that free North American republic where blacks are and will always be regarded as an inferior race to whom no alternative can ever be conceded. Whatever the black does, if he obtains a doctorate, if he writes a book, if he makes a million dollars, if in concert he interprets Beethoven like Brindis de Salas[32]. . . contact with him will still be avoidable. A white person should get off the street car or get up from the table at the bar when a black fellow threatens proximity of the emanations of his skin which, as everyone [white] knows, looks like that of the cockroach.[33]

Because Johnson went on to beat Sanders, Clarence goes on to say that this time "the cockroach" had taught racists a much-needed lesson.

Minerva also featured less volatile items about blacks in the United States. A regular column called "Echoes from Tampa" often carried news of the black organization known as the Martí-Maceo Union. It reported on the brave and "multiple efforts made by a class of people both noble and humble" to maintain a vibrant social and cultural scene.[34] There was also news on the sports page and in "Echoes From Tampa" about black sporting events in the United

States, especially in baseball and boxing. When black baseball teams would visit Cuba, the sports page would advertise their arrival. One headline proclaimed the arrival of "Visiting Teams, among them [New York's] Lincoln Giants." It added that the U.S. teams were "composed exclusively of black players." It was hoped that Cuba's black community would come out and support these all-black teams from the United States. The magazine also covered the activities of American blacks visiting the island. Those who were hosted by one of the island's own black societies would get the most press. One example was this item, which appeared in a September 1911 issue of *Minerva:* "The coachmen's center celebrated a soiree in honor of American tourists and prominent personalities of the colored race in the United States, Mr. John E. Ford, Dr. James E. Shepart, John Merrick, C. C. Spaulding and Acron M. Moore. The evening was a resounding success among leading members of Havana society."[35]

In 1912 the magazine again came to an end, after two years of publication. Although no official reason was given for the suspension, one can assume the primary reason was the black revolt that began in Oriente province in May of that year and spread throughout the island during the summer. There was a general crackdown on all blacks at that time in response to what became known as the "Race War." Black societies and organizations were especially vulnerable. New magazines, however, did resurface within the next few years.

Conclusion

Minerva magazine, during both its first and second periods, served to give voice to black Cuban women and the black community as a whole. Even though the magazine did not focus primarily on women during its second period, it continued to publish more women writers and featured more women's issues than any of the other black magazines of the time. Among the regular contributors in the second period were Laura Clarence, Cristina Ayala, Ursula Coimbra de Valverde, Gloria Alonso, Angelina Edreira, Ana María Marcos, Nieves Prieto, María J. Michelena, Dr. María Latapier, and Anabella and Vitalina Morúa Delgado. Interestingly, some of the women wrote during both periods. This illustrates, I think, that the changes in the magazine were not an expression of differing perspectives brought by different writers but of a changed consciousness on the part of black Cubans. The era of biological racism that had descended in much of the West required all blacks to be more race conscious. Whether this was good for the struggle against sexism within the black community is yet another question. *Minerva* did in this second period serve as a bridge between those old nationalists and an emerging generation of intellectuals and activists. Juan Gualberto Gómez was the magazine's honorary director, and he, along with contemporaries such as General Campos Marquetti, continued to write for the magazine alongside unestablished new writers, such as Regino Boti and a very young Nicolás Guillén.

NOTES

Acknowledgment: This essay was translated by Francine Cronshaw.

1. Blanche Zacharie de Baralt, *Sociología en impresiones de la República de Cuba en el siglo XX* (England, 1913), 156–65.

2. "Prosigamos," *Minerva: Revista Quincenal Dedicada a la Mujer de Color* [Havana] 1, no. 6 (Dec. 15, 1888): 1 (hereafter *Minerva*).

3. Miguel Gualba was the director of *Minerva* magazine, manager of *La Fraternidad* newspaper, and secretary in its early period of the Directorio Central de las Sociedades de la Raza de Color. The central directorate was created in Cuba at the initiative of Juan Gualberto Gómez in 1887, to unite all the black and mulatto societies in Cuba in order to prepare them for the war that was quickly approaching. He maintained that the struggle was against Spain, not against whites.

4. *Minerva* 1, no. 1 (October 15, 1888): 5.

5. Joanne Braxton, introduction to Mrs. N. F. Mossell, *The Work of the Afro-American Woman,* Schomburg Library of Nineteenth Century Black Women Writers Series (New York: Oxford University Press, 1988), xxviii.

6. Evelyn Brooks Higginbotham, "African-American Women's History and the Metalanguage of Race," in *"We Specialize in the Wholly Impossible": A Reader in Black Women's History,* ed. Darlene Clark Hine, Wilma King, and Linda Reed (Brooklyn, N.Y.: Carlson Publishing, 1995), 4.

7. Higginbotham explains the metalanguage of race: "we must expose the role of race as a metalanguage by calling attention to its powerful, all-encompassing effect on the construction and representation of other social and power relations, namely, gender, class, and sexuality, . . . [and] we must recognize race as providing sites of dialogic exchange and contestation, since race has constituted a discursive tool for both oppression and liberation" (ibid., 4).

8. Braxton, in Mossell, *The Work of the Afro-American Woman,* xxxviii.

9. "Sumario," *Minerva* 1, no. 4 (Nov. 30, 1888): front cover.

10. Henry Louis Gates, who together with the Schomburg Center for Research in Black Culture has spearheaded a project aimed at reprinting little-known texts by black women in the nineteenth century, has called the period between 1890 and 1910 "the Black

Woman's era" in the African-American literary tradition. See his foreword in Mossell, *The Work of the Afro-American Woman,* xvi.

11. Rafael Serra was a Cuban journalist and patriot who collaborated with José Martí during the latter's years of exile. A significant poet, Serra served in the Chamber of Representatives during the "pseudo-republic" period. He died in 1909.

12. América Font, "Mis opiniones," *Minerva* 1, no. 4 (Nov. 30, 1888): 1.

13. "La ignorancia," *Minerva* 1, no. 5 (Dec. 15, 1888): 4.

14. María Storini, "Una carta," *Minerva* 1, no. 4 (Nov. 30, 1888): 3.

15. Storini, in her letter to the editor (ibid.), indicated that an association should be created for instructing women, in particular black women. It would be similar to the program established in Madrid in 1871–72, on the initiative of Fernando Castro, the rector of Madrid's Central University. The institution had as its goal the promotion of the education and instruction of women in all spheres of social life.

16. Ibid.

17. Amira, "Carta abierta a la srta. C. B.," *Minerva* 1, no. 4 (Nov. 30, 1888): 1.

18. "Raza negra, elevate," *Minerva* 1, no. 4 (Nov. 30, 1888): 2.

19. According to the Blood Code, in effect in Cuba during the colonial period and lasting until after the Ten Years' War, blacks were not allowed to pursue higher education, nor was anyone who could not prove that they were descended from Catholic Christians.

20. Africa Céspedes, "Reflexiones," 4.

21. Cristinia Ayala, "Me adhiero," *Minerva* 2, no. 2 (Jan. 26, 1889): 2.

22. Enrique Cos, journalist and administrator of *Minerva* magazine, had been the first black student enrolled in Institute No. 1 of Havana. He collaborated with Juan Gualberto Gómez in his struggle for black emancipation and Cuban independence.

23. During the first decade of the "pseudo-republic," a group of persons belonging to the black race created a grouping called Independents of Color, which became a political party. It was initially recognized as such by the interventor government of the United States; blacks were otherwise marginalized at that time. Political struggle subsequently turned into armed struggle, and the movement of the Independents of Color was brutally repressed, and its leaders, independence army officer Pedro Ivonet and working class leader Evaristo Estenoz, were murdered.

24. "Imputaciones calumniosas," *Minerva* 4, no. 13 (July 1912): 7.

25. "Existe en Cuba la clasificación oficial de raza?" *Minerva* 1 (January 11, 1911): 16.

26. Ibid.

27. Alberto Castellano, "La labor de Minerva," *Minerva* 3, no. 7 (September 1911): 3.

28. Russia's leading poet, Alexander Pushkin, was born in Moscow on May 26, 1799. He carried African blood in his veins since his paternal grandfather was a black who had been brought to Russia as a child by Peter the Great. In his adopted country Pushkin's father established the Amiballoff family. Pushkin's mother belonged to one of the oldest and noblest families of the Russian empire and herself descended from Rottcha Caballero Alemán, who settled in Moscow in the thirteenth century.

29. E. T. Elvira, "Notas quincenales," *Minerva* 4, no. 12 (May 12, 1912): 16.

30. Alberto Castellano, "La labor de Minerva," 3.

31. Elvira, "Notas quincenales," 16.

32. Claudio Brindis de Salas was a prominent Cuban violinist, known as the "king of the octaves," and a member of the Legion of Honor.

33. Laura Clarence comments on Emilia Pardo Bazán, "La sonrisa blanca" [The white smile], *Minerva* 4, no. 10 (July 12, 1912): 16.

34. "Ecos de Tampa," *Minerva* 4, no. 7 (April 7, 1912): 2.

35. *Minerva* 3, no. 7 (September 1911): 3.

2

Telling Silences and Making Community

Afro-Cubans and African-Americans in Ybor City and Tampa, 1899–1915

NANCY RAQUEL MIRABAL

Any investigation of collective identity today, if it is not to become an essentialist quest for a national spirit or soul, must necessarily bear in mind that knowledge is constructed and that its construction is endlessly renewed.
Amaryll Chanady, "Latin American Imagined Communities and the Postmodern"

[I]f we want to be whole, we must recall the past, those parts we want to remember, those parts that we want to forget.
Barbara Christian, "Somebody Forgot to Tell Me Something"

On October 26, 1900, twenty-three people attended the first meeting of the Martí-Maceo Society of Free Thinkers of Tampa, at the home of Ruperto and Paulina Pedroso, located on Eighth Avenue in Ybor City.[1] With a copy of the newspaper *El Pueblo Libre* in his hand, Teófilo Domínguez explained to the Afro-Cuban men seated in the small living room why it was necessary that "men of dignity" form an independent institution similar to the one in Cuba known as the Antonio Maceo Free Thinkers of Santa Clara. The object of the club, Domínguez explained to the men, should be to "help finish their intellectual education." Surveying the gathering, Ruperto Pedroso made a point of admonishing members that they "not look at the numbers present," which appeared dismal in comparison to other club gatherings, but to "look at the idea which should prevail." Although many in the room (including señores Palacios, Agüero, Alfonso, and Caballero) agreed with Domínguez, one member, a señor Acosta, stood up and admitted to the others that he thought this "institution was going to be part of the other one." While no one in the room formally declared what this "other" institution was or why it was so important that the new society be independent, Ruperto Pedroso suggested that the "matter be explained again."[2]

The minutes of the meeting do not reveal what the "matter" was or if anything was indeed explained to Señor Acosta. There are hardly any references to the fact that only a few months earlier the male Afro-Cuban members of a newly organized racially integrated Cuban club known as El Club Nacional Cubano, October 10 had been expelled.[3] There is no indication from the words recorded that the very reason for the meeting in Ruperto and Paulina Pedroso's small home was to organize a separate Afro-Cuban club. The minutes say little about the changes in Ybor City after the end of the Cuban War for Independence in 1898 and the subsequent military occupation of Cuba by the United States. There is no mention of the sudden shift in the political climate, the Weight Strike of 1899 in Tampa,[4] or the reasons behind the dissolution of the local chapter of the Partido Revolucionario Cubano (Cuban Revolutionary Party) only eight months after the end of the war.[5]

The first meeting of what was later to be the club called La Unión Martí-Maceo lasted late into the evening, adjourning at half past midnight. Yet the minutes that Pablo Folas took that evening, filled with suggestive silences and omissions, only hint at what must have kept the members arguing for hours in the Pedrosos' living room. While the minutes, as a formal account of club proceedings, omit any information not formally tied to the meeting agendas, the secretary nonetheless possessed some control over what ultimately became public record. With this in mind, we can begin to examine why Folas chose not to reveal the thoughts, conversations, and arguments that led to the formation of "the only club of this sort in the state of Florida."[6]

The recognition that choices are made, that historical records are neither factual nor static but active and constructed, indicates that sources, as Michel Rolph Trouillot has written, are "produced" and are part of a larger historical process.[7] Examining sources as elements of a continuous and multilayered "production" creates room for reading silences, for complicating what is said and interpeting how it is said. It serves as a reminder that sources that operate as the public transcript are, as James C. Scott has noted, "not the whole story."[8] This understanding, in turn, enables us to move past what is written to investigate not only those parts of the story that remain untold but also why and how the writing and the "not writing" take place. As a result, we can begin to view the withholding of words, the silencing of experiences, and the fragmenting of memories as strategies employed by Afro-Cuban women and men to negotiate being black, Cuban, and immigrants in post-Reconstruction Florida.[9] For the members of the Martí-Maceo Society of Free Thinkers to have formally documented the reasons behind the organization of a separate Afro-Cuban club would have meant publicly acknowledging that their lives were shaped by factors not only outside of the Cuban immigrant community but also within it—that along with their racial identity, being Cuban itself was subject to redefinition once they were in Florida.

When Afro-Cubans arrived in Ybor City they were faced with an imposed definition of race that did not take into consideration their immigrant status or ethnic identity. Since Florida's "Black Codes" defined any person with one eighth Negro blood as black, Afro-Cubans who immigrated to Florida during the late nineteenth and early twentieth centuries were assigned to the same legal category as African-Americans. However, as Cubans living and working in an immigrant community, they occupied a fluid, in-between position where they were neither white nor necessarily black.[10]

At the time, the United States lacked immigration policies restricting Cuban entry into Florida; Afro-Cuban women and men were able to move back and forth between Cuba and the United States with relative ease.[11] This mobility, as well as the possibility of finding work and being part of an established immigrant community, facilitated the creation of "in-between" spaces and strengthened them. Such spaces allowed Afro-Cubans to create an identity that preserved and reflected their Cuban cultural heritage while enabling them to resist being defined racially by the state of Florida.

While Afro-Cubans were able to avoid some forms of racial and economic disenfranchisement, they could not altogether escape certain racial laws and policies. By the late nineteenth century, a series of Jim Crow laws had been passed by the Florida legislature that further entrenched the state's already extensive practices of racial segregation. In 1885 the Florida legislature drafted a constitution to replace the 1868 constitution, which had extended certain rights and privileges to African-Americans. The new constitution effectively revoked those rights and sought both to disenfranchise African-Americans and to dissolve the Republican Party. Four years later a series of Jim Crow laws were passed giving legal sanction to racial segregation in Florida. The 1889 laws were so far-reaching that by 1900 racial segregation had become more widespread than it was in 1865.[12]

For Afro-Cubans this meant that even though they lived and worked in racially integrated neighborhoods and cigar factories, they were still expected to use separate schools, theaters, hospitals, and churches and travel in segregated streetcars and trains.[13] It meant not only having to negotiate multiple levels of racial segregation but also of integration. Afro-Cubans had to "know their place" even when what constituted "their place" was continually changing. The fluid and yet persistent nature of racial definitions and customs emphasized the tenuous and changeable nature of such contested spaces, making it clear to Afro-Cuban immigrants that if they were to have a space to work, live, and socialize, those spaces needed to be asserted and cultivated at all times.

The Havana of America

In 1895, nine years after Vicente Martínez Ybor built the first cigar factory in the Tampa area and established a company town known as Ybor City, close to 130 cigar factories had already been constructed in Tampa.[14] The large number of cigar factories and the steady influx of Cuban workers transformed Ybor City into an economically independent and bustling immigrant community. Boarding houses, grocery stores known as bodegas, restaurants, funeral homes, and barbershops (such as the one advertised as "la barbería cubana más notable de la ciudad") catered to a growing and ever-changing Cuban community.[15] Known as the Havana of America, Ybor City, with its immigrant population, Spanish-language newspapers, "hole in the wall cafes,"[16] and Cuban social clubs, eased the transition of Cuban immigrants and exiles into the United States.

The majority of Afro-Cubans who immigrated to Ybor City found work in the cigar factories stemming tobacco leaves and rolling cigars.[17] Employment in the cigar factories provided immigrants with the "good salaries" needed to "live well and occasionally make trips to Cuba."[18] Moreover, the factories enabled Afro-Cubans to find work during a time of economic and political instability. By the mid-1880s Cuba was in the midst of a severe economic depression that caused banks to close, businesses to fail, and workers to lose their jobs. At the same time, the failure to secure independence from Spain via two revolutionary wars, the Ten Years War and La Guerra Chiquita (the little war) of 1879–80, kept Cuba under the control of the Spanish government. Amid economic and political turmoil, the abolition of slavery was finally completed. In 1886, during a time of severe unemployment, two hundred thousand former slaves joined the Cuban labor force as wage earners.[19] Under these circumstances, thousands of Cubans traveled to Ybor City and Tampa in search of employment.

For Afro-Cuban immigrants who worked in the cigar industry, the factories represented an identifiable Cuban space where they could exchange information, organize unions, raise funds for the nationalist movement, form social clubs, and listen to the *lectores* read in Spanish. *Lectores,* or readers, sat on a scaffold a few feet above the cigar workers and read aloud from a variety of newspapers and books as the workers rolled cigars. Rooted in Cuban and Puerto Rican cigar-making and manufacturing traditions, the *lector* was brought to the United States by Cuban and Puerto Rican cigar workers during the mid-nineteenth century. Although *lectores* were chosen by the cigar workers for their ability to engage listeners, they had little control over the materials they read in the factories. It was usually up to the workers to decide what newspapers, novels, literature, and books the *lectores* would read each day. As the *lector* Abelardo Gutiérrez Días noted, one was expected to "read the materials demanded by workers, not judge them."[20]

Cigar manufacturers permitted certain Cuban customs like *el cafecito* at the bench, a flexible work schedule, *la lectura,* and an unlimited personal supply of cigars as a way to facilitate the entry of Cuban cigar workers into the U.S. labor force. By 1908 close to 90 percent of Cubans in the workforce of Tampa and Ybor City were involved, one way or another, in the cigar industry. Therefore, it was to the benefit of the management to create work environments similar to those in Cuba.[21] With time, however, the customs used to help Cuban cigar workers adapt to labor conditions outside of Cuba came to symbolize workers' autonomy and individualism within the workplace.

Having some control over their work space, as well as the process by which they selected the leaves, measured the tobacco, and rolled the cigars, was critical to preserving the cigar factories as spaces where Cubans could define and redefine themselves as workers and as part of a changing Cuban immigrant community. So important had these spaces become to Cubans in and outside of the cigar industry that attempts by manufacturers to alter or minimize their control were met with cigar workers' refusal to work. From 1886 to 1893 alone, the "local factories suffered at least fourteen strikes."[22]

Although cigar factories were racially integrated, they were by no means free of gender, class, ethnic, and, to an extent, racial distinctions. These differences shaped the type of employment offered to cigar workers and situated them in what has been called an "occupational hierarchy." Although Afro-Cubans earned the same wages as other workers for comparable labor, they consistently occupied the lowest rungs of the occupational hierarchy. For Afro-Cuban men the hierarchy was relatively fluid, allowing them to work not only cleaning the factories and hauling tobacco leaves but also rolling less expensive cigars.[23] Afro-Cuban women, on the other hand, were offered few jobs apart from stemming tobacco leaves.[24] It was an undesirable job that by the 1870s, as Patricia Cooper has written, was fast-becoming a separate occupation, with manufacturers usually hiring women for this "dirty, dead-end, low-wage labor."[25]

Not only was labor stratified on the basis of sex, but so were the spaces where women worked. Afro-Cuban women labored alongside other immigrant women in work areas separated from the men. Between 1885 and 1920 the number of women employed in the cigar factories increased from 10 percent to almost 40 percent of the workforce.[26] Within these spaces women disseminated information, formulated arguments, and on the whole helped them to create a community within the factories, in labor unions, and in the larger Tampa community. Their discussions, however, were not limited to the cigar factories. Their networks reached women who worked as seamstresses, midwives, cooks, domestic workers, and boarding-house keepers. During the mid-1890s these networks became particularly important to Cuban women involved in the effort to liberate Cuba from Spain. Cuban women moved their activism beyond their separate work sites to join Cuban male cigar workers as well as those who worked outside the cigar industry in raising funds and forming revolutionary clubs.[27]

While the number of Afro-Cuban immigrants living in Ybor City remained relatively small, they were well represented within the nationalist movement. Afro-Cuban women and men served as delegates to the Tampa chapter of the Partido Revolucionario Cubano, wrote for revolutionary newspapers, contributed donations, and "performed their duties zealously."[28] Some, like Paulina and Ruperto Pedroso, came to symbolize the very struggle for a free Cuba. The Pedrosos donated money, medical care, and almost all of their possessions to the war effort. They even sold their house in Ybor City to help raise needed funds.[29] Others like Cornelio Brito and Bruno Roig helped to form revolutionary clubs and educational centers, including La Liga de Instrucción de Tampa.[30] Yet despite the efforts of the Afro-Cuban immigrants, they were given little recognition as a community for their work and offered few positions of power within the movement.

Aware of the obstacles presented by racism and class differences in past nationalist efforts, José Martí worked to build a movement that could withstand deep-rooted divisions. Establishing such a movement outside of Cuba necessitated that Martí emphasize the very element missing among Cubans living and working in the United States: Cuba. Central to the movement was the construction of a shared Cuban identity, a *cubanidad* based on the belief that being Cuban and having connections to Cuba superseded differences of race, gender, and class, as well as immigrant and exile status. In his speeches, including one given on the steps of the Club Ignacio Agramonte in Ybor City, Martí urged Cubans to work together and view the revolution as one belonging to all Cubans regardless of color.[31] In essays published in *Nuestra América, La Nación,* and in *Patria,* the publication of the Partido Revolucionario Cubano, Martí consistently stressed the need for a Cuba free not only from Spanish control but from racism, political oppression, and economic exploitation. Although Martí was able to unify Cubans to the point of transforming Tampa into "one of the most important enclaves of revolutionaries in the United States,"[32] he was never fully able to neutralize divisions within the community.

Martí's words constitute one of the few historical sources that speak directly to the existence of division and conflicts among Cuban immigrants. His essays, speeches, and actions interrupt and disrupt the silences by challenging the common perception that "racial prejudice among Cubans never existed."[33] Martí's persistent calls for unity reveal that tensions among Cuban exiles and immigrants did exist and that such tensions complicated the project of creating a shared Cuban community and identity outside of Cuba.[34] In stirring the silences surrounding Cubans in Ybor City, Martí's work provides us with an opening to question why discussions concerning race among Cuban immigrants have been silenced, fragmented, and withheld. Why, in spite of Martí's open and public criticism of racial divisions and separations, was it important for white Cuban immigrants to consider, and more importantly to remember, Cubans as a unified community?[35]

1898: Interventions, Occupations, and the Transformation of Exile

In April of 1898 the United States intervened in the Cuban War for Independence. Its ensuing military and political occupation of the island drastically altered definitions of exile, immigration, and nationalism. The U.S. actions, along with Martí's untimely death in 1895, signaled an end to the exile nationalist movement, causing revolutionary clubs to close and the Partido Revolucionario Cubano, founded by Cuban exiles, to disband. Cubans who had been in exile were for all intents and purposes free to return to Cuba. Yet the Cuba they would return to was now under the firm political and economic control of the United States. Military occupation of the island until 1902 and the implementation of the Platt Amendment effectively limited Cuban sovereignty and altered the status of Cuba as nation.

Cuban immigrants were now faced with the dilemma of settling in Ybor City or returning to Cuba during a time of economic devastation and political instability. The decision to remain in Ybor City meant having to re-envision a community that was no longer in exile nor able to use the goal of Cuban liberation as its main tool for unification. As a result, questions concerning what it meant to be Cuban outside of Cuba during a time of U.S. occupation and influence figured prominently in the process of remaking community. Some sites where Cuban immigrants grappled with such questions were the cultural clubs and mutual aid societies. Organized before, during, and after the Cuban War for Independence, these groups not only provided Cuban immigrants with a place to meet, discuss, argue, and socialize but they also offered members badly needed medical insurance, unemployment benefits, and temporary economic relief.

When a group of veterans of the Ten Years War organized the Club Nacional Cubano, close to a year after the U.S. actions in Cuba, it was with the intention of establishing a place to meet. One of the few racially integrated clubs in Ybor City and Tampa, it was, as José Ramón Sanfeliz remembered, "composed of white and black members—a sort of rice with black beans."[36] While the common thread of involvement in the nationalist struggle operated as a powerful tool for unification, it was not enough, in this period, to make and sustain community. Within a few months and with little explanation, the male Afro-Cuban members were expelled and the club disbanded. For Sanfeliz, the decision to separate was not based on racism, since for him "there was no distinction of races"; rather, it was simply something that "happened" in the process of reorganizing a new club called El Círculo Cubano. As Sanfeliz noted, it was only when El Círculo Cubano was formed that the Afro-Cuban members were, as he put it, "left out."[37]

In a study conducted by the Federal Writers' Project on the origins of La Unión Martí-Maceo, the writers describe its formation without ever mentioning the October 10 Club or the ejection of the Afro-Cuban male members. The writers merely note that while the "Cuban whites organized a recreation club to celebrate their festivals, the Cuban coloreds found themselves without a place to do the same." This, the writers state, is what prompted Afro-Cubans to "organize a club of their own."[38]

The most common explanation for the split, the one offered in José Rivero Muñiz's study, has been Florida's Jim Crow laws. For Muñiz it was racial segregation "in this part of the United States" that caused the "dissolved clubs to proceed in the manner that best suited their respective needs."[39] While it is certainly possible that segregation played a role in the decision to eject the Afro-Cuban male members, it does not explain why Cuban immigrants failed to consider the consequences of racial segregation when they first formed the club in 1899, how segregation was enforced in the immigrant community, or why certain institutions like the cigar factories remained racially integrated before, during, and after the split.

The sources detailing the split rarely considered the thoughts, emotions, and experiences of the Afro-Cuban members who were left out. We know little of the reaction of the Afro-Cuban members or the impact the decision had on the Afro-Cuban community. The expulsion of the Afro-Cuban members belies the longstanding effect the decision actually had on the relationship between both clubs and within the Cuban community. The split formalized and, in a sense, reinforced the existence of a "color line" among Cuban immigrants. Although rarely articulated or formally addressed, the color line affected and shaped the actions, decisions, and experiences not only of the Afro-Cuban club members but of the entire Cuban immigrant community. The decision of white male Cuban members to eject the Afro-Cuban male members of the October 10 Club reinscribed the Afro-Cuban members, and by extension the Afro-Cuban immigrant community in Ybor City, as "black."[40]

By the time the Martí-Maceo Society of Free Thinkers officially merged with the mutual-aid society La Unión in 1904 to form La Unión Martí-Maceo,[41] Afro-Cubans were already making these societies a center of activity in their community. Afro-Cuban immigrants would go to La Unión Martí-Maceo to find out about job openings and housing opportunities, to socialize, and of course to discuss political developments in Cuba. In addition to being a place where Afro-Cubans could gather, the club offered any member who paid a weekly dues of twenty-five cents complete medical care and financial compensation for lost income during illness or injury. Although not allowed to become formal members until the 1920s, Afro-Cuban women were pivotal to the club's success. They exercised decision-making powers and remained active in club affairs through the formation of the *comité de damas* (women's committee).[42] Referred to in the records as early as June 16, 1901, the women who made up the *comité de damas* were responsible for organizing social functions, keeping records, raising funds, and, after 1904, dispensing economic and unemployment benefits. While the committee exercised power through formal avenues, many of the women involved in, as well as independent of, the *comité de damas* practiced what Patricia Hill Collins has called a "less visible but equally important form" of social and political activity.[43] Whether through their relationships with club members or their presence at club functions, Afro-Cuban women used multiple and distinct avenues, such as discussions and informal gatherings, to suggest and make changes.

An important characteristic of the club was its fervent interest in the political, social, and economic developments in Cuba as well as its devotion to Cuban immigrant issues. The club was so strictly organized around Cuba and being Cuban that its charter prohibited members from endorsing any political organization in the United States and called for all funds and properties to be turned over to the Cuban government in the event of the club's dissolution.[44] These provisions not only made it difficult for the club and individual members formally to support issues that were not directly connected to Cuba or to Cuban immigrants, but it also effectively closed them off from the African-American community. This reality was not lost on Juan Mallea's father, an early member of La Unión Martí-Maceo, who, as Mallea recounted, told the other members that they "were doing the same thing that others were doing to African-Americans."[45]

On the Part of Culture: African-Americans and Afro-Cubans

In 1900, the same year in which the Martí-Maceo Society of Free Thinkers was formed, close to 4,400 African-Americans lived in Hillsborough County, Florida. African-Americans made up over 20 percent of the population and were concentrated in racially segregated Tampa neighborhoods known as College Hill, Central Avenue, Dobyville, and an area northeast of the business district called the Scrub. Housing in these areas was often the city's poorest, while their disease, illiteracy, and infant-mortality rates were its highest.[46]

Florida's legally enforced racial segregation, the Black Codes, and the efforts of local officials to restrict voting rights combined to disenfranchise African-Americans politically and economically. Only those African-Americans who paid the poll tax were "deemed qualified electors and authorized to vote at any general, special or municipal election."[47] Attempts to run African-American candidates for office were often met with threats and violence. In 1910, roughly a year after an African-American candidate ran unsuccessfully for municipal judge, the White Municipal Party was created to eliminate the African-American vote from the primaries and to annihilate any form of African-American political activism. Organized to "allow 'responsible' whites to debate the real issues," the White Municipal Party in Tampa remained a force in local politics until the mid-1930s.[48]

While the White Municipal Party effectively limited institutional political representation, it could not keep African-Americans from being political. African-American women and men created organizations such as the Afro-American Civic League, Tampa's Urban League, and the City Federation of Colored Women's Club, in which they could organize in response to the growing political, economic, and social repression in Tampa. Action was not confined to political institutions, however. African American women and men extended their political activities and discussions to homes, businesses, and work settings, as well as to meetings in churches such as St. James Episcopal Church and St. Paul's African Methodist Episcopal Church.[49]

The relationship between African-Americans and Afro-Cubans during this period was strongly shaped by Florida's racial laws. Although a substantial number of Afro-Cuban immigrants lived in a racially integrated community, extensive segregation laws in Tampa left Afro-Cuban immigrants with little choice but to go to the Scrub, and other parts of the African-American community, to receive medical attention, attend schools, and visit the only theater that admitted black patrons. Despite the inevitable interactions that took place between the two communities, Afro-Cubans preferred to distance themselves socially and politically from African-Americans. They were able to do so by carving out spaces where they could both interact with white Cubans and form organizations that catered solely to their own needs.

Ironically, during the late nineteenth and early twentieth centuries, the social and political ties between African-Americans and Cuba, as nation, were intricately involved and raveled. The connections extended beyond Tampa, where African-Americans sent to fight in the Spanish-American War were stationed,[50] to the war itself, where black soldiers were faced—as an African-American chaplain had observed—with the "glorious dilemma" of relieving Cubans of Spanish tyranny, only to push them "into the condition of the American Negro."[51] Race, as Amy Kaplan has deftly argued, loomed large in the minds of U.S. government and military officials, who used race both to control African-American troops and to justify the repression and colonization of Cubans. Blackness and its attributed meanings had been constructed to the point where, as Kaplan observes, "the same argument about the need for white officers to discipline black soldiers was made about the need for the United States government to discipline the Cubans by radically circumscribing their status as nation through the conditions of the Platt Amendment.[52]

Even if it meant blurring lines of distinction, such as ethnicity, culture, and political and national allegiance, the U.S. military and government, and at times the press, socially constructed "blackness" to suit their political and economic agendas. Blackness was infused and inscribed with meanings that depicted all Cubans as lazy, unable to govern their own affairs (let alone a nation), in need of direction and guidance, and potentially subversive. These meanings imply that Cubans needed to be controlled and disciplined by white officers. By the same token there also existed a recognition that African-Americans serving in the military were undeserving of any form of rank or prestige. The meanings tied to blackness and power were very clear to the black press in the United States, who in reporting the war sided with their "brown brothers" and, as Kaplan has pointed out, "decried the exportation of post-Reconstruction disfranchisement, Jim Crow laws, and the resurgence of violence and virulent racism to the new outpost of empire."[53] In writing about the implications and possible ramifications of United States colonialism, African-American journalists pushed definitions of "blackness" to include those Cubans, female and male, who might not necessarily view themselves as "black."

The collective memory of experiences and lives woven through the constructions and uses of "blackness" were not as binding nor as evident as one would think ten years later in Ybor City. Any longstanding memory or legacy of connections between African-Americans and Afro-Cubans seemed to have given way to everyday concerns and efforts to simply "resolver."[54] On February 19, 1908, members of La Unión Martí-Maceo met to discuss and later vote on Señor Gonzales's offer to set up a school free of charge for "hombres de color de ambas nacionalidades" (men of color of both nationalities). The proposition was unanimously rejected by the members, even though one of the founding tenets of the club was a commitment to the "intellectual education" of the members. Although little discussion appears in the club records, the secretary did note that *el señor* Acosta had asked that the members not say anything in public concerning the decision.[55]

Seven years later, on October 17, 1915, Afro-Cuban male members voted to permit all eligible "Black individuals regardless of nationality" to become members of La Unión Martí-Maceo. That night close to sixty-two members showed up to argue, discuss, dissent, and finally accept the membership of African-American males. After a long discussion, Facundo Acción proposed that a vote be cast. Of the members present, only twenty-six voted in favor of the decision; four voted against it, and thirty-two abstained. Although African-American males were now offered membership into the club, they had to be recommended by a current member and speak Spanish.[56]

These stipulations enabled Afro-Cuban members not only to control the eligibility of African-American membership but also to designate the club as a distinctly Cuban space in the face of rapid and unavoidable change. The vote to accept African-American male members shows that on some level interactions and perhaps even solidarity had developed between the two communities.[57] This, with the declining number of new members and a waning interest in the club, motivated Afro-Cubans to consider African-American male membership as a way to keep the club and mutual-aid society alive. Yet, as the stipulations and abstentions demonstrate, many Afro-Cuban members were still reluctant to open the club to African-Americans.

The making of an Afro-Cuban community and identity in Ybor City was shaped by the multiple applications and uses of silences. In addition to being woven within and throughout public records and sources, official documents and published texts, silences were also present in the everyday. Operating on a more intimate and quotidian level, silences were often a necessary tool for forging alliances and sustaining community. As strategy, silences enabled Afro-Cubans to theorize for themselves their identity and negotiate an "in-between" space during a period when such complexities were rarely recognized, accepted, or easily negotiated.

The silences present in the minutes of the meetings of La Unión Martí-Maceo provide a glimpse into the workings of silences among the Afro-Cuban community in Ybor City. As symbol, they serve as a reminder that Afro-Cubans not only understood their "place" within the United States but that they were intent on restructuring that "place" to accommodate their race, ethnic identity, language, and culture, despite the strict legal definitions of race as well as accepted notions of "blackness" in post-Reconstruction Florida.

By their very nature silences are difficult to pinpoint, theorize, recognize, and, of course, document. Yet, once interpreted and theorized, silences can reveal the workings of power, of distinct forms of perceptions, complicated modes of resistance as well as of accommodation. They remind us that to forget—or better, to choose *not* to remember—is also in itself a powerful act.

NOTES

Acknowledgment: A big thank-you goes to Javier Morillo-Alicea for bringing to my attention Amaryll Chanady's essay "Latin American Imagined Communities and the Postmodern" in her edited collection, *Latin American Identity and Constructions of Difference.* Thanks also go to Doris Dixon for knowing just what I needed to know.

Portions of this essay that were originally in Spanish have been translated by the author unless otherwise indicated.

1. In 1887 Ybor City was incorporated into Tampa proper.

2. La Unión Martí-Maceo records, minutes of the meetings, October 26, 1900. Special Collections, University of South Florida, Tampa.

3. According to Susan Greenbaum, the formal name of this club was El Club Nacional Cubano, October 10. The club has been referred to as the October 10 Club as well as El Club Nacional Cubano in both primary and secondary sources. In 1902, approximately three years after the Afro-Cuban members were asked to leave, the club was renamed El Círculo Cubano.

4. During the Weight Strike of 1899, workers walked out after cigar manufacturers instituted a weight system in the old Ybor factory. In addition to the Weight Strike of 1899, cigar workers also went on strike in 1901, 1910, 1920, and 1931.

5. The Florida chapter of the Partido Revolucionario Cubano was founded by Cuban exiles and immigrants on January 5, 1892, in Tampa. The PRC was set up after José Martí and other Tampa-based Cuban nationalists drafted the "Tampa Resolutions" and the "Bases of the Cuban Revolutionary Party" in November 1891. It soon became one of the most powerful Cuban nationalist revolutionary organizations formed in exile.

6. "Study of La Unión Martí-Maceo: Cuban Club for the Colored Race." (N.d.) Federal Writers Project, Work Projects Administration. Special Collections, University of South Florida.

7. Michel Rolph Trouillot, "Good Day Columbus: Silences, Power and Public History, 1492–1892," *Public Culture* 3, no. 1 (1990).

8. James C. Scott, *Domination and the Arts of Resistance: Hidden Transcripts* (New Haven: Yale University Press, 1990), 3.

9. Please see Earl Lewis, *In Their Own Interests: Race, Class and Power in Twentieth Century Norfolk, Virginia* (Berkeley: University of California Press, 1991); Tera W. Hunter,

"Domination and Resistance: The Politics of Wage Household Labor in New South Atlanta," *Labor History* 34, nos. 2–3 (1993); Elsa Barkley Brown, "'What Has Happened Here': The Politics of Difference in Women's History and Feminist Politics," *Feminist Studies* 18, no. 2 (Summer 1992); Nancy Hewitt, "Compounding Differences," *Feminist Studies* 18, no. 2 (Summer 1992); and Robin D. J. Kelley, "'We Are Not What We Seem': Rethinking Black Working Class Opposition in the Jim Crow South," *Journal of American History* 80, no. 1 (June 1993), for important and insightful studies that look at how race, class, gender, sexuality, and politics shape and reconfigure the uses of language, everyday strategies, and resistance.

10. Clara Rodríguez, "Puerto Ricans between Black and White," in Clara Rodríguez, Virginia Sánchez Korrol, and José O. Alers, eds., *The Puerto Rican Struggle: Essays on Survival in the United States* (Maplewood, N.J.: Waterfront Press, 1980). Rodríguez argues that early Puerto Rican migrants in New York City rejected "racial identification on American terms" and refused assimilation by "holding on to their cultural identity very strongly." I find Rodríguez's discussion of fluid "in-between" spaces to be particularly useful when discussing the early history of Puerto Rican and Afro-Cuban migrants. In addition to Rodríguez, please see both the *Memoirs of Bernardo Vega: A Contribution to the History of the Puerto Rican Community in New York,* ed. César Andreu Iglesias and trans. Juan Flores (New York: Monthly Review Press, 1984) and Bernardo Ruiz Suárez, *The Color Question in the Two Americas,* trans. John Crosby Gordon (New York: Hunt Publishing, 1922).

For a study of "in-between" positionality outside of the Puerto Rican and Cuban community, and another example of how race and ethnicity impacted immigration, identity, and community formation, please refer to Marilyn Halter's *Between Race and Ethnicity: Cape Verdean American Immigrants, 1860–1965* (Urbana: University of Illinois Press, 1993). In a different context, Homi K. Bhabha also discusses the recognition and making of "in-between" spaces in his introduction to *The Location of Culture* (London: Routledge, 1994). For Bhabha such "in-between" spaces move beyond middle-ground positions that complicate identity constructions to a "terrain of elaborating strategies of self-hood-singular or communal that initiate new signs of identity, and innovative sites of collaboration and contestation, in the act of defining the idea of society itself." It is also important to note that the creation and cultivation of such spaces were and are by no means limited to immigrants. African-Americans have consistently questioned the "color line." In particular, African-American writers like James Weldon Johnson, Jessie Fauset, Nella Larson, and Toni Morrison, to name a few, have examined and challenged race by analyzing "passing" and how passing restructures and reconfigures meanings of power, community, identity, self, and institutions.

11. Gary R. Mormino and George E. Pozzetta, *The Immigrant World of Ybor City: Italians and Their Latin Neighbors in Tampa, 1885–1985* (University of Illinois Press, 1987), 76. While Mormino and Pozzetta's assertion brings to light questions concerning immigration, state authority, and U.S.-Cuban relations, they do not fully examine why, during a pe-

riod of intense nativist sentiments, anti-immigration legislation, and quotas, Cuban immigrants were able to move so easily from Cuba to the United States.

12. Jerrell H. Shofner, "Custom, Law and History: The Enduring Influence of Florida's Black Codes," *Florida Historical Quarterly* 45 (January 1977): 277–98; "Florida in the Balance: The Electoral Count of 1876," *Florida Historical Quarterly* 7, no. 2 (October 1968); and *Nor Is It Over Yet: Florida in the Era of Reconstruction, 1863–1877* (Gainesville: University Press of Florida, 1974). In addition to Shofner, refer to Ralph Peek's "Military Reconstruction and the Growth of Anti-Negro Sentiment in Florida, 1867," *Florida Historical Quarterly* 47, no. 4 (April 1969); and Joe M. Richardson's "Florida's Black Codes," *Florida Historical Quarterly* 47, no. 4 (April 1969).

13. By 1907 electric cars, waiting rooms, and ticket windows were all legally segregated. See the State of Florida Statutes, Chapter 5617, section 2860, May 7, 1907, and Chapter 5619, section 2860f, May 15, 1907, respectively.

14. Durward Long, "The Making of Modern Tampa: A City of the New South, 1885–1911," *Florida Historical Quarterly* 49 (1971): 341.

15. Translated this means "the most notable Cuban barbershop in the city." Advertised in *La Doctrina de Martí,* December 25, 1897. Colección Cubana, La Biblioteca Nacional José Martí, Havana.

16. When writers from the Florida branch of the Federal Writer's Project entered Ybor City in 1941, they declared it the "Havana of America." The writers noted the shop windows in Spanish and English, the "click of dominoes," and the "odors of hot Cuban bread, roasting coffee and the tang of bright leaf tobacco mellowing in the dungeons of the cigar factories." Descriptions contained in "Ybor City: Tampa's Latin Colony," produced by the Florida branch of the Federal Writers Project of the WPA, March 31, 1941. Special Collections Department, University of South Florida, Tampa.

17. In 1900 over 90 percent of Afro-Cuban men and 15 percent of Afro-Cuban women in the workforce labored in the cigar industry. Statistics quoted in Susan Greenbaum's "Afro-Cubans in Ybor City: A Centennial History," University of South Florida, Tampa, 1986, p. 9.

18. Quoted in a "Study of La Unión Martí-Maceo: Cuban Club for Colored Race," (n.d.) Federal Writers' Project, Work Projects Administration. Courtesy of Special Collections, University of South Florida, Tampa.

19. Louis A. Pérez Jr., *Cuba between Empires 1878–1902* (Pittsburgh: University of Pittsburgh Press, 1983), 22–23.

20. Louis A. Pérez Jr. in "Reminiscences of a Lector: Cuban Cigar Workers in Tampa," *Florida Historical Quarterly* 53 (April 1975). Not only did *lectores* inform cigar workers of social, political, and economic developments in Cuba and the United States, but many were also labor agitators and advocates for a free Cuba. Their powerful presence in the factories resulted in long-standing tensions with the managers and owners. According to Pérez, these tensions ended in 1931 when cigar manufacturers, with the support of city and county authorities and vigilante groups, decided to "abolish the lectura." In addition to Pérez, please see Julio Ramos's *Amor y anarquía: Los escritos de Luisa Capetillo* (San Juan: Ediciones Hu-

racán, 1991) for an account of a woman *lector* in Puerto Rico who also traveled to Ybor City. Capetillo's discussion is particularly insightful concerning the important position of *lectores* in Puerto Rican and Cuban communities in the United States. I am grateful to John McKiernan for introducing me to Capetillo's story.

21. Durward Long, "The Making of Modern Tampa: A City of the New South, 1885–1911," *Florida Historical Quarterly* 49 (1971): 333–45. Long states that between 1885 and 1911 the percentage of foreign-born cigar workers in the Tampa cigar industry ranged from 75 to 95 percent, with Cubans making up the largest portion of that group.

22. Statistics quoted in Nancy Hewitt, "The Voice of Virile Labor: Militancy, Community, Solidarity and Gender Identity among Tampa's Latin Workers," in Ava Baron, ed., *Work Engendered: Toward a New History of American Labor* (Ithaca: Cornell University Press, 1991), 142.

23. Gary R. Mormino and George E. Pozzetta, *The Immigrant World of Ybor City: Italians and Their Latin Neighbors in Tampa, 1885–1985* (Urbana: University of Illinois Press, 1987), 100. Mormino and Pozzetta place Spaniards who worked as managers, salesmen, accountants, and skilled clerical staff at the top of this hierarchy. At the bottom were mostly Afro-Cuban women and men, early Italian immigrants, and African-Americans who were employed in jobs that were not directly tied to tobacco. At the same time, this hierarchy was fluid and subject to change. As a result of political and economic shifts over the years some groups (such as Italian immigrants) moved up the ranks while others (like African-Americans) found it more difficult to advance within this "hierarchy" of labor.

24. Tobacco stemming consisted of women stripping the midrib of the tobacco leaf.

25. Quoted in Patricia A. Cooper, *Once A Cigar Maker: Men, Women and Work Culture in American Cigar Factories, 1900–1919* (Urbana: University of Illinois Press, 1987), 15. According to Cooper, stemming was initially a boy's occupation and it was viewed as a stepping-stone to a cigar-making job.

26. Nancy Hewitt, "The Voice of Virile Labor," 148.

27. Cuban newspapers published in Tampa often referred to the important role of women in the nationalist movement. *La Verdad* announced the start of a new column focusing solely on women: "Con este fin útil y saludable comenzamos a publicar en *La Verdad,* 'La defensa de las mujeres' por Feijó" [With this useful and laudable purpose we begin to publish in *The Truth* "The Defense of Women" by Feijó]. Colección Cubana, Biblioteca Nacional José Martí, Havana, 1896. Cuban women were also praised for their efforts to secure a "Cuba libre" by Néstor Carbonell in an article entitled "Heroes!" *El Oriente Periódico Separatista Independiente de Tampa* 1897 Colección Cubana, Biblioteca Nacional José Martí, Havana. While such articles offer insight into the role women played in the movement, they raise the question of why men wrote them and what their motivation was for describing and promoting the "ideal" role of women in the movement.

On another note Nancy Hewitt has shown that by 1897 more than two hundred Cuban women found their way into print as leaders of the Partido Revolucionario Cubano's affiliates as well as organizers of Ybor City's first female revolutionary club, Obreras de la

Independencia (Women Workers for Independence). There is no mention, however, of how many of these women were Afro-Cuban. For details please see Hewitt, "Paulina Pedroso and Las Patriotas of Tampa," in Ann Henderson and Gary Mormino, eds., *Spanish Pathways in Florida, 1492–1992* (Sarasota: Pineapple Press, 1991).

28. Quoted in Federal Writers Project, "Study of La Unión Martí-Maceo."

29. Sources that discuss Paulina and Ruperto Pedroso include Nancy A. Hewitt, "Paulina Pedroso and Las Patriotas of Tampa"; Joan Marie Steffy, "Cuban Immigration to Tampa, 1868–1898," Master's thesis, History Department, University of South Florida, 1975; and Susan Greenbaum, Afro-Cubans in Ybor City."

30. La Liga de Instruccíon de Tampa was modeled after La Liga in New York, which was established by a group made up of mainly Afro-Cubans and Puerto Ricans. La Liga was set up to be a "training school for the revolution" with classes and lectures held in the evenings and throughout the week. In the introduction to *Our America by José Martí: Writings on Latin America and the Struggle for Cuban Independence,* trans. Elinor Randall, Juan de Onís, and Roslyn Held Foner (London: Monthly Review Press, 1977), Philip S. Foner discusses the formation of the club. For details concerning the organization of La Liga de Instrucción in Tampa see Steffy's "Cuban Immigration to Tampa, 1868–1898."

31. The Liceo speech was given on November 26, 1891. Reference to the speech is made in Steffy's "Cuban Immigration to Tampa, 1868–1898" and Gerald Poyo's *"With All and for the Good of All": The Emergence of Popular Nationalism in the Cuban Communities in the United States, 1848–1890* (Durham, N.C.: Duke University Press, 1989).

32. Dwight Middleton, "The Organization of Ethnicity in Tampa," *Ethnic Groups* 3 (December 1981): 28. In addition to Middleton, see Poyo's *"With All and for the Good of All"* for a discussion on the revolutionary activity of Cubans in Tampa.

33. José Rivero Muñiz, "Los Cubanos en Tampa," *Revista Bimestre Cubana* 74 (1958).

34. Although not within the scope of this chapter, the questionings reveal the need for a deeper and more complex contextualization and examination of the multiple discourses and definitions of race and ethnicity both within and outside of the Cuban immigrant community. Because Afro-Cuban immigrants did not live in isolation from other communities, they were subject to and often shaped by differing and changeable conceptions of race as theorized by outside communities. The questionings and at the same time location of Cuban racial identity within the United States by outside communities made it difficult for Cuban immigrants not to rethink what it meant to be black and white, as well as Cuban, during the turn of the century in Florida. At the same time, such constructions were not based solely on race; ethnicity, class, gender, and immigrant status all contributed to the racialization of the Cuban community in Ybor City.

35. In speaking of a unified community I am in part looking at the efforts of members of the Cuban community, often both white and black, to downplay racial, class, and in some instances gender differences. At the same time, I want to note that Martí's declarations survive as a direct result of Martí's stature as poet, revolutionary architect, and national figure. The connection between the construction of the historical figure and the survival of words and texts is

crucial. At the same time that we recognize the relationship between historical legacy and the survival of words and text, we must also deeply consider the loss of words, texts, and historical memory of those who do not occupy the same historical position as Martí.

36. Federal Writers' Project, 'The Life History of José Ramón Sanfeliz," Work Projects Administration, (n.d.). Courtesy of the P. K. Younge Collection, University of Florida, Gainesville.

37. Ibid.

38. Federal Writers Project, "Study of La Unión Martí-Maceo."

39. José Rivero Muñiz, "Los Cubanos en Tampa." Also quoted in Dwight Middleton, "The Organization of Ethnicity in Tampa," 290.

40. In addition to the records of La Unión Martí-Maceo and El Círculo Cubano (Special Collections, University of South Florida, Tampa), also see Aline Helg's *Our Rightful Share: The AfroCuban Struggle for Equality, 1886–1912* (Chapel Hill: University of North Carolina Press, 1995). Helg effectively demonstrates how, in spite of "myths" about racial equality and a shared Cuban identity, "race still dominated many aspects of political and socioeconomic relationships in Cuba, resulting in blacks' continuing marginalization." The question that I am most interested in is how the relationship between "myth" and "marginalization" was transferred and manifested by Cuban immigrants once they were in the United States. While club records offer some clues, those records refer mainly to club activity, which on some level is restricted by club bylaws, charters, rules, and regulations.

41. La Unión was an organization begun by Juan Franco, a cigar maker who also belonged to Martí-Maceo. Once the merger took place, economic benefits were added to club. Please see Susan Greenbaum, "AfroCubans in Ybor City," page 8, for more details.

42. La Unión Martí-Maceo records, minutes of the meetings, June 16, 1901. Special Collections, University of South Florida, Tampa.

43. Patricia Hill Collins, *Black Feminist Thought: Knowledge, Consciousness, and the Politics of Empowerment* (Boston: Unwin Hyman, 1990), 141.

44. Information concerning the charter taken from an interview of Juan Mallea by Enrique Cordero, Special Collections, University of South Florida, Tampa. The charter itself has yet to be located, and, according to Juan Mallea, the club's bylaws were destroyed in a fire in 1909.

45. Interview of Juan Mallea conducted by Enrique Cordero, 1983. Special Collections, University of South Florida, Tampa.

46. Mary Burke, "The Success of Blanche Armwood, 1890–1939," *The Sunland Tribune: Journal of the Tampa Historical Society* 15 (November 1989); Mormino and Pozzetta, *The Immigrant World of Ybor City,* 55–58.

47. African-American voting rights in Florida have a long history of political and legal manipulation. In addition to enacting the poll tax, the legislature of 1889 also reenacted the multiple ballot box system, which required that each ballot be cast in the proper box; otherwise the vote would be thrown out. Since a number of African-American males could not read the labels on the boxes, their votes were jeopardized. In 1901 the Florida legisla-

ture made it legal for the executive or standing committee that called a primary election to declare the terms and conditions on which "legal electors" would be allowed to vote in the primary. This provision enabled all-white primaries to exist simply by claiming that African-Americans were not members of a political party.

Attempts to restrict the African-American vote continued in the Florida legislature, culminating in 1915 with a proposed amendment to the Florida constitution. This amendment, although defeated when it was put to a vote, required that a voter be able to read, write, and interpret any section of the Florida constitution at the time of voting. Voting rights, access to the political system, and the integration of African-Americans into the political arena were resisted on all levels, mainly by Florida state legislators and city officials. For more details, please see Jesse Jefferson Jackson, "The Negro and the Law in Florida: Legal Patterns of Segregation and Control in Florida, 1821–1921," Master's thesis, Florida State University, 1960.

48. Robert P. Ingalls, *Urban Vigilantes in the New South: Tampa, 1882–1936* (Knoxville: University of Tennessee Press, 1988), 177. Ingalls mentions the existence of the White Municipal Party as late as 1931 during a discussion of the mayoral election of Robert E. Lee Chancey. In addition to Ingalls, see Mormino and Pozzetta, *The Immigrant World of Ybor City,* 53.

49. Please see Elsa Barkley Brown's "Negotiating and Transforming the Public Sphere: African-American Political Life in the Transition from Slavery to Freedom," *Public Culture* 7, no. 1 (Fall 1994), for an important and valuable discussion on the need to expand definitions of political activism and political space.

50. With the outbreak of the war all African-American units of the regular army, including the infantrymen, were sent to Tampa because its port was considered one of the best suited for embarkation to Cuba. From the moment the troops arrived in Tampa, they were treated with hostility and resentment. Local newspapers continually criticized the decision to station African-American troops in Tampa, while many in the native Anglo community did everything in their power to demean and humiliate the troops. Tensions between the African-American troops and the native Anglo community was so great that on the eve of the embarkation for Cuba a riot broke out. Please see Willard B. Gatewood Jr., "Negro Troops in Florida, 1898," *Florida Historical Quarterly* (July 1970), for more details concerning the reaction to the troops stationed in Tampa.

51. Ibid., 15.

52. Amy Kaplan, "Black and Blue on San Juan Hill," in Amy Kaplan and Donald Pease, eds., *Cultures of United States Imperialism* (Durham, N.C.: Duke University Press, 1993), 21.

53. Ibid., 228.

54. Translated, this means "to resolve." In using the word *resolver* I am referring to the preoccupation—and at times struggle—to make ends meet, care for family, and similar concerns that constitute the daily lives of Afro-Cuban immigrants.

55. La Unión Martí-Maceo records, minutes of the meetings, February, 19, 1908. Special Collections, University of South Florida, Tampa.

56. La Unión Martí-Maceo records, minutes of the meetings, October 15, 1915. Special Collections, University of South Florida, Tampa. One passage mentions that after the

votes were cast, "it was agreed that article 82 be such that article 8 prohibits. The letter of nonconformity to the state was approved." This is somewhat ambiguous since it is not clear what type of letter needed to be sent to the state and the reasons for it.

57. I am indebted to Wilson Valentin for bringing to my attention the fact that solidarity and unions were created at the same time that separation and distinctions also occurred.

3

The African-American Press and United States Involvement in Cuba, 1902–1912

DAVID J. HELLWIG

> The people of Cuba know what they want, and any action of the United States which prevents them from getting it will be a crime against the spirit of liberty and fair play, of which we claim to be the chief defenders for others but practice very little at home.
> *New York Age,* September 27, 1906

Scholars have analyzed United States intervention in Cuba at the turn of the twentieth century from a variety of perspectives. Most studies focus on the events related to the Spanish-American War and American military occupation of the island from 1899 to 1902. While they often consider the responses of white Americans to the nation's changing role in world affairs, seldom are the views of black Americans examined. Yet African-Americans have long been interested in Cuba. In the middle of the nineteenth century they were alarmed by Southern attempts to acquire Cuba as a new slave state; during the last two decades of the century they closely followed the long struggle of the Cuban people to achieve independence from Spain.[1]

This chapter builds upon the work of Willard B. Gatewood Jr., who in the 1970s published two books that dealt with the reactions of black Americans to U.S. involvement in Cuba between 1898 and 1902.[2] It focuses on two key events in the decade following the withdrawal of troops in May 1902: the reestablishment of U.S. military rule following the fall of the

A version of this chapter was published in *Mid-America: An Historical Review* 72, no. 2 (April–July 1990).

Estrada Palma government in 1906, and the insurrection known as the Race War of 1912. Since both events had strong racial overtones, they elicited numerous editorials in the black press.

The twenty newspapers and magazines examined for this study constitute a wide but not necessarily representative sample of black opinion. Even more so than the white press, the black press was predominantly urban and middle class in orientation. While the typical African-American in the early twentieth century lived in the rural South, most periodicals were published in northern cities. Many presented themselves as militant advocates of racial advancement, although few were. Instead, most reflected the accommodationist views of Booker T. Washington, founder of Tuskegee Institute and the most influential black adviser to Presidents Theodore Roosevelt and William H. Taft. Many editors shared his conservative social and economic philosophy; others depended on secret financial aid from Washington for survival.[3] It is most unlikely that any of the editors had direct knowledge of Cuba; typically the black press based its coverage of international news on reports in the white press. The opinions reported in this study were gathered primarily from editorials assessing the significance of the previous week's events for the local community.

Except for Haiti, no New World society received as much attention from black North Americans in the nineteenth century as did Cuba. To them the island was not an accessible holiday retreat for the wealthy or an outlet for investment but rather the setting for an experiment in race relations offering hope that former slaves and slave masters could live together harmoniously. Like earlier efforts, the final struggle of the Cuban people for independence that began in 1895 attracted the attention and sympathy of black Americans. Although just one-third of the island's population was of African descent, African-Americans saw the War for Independence as a black undertaking. They identified with the large nonwhite segment of the Cuban population and noted parallels in the struggle against Spanish oppression and their own quest for first-class citizenship. Since in the late nineteenth century black Americans tended to view Cuban race relations as close to ideal, some thought the new nation might provide a refuge for American blacks. They could contribute generous doses of much-needed Yankee ingenuity and technology to the poorly developed island as they escaped the ever-tightening proscriptions assigning them to inferior status in the United States.

Consequently, the heavily Republican black press generally applauded U.S. intervention in the war with Spain in 1898. It was an opportunity for black youths once again to affirm their loyalty to the nation as they helped in the creation of a new black republic. The conduct of the war was closely followed and its successful conclusion duly recognized. Shortly thereafter, however, coverage of Cuban developments declined dramatically. On occasion a note appeared regarding resistance to the Platt Amendment[4] or the controversy over the Tariff Reciprocity Treaty.[5] A few papers, such as the *Star of Zion,* the official organ of the African Methodist Episcopal Zion Church, hailed the withdrawal of American forces from Cuba in 1902.[6] But even the long-awaited achievement of Cuban independence received scant notice.

The steady decline of interest in Cuba in part reflected a general loss of enthusiasm for American expansion. As in white America, the resistance of Filipino rebels under Emilio Aguinaldo fostered anti-imperialist sentiment in black America. Although the press seldom linked events in Asia and Cuba, it followed the guerrilla war and deplored the use of force by the United States to subjugate non-white Filipinos.[7] Talk of the "white man's burden" in Asia had implications for the Western hemisphere. Cuba and even more so Puerto Rico contained a large, visible colored population. Both the proponents and opponents of American expansion in the Caribbean used racially based arguments to support their position.[8]

Another factor dampening African-American interest in Cuba was the conviction that the nation had abundant problems at home, foremost of which was the deteriorating pattern of race relations. Segregationist policies introduced gradually in the post-Reconstruction South spread rapidly in the last decade of the nineteenth and first years of the twentieth centuries. Political disfranchisement and economic dependency reinforced Jim Crow. White politicians sought to disassociate the Republican Party from blacks in an effort to gain white votes in the South and elsewhere. In *The Black Press Views American Imperialism,* George P. Marks notes that even during the Spanish-American War African-American patriotism was "restrained, critical, and often bitter." Some editors, such as John Mitchell of the *Richmond Planet,* had resisted the clamor for war against Spain, arguing that the duty of the American government was to protect black American citizens in the South from hostile and increasingly violent whites and not the people of Cuba from their oppressors.[9]

With the decline in volume came a change in the tone of comments about Cuba. Black Americans came increasingly to fear the consequences of the American presence on the island. Their prime concern was that North American racial beliefs and practices would accompany other Yankee influences. Shortly after the establishment of the U.S. military government, the press noted the introduction of prejudice by military authorities into what African-Americans saw as a racially harmonious society. These reports were confirmed by black Americans in Cuba and by Afro-Cubans.[10] As Gatewood has observed, "Negroes came to understand that the mission of America to Cuba actually meant the 'mission of the Anglo-Saxon.'"[11] Recurrent calls for annexation of the former Spanish colony aroused fears that the war for Cuban independence would prove to have been fought in vain and that black brothers and sisters in Cuba would be permanently subjected to the indignities experienced by their relatives to the north. As a result, black Americans could no longer dream of improving their position through emigration, a possibility that at best had been a remote one.[12]

When American troops withdrew in May 1902, the government of Cuba passed from General Leonard Wood to Tomás Estrada Palma, a leader of the Ten Years War (1868–78) who had spent most of the preceding quarter century in the United States. In many ways Estrada Palma was an ideal choice to head the new nation. He was acceptable to the American government and, because of his long exile, not clearly identified with any faction in Cuba.[13] Although Cuba was not without serious problems related to poverty, sectionalism, and competition for the spoils of office, the period from 1902 through 1905 was one of relative tranquility and prosperity, if not "the best years of the republic," as a leading North American student of Cuban history wrote in 1927.[14]

The election campaign in the fall of 1905, however, set into motion a series of events that ultimately led to the re-establishment of U.S. administration of the island. Estrada Palma's decision to seek re-election and the subsequent efforts of his supporters to secure victory resulted in charges of corruption and the outbreak of violence. The Liberals, convinced that Estrada's Moderate Party was determined to win by fair or foul means, boycotted the December election. Rumors of rebellion and scattered episodes of open resistance to the government persisted for several months until August 16, 1906, when a revolt in the province of Pinar del Río led to widespread armed resistance.[15]

A major objective of the rebels was to cause the United States to intervene, thereby bringing an end to rule by Estrada Palma and the Moderates. Although the Roosevelt administration wanted to avoid dispatching troops to the island, it supplied the government forces with munitions and on September 11 sent two warships to Havana and Cienfuegos. Soon thereafter

Secretary of War William H. Taft and Assistant Secretary of State Robert Bacon left for Cuba to mediate the conflict. Estrada, however, refused to compromise, believing U.S. intervention preferable. On September 28 he resigned and in effect turned the government over to Taft and the American army. The second intervention under Governor Edward Magoon, who replaced Taft in October, lasted until January 1909.[16]

Most African-American journals that commented on the Cuban situation—and virtually all did so—expressed reservations about the intervention; these were rooted in concerns first voiced during the occupation that followed the Cuban-Spanish-American War. Their main fear was that American action represented a victory for those in the United States and on the island who favored annexation and that in the process Afro-Cubans, and indirectly all black people, would suffer a defeat in their quest for justice.

One of the few editorial comments written prior to the sending of ships and the peace mission to Cuba in mid-September 1906 indicated the tendency of black Americans to assess events in Cuba in racial terms. On August 25, nine days after the outbreak of the revolt, the *Boston Guardian* remarked that "it looks like from the Cuban revolution that lily-whiteism is not as tamely submitted to by Colored Cubans as by Colored Americans." The *Guardian* refrained from accusing the United States government of contributing to the worsening racial climate in Cuba, but the *Cleveland Gazette, Voice of the Negro,* and others did not. The disorders in Cuba as seen by the *Gazette* were the result of a color line created in part by the "half-American baked" president (Estrada Palma) and by the settling of prejudiced Americans in Cuba after the Spanish-American War. The *Voice of the Negro* agreed that one source of the turmoil was the introduction of "degenerate prejudice" into the island by American citizens. While the United States clearly had the right to intervene under the Platt Amendment, it did not have the right to annex the island. Such action would be a "serious setback to the cause of liberty" since the United States had proven its inability to govern territories with large numbers of people of color.[17]

Some papers that downplayed the racial aspect of the disturbances saw the United States as being manipulated by groups of Cubans and American citizens. The *Richmond Planet,* for example, accused President Roosevelt of playing into the hands of those Cubans who desired annexation by threatening intervention if order were not quickly restored. In effect, Roosevelt was saying that if Estrada Palma did not continue in office, no one else would do so. In a September 1906 editorial, the *New York Age* also expressed fear that the U.S. intervention being encouraged by the unpopular Estrada Palma government might lead to annexation or to the establishment of an American protectorate. Even though a few months later the paper observed that the Cubans were bringing trouble upon themselves by their incessant internal strife, it continued to voice concern at the activity of powerful American interests seeking annexation.[18]

In commenting on events in Cuba and U.S. responses, blacks (like other Americans) sometimes related external affairs to domestic policies. Two papers found in the Cuban situation an opportunity to attack the federal government's indifference to the plight of black citizens while assuming the burden of preserving order and protecting lives in Cuba. "Our government is a peculiar structure," observed the *Atlanta Independent*. "It undertakes to guarantee and enforce a republican form of government in a foreign country but it is powerless to protect its own citizens." In an obvious reference to the Atlanta race riot of September 1906, in which at least twenty-five black citizens lost their lives and over one hundred were seriously wounded, the *Baltimore Afro-American* suggested that instead of sending Taft to Havana he should have been ordered to Georgia.[19]

In contrast to the events leading to intervention in the fall of 1906, developments in Cuba during the Magoon regime received little attention in the African-American press. And as was the case seven years earlier, the end of American control in January 1909 elicited scant but favorable notice. The *Nashville Globe* applauded the election of Jose Miguel Gómez as president in November 1908. It predicted that he would be more successful than Estrada Palma had been because his service in the struggle against Spain and his dark skin brought him closer to the masses. Indeed, had Gómez lived in the United States, he would have been classified as a Negro. In an unusually complimentary January 1909 editorial, the *Indianapolis Recorder* praised the United States for working in good faith to establish a government "of Cubans by Cubans for Cubans." After what had been in effect a false start toward self-rule under Estrada Palma, Cuba was now beginning an experiment in self-government in good shape.[20]

Yet as those familiar with the history of Cuba are well aware, American administration had not altered the conditions that gave rise to the disorders of 1906. Furthermore, the intervention, while widely deplored in Cuba and far from popular in the United States, actually contributed to political instability. The U.S. actions encouraged those who had failed in the quest for power to resort to rebellion as a means of promoting further intervention and the removal of their opponents from office.[21] In addition, one of the problems faced by Cuba—racial conflict—became more severe during the second intervention and ultimately contributed to the Race War and near-intervention of 1912. In the first years of the twentieth century most white Cubans and North Americans did not consider racial tensions a major problem facing the new nation. Although slavery was not completely abolished until 1886, the society did not have the heritage of racial violence or rigid segregation found in the United States. Moreover, dark-skinned Cubans who would have been classified as Negroes in the United States played a key role in the independence movement. A large number of mixed-race people further contributed to the image of the island as free of deep-seated racial antagonism.

Despite the popular image of Cuba as a racial paradise—one initially confirmed even by black American soldiers in 1898—Afro-Cubans did not enjoy full equality with whites. They had less education, poorer housing, and lower occupational standing than whites. The equality and extensive miscegenation among the lower social classes did not extend into the upper classes. Furthermore, fear of black political power among the largely white elite had retarded the growth of the independence movement and had weakened rebel efforts during the Ten Years' War and the final struggle to overthrow Spanish rule.[22]

Afro-Cubans had distinguished themselves in the struggle against Spain. With independence, however, their position in Cuban society deteriorated. Under U.S. military rule from 1898 to 1902, participation of blacks in the government was minimal and Cuban military units became organized on a segregated basis. When blacks protested, whites blamed the Americans and promised changes once self-government was restored. During the Estrada Palma years, Afro-Cubans complained even more of discrimination in public service, the armed forces, education, and in foreign-owned companies. Gradually race entered politics, and in 1905 the Liberal Party sought black votes by committing itself to the eradication of existing inequities. The uprisings leading to the revolt of August 1906 involved a disproportionate number of nonwhite Cubans, although by no means did all blacks support the insurgents.[23]

Even with the end of the Estrada Palma regime, the restoration of order, and the growth of the Liberal Party under the Magoon provisional government, large numbers of blacks remained restless. Early in 1907 various political groups began to solicit black support in anticipation of the 1908 elections. One result of the growing political consciousness of Afro-Cubans was the rise of an independent Afro-Cuban political movement, a development that alarmed much of the white population. When in the congressional elections of August 1908 not a single black was elected, disgruntled blacks formed the Partido Independiente de Color (PIC), composed primarily of workers, veterans of the War for Independence, and participants in the 1906 revolt. Although the PIC was allowed by the American provisional government to take part in the November 1908 general election, in February 1910, a year after the end of American control, the Cuban Congress outlawed political parties and organizations based on race, class, place of birth, or profession. The provision, known as the Morúa Law after Senator Martín Morúa Delgado, himself a black man, was obviously directed against the PIC.[24]

Bitterness at the persistence of racial discrimination and resentment over the exclusion of the PIC from the forthcoming presidential election contributed to the outbreak of the insurrection known as the Race War of 1912 in May of that year.[25] The PIC rebel leaders hoped to achieve either legalization of their party or a third U.S. intervention. Political unrest and armed revolt by the PIC sparked disorders in the countryside, especially in Oriente province. Over the past decade economic conditions for farmers and peasants in the province, which included a large Afro-Cuban population, had steadily declined. Loss of land, increased population density, immigrant competition, and depressed export prices meant that rural Cubans of color, like their urban counterparts, faced a future in sharp contrast to the hopes generated by independence.[26] Fear that the massive upheavals in Cuba might endanger American lives and property led the Taft administration to dispatch ships and troops to the island. But the desire of both the American and Cuban governments to avoid another intervention, and the success of the Cuban army in bringing a quick end to the insurrection, prevented the landing of large numbers of Yankee troops and the re-establishment of American rule.[27]

With one important exception, prior to the spring 1912 upheaval black American newspapers gave only sporadic attention to racial politics in Cuba under the provisional government and the Gómez presidency. The formation of the PIC in 1908, for example, went virtually unnoticed. The *New York Age,* which commented on the event, professed not to know the complete story about the formation of the party. But it did recognize that prejudice on the island had grown under American occupation. "Not only the Constitution but American race prejudice also follows the American flag," it remarked.[28]

The one event between 1906 and 1912 that attracted attention from the African-American press was the refusal of an American- owned hotel in Havana to serve two Afro-Cuban congressmen in early January 1910. The action led to the gathering of a crowd of several hundred and an ensuing riot. Prompt corrective action by the Cuban government failed to placate all concerned, and tensions remained high in the capital.[29]

Black American press reaction to this event rivaled that devoted to American intervention in 1906. Without exception the press saw the incident as a manifestation of the spread of American-style racism. Some, such as the *St. Paul Appeal* and the *Savannah Tribune,* said little except to report the event and the reaction to it, which resulted in a change of hotel policy. The *Nashville Globe* included in its editorial note a warning that black Cubans should remain alert to efforts to introduce race hatred into their society.[30]

Other journals commented at length and drew various lessons from the episode. The *Indianapolis Freeman* interpreted the Cuban responses to discrimination as evidence that race prejudice would not prosper in societies where colored races were predominant despite North American efforts to export colorphobia. The *Star of Zion* cited the disturbances as good reason for the country to avoid involvement in nonwhite areas of the world and to resist pressures to annex Cuba in particular. Acquisition of territories with populations similar to that of Cuba, it warned, would only further complicate America's already tangled and troublesome race problem. "What if Cuba were a part of our possessions with its large and influential Negro citizenry?" it wondered.[31]

The *Cleveland Gazette* and the *New York Age* looked at the hotel's denial of service in terms of the impact of American racism on its relations with Cuba and Latin America in general. The great majority of Cubans, the *Gazette* reported, had no love for the United States, a sentiment attributable to American greed and "damphool" color and race prejudice. As far as the Cubans were concerned, annexation would be worse than return to Spanish control. The *Age* worried that the Havana race riot was only a skirmish in a great battle between North American race oppression and South American race freedom. Unless the nation learned from its neighbors not to damn a person because of race, its relations—commercial and otherwise—with the mixed republics to the south would continue to deteriorate and "Christian America" would fail to fulfill its mission to lead South America to progress and prosperity.[32]

From time to time in the succeeding months black newspapers commented on the persistence of racial tensions in Cuba,[33] but it was not until the outbreak of violence in May 1912 that they once again focused on Cuban developments. Editorials about the revolt and its immediate aftermath indicate that black Americans agreed about the causes of the Race

War and U.S. policy, past and present, regarding Cuba. They were not of one mind, however, on the desirability of combating racial discrimination through a separate political party or by resorting to violence.

In the view of the black American press, the disturbances in Cuba were the culmination of a long period of worsening relations that had begun with the U.S. intervention fourteen years earlier. Afro-Cubans who had valiantly fought for liberty under the gallant leadership of martyred black heroes, such as Antonio Maceo, had thrown off Spanish-style oppression only to encounter Southern American–style oppression. The spilling of blood on Cuban soil, wrote the *Philadelphia Tribune* in May 1912, was "the yield of the harvest from the seed of race prejudice" sown by the United States and carried to the island. But for the "over-bearing, unfair methods of white people" who migrated from the United States, the island would have continued to experience racial harmony. So contagious was the "white fever" that had blown over from the American South that Cuba was considering legislation to bar black and Asian immigrants, the *Washington Bee* added.[34] When blacks organized to protect themselves through political action, their party had been outlawed, creating a crisis.[35]

Another theme in the black press in the spring and summer of 1912 was suspicion of United States intentions in Cuba. Although little sentiment existed for annexation of the troubled republic and the Taft administration, like its predecessor six years before, sought to avoid a politically unpopular direct intervention, black editors feared that the United States would use the disturbances as a pretext for annexing the island. Such a step, they asserted, would be detrimental to the cause of Cuban liberty. It would also pose innumerable problems for racially torn America, which had yet to learn that in other areas of the world people of color would not submit to the indignities tolerated by African-Americans.[36] Indeed it was the rejection by the proud colored Cubans of the repugnant American pattern of race relations that had caused the present troubles, observed the *Philadelphia Tribune*.[37]

Most African-American journals gave the Cuban rebels tacit if not enthusiastic support, but two leading papers, the *New York Age* and the *Indianapolis Freeman,* were critical of the revolt. The Negroes of Cuba, the *Age* warned, had nothing to gain and much to lose by taking up arms against the Gómez government. Grievances should be settled through the use of the ballot. By turning to force, Negroes would suffer in the long run. Furthermore, white Americans alarmed by the uprising in Cuba would make conditions worse for the race in this country.[38]

The *Age* expressed its reservations in just one editorial, but the *Freeman* had a great deal to say about the uprising. It did not question the validity of the complaints voiced by Afro-Cubans. Yet even though Negroes were not getting a "square deal," neither could one claim that they lived in bondage. After all, they enjoyed much greater freedom than blacks in the United States. While the editor professed to recognize the value of rebellion as an assertion of manhood, such behavior was costly and unlikely to produce the desired results. Since the Cubans lacked the numbers and resources to succeed in either rebellion or independent political activity, they would be wise to do as blacks did in the United States—work through existing political arrangements—especially since they received more "political and civil consideration in general than Negroes of the United States."[39]

With the defeat of the rebels in July 1912 and the return of relative tranquility, black American interest in the island's affairs subsided once again. Another upheaval led to a third American intervention in 1917, but the African-American press said little about it.[40] For one thing there was no overt racial dimension to the violence in 1917. Also by then black Americans, like others, were preoccupied with the spread of war in Europe and the seemingly endless turmoil in revolutionary Mexico.[41]

Although black editors did not always view events in Cuba and the United States policy identically, they considered them of importance to the nation and to the well-being of African-Americans. Blacks could no more divorce their interests and concerns from the way they looked at the world around them than could other Americans. Their experiences may have led them to distort what was happening in Cuba and American actions there, but they also enabled them to perceive aspects of the situation that whites failed to see. Race may not have been as vital a factor in the internal politics of the island as the editors tended to assume. Yet by being all too familiar with the pervasiveness of racial thinking and decision-making, black North Americans were prepared to provide a sympathetic audience for Afro-Cubans excluded from full participation in the affairs of the new republic. Likewise, if racial considerations were not as central to the controversy over the annexation of Cuba as the African-American press claimed, the journalists were correct in alerting readers to the strong theme of racist thought among American expansionists. If the press often overstated the extent to which Cuba was a black nation, it was perceptive in noting that Cuba and much of Latin America had a large nonwhite population and that Americans in both the public and private sectors had to act differently in dealing with people of color in Latin America than was the norm in North America. The dual consciousness of black Americans stemming from their status as oppressed people in their land of birth clearly provided them with a unique if not always accurate perspective on developments in Cuba and United States policy.

NOTES

Acknowledgments: The author would like to acknowledge the assistance of Dr. Frederick Hay of Kansas State University, Dr. Brenda Gayle Plummer of the University of Wisconsin–Madison, and Dr. George Yoos of St. Cloud State University in the preparation of this essay.

1. For a brief overview of black interest in Cuba see Johnetta B. Cole, "Afro-American Solidarity with Cuba," *Black Scholar* 8 (Summer 1977):73–80.

2. Willard Gatewood, ed., *"Smoked Yankees" and the Struggle for Empire: Letters from Negro Soldiers* (Urbana: University of Illinois Press, 1971); Gatewood, *Black Americans and the White Man's Burden, 1898–1903* (Urbana: University of Illinois Press, 1975).

3. Washington's influence on the Afro-American press is examined in August Meier, "Booker T. Washington and the Negro Press: With Special Reference to the *Colored American Magazine*," *Journal of Negro History* 38 (January 1953): 67–90.

4. See, for example, *Indianapolis Freeman,* April 20, 1901, and *Indianapolis Recorder,* June 8 and 15, 1901.

5. *Indianapolis Freeman,* January 25 and March 29, 1902; Gatewood, *Black Americans and the White Man's Burden.* For details regarding the Platt Amendment and the Tariff Reciprocity Treaty see Louis A. Pérez Jr., *Cuba between Empires, 1878–1902* (Pittsburgh: University of Pittsburgh Press, 1983), 317–27 and 346–65.

6. *Star of Zion,* Charlotte, N.C., June 5, 1902. On October 9, 1902, however, the paper expressed concern about the continuing presence of a few American troops in Cuba.

7. George P. Marks III, "Opposition of Negro Newspapers to American Philippine Policy, 1899–1900," *Midwest Journal* 4 (Winter 1951–52); Gatewood, *Black Americans and the White Man's Burden,* 1–25, 181–221, and 261–92; Richard E. Welch Jr., *Responses to Imperialism: The United States and the Philippine-American War, 1899–1902* (Chapel Hill: University of North Carolina Press, 1979), 107–16.

8. Phillip W. Kennedy, "Race and American Expansion in Cuba and Puerto Rico, 1895–1905," *Journal of Black Studies* 1 (March 1971): 306–16; Rubin F. Weston, *Racism in U.S. Imperialism: The Influence of Racial Assumptions on American Foreign Policy, 1893–1946* (Columbia, S.C.: University of South Carolina Press, 1972), 137–62 and 183–94.

9. George Marks III, ed., *The Black Press Views American Imperialism (1898–1900)* (New York: Arno Press, 1971), 51; Gatewood, *Black Americans and the White Man's Burden,* 30–34; Gatewood, "A Negro Editor on Imperialism: John Mitchell, 1898–1901," *Journalism Quarterly* 49 (Spring 1972): 43–50.

10. The growth of disillusionment regarding U.S. policy in Cuba is outlined in Gate-

wood, *Black Americans and the White Man's Burden,* pp. 159, 175–77. Racial attitudes and policies of U.S. decision makers regarding Cuba are considered in Pérez, *Cuba between Empires,* pp. 219–20, 307–8.

11. Willard Gatewood Jr., "Black Americans and the Quest for Empire, 1898–1903," *Journal of Southern History* 38 (November 1972): 555.

12. Gatewood, *Black Americans and the White Man's Burden,* pp. 158, 164–74, 177–78.

13. Allan R. Millet, *The Politics of Intervention: The Military Occupation of Cuba, 1906–1909* (Columbus: Ohio State University Press, 1968), 46–48; David A. Lockmiller, *Magoon in Cuba: A History of the Second Intervention, 1906–1909* (Chapel Hill: University of North Carolina Press, 1938), 17–27; Louis Pérez Jr., *Cuba under the Platt Amendment, 1902–1934* (Pittsburgh: University of Pittsburgh Press, 1986), 89.

14. Charles E. Chapman, *A History of the Cuban Republic: A Study in Hispanic American Politics* (New York: Octagon Books, 1927, 1969), 152–75.

15. For background on events leading to the second U.S. intervention, see Millet, *The Politics of Intervention,* 27–39; Lockmiller, *Magoon in Cuba,* 27–39; Chapman, *History of the Cuban Republic,* pp. 176–98; Pérez, *Cuba under the Platt Amendment,* pp. 89–98.

16. Lockmiller, *Magoon in Cuba,* pp. 39–63; Louis Pérez Jr., *Cuba under the Platt Amendment,* 63–112; Chapman, *History of the Cuban Republic,* 199–230.

17. *Cleveland Gazette,* September 22, 1906; *Voice of the Negro* (Atlanta) 3 (October 1906): 393–94.

18. *Richmond Planet,* September 22, 1906; *New York Age,* September 27, 1906, January 31, 1907.

19. *Atlanta Independent,* September 15, 1906; *Baltimore Afro-American,* October 13, 1906. For other comments on events in Cuba in late 1906 see *New York Age,* October 11, 1906. The importance of developments in Cuba for domestic black politics is suggested in a letter from Charles W. Anderson, the U.S. collector of internal revenue in New York City, to Booker T. Washington on November 10, 1906: "Governor Magoon of Cuba seems to be drawing the color-line, if we are to credit newspaper reports. Gualberto Gómez, the colored Cuban leader, is very much dissatisfied with Magoon, and the entire Liberal party are claiming that he is filling the offices with men who stood behind Palma. They accuse him of reversing the attitude of Taft. All these things will form different counts in the indictment, which the enemy will make." Louis R. Harlan and Raymond W. Smocks, eds., *The Booker T. Washington Papers* (Urbana: University of Illinois Press, 1980), 9:124.

20. *Nashville Globe,* November 20, 1908; *Indianapolis Recorder,* January 9 and January 23, 1909.

21. Pérez, *Cuba under the Platt Amendment,* 97, 104, 338.

22. The status of Afro-Cubans in the late nineteenth century is considered in Verena Martínez-Alier, *Marriage, Class and Colour in Nineteenth-Century Cuba* (New York: Cambridge University Press, 1974); Franklin W. Knight, *Slave Society in Cuba during the Nineteenth Century* (Madison: University of Wisconsin Press, 1970); Franklin W. Knight, "Slavery, Race and Social Structure in Cuba during the Nineteenth Century," in Robert B.

Toplin, ed., *Slavery and Race Relations in Latin America* (Westport, Conn.: Greenwood Publishing, 1974), 219–23; Rebecca J. Scott, *Slave Emancipation in Cuba: The Transition to Free Labor, 1860–1899* (Princeton, N.J.: Princeton University Press, 1985).

23. Rafael Fermoselle-López, "Black Politics in Cuba: The Race War of 1912" (Ph.D. diss., American University, 1972), 11, 35–36, 48–60, 83. This study has been published as *Política y Color en Cuba: La Guerrita de 1912* (Montevideo: Ediciones Geminis, 1974).

24. Fermoselle-López, "Black Politics in Cuba," 124–37, 207. For other accounts of the background of the Race War of 1912, see Thomas T. Orum, "The Politics of Colors: The Racial Dimensions of Cuban Politics during the Early Republican Years, 1900–1912" (Ph.D. diss., New York University, 1975); Chapman, *History of the Cuban Republic*, 260, 308–10; Hugh Thomas, *Cuba: The Pursuit of Freedom* (New York: Harper and Row, 1971), 514–24; Pérez, *Cuba under the Platt Amendment,* 48–52.

25. Although African-Americans stressed racial discrimination as the central if not the only cause of the 1912 uprising, many contemporaries and historians have interpreted the event otherwise. For discussion of various theories regarding the rebellion see Fermoselle-López, "Black Politics in Cuba," 183–211.

26. The rural aspects of the 1912 revolt are stressed in Louis A. Pérez Jr., "Politics, Peasants, and People of Color: The 1912 'Race War' in Cuba Reconsidered," *Hispanic American Historical Review* 66 (August 1986): 509–38.

27. Fermoselle-López, "Black Politics in Cuba," 190.

28. The *New York Age,* October 1, 1908.

29. *New York Times,* January 3 and 4, 1910.

30. *St. Paul Appeal,* January 8, 1910; *Savannah Tribune,* January 8, 1910; *Nashville Globe,* January 7, 1910.

31. *Indianapolis Freeman,* January 8, 1910; *Star of Zion,* January 20, 1910.

32. *Cleveland Gazette,* February 10, 1910; *New York Age,* January 13, 1910.

33. *New York Age,* February 3, 1910, July 20, 1911; *Indianapolis Recorder,* April 30, 1910; *Cleveland Gazette,* May 21, 1910, February 24, 1912; *Baltimore Afro-American,* December 10, 1910; *Indianapolis Freeman,* March 9, 1912. Although he gave no specifics, Booker T. Washington noted in 1911 that since 1908, when the PIC was formed, race relations had deteriorated in Cuba (Harlan and Smock, eds., *Booker T. Washington Papers,* 10: 176–77). For often contrasting assessments of race relations in Cuba by two prominent black Americans who visited the island on the eve of the 1912 revolt, see the letters by Madame E. Azalia Hackley in the *Philadelphia Tribune,* March 20 and April 6, 1912, and by J. Arthur Davis in the *New York Age,* June 6, 1912.

34. *Philadelphia Tribune,* May 25, 1912; *Washington Bee,* July 13, 1912.

35. *Baltimore Afro-American,* May 25, 1912; *Cleveland Gazette,* June 8, 1912. See also the assessments of the conflict in Cuba by John E. Bruce (as "Bruce Grit") in the *Denver Statesman,* June 1, 1912.

36. *Pittsburgh Courier,* June 14, 1912; *Philadelphia Tribune,* June 8, 1912; *Denver Statesman,* June 1 and 8, 1912.

37. *Philadelphia Tribune,* May 25, 1912.

38. *New York Age,* June 6, 1912.

39. *Indianapolis Freeman,* May 25, June 15, and August 3, 1912. For another critique of the uprising see James B. Clarke, "The Cuban Revolution," *Crisis* 4 (October 1912): 301–2. An earlier article in the *Crisis* by Arthur A. Schomburg, "General Evaristo Estenoz" (vol. 4 [July 1912]: 143–44), had been sympathetic to the revolt. The usually outspoken editor of the *Crisis,* W.E.B. Du Bois, presented no editorial comment on events in Cuba from 1910 through 1912.

40. For examples of comments about Cuba after 1912, see *Chicago Defender,* February 21, 1914; *Philadelphia Tribune,* March 3, 1917; *Baltimore Afro-American,* May 12, 1917.

41. See this author's "The Afro-American Press and Woodrow Wilson's Mexican Policy, 1913–1917," *Phylon* 48 (December 1987): 261–70.

4

Encounters in the African Atlantic World

The African Methodist Episcopal Church in Cuba

JUALYNNE E. DODSON

> Although I've been greatly opposed by others of wicked, jealous and covetous mind, by the help of the Lord, I've succeeded in establishing four preaching centers [in Cuba]. . . . At Jacajo, the people appreciate the work greatly, but the property being that of the United Fruit Company, a [place of worship] can not be obtained.
> Rev. R. A. Cevestus Duggan, 1920

Although there have been major and important achievements toward reclaiming the Africanist presence in the Americas, we are still a long way from fully understanding the complexities of human relationships created by that presence. This collection of essays probes one set of encounters provoked by that presence; my chapter specifically examines interactions between the African Methodist Episcopal (AME) Church of the United States and Afro-Cubans. Compounding the complexities associated with unraveling relations between Afro-Cubans and the AME Church are the intersecting realities of colonialism, racism, and economics.[1] In any exploration of these relations it is important to include the impact of United States military occupation of Cuba (1898–1902) as well as the sixty-one years of imperialist influence that followed. Neither can the analysis omit the complexity arising from tensions between Protestantism and Catholicism in the Americas. While an examination of African-derived religions in this context would be important as well, these traditions rarely came up in the documents about the AME Church upon which this essay is based. The narrow frame of this work, therefore, does not include the African-derived traditions.

From Columbus's first entry into the Americas, the Roman Catholic

Church dominated religious and most nonreligious affairs in Spanish Cuba. With the settling of North America as Protestant territory, the rivalry between the two branches of Christianity crossed the Atlantic. In 1895, when Cubans began a second struggle for national independence, supporters of the rising imperialist strength of the United States envisioned a Protestant expansion into the Caribbean and Latin America, under Catholic influence for more than three hundred years. As the United States publicly considered military intervention into Cuba in 1898, secular and religious newspapers heralded the move as more than a military undertaking. Even President William McKinley began to transform the operation "into a crusade [that] . . . rationalized imperialism as a missionary obligation." Among Protestants, the Methodist congregations were particularly strident, proclaiming that a U.S. presence would "destroy 'Romish superstition' in the Spanish West Indies."[2] However, the prevailing imperialist sentiment was not exclusive to Methodists. Most among U.S. religious communities held that intervention was good: it meant the "coming to poor Cuba. . . . [of] Christian civilization,"—implying, of course, that Catholicism was somehow outside of that definition.[3] Although Catholics in the United States initially expressed concern about such blatant attacks on their faith and their church, most yielded to their national (rather than religious) allegiance and joined in the imperialist fervor. Support for involvement in the Cuban war against Spanish colonialism traversed the boundaries of Christian traditions.[4]

The slogan "The cross will follow the flag" captured this national sentiment. Military occupation moved forward into Cuba, and missionary zeal accompanied it. It was a time of nationalist coalescing, a time when Protestantism unabashedly aligned itself with the ideals of patriotism and imperialism.[5] Part of the complex of events surrounding the Cuban struggle for independence and U.S. intervention was an independent black denomination, the African Methodist Episcopal Church. In fact, nowhere were complexities more apparent than in the religious yet nationalistic organizing of the AME Church in Cuba.

Making Connection

The African Methodist Episcopal Church had its origins in Philadelphia in 1787, when a small group of free blacks acted upon their desire for self-determination in religious affairs. The group was clearly protesting white-skin privilege in worship, but they were simultaneously expressing disagreement over their preferred practice of Christianity and the way it was practiced by European Americans. On a now-famous November Sunday in 1787, every African-American person in St. George Methodist Church walked out, never to return. After meeting as a mutual aid society for more than a year, some among the protesters formed the Bethel African Methodist Church of Philadelphia and proceeded to seek legal incorporation for the congregation. Members claimed the right to organize independently of the white parent church. Bethel took its petition for independence to the courts of Pennsylvania, and a decision in their favor was issued. The legal precedent made Bethel Church the focus for organizing African Methodism into a linked connection of independent congregations. In 1816 leaders of these congregations met in Philadelphia and formed the denomination called the African Methodist Episcopal Church.

By 1886 the AME Church was the world's largest denomination of African-Americans. It had more than four hundred thousand members, nearly three thousand ordained ministers, and more than three thousand church buildings, and it had sent missionaries to Haiti, Santo Domingo, and Africa.[6] In 1893 the Missionary Department received a letter from a Reverend Durmer in the city of Santiago de Cuba. Exactly who Durmer was, how he came to be in Santiago, or how he had learned of the denomination is not known. Nevertheless, Durmer's letter requested that Church leaders consider organizing in Cuba inasmuch as the country had a large black population.[7] But the letter was more than a request for Protestant expansion among the Catholic-dominated community, for despite their Cuban nationalism, Afro-Cubans shared historical experiences of social oppression with other African-Americans in the hemisphere. Durmer's request to the AME Church to begin working in Cuba was based on that shared experience, making it an African nationalistic request. A socially constructed consciousness of such common historical experiences undergirded Durmer's petition.

By 1898 the post–Civil War programs of Reconstruction had been completely abolished; thousands of once-enslaved and first-generation African-American voters were "grandfathered" and gerrymandered into a disenfranchised status; economic downturns resulting in severe underemployment pushed a majority of the population into abject poverty. The use of intimidating violence against black citizens to insure white supremacy was overtly and legally sanctioned by national attitudes, social practice, and legal proclamations. The Supreme Court's 1896 "separate but equal" decision in *Plessy v. Ferguson* made racial segregation the law of the land.[8]

In Cuba the black population also confronted a society based on discrimination; here too their African ancestry was assigned an inferior status. Despite their high numerical representation in the first struggles for national independence (1868–98) and the outlawing of slavery in 1886, Afro-Cubans did not enjoy fair treatment or equality of opportunity.[9]

When the Reverend Durmer contacted the AME Church in 1893, racial discrimination limited the economic, political, and social advancement of dark-skinned Cubans. While this was not the U.S. style of institutional segregation that resulted from *Plessy v. Ferguson,* racial discrimination against Afro-Cubans was real and measurable. Dark-skinned Cubans began to place their hopes for equality in the armed struggle against the final vestiges of Spanish colonial rule. In that struggle some 40 percent of the senior commissioned ranks of the Liberation Army were men of color, including the "Bronze Titan," Antonio Maceo.[10] Afro-Cuban expectations for equality of citizenship now resided in their demonstrated contributions to national independence.

In the United States, although the 1896 Supreme Court decision radically circumscribed African-Americans' aspirations for social and political equality, church membership was rising. Independent black congregations and denominations responded to the unmet social and economic needs of their community. The institutional apparatus of white U.S. society had long ignored the latter. Like other denominations, the AME Church expanded into arenas of education, social services, real estate, publication, employment, and politics. These activities demonstrated that collectively, including all denominations and congregations, the African-American community had a *social institution;* it was the Black Church.[11]

Their success with self-help endeavors, coupled with American society's violent practices of racial oppression, convinced many AME leaders that race-conscious self-help, linked with social and spiritual uplift, was an appropriate strategy for African people outside of the United States. The AME Church did not send missionaries to Cuba in 1893, as the Reverend Durmer had requested, but it did begin monitoring the country's social and political climate from a missionary base maintained in Santo Domingo.[12] In 1895 the Rev. C. S. Smith, historiographer and bishop, also undertook to "make a cruise of the West Indies, stopping at all the principal places including Cuba."[13] By 1895 Cubans were engaged in armed struggle against Spanish rule for the second time, and the leadership of General Antonio Maceo was a visible success. Maceo impressed church officials, as did the centrality of Afro-Cuban contributions to the liberation effort. The AME Church's legislative body unanimously passed a resolution expressing approval of Cuba's struggle for self-determination and, along with other African-American organizations, appealed to the U.S. government to recognize the freedom fighters.[14]

Dedicated men of the denomination were among the four African-American regiments to mobilize and fight in Cuba. At least two African Methodists were chaplains who carried authorization from the AME Church.[15] Rev. H. C. C. Astwood was officially appointed superintendent of AME missions in Cuba in April 1898, an appointment that coincided with his assignment as U.S. consul in the Dominican Republic. To combine ministerial responsibility with military or other employment in a specific geographical space was not a new strategy for religious organizations. African Methodists relied on it as a way to expand denominational work beyond the limited economic capabilities of the Church.[16]

In Cuba the Reverend Astwood organized the first gathering of African Methodists in the eastern city of Santiago de Cuba on August 17, 1898. From this site he reported eleven members with two licensed exhorters. In the capital city of Havana, two congregational groups were organized, but when Astwood's governmental assignment ended, the AME Church was unable to finance a replacement. There was an attempt to sustain the Cuban efforts with visits from Bishop Charles S. Smith, but Church development on the island remained weak. The appointment of H. C. C. Astwood nevertheless marked the beginning of the Church's formal presence in Cuba. It was a relationship founded on shared racial consciousness developed through common historical experiences with social oppression. The relationship was an alliance for resistance and upward mobility through spiritually centered self-help among African-Americans. However, it was not a relationship in which Cuban realities necessarily informed the actions of the denomination.

For example, Afro-Cubans were a Spanish-speaking people. The surnames Durmer and Astwood do not suggest that the two religious men were themselves of Spanish-speaking origin, however. Neither were they apparently citizens of Cuba. In fact, as we shall see, it is questionable whether any of the early ministers to Cuba even spoke Spanish. The Church's ministers in Cuba were not specifically suited for that work. Church officials accepted the convenience of combining their denominational appointment with Astwood's consular assignment. Thus the early contacts between the AME Church and Afro-Cubans, while facilitating a relationship, were somewhat problematic.

As the twentieth century approached and AME missionary efforts waned in Cuba, Bishop Henry McNeal Turner became interested in the possibilities of growth among Afro-Latinos. He had been the first man born in the South to be elected to the office of bishop since before the Civil War. He was an ardent black nationalist who espoused the freedom and rights of African peoples internationally. He has been called the last radical leader of the nineteenth-century Black Church.[17] It was Turner who was responsible for establishing an AME presence in South Africa, and it was from a subsidiary of his Sixth Episcopal District that Turner supported the Rev. H. C. C. Astwood's 1898 appointment in Cuba. As the new century opened, Bishop Turner focused his nationalistic vision on blacks in Mexico and Cuba. Although he was near the end of his career, he used his episcopal position to pursue this nationalistic missionary vision.[18]

Bishop Turner appointed the Rev. D. S. Wells to the supervising position of presiding elder to Cuba in 1901. Like H. C. C. Astwood before him, and others who would follow, Wells had only partial success. From Cienfuegos, a city southeast of Havana, Wells was "instrumental in bringing sixty-five native Cubans and Spaniards into the AME Church." But his tenure was short lived; in 1903 Wells was given an appointment back in the United States.[19] Such brief sojourns point to the obstacles AME ministers faced in sustaining a relationship with Afro-Cubans, but they are also indicators of organizational impediments that were directly related to the impoverished condition of African-Americans in the United States.

The denomination's domestic and international expansion could not occur without financial support. The base for that financial support was congregants of local churches as well as the broader U.S. African-American community. Contributions from these sources were generous, but the economic instability and impoverishment of the black population meant that the AME Church often found itself in precarious financial straits. There is consistent evidence that leaders were concerned about Christian missionary work of their Church, and they regularly provided financial resources for such activities. However, finances also appear at the center of many denomination conflicts, and organizational preservation was an equal priority in the allocation of funds.[20] Even the achievement of a presence in Cuba, Jamaica, other Caribbean sites, and South Africa had been accomplished by combining ministers' missionary appointments with employment assignments. A dilemma often occurred when a minister's employment changed; the denomination then had to wrestle with whether to use its limited resources for home missionary work, for sustaining its organizational structure, or for international endeavors. Rarely did the decision favor Cuba.

Bishop Turner's missionary vision had opened the twentieth century. His appointment of a presiding elder did improve the Church's encounters in Cuba. However, economic instability made it difficult to transform encounters into sustained relationships. Cuba barely appeared in the AME Church's 1904 report on missionary activities, for example.[21] Bishop Turner apparently attached high significance to a policy of sustaining relations in Cuba and committed support from resources available to him, but the national legislative body of his Church did not follow his example. Nevertheless, a connection had been made between the two groups of African-Americans.

Race and Protestant Missions

The U.S. military intervention into Cuba's War of Independence brought a well-tested alliance to the island nation—Protestant extension and capitalism. The successful duo would persist beyond the 1902 military evacuation, and it guaranteed missionary accomplishments for white denominations. The discriminatory practices faced by African-Americans in the United States, which were intensified by legalized racial segregation and the ideology of biological racism, were exported to Cuba through U.S. economic penetration and Protestantism. Their arrival signaled a further institutionalization of racism in Cuban society. The linkage between Protestantism and imperialism further complicated relations between African Methodists and Afro-Cubans.

As capitalism developed its foothold in Cuba, U.S. businesses supported the missionary activities of white Protestant denominations. The AME Church, on the other hand, received no financial or structural support. African Methodist ministers approached businesses for assistance, but no evidence has been found to show that companies responded positively. There is also no evidence to link the Church with the 1902 geographic partitioning of Cuba into missionary fields.[22] After entry into the country, the major white denominations agreed to confine their proselytizing and missionary work to designated areas. This, it was thought, would eliminate competition between them. Missionaries from the AME Church were not included in the division, although they were present on the island. This left black ministers free to meet and work with Afro-Cubans throughout the country, but it also left them without the social and economic support and sanction associated with Protestantism's overall mission to Americanize the country. The AME Church was unable to take advantage of the flexibility of its position as outsider and benefit from its black nationalist focus.

Americanization was one reason white Protestant denominations could move ahead aggressively and successfully in the conversion of Cuban citizens. This process included the adoption of American social and racial practices and the use of English. Cubans who converted to Protestantism and joined Protestant congregations had access to the economic and social opportunities created by U.S. imperialism and might attain a position of privilege in the new political economy. In fact, local white churches offered English-language classes as a companion to religious instruction. Facility in English quickly became a prerequisite for many upwardly mobile jobs in the new Cuban economy.

Membership in local Protestant congregations increased, particularly among Cuba's working and poorer classes, who had not been part of the predominantly white-skinned ruling class and whose aspirations for upward mobility were enhanced by opportunities offered by church membership. Most urban communities had several local congregations, but there were also local churches throughout the island. Protestant schools, whether independent or church affiliated, were well attended. However, leadership and control of denominational expansion remained in the hands of U.S. nationals, with some Cuban appointees—not dark skinned—occasionally sharing some functions. The actual number of Cuban Protestants was minimal—seven to nine thousand—compared to the national population of approximately six million, but Protestant social and political influence was substantial. Their churches offered educational opportunities and they were closely associated with Americanization. In January 1907 a meeting of the denominations was called (the African Methodist Episcopal Church was not included) and statistics in the following table were reported:

White Protestant Presence in Cuba, 1907

Denominations	10
Congregations	145
Preaching Points	88
Members	7,781
Schools	29
Teachers	95
Students	22,477

Source: Marcos A. Ramos, *Protestantism and Revolution in Cuba* (Miami: Research Institute for Cuban Studies, University of Miami, 1989), 25.

Americanization and Protestantism were partners in race relations as well. Racial or skin-color discrimination in Cuba was converted from informal social practices into formally structured realities. Segregation of dark-skinned Cubans in public parks and social clubs was accompanied by prohibitions preventing Afro-Cubans from attending certain schools operated by the Methodist and Presbyterian Churches. These were among the most prestigious schools not under the influence of the Catholic Church. Cubans with strong nationalistic ties, those who were very anti-Spanish or those concerned with self-improvement, were particularly attracted to these Protestant schools, and many twentieth-century leaders and intellectuals attended them.[23] In several instances (in the city of Cárdenas of Matanzas Province, for example), the schools were located near large black populations. Nevertheless, white churches actively discouraged dark-skinned Cubans from attending. An informal practice of dissuasion in time solidified into formal patterns whereby Protestant education was structured to privilege light-skinned Cubans.[24] Jim Crow practices of the United States were transplanted, if only de facto, into Cuban social life.

Afro-Cubans who experienced such racist practices might easily have been drawn into an alliance with the independent and race-conscious AME Church. After all, independent organizing for self-help was part of the Cuban social landscape of the period. The Agrupación Independiente de Color was organized in 1907 to express dark-skinned Cubans' frustration with their increased exclusion from government employment and public office following the War of Independence. The initial organizers were largely veterans who had been consistently mistreated, even as everyone acknowledged their disproportionate representation and significant contributions to the independence effort. The Agrupación evolved into a full political party, the Partido Independiente de Color (PIC), whose goals were to ensure that Afro-Cubans received full and equitable participation in the postwar expansion of the government and its services, something sought but not achieved since the Ten Years War of 1868–78.

The complaint of racial discrimination was a legitimate one. Aline Helg's 1995 work, *Our Rightful Share: The Afro-Cuban Struggle for Equality, 1886–1912,* details the factors that led to the formation of the PIC. Its presence posed a serious challenge to the traditional control of the black electorate by the nation's Liberal Party. Thus, every effort was made to eliminate the party, including arrest and harassment of its leaders as well as laws prohibiting political parties based on race.[25] In May 1912 the Partido Independiente de Color resorted to armed rebellion. The conflict, contained mostly in the eastern Oriente Province, lasted several months. The potential for another intervention by the United States, legitimized by the Platt Amendment to the Cuban Constitution, helped push government officials to a quick and ruthless response to the rebellion. More than one thousand black Cubans were killed in what can only be described as a massacre.[26] Clearly, Afro-Cubans were sensitized by the racial inequality of their country, and a receptivity to alliances with African Methodism could easily have developed during these early years of the century.

In November 1916, Frances A. Pearson, of Calle Santo Tomás #60 Alto in the city of Santiago de Cuba, sent a letter to the new secretary of missions of the AME Church, the Rev. John. W. Rankin. The letter was a request for pastors to come help "Spanish speaking people" and it ended with a Protestant appeal: "May it please the A.M.E. Church to assist in evangelizing Cuba."[27] It is not clear if Pearson received any response, but by 1920, as part of the regular procedures of the denomination, the Missionary Department received an official quarterly report from a minister assigned to congregations in the Caribbean. The Rev. R. A. Cevestus Duggan reported four centers of AME progress in Cuba, with the most important identified as Preston, Nipe Bahia, and Oriente de Cuba. Mr. Henry Ramsay was identified as circuit steward and George Taite and T. E. O'Riley as local preachers.[28]

At first glance, such activity indicates that the Church had overcome many obstacles and was beginning to have some successes. However, Duggan's October 1920 report also spelled out details of the missionary work and discussed encounters that compounded relations between African-Americans of Cuba and the United States. Duggan's report stated:

[A]lthough I've been greatly opposed by others of wicked, jealous and covetous mind, by the help of the Lord, I've succeeded in establishing four preaching centers, i.e. Banes, Jacajo, San Jeriner and Preston. As I get no support from any source whatsoever . . . I cannot run the risk to rent said Hall and have to confine to outdoor services for the present. At Jacajo, the people appreciate the work greatly, but the property being that of the United Fruit Company, a Hall can not be obtained.[29]

The "wicked, jealous and covetous mind[ed]" opposition originated among whites from both the United States and Cuba, Catholics as well as Protestants. The absence of "support from any source whatsoever" was a reference to AME officials more than to the Cuban community. Everyone was aware of the impoverished nature of Cubans, so there were no expectations of their financial support. The denomination, on the other hand, had authorized work in the country and, based on the tone of Duggan's report, was expected to support that work. Because there was no support forthcoming, he was forced "to confine to outdoor services" as he could not "run the risk to rent" a hall for worship. Duggan's reference to the United Fruit Company points to yet another complexity in the encounters of African-Americans in Cuba.

The United Fruit Company, like most agricultural enterprises in Cuba during the period, had built a successful business based on labor patterns developed during slavery. Similar racist labor patterns had also existed throughout the Americas.[30] Such companies owned the land under cultivation, as well as the processing factories, worker housing, church buildings, and local businesses serving employees; thus employees and the economic survival of the community were bound to the company.[31] Through charitable donations to religious denominations, these businesses created an image of social responsibility that, in turn, contributed to maintaining their power and control in the communities.[32] However, the Cuban firms were not inclined to make donations to black congregations, particularly those associated with the independent and (black) nationalistic AME Church. And if an excuse or rationalization was needed for excluding certain local churches, businesses could point to contributions they made to congregations composed of their employees, churches with no association with organizing social discontent. Such churches were consistently aligned with white Methodist denominations and/or composed of immigrant workers (usually West Indians).[33]

The Rev. Cevestus Duggan was referring to these complexities when he sent his report in October 1920. He was substantially limited by the economic strictures of the United Fruit Company, he was experiencing racist exclusion from religious philanthropy, and he was expressing the difficulties of attempting to organize without the United Fruit Company's support. If there was hope, Duggan saw it in the fact that "the people appreciate the work greatly." By December the Rev. Thomas H. Spencer, another missionary in Cuba, submitted his quarterly report from the town of Boquerou on Guantánamo Bay, in Oriente Province. He had held meetings in a church building that had been constructed twelve years before and was located close to the U.S. naval base.[34]

It is not mere summation to acknowledge African ancestry as a force in the work of these and other AME ministers. These encounters in the African

Atlantic world were seen as connections between long-separated family members, and missionary reports from Cuba referred directly to an organizing strategy of uniting those of African heritage. A decade after the 1920s reports had come from the eastern province, the Rev. W. H. Mayhew was just as direct. He was the superintendent in charge of Caribbean work and "contributing editor for West India Islands" for the AME newspaper, *Voice of Missions*. In January 1930, Mayhew suggested that there should soon be great progress for African Methodism, and to achieve it all that was needed was to "arouse racial consciousness among the citizens" of the Caribbean, who were bound to suffer from the institutional racism that had accompanied U.S. Protestantism into Cuba. This supposition proved problematic. The very presence of AME missionaries in their country actually startled Afro-Cubans. As Mayhew observed, "We should be acquainted with the fact that African Methodism is in its stage of infancy as yet in these lands, a phenomenon where Negro ministry is yet a popular surprise." His assessment was that the Church could expect encounters and connections with Afro-Cubans to be solidified by "arousing racial consciousness."[35]

In 1938 the geographic center for African Methodist work in Cuba had shifted west to the capital city of Havana. John Deveaux, an enterprising West Indian but not an AME official, had contacted the denomination and offered his organizing services as well as those of "[o]ur Knights of Phythias in Cuba." Deveaux was working in Havana as a modern-day "community organizer" through such Cuban fraternal organizations or "logias."[36] He expressed praise for African Methodism and enumerated development opportunities for the denomination in Cuba. Bishop Reverdy Ranson, who had succeeded Bishop Turner as radical leader of the Church, received Deveaux's correspondence and prepared an official delegation to make a visit. The Cuba Commission was to determine the interest of the population in organizing self-supporting AME congregations.

Although its numerical presence was small and ignored by most white denominations, by the 1930s the AME Church had connected with the black population in Cuba and established a foundation for its organizing effort. The strategy to build local church organizations was the same one that had brought success in the United States: activities focused on social uplift and racial consciousness. But while its emphasis on racial consciousness enhanced the potential of the Church to connect with Afro-Cubans, it gave little attention to the broad national identification that also informed their consciousness.

Until the 1930s, AME missionaries were not Cuban citizens, and indications are that only Mayhew had facility with Spanish.[37] In those communities where successful organizing was reported, most residents were
West Indian immigrants to Cuba and English speakers. Even though they
were of African heritage, these immigrants experienced resentment from
Cuban nationals during the difficult economic and political times that followed independence. The AME Church was physically *in* Cuba, but none
of its spokespersons were *of* the people. If encounters between the two
groups were to be transformed into lasting relationships, a more integrated
type of connection was necessary.

The Final Push

While African Methodism had experienced some growth in the communities
of Oriente province, the correspondence of the 1930s does not use the term
"congregation." This is an important omission because local congregations are
the smallest self-supporting unit of the AME polity. Without them, a specific
locality did not truly have official denominational status or recognition. One
reason for the absence could be that the correspondence of this period came
mostly from John Deveaux and he was not African Methodist, nor Methodist,
and possibly not even a practicing Christian.[38] It also could have been that
Deveaux was not familiar with the details of activities that occurred in the east;
the foundations of his work, after all, were in Havana. Whatever the reasons
for the lack of references to congregations, the correspondence between John
Deveaux and Bishop Ransom was filled with plans for an impending visit
from the AME Church's Cuba Commission.[39]

The commission was planning its visit during a period of Cuban history
that was very different from earlier ones. This was a time of significant political transition. Since the 1898 War of Independence the nation had functioned under a constitution, but there had been little stability and interven-
tions from the United States dominated state affairs. Suppression of the 1912
Afro-Cuban protest against racism was followed by yet another military intervention in 1917, which continued in the eastern region through 1922. The
political climate grew more volatile as the Cuban population regained its nationalistic bearings. Urban and agricultural workers united their various organizations, and writers and artists consolidated their groups.[40] Afro-Cubans
once again figured among the leadership of this organizing.

The Church's Cuba Commission would need to prove the integrity of its desire to expand on the island if it did not want a serious assault from Cuban nationalism. Deveaux's proposition was timely. His presence in Havana and offer to organize with the denomination through "Our Knights of Phythias in Cuba" could provide an initial force with which to begin. The delegation of outsiders also would need approval from the military authorities in charge at the time. There had been several upheavals in the Cuban military command, but in the mid-1930s Fulgencio Batista had overthrown yet another government.

As part of the preparation for a planned but delayed 1938 visit, Bishop Reverdy Ransom wrote John Deveaux about the purpose and intent of the AME commission. He outlined the Church's focus as a black nationalistic one appealing to Cubans of African ancestry. The bishop was equally clear in articulating the Church's "absolute" support for African people's right to freedom and equality in all arenas of social life. Ransom wrote the following:

> Our chief plea shall be to Negroid people to organize under the auspices of the African Methodist Church. As you know, we stand for absolute Equality and Manhood of dark skinned people throughout the world. We do not desire to segregate ourselves, but in the face of racial segregation and antagonism on account of the Colored race, we are compelled to take our stand for absolute political, social, economic and religious Freedom and Equality. If the people of Cuba who we shall meet desire to subscribe to this position, we shall be glad to welcome them into our brotherhood and fellowship.[41]

Although the correspondence may have been shared with the military authorities, the bishop composed another letter. The agency to whom he wrote was the Constitutional Army of Cuba, and Colonel Fulgencio Batista was the official to whom Ransom made the request. However, the bishop was more diplomatic and much less candid about the issues of black nationalism and independence of African Methodism. In November he wrote Colonel Batista the following: "Our Mission is not to attempt to proselytize or supplant in any way other religious denominations. We simply seek out brethren of like faith in the Lord Jesus Christ and of common interest in the welfare of our people in the Americas."[42] Approval to travel throughout the country was issued on December 21.[43]

In January 1939, an AME-led commission of eight bishops, five other denominational leaders, and two women of the church toured Cuba. The inclusion of women in the delegation did not represent any intent to organize Cuban women but rather reflected a health condition of Mr. John R. Hawkins that required the assistance of his daughter, Mrs. Ester Wilson. Consistent with the gender mores of the time, the delegation needed another woman to accompany Mrs. Wilson. The delegation toured six cities: Havana, Matanzas, Pinar del Río, Santa Clara, Camagüey, and Santiago de Cuba. The visit was considered a success for in addition to English-speaking West Indian immigrants it identified Cubans interested in denominational membership. In Santiago de Cuba, 450 persons were reported to have expressed written desire to join the Church. On the basis of reports from this visit and the list of potential new members, the Church's national body gave its strongest support to the work in Cuba.[44]

The Council of Bishops approved eight hundred dollars of financing "to assist in opening at once churches in Cuba." They allocated one hundred dollars per month as a ministerial allotment for work from July 1939 through May 1940 and an additional fifty dollars a month for the Rev. José W. Jarvis to serve as superintendent of the AME Church in Cuba, in addition to his ministerial duties. Not only was the denomination providing finances for Jarvis's work, but his name suggested association with a Latin American heritage, he spoke Spanish, and he would be the first minister designated to work specifically in Cuba. Finally, the Church appeared serious about expansion among Afro-Cubans. In July 1939, Bishop Ransom returned with Jarvis to Cuba, where they organized a school and several congregations. Ransom's report to the Missionary Department was enthusiastic: "In round numbers, there are two thousand people in Santiago who desire to be received into the church at once. They say they can start us off with five hundred children in the school in that connection. Our job is to secure a building and open it for church purposes and open a school in connection with it. This done, they say they can carry themselves almost at once with very little future aid."[45]

A significant fact about the work in Santiago was that recorded documents from the organizing meeting contain the names of Cuban nationals. When interviews were conducted in 1990 with relatives and descendants of these organizers, all were dark-skinned Afro-Cubans. In 1939, therefore, the AME Church had established connections with Cuban nationals of African ancestry.[46]

Conclusion

For a very brief moment, the AME Church appeared to be stabilizing its toehold in Cuba. There were congregations in eastern and western portions of the island. There was a ministerial representative who spoke Spanish and was very familiar with the denomination's organizational functioning in the United States. In addition, when other Protestant denominations organized the Cuban Council of Evangelical Churches in 1940, the AME Church was a charter member with its representative, the Rev. José Jarvis, signing for the body.[47]

However, cultural misunderstandings would ultimately prove self-defeating for denominational stability and growth. The Afro-Cuban population had expectations about membership in the AME Church that differed from established patterns of congregational affiliation. The parent body presumed that local Cuban congregations, like those in the United States, would not only be self-supporting but would contribute regularly to the international work of the denomination. However, Afro-Cubans were more impoverished than blacks in the United States, and they expected AME affiliation to enhance their struggle for educational, economic, and social opportunities. The U.S. denomination did not have sufficient resources, nor would it commit those it did have, to develop an impoverished black community outside of the United States. The needs of the home population were too pressing. Although there are reports of activity in Cuba into the 1960s, the AME never truly became a social, political, or spiritual influence there.

NOTES

1. In this chapter "Church" (with a capital "C") refers to the national denominational body of the African Methodist Episcopal Church. The lowercased word "church" refers to local congregations.

2. Sydney L. Ahlstrom, *A Religious History of the American People* (New Haven, Conn.: Yale University Press, 1972), 798–99.

3. Ibid., 848–51.

4. Ibid., 877–80. Robert E. May, *The Southern Dream of a Caribbean Empire* (Baton Rouge: Louisiana State University Press, 1973).

5. Ahlstrom, *A Religious History*, 880.

6. L. L. Berry, *A Century of Missions of the African Methodist Episcopal Church, 1840–1940* (New York: Gutenberg Printing Co., 1942), 43–46. Benjamin Arnett, *The Budget of 1904* (Philadelphia: Rev E. W. Lampton and Rev. J. H. Collet, 1904), 173–74.

7. AME Missionary Collection, New York, Schomburg Center; Box 1, letter from Reverend Durmer.

8. John Hope Franklin and Alfred A. Moss Jr., *From Slavery to Freedom: A History of African Americans,* 7th ed. (New York: McGraw Hill, 1994), chaps. 12, 13, 15.

9. Rebecca Scott, *Slave Emancipation in Cuba: The Transition to Free Labor, 1860–1899* (Princeton: Princeton University Press, 1985), 45–62. Scott's book is a detailed exploration of the topic, but she does not commit to specific numbers. However, her presentation makes clear that Afro-Cuban participation in the 1868 war exceeded their proportional representation in the general population. Also see Aline Helg, *Our Rightful Share: The Afro-Cuban Struggle for Equality, 1886–1912* (Chapel Hill: University of North Carolina Press, 1995).

10. Louis Pérez Jr., *Cuba: Between Reform and Revolution* (New York: Oxford University Press, 1988), 158–61.

11. See William E. Montgomery, *Under Their Own Vine and Fig Tree: The African-American Church in the South, 1865–1900* (Baton Rouge: Louisiana State University Press, 1993), 231–33; C. Eric Lincoln and Lawrence H. Mamiya, *The Black Church in the African American Experience* (Durham, N.C.: Duke University Press, 1990); E. Franklin Frazier, *The Negro Church in America* (New York: Schocken, 1964), as well as Franklin and Moss, *From Slavery To Freedom,* chap. 14.

12. For discussion of AME missionary activities in the Caribbean prior to 1906, see L. L. Berry, *A Century of Missions,* 79, and Charles S. Smith, *A History of the African Methodist Episcopal Church* (Philadelphia: Book Concern of the AME Church, 1922), 2:86.

13. Smith, *A History of the African Methodist Episcopal Church,* 2:186.

14. Ibid., 2:201.

15. See William Seraile, *Voice of Dissent: Theophilus Gould Steward (1843–1924) and Black America* (New York: Carison Publishing, 1991).

16. Henry McNeal Turner is a prime example of this type of appointment. Indeed, he is noted for using his employment position to expand church efforts and thereby advance his standing within the church. See Stephen Ward Angell, *Bishop Henry McNeal Turner and African-American Religion in the South* (Knoxville: University of Tennessee Press, 1992). Also see Seraile, *Voice of Dissent.*

17. See Gayraud Wilmore, *Black Religion and Black Radicalism,* 2d. ed. (New York: Orbis Press, 1994), chap. 6.

18. Dennis Dickerson, "Bishop Henry M. Turner and Black Latinos: The Mission to Cuba and Mexico," *A.M.E. Church Review* 108, no. 349 (January–March 1993): 51–55.

19. Ibid.

20. Minutes of meetings of the General Conference, the denomination's legislative body, are filled with discussions about finances. These meetings were held every four years. Lower levels of the Church governing structure met more often, and they also made decisions about financial matters and denominational conflicts. See Smith, *A History of the African Methodist Episcopal Church,* vol. 2, pp. 75, 144, 183–84.

21. See AME Missionary Collection, Schomburg Center for Research in Black Culture, New York. This collection includes budgetary records as well as correspondence pertaining to Cuba, but there are no records of positive relations with U.S. businesses in the country.

22. Marcos A. Ramos, *Protestantism and Revolution in Cuba* (Miami: Research Institute for Cuban Studies, University of Miami, 1989), 36–37.

23. Ibid., 26–27.

24. See Helg, *Our Rightful Share.* These legal prohibitions are consistently recited as proof that Cuba never had legalized racial segregation and, therefore, never had institutional racism. Both light-skinned Cubans and Afro-Cubans maintain this position, although the latter continue to discuss their experiences with formal and informal patterns of racial discrimination. Nevertheless, interviews and conversations with working-class Cubans, Cuban scholars, and experts on Cuban scholarship suggest that these laws have become a rhetorical touchstone and that the denial of Cuban racism is part of an enforced national political allegiance. See Jualynne Dodson, field interview notes, October 1995, Washington, D.C.; January 1996, Cerro District, Havana, Cuba.

25. Helg, *Our Rightful Share;* also see Louis Pérez Jr., *Between Reform and Revolution,* 211–24.

26. AME Missionary Collection. Folder Correspondence "P" 1916, Box 1. Schomburg Center for Research in Black Culture, New York.

27. AME Missionary Collection, "Missionary's Letter to the Secretary of Missions," October 7, 1920, Folder Correspondence, Box 1. Schomburg Center for Research in Black Culture, New York.

28. AME Missionary Collection, ibid., September 30, 1920.

29. Verena Martínez-Alier, *Marriage, Class and Colour in Nineteenth-Century Cuba* (Ann Arbor: University of Michigan Press, 1974), and Richard Graham, ed., *The Idea of Race in Latin America, 1870–1940* (Austin: University of Texas Press, 1990) are excellent discussions of race relations and racism in Cuba and Latin America generally.

30. For an excellent study of just how complete a company's control over a community could be, see Liston Pope, *Millhands and Preachers: A Study of Gastonia* (New Haven: Yale University Press, 1942).

31. For a discussion of white philanthropy and race see John H. Standfield, *Philanthropy and Jim Crow in American Social Science* (Westport, Conn.: Greenwood Press, 1985), although his focus is on white philanthropy in the social sciences.

32. Jualynne Dodson, field interview notes, January 1990, January 1992, and January 1995. I obtained this information on the United Fruit Company's direct support to a small Jamaican congregation through personal interviews with Mrs. Nugent, an original member of the Mt. Sinai Church of Banes, and with the Rev. Felicita Oakley, current pastor of the congregation. For a video documentary of one such Jamaican community, see Gloria Rolando, "My Footsteps in Baragua" (Havana: 1996).

33. I have identified Afro-Cubans who lived in this community and remember the congregation. Systematic research interviews were scheduled, but difficulties in traveling to Cuba prevented this follow-up. I am looking forward to the contact.

34. W. H. Mayhew, *Voice of Missions,* January 1930.

35. Jualynne Dodson, field notes, June 1990, Havana, and July 1994, Santiago de Cuba. During the 1994 research visit, Afro-Cubans described how "logia"—Masons, Odd Fellows, Knights of Phythias—functioned as mutual-aid, self-help associations for the Afro-Cuban population. These groups also were positively associated with the Cuban War of Independence and Protestantism, and opposed the anti-independence postures of the Catholic Church.

36. This assumption is based on the fact that Mayhew had such longevity in missionary work in Spanish-speaking areas of the Caribbean as well as on my conversations with the historiographer of the AME Church (Dodson interviews with Dennis Dickerson, February 1992, New York).

37. Dodson, field interview notes, June 30, 1990, Marianao District, Havana. Interview with Cristina Díaz, sister-in-law of John Deveaux.

38. AME Missionary Collection, Schomburg Center for Research in Black Culture, New York. Boxes 1 and 2, correspondence for 1938.

39. Pérez, *Cuba: Between Reform and Revolution,* chaps. 8 and 9.

40. AME Missionary Collection, Schomburg Center for Research in Black Culture, New York. Box nn, November 21, 1938, and December 1938.

41. Ibid., November 21, 1938.

42. Ibid., December 21, 1938.

43. AME Church, *Proceedings of the Spring Session of the Council of Bishops* (Philadelphia: n.p., June 22–23, 1939), 4–8; Berry, *A Century of Missions,* 203–4.

44. Berry, *A Century of Missions,* 203–4.

45. Ibid.

46. Dodson, field interview notes, January 1990: Lauro Betancourt and Juan Bernardo Betancourt, sons of Juan Betancourt, who they say was treasurer of the AME organizing group in Santiago de Cuba.

47. Organizing Charter of the Cuban Council of Evangelical Churches, Matanzas, Cuba (n.p.: 1940).

5

Cuba's Roaring Twenties

Race Consciousness and the Column "Ideales de una Raza"

ROSALIE SCHWARTZ

It never occurs to me to seek solutions outside ourselves. We are an inexhaustible source of energy and force, though untapped.
Enrique Andrew, "Ideales de una Raza," 1928

Afro-Cubans and the Challenge of Race

The 1920s era that roared through the United States bellowed just as insistently in Cuba. Both countries greeted 1920 with confidence and optimism but faced 1930 considerably chastened. And in both nations, citizens of African descent fought racial discrimination, separation, and prejudice that contradicted constitutional guarantees of equal status. Afro-Cubans had spilled their blood to achieve Cuba's freedom from Spain and expected the republic to acknowledge their loyalty and to reward their sacrifice with full inclusion in the independent nation. They justifiably resented being confined to the lowest ranks of Cuba's social hierarchy.

Although colored Cubans had enjoyed a measure of social and economic mobility during two decades of post-independence economic expansion, by the mid-1920s a growing middle stratum realized that even education and professional status did not confer acceptance by the dominant white society. After the artificially high demand for Cuban sugar during World War I, overproduction worldwide pushed sugar prices into a freefall. Economic uncertainty pervaded the island; and as financial pressures squeezed Cubans in all social categories, equity for Afro-Cubans seemed more remote than ever.

Rapid economic growth may have worked against Afro-Cubans who pros-pered, in fact. While the elite might admit a few prominent people of color to the upper social ranks in periods of slow development, economic growth of the magnitude experienced in Cuba necessitated a more stringent color line, as a greater number of upwardly mobile Cubans assaulted social barriers.

Social exclusion irrespective of merit exacerbated the discontents of a dis-advantaged race. Demonstrations of racial solidarity, however, prompted ac-cusations that Afro-Cubans aspired to dominate whites, charges accompanied by somber, exemplary references to the republic of Haiti—the sugar-growing, slave-dependent colony that had achieved independence and fallen under the rule of its former slaves. This analogy required no further elaboration in order to play on long-held fears.

Keenly aware of their own grievances and those of their North Ameri-can racial brothers and sisters, Afro-Cubans debated critical issues. For ex-ample, should they join with poor whites in class-based solidarity and wage armed struggle to enforce economic and social parity, or should they achieve racial cohesiveness and then apply political pressure for equality as a color-based group within a pluralistic society? Should Afro-Cubans preserve their cultural distinctiveness or blend in, play by the current rules and achieve sta-tus as individuals or insist on a leveled playing field for everyone?

For race-conscious Afro-Cubans, the United States became a template against which they could measure and assess their own circumstances. Afro-Cuban lawyer and poet Bernardo Ruiz Suárez suggested to a New York audience of African-Americans in 1922 that legal restrictions had actually strengthened black identity in the United States, while Cuban blacks had de-ceived themselves by thinking that legal equality would bring about full social participation. Afro-Cubans who had enjoyed a measure of economic pros-perity, Ruiz Suárez lamented, operated as individuals rather than as part of a collectivity. Although bound by their common heritage of slavery and dis-crimination, Afro-Cubans disagreed on goals for their future and on the meth-ods to achieve them. The Cuban of color who promoted racial solidarity and economic independence often found his appeal suppressed in the name of na-tional unity.[1]

Did the strict black-white color line in the United States create a com-munal strength and identity that Cuba's three-tiered black-mulatto-white categorization inhibited? Color distinctions within the Afro-Cuban com-munity often impeded group action, and Ruiz Suárez heralded a growing internal cohesion fostered to combat the prejudices of white society. Mulattos and blacks needed to break down the skin-tone exclusivity that characterized Afro-Cuban social circles and to extend fellowship to colored persons of varying hues.[2]

Afro-Cubans also cultivated relationships with members of their race in other locations and focused most closely on those in the United States, although they were conscious of the similarities and differences in their respective circumstances. Educational, religious, economic, health, and communications facilities founded and supported by African-Americans afforded leadership positions for blacks that were unavailable in Cuba. Yet, the overall racial structure in the United States held little attraction for Cubans; they rejected the segregation that forced independent institutions even as they recognized their advantages for building a community.[3]

Solidarity among Afro-Cubans, tentative as it was in the early 1920s, brought little change in their social position. They issued optimistic public statements, affirmed their accomplishments, and attempted to impress upon the majority society the value of African culture for all Cubans. They claimed the right to participate fully in Cuban society without disappearing into the white race. As positive a case as Afro-Cubans may have projected, however, the distribution of wealth and power remained skewed. Support and sympathy translated into few concrete improvements. Praise and appreciation did not ameliorate the substantive social problems of the racially defined collectivity.

In their search for equality Afro-Cubans engaged in intragroup dialog and debated with white Cubans. They also combed news and literary sources for helpful information on the experiences and strategies of African-Americans—not imitatively but with admiration for achievement and awareness of social and cultural differences. Both communities struggled to share rightfully in the benefits of their respective societies.

Social Strategies and Havana's Black Newspaper Column

As rising social expectations and increased color consciousness confronted the status quo, Afro-Cubans loudly began to declare what most Cubans denied or deliberately overlooked: republican Cuba had not solved the color problems that a colonial slave society had engendered. Spokespersons for the group, mostly from the middle class, took great pains to present the case for racial acceptance in a nonadversarial way, suggesting that blacks and whites work together to create social harmony. On the other hand, the efficacy of race-based collective action had not escaped their notice. Outrage against the 1919 lynching of a Jamaican black near the Havana suburb of Regla had brought Afro-Cubans together in their own defense. Their manifesto demanded guarantees against any recurrence of the "racial calamity," and a supportive response from President Mario Menocal reinforced the value of group protest.[4]

Meanwhile racial tensions increased, and the dominant white society played ostrich. *Diario de la Marina,* Havana's most widely read and most conservative daily newspaper, banned the word *negro* (black) from its columns, ostensibly to avoid offending Afro-Cuban readers. Few people were deceived by this patent falsehood; the policy simply precluded discussions of race relations. Afro-Cubans, restrained from airing their apprehensions and faced with the reality of prejudice and discrimination, asserted themselves publicly only occasionally, but they analyzed their predicament ceaselessly in their own circles: "As always when two or three black men get together, the talk turned to the subjection of the Afrocuban and the failure of the doctrine of Martí. We lamented that we did not have our own press or newspaper to present our campaign for revindication."[5]

This particular conversation engaged a group of friends as they traveled by streetcar in 1928 from the mostly white Havana seaside suburb of Marianao to the preponderantly Afro-Cuban city center. One participant, Gustavo Urrutia, determined to remedy the situation and presented his proposal for a public racial dialog to *Diario de la Marina.* Urrutia's boldness resulted in the column "Ideales de una Raza," and Afro-Cubans found a voice.

Hardly a social or political radical, Urrutia had supported the idea that individual effort would bring social acceptance. After all, he had gained recognition as an architect in spite of his skin color. Since race had not impeded his own aspirations, he had discounted the need for collective action. His proposal to *Diario,* in fact, suggested only a weekly page in the newspaper to publicize the benefits of interracial cordiality. However, as Cuba's economic picture darkened in the pre-Depression era and social distinctions solidified, the liability of dark skin grew more apparent. Discussions of racial issues in the weekly "Ideales de una Raza" ranged widely in scope, but gradually became more combative than cordial.

Urrutia's dual strategy for his "Ideales"-based campaign might be summarized as, first, to solidify a collective consciousness among Afro-Cubans, and then to explain the new mentality to Cuba's white population. Urrutia hoped, first of all, to shake Afro-Cubans loose from the intangible, but perceptible, inertia that grew out of the frustrations of race prejudice and to channel an undercurrent of agitation that swirled aimlessly. He seized on the widely circulated *Diario* as an excellent forum in which to vent dissatisfactions and to seek solutions.

From 1928 to 1931 "Ideales de una Raza" exposed racism in the hope of deepening all Cubans' consciousness on the issue. Denial of the race prejudice that clearly plagued Cuba particularly irked Urrutia. With ironic but bitter humor, one "Ideales" sketch laid bare the hypocrisy of Cubans who closed their eyes to the race-based hierarchy. Succinctly told, a pair of wealthy white men competed in affirmations of love for their black servants. They proclaimed strong personal bonds between themselves and their loyal, hard-working, discreet employees. They also adored their colored mistresses and paid effusive tributes to all blacks. Alas, one of them discovered that he and his black chauffeur were both enamored of the same *mulatta*. Camaraderie crumbled. The boss had the chauffeur thrown in jail and condemned the malevolent character of the whole African race.[6]

Cognizant of Cuba's shortcomings, the "Ideales" column was also aware of the harsh North American racial code, and it published cautionary tales for Afro-Cubans. A particularly ugly incident at the very highest level of American society created a *real* tempest in a teapot in the United States and sent a wave of revulsion through "Ideales" readers. Lou Henry Hoover, wife of newly elected president Herbert Hoover, invited congressional wives to a White House tea in 1929, never anticipating the negative response to her seemingly unremarkable inclusion of the wife of Oscar de Priest, Chicago's black congressman. Several southern members of Congress, however, reacted with threats to censure the president for a so-called racial affront, using the social occasion to make a political point. De Priest had offended his colleagues by proposing two African-Americans for appointment to the military academy at West Point and one for the naval academy at Annapolis. No black student had been enrolled at Annapolis since 1875, and the Southerners wanted to keep it that way.[7]

A preference for Cuba's less stringent discrimination was again the object lesson when "Ideales" recounted another equally offensive occurrence. The U.S. government generously sent all Gold Star mothers to France to visit the graves of sons killed in World War I, but it separated the mothers into racially distinct groups. Writing for "Ideales," Urrutia castigated such behavior as the type of folly that followed an irrational segregation of the races.[8] Cubans had not fallen that far from standards of fairness, he implied, at least not yet.

On the other hand, Urrutia's columns expressed admiration for the ideal of racial cooperation advanced by the National Association for the Advancement of Colored People (NAACP). Most Cuban fraternal associations adopted NAACP principles of blacks and whites working together toward conflict resolution. Although ideological disagreements separated the followers of W.E.B. Du Bois and Booker T. Washington in the United States, Cubans praised them both as race leaders worthy of emulation. Urrutia applauded Washington as one of humanity's great benefactors and called his efforts to regenerate the heirs of slavery through education and training "inspired and noble work."[9]

Quite clearly, Afro-Cubans respected the achievements of African-Americans but feared the hard racial line that impelled them. Writings in "Ideales" conceded that separatism generated the vitality that they observed and admired among African-Americans and that a categorical definition of blackness had created a solidarity that the vague Cuban differentiation by skin tone could not instill. The dangers of the American system were obvious, however, and ambivalent molders of Afro-Cuban consciousness trod warily along the edge of a precipice, trying to build solidarity without falling into the pit of segregation.

Harlem and Havana

Of all the facets of life in the United States that fascinated Afro-Cubans in the 1920s, Harlem cast the most captivating spell. Geographic proximity, long-standing ties between the United States and Cuba, and commitment to social betterment made kindred spirits of activists and writers in the two black communities. To race-conscious Afro-Cubans, Harlem—race capital of African-Americans—epitomized the struggle taking place in the United States. Urban middle-class groups of color in Harlem and Havana shared the experiences of social disruption that resulted from rapid social change. Large-scale capitalization of enterprise had brought demographic and economic modifications to both the United States and Cuba in the preceding generation.

Industrialization of sugar production moved Afro-Cubans from west to east in Cuba. The growth of Havana took them from countryside to town. A similar expansion of mechanized mass production motivated

African-Americans to move from south to north, from cotton farms to factories. World War I opened economic opportunities in both countries and magnified and intensified the population flow that scattered families. More agriculturalists became wage earners; middle sectors expanded and diversified. Mobility and job competition increased racial tensions, while a generation of colored citizens who had not been born under slavery chafed under demeaning social restrictions.

African-Americans had been migrating north and west since the Civil War, but the exodus from the South gathered considerable momentum after 1890. A substantial number of educated blacks and skilled workmen sought to improve their lives in the bustling atmosphere of northern commercial activity. The early migratory stream unleashed a healthy tension between the established black communities and newcomers in cities where they took up residence. A settled middle-class core joined the typically young, unskilled, and unmarried migrant to form the vibrant African-American ghettoes of the northern cities in the 1920s.[10]

As the African-American segment of New York's population tripled in the decade between 1900 and 1910, the Manhattan neighborhood called Harlem emerged as a racially distinct community, but it was not by any means a slum. Harlem drew black artists, writers, and scholars like a magnet. A notable coterie affirmed their blackness through their work and labored in the same cause that moved Afro-Cubans in Havana: racial equality.

Habaneros—residents of Cuba's capital city—turned to "Ideales de una Raza" for accounts of visits by prominent African-Americans to their city, guests who were welcomed with great warmth and generosity. Mary McLeod Bethune, founder and president of Bethune-Cookman College; R. P. Sims, president of West Virginia's Bluefield Institute; and William Pickens, NAACP public relations secretary, came to observe Cuba's schools and to compare the prospects for Afro-Cubans with their own.

The Club Atenas, the recreational and cultural society founded by Havana's most prominent Afro-Cubans, held public receptions and gave their countrymen an opportunity to meet distinguished visitors. Since its founding in 1917, the club had promoted the collective betterment and cordial fraternity of Afro-Cubans through sports, education, and cultural programs. "Ideales" publicized the various conferences and social gatherings organized around the visits, occasions that fostered Afro-Cuban pride and also conveyed to white society the accomplishments of blacks in the United States and in Cuba.[11]

Havana's Afro-Cubans extended their grandest welcome to Langston Hughes, poet of Harlem's street life. His visit to Cuba in 1930 roused the sincere and overflowing adulation of the community's social and intellectual circles. Cubans read Hughes's poems in major North American periodicals, and some of his work appeared in translation in Cuban publications. Appreciative audiences gathered at Club Atenas to honor the poet and greeted Hughes as one of the most respected interpreters of the new and vigorous sensibilities of African-Americans.

Cubans particularly admired the universality of Hughes's poetry; his words seemed to capture their feelings as well. The Spanish-speaking Hughes had previously visited Cuba and had found a kindred spirit in Nicolás Guillén, the Cuban poet celebrated for his evocation of the island's African heritage. Guillén praised Hughes for his ability to portray the vibrant life of Harlem's black population and acknowledged Hughes's influence on his own creative expression.

Tied by experience and sensibility, the two poets found their voices among the masses of black people in their respective adopted cities. Hughes had left the American Midwest for Harlem, and Guillén took his inspiration from the vitality and pathos of Havana's black poor. Their shared commitment to the thoughts and feelings of the offspring of African slaves fostered a deep friendship in the 1920s, and they grew even closer when they both covered the Spanish Civil War as journalists.[12]

The Harlem-Havana connection flourished through the efforts of poets like Hughes and Guillén, through socially committed citizens like Gustavo Urrutia, whose outspoken advocacy of racial equality in "Ideales" gave heart to members of both communities, and through the work of associations like the Club Atenas. The connection drew even greater strength from the exertions of Arthur Schomburg, the renowned student and recorder of black experiences in various areas outside Africa.

Schomburg, a Puerto Rican of African descent, spent years of study and work as a teacher after his 1891 arrival in the United States. He amassed a considerable collection of artifacts and documents as he pursued his fascination with Africa and its influence on America. By the time black awareness exploded in Harlem and Havana in the 1920s, Schomburg had collected more than six thousand volumes, three thousand manuscripts, and two thousand works of art on African and African-American themes.

When the Carnegie Corporation funded the New York Public Library's purchase of his books and artifacts, Schomburg became curator of the collection. Because of his personal interests and in his capacity as curator, Schomburg kept the New York–Havana mail routes busy with a constant flow of correspondence. He opened the world of U.S. publications on black themes to Urrutia and Guillén, and through them to the Cuban public. Schomburg sent Urrutia the latest studies on African-American social problems and literary works by black authors. Urrutia responded with works by Cuban authors and "Ideales" pages, which Schomburg bound in a volume for presentation to the library.[13]

Arthur Schomburg and Nicolás Guillén also kept up a steady correspondence and exchanged literary works. Schomburg focused a keen and knowledgeable eye on the Cuban art scene through Afro-Cuban painter Pastor Argudín and often relayed messages among literary publisher Nancy Cunard in Paris, Langston Hughes on his travels, and Guillén and Urrutia in Havana. Their correspondence carried the warmest expressions of affection and mutual respect for efforts undertaken on behalf of an international black community and communicated their activities to an extended audience.[14]

Awakened race consciousness formed a bond among artists and writers, and they reinforced pride in black achievement by maintaining a close watch on, and expressing appreciation for, the successes of their colleagues. When Cuban sociologist Fernando Ortíz visited New York in 1930, he proclaimed Harlem the world capital of the colored race, and called Gustavo Urrutia a comparable race champion among Havana's Afro-Cubans.[15]

"Ideales," Economic Nationalism, and Class Struggle

In the challenging, invigorating, roaring 1920s, Afro-Cubans and African-Americans walked similar tightropes. They worked to end prejudice and discrimination in order that they might prosper and live with dignity. But patriotism, self-sacrifice, military accomplishments, and morality itself were perhaps antiquated arguments for social acceptance. Despite a climate of opinion that recognized the progress of blacks and provided spiritual uplift, blacks could not overlook the material shortcomings of day-to-day life. Since the end of slavery, some Afro-Cubans and African-Americans had altered their condition and elevated their social status, but the majority lacked access to economic and political power. In an era when acquired wealth superseded conditions of birth as status determiners for the dominant white society, riches conferred social prestige on many people in the United States and in Cuba. Dreams of business success motivated citizens across the racial spectrum. If wealth influenced social considerations, Gustavo Urrutia forthrightly argued, Afro-Cubans and African-Americans alike needed economic leverage—not merely good character—to shape events.[16]

Afro-Cubans filled the pages of "Ideales" with opinions on their keenly felt predicament. They needed and wanted economic strength but had to communicate this desire to their racial brothers and sisters without stirring fears among whites, who monopolized sources of wealth. After all, in a period of declining prosperity, racial discrimination helped to control economic competition. Thus the economic benefits of prejudice impeded resolution of racial conflicts. Afro-Cubans needed their own economic power base but hesitated to provoke increased discrimination by being perceived as economic competitors. Through "Ideales" they presented the logic of their case, assuring the white community that Afro-Cuban economic viability improved the well-being of all Cubans and did not threaten white economic control.[17]

Promotion of community strength through economic nationalism, however, carried the same risk as organization on the basis of cultural nationalism—that is, segregation. Arguing for economic independence, nevertheless, Gustavo Urrutia charged that his fellow Afro-Cubans lived in servitude to the Cuban economy, rather than as a free people, because they did not produce their basic necessities. Possessors of potential—rather than actual—wealth, they consumed goods that they did not manufacture and thus found themselves at the mercy of white purveyors. Although Afro-Cubans composed one-third of the population, they owned only 11 percent of Cuba's farms. Moreover, their landholdings represented the smaller and poorer farms, and they suffered the consequences of economic dependence on white society.

This argument found unexpected support from Cuban historian and social analyst Ramiro Guerra y Sánchez, from whom one might expect a less gradualist challenge to the status quo. Through the medium of the "Ideales" page, Guerra y Sánchez advised the Afro-Cuban leadership to urge the black masses to purchase individual plots of land in order to become self-sufficient and productive members of society and have something to leave to their children. By gaining an economic base, he wrote, Afro-Cubans could build toward enhanced influence in the political arena.[18]

Urrutia had no quarrel with the benefits of land ownership. The liberal capitalist ethic, to which the majority of Afro-Cubans subscribed, valued property. In answer to Guerra y Sánchez, however, Urrutia argued that the economic situation of most Afro-Cubans prohibited the accumulation of capital sufficient to purchase the necessary acreage. Afro-Cubans had organized efforts directed toward industrial and agricultural enterprise, but their disadvantaged position within the total society removed control of such undertakings from the power of the community's leadership. The Cuban social system perpetuated an indigence among Afro-Cubans against which the efforts of the race unfortunately had little effect.[19]

Urrutia's response identified an essential contradiction in the argument for economic nationalism. That is, white society controlled admission to institutions of higher learning, the necessary path to better-paid employment or professional status. Private colleges openly excluded Afro-Cubans, while directors of public schools used more subtle means to deny them access.[20] Thus discrimination on the part of whites made it incumbent upon blacks to organize as producers of wealth, but the same discrimination stood in the way of their doing so. Those Afro-Cubans who struggled against inequality and managed to become professionals or to open businesses continued to suffer the consequences of prejudice, since white Cubans patronized members of their own race.

Consignment of the majority of blacks to the least rewarding jobs deprived Afro-Cubans of the economic base they needed to support black businesses and professions, Urrutia argued. If most Afro-Cubans had no work, then Afro-Cuban business owners and professionals had few clients and eventually faced failure. If they produced and possessed little of their own, Afro-Cubans necessarily relied on the good will and generosity of the dominant community. Only economic independence and business success could break the chains of social inferiority, experience suggested, but imposed social restrictions and racial prejudice inhibited business success and economic independence.[21]

However realistic the analysis or appealing the strategy, economic nationalism based on racial solidarity nevertheless ran counter to a fundamental goal of Havana's black middle class, which was to live in a society that offered equal access to opportunities, as was promised in the independence movement. Most of those who responded to Urrutia through "Ideales" shunned the idea of separate institutions. Some questioned the ability of Afro-Cubans to create themselves as an independent economic entity without help; others viewed a racially based economic solution as a step backward toward isolation.

Journalist Belisario Heureaux, for example, served as president of Club Atenas's committee for economic interests. Heureaux agreed that Afro-

Cubans lacked control over Cuba's economic base and that whites had monopolized the sources of wealth production. He disputed Urrutia's conclusion, however, arguing that the functional division of modern societies fell along class lines, not racial ones. Afro-Cubans faced a class battle and could not effect significant change in the distribution of wealth by their efforts alone. Rather than work toward racial self-sufficiency, they should align themselves with members of the white working class to redistribute wealth.[22]

Moreover, Club Atenas member Ramón M. Valdés Herrera pointed out, control of industry and commerce by foreign capitalists made Cuba itself a dependent society. White Cubans did not in fact control the island's economy. The removal of profits from the country had limited employment expansion by removing money from national circulation. Externally determined job shortages created the competition that aggravated prejudice and encouraged discrimination. Prior to a discussion of racial equality, Valdés Herrera maintained, Cubans had to gain real control over their country's resources and productive mechanisms.[23] Only then could they make a valid argument concerning distribution of wealth and power among Cubans.

The competing interests of class, race, and economic nationalism also confounded the Afro-Cuban community on the issue of imported laborers. Not just sugar industry workers but Cuban tobacco farmers, carpenters, masons, tailors, painters, shoemakers, cooks, and servants competed with Jamaicans and Haitians of African descent who flooded Cuba in search of jobs and, by their numbers, lowered wage rates. Most Afro-Cubans supported a law reserving 75 percent of jobs for native Cubans. The measure never passed, but community support for the restrictions clearly undermined both racial and class solidarity.

As Afro-Cubans struggled through this intellectual (but nevertheless real) quagmire, African-Americans encountered similar contradictions. Economic nationalism, championed by Garveyites in the early 1920s, reinforced separatism; class struggle diluted racial solidarity and entailed the risk of co-optation by small but increasingly vocal Marxist political movements. While these debates raged, racial discrimination did not abate.

Marcus Garvey's message of black pride and economic self-sufficiency, his exhortation, "Up you mighty race, you can accomplish what you will," appealed first to communities of Jamaican immigrants in Cuba. As chapters of Garvey's Universal Negro Improvement Association spread in Cuba, members insisted that *Negro World,* the Garveyite paper, devote space to poetry, songs, articles, and features in Spanish. Lively discussions at UNIA meetings included such topics as the development of economic enterprises, self-improvement, and pride in Cuba's African heritage. Growing interest in the movement encouraged Garvey to appoint Eduardo V. Morales as high commissioner for the UNIA in Cuba. Morales's spirited Spanish-language speeches brought hundreds of Afro-Cubans flocking to the Garveyites' Liberty Halls to hear the message of racial uplift.[24]

For several years Gustavo Urrutia and the "Ideales" column tried to galvanize Afro-Cubans and to breach the wall of racial discrimination. Urrutia continued to encourage progress for Afro-Cubans within the confines of capitalism, even as the Depression of the 1930s drastically eroded already limited opportunities for personal economic viability. By 1933 almost one million persons, out of a population of about four million, belonged to families in which the head of the household had no employment. More than half of the population lived at a "submarginal" level.[25]

As the economic situation deteriorated, Urrutia and Nicolás Guillén, two of the most prolific and influential Afro-Cuban writers and activists of the 1920s, radicalized their assessment of Cuba's economic situation and of the position of blacks in the universal capitalist structure. Urrutia, the long-time champion of commercial enterprise and capital accumulation, openly expressed doubts that Afro-Cubans could ever obtain equal opportunity under an individualistic capitalist system. Afro-Cubans belonged to the "proletarian masses of the world," he wrote in 1933, and must link their own future to the broad mass of laborers, regardless of color. Calling for a socialistic regime, Urrutia challenged Cuban officials to distribute available work equally among all citizens.[26]

Urrutia had explained his ideological evolution in a 1932 *Diario de la Marina* article, "The New Negro." Urrutia's familiarity with the writers of Harlem's renaissance may have prompted his borrowing of Alain Locke's term for an awakened, militant black community. His extensive activity among, and intimate knowledge of, Afro-Cubans had convinced him that a "new black man" had emerged, a Cuban changed in attitude and mentality by experience and by the open, ongoing dialog between the races. Although he spoke for less than a majority of Afro-Cubans when he called for an orderly evolution to socialism, he championed radical change. Ever mindful of the opinion of Cuba's whites, however, he discreetly avoided any advocacy of violent revolution.[27]

The economic calamity of the 1930s transformed the discontents of a socially subjugated Afro-Cuban middle class into desperation among all social categories. Crisis conditions overwhelmed notions of reformist gentility as government corruption flourished and brutality against protesters intensified. Race prejudice increased, rather than diminished, despite Urrutia's forceful arguments. Intellectual discourse on race relations and the worthiness of Afro-Cubans to enjoy equal opportunities appeared a self-indulgent luxury in the face of a daily struggle for existence. Always the close observer of local conditions and universal trends, Urrutia hacked away at failed policies in an effort to carve a new path for Cuba.

Many African-Americans trod the same path leftward as the Depression drove both white and black workers into breadlines. Lack of economic power, a force that proved more relentless than racial prejudice, had deprived people of status and dignity. The inability to control one's destiny crossed color lines. In the years since the Russian Revolution, communist political parties in Cuba, the United States, and elsewhere, struggled to organize exploited populations. Hunger worked more effectively than pamphlets, however, to convince impoverished people that society was structured against their best interests. The ranks of the Communist Party swelled in Harlem as they did throughout the United States.

Cubans learned the same cruel lessons. Nicolás Guillén's life and work reflected his evolving class consciousness. While the poems of *Motivos de son* (1930) centered on Afro-Cuban cultural identity, *Sóngoro cosongo* (1931) expressed a clearer sense of concern for the social condition of blacks in Cuba; and a focus on the economic and political causes of racial discrimination infused *West Indies, Ltd.* in 1934. Guillén came to view Afro-Cubans as but one segment of the exploited masses who languished in a poverty-creating system of economic imperialism in which powerful capitalists held sway over workers in their own and in subservient, impoverished countries. He participated in the 1933 Cuban Revolution and became a member of the Communist Party in Valencia, Spain, in 1938 while covering the Spanish Civil War.[28]

The Cuban Revolution of 1933 did not end the socioracial fragmentation that characterized the 1920s, however. It was an economic and political battle, not a race war; and the goals of its more radical participants were thwarted by the very imperialism that Guillén decried. The United States rejected a government committed to national, not foreign, interests and installed its own choice, Fulgencio Batista, as head of state.

"Ideales" had exposed Cuba to the contribution of its black citizens and supported reform over violent change. Dialogue on racial questions had focused on the efforts that Afro-Cubans had made in their own behalf. The weekly page in *Diario de la Marina* had helped to define goals and strategies, had described the material conditions of Afro-Cubans, and had challenged the national conscience, but even Gustavo Urrutia ultimately conceded the impotence of racial politics and moral arguments to effect a redistribution of power and wealth. Middle class, urban Afro-Cubans had pressed legitimate claims against society, but most Cubans interpreted the arguments for equality as a prelude to racial conflict and assumption of power by impoverished black masses. Race consciousness and pride imparted a cohesiveness and purpose to the struggle of Afro-Cubans, but even their most articulate spokesmen could not overcome the contradictions of class and caste. "Ideales de una Raza" represented their earnest efforts to establish principles of mutual respect among Cubans of all color. Like their American counterparts, Afro-Cubans learned that ideals expressed in a society's fundamental guiding documents do not readily translate into social realities.

NOTES

Acknowledgment: The material for this chapter comes from "The Displaced and the Disappointed: Cultural Nationalists and Black Activists in Cuba in the 1920s," Ph.D. diss., University of California, San Diego, 1977. Parts of this essay that were originally in Spanish have been translated by the author unless otherwise indicated.

1. Bernardo Ruiz Suárez, *The Color Question in the Two Americas,* trans. John Crosby Gordon (New York: Hunt Publishing Co., 1922), pp. 22, 33, 45–47.

2. Ruiz Suárez, *Color Question,* 86.

3. See "Ideales de una Raza," *Diario de la Marina* (Havana), June 16 and April 28, 1929, for comparisons of race relations in Cuba and the United States.

4. Gustavo Urrutia, "Armonias," *Diario de la Marina,* May 10, 1938.

5. Mercer Cook, "Urrutia," *Phylon* 4 (1943): 226; Gustavo Urrutia, "Armonias," *Diario de la Marina,* May 5, 1938. José Martí, the father of Cuban independence, wrote extensively of the racial harmony that would prevail in the republic he gave his life to create.

6. "Ideales," April 7, 1929.

7. Urrutia, "Ideales," June 2, 23, and 30, 1929.

8. Urrutia, "Ideales," August 17, 1930.

9. Urrutia, "Ideales," November 25, 1928.

10. Gilbert Osofsky, *Harlem: The Making of a Ghetto* (New York: Harper and Row, 1968), 18–20.

11. Club Atenas's founding members, sixty-eight of them, included lawyers, engineers, property owners, a dentist, and several journalists, along with tobacco workers, a

telegrapher, a tailor, and several students. See Nicolás Guillén, "El camino de Harlem," in "Ideales," April 21, 1929; "Ideales," August 31, 1930.

12. "Ideales," March 2, 1930; Pedro Marco, "Canción de la calle," in "Ideales," March 16, 1930; Nancy Morejón, "Conversación con Nicolás Guillén," *Casa de las Américas* 23 (July–August 1972): 128.

13. *The Schomburg Center for Research in Black Culture Journal* 1 (Fall 1976): 1–4; see Arthur Schomburg's letters, Schomburg Collection, New York Public Library.

14. See Schomburg letters, correspondence with Nancy Cunard, Pastor Argudín, Langston Hughes, Gustavo Urrutia, Nicolás Guillén.

15. Arthur Schomburg, "My Trip to Cuba in Quest of Negro Books," *Opportunity* 11–12 (1933): 48–52; "Como nos ven," in "Ideales," March 16, 1930.

16. Urrutia, "Armonías," March 2, 1930, and December 8, 1929.

17. "Ideales," August 10, 1930.

18. Ramiro Guerra y Sánchez, "Hay que terminar," in "Ideales," January 6, 1929.

19. Urrutia, "Armonias," January 20, 1929.

20. "Ideales," April 20, 1928; Francisco Calderio (Blas Roca), *Los fundamentos del socialismo en Cuba* (Havana: Editorial Páginas, 1943), 76–77.

21. Urrutia, "Armonias," July 7 and 15 and December 15, 1929, and March 23, 1930.

22. *Revista Atenas* 2 (Aug.–Sept. 193l): 4; "Comentos sin comentarios," in "Ideales," January 27, 1929.

23. Ramón M. Valdés Herrera, "Nacionalicemos a Cuba," *Revista Atenas* 2 (Aug.–Sept. 1931): 3.

24. For Garvey's activities in Cuba and the spread of the UNIA, see *Negro World,* November 6, 1920; February 19 and 26, 1929; April 2, 9, and 23, 1921; July 2 and 16, 1921; December 17, 1921; January 21, 1922; and February 11, 1922.

25. For the impact of the Depression on the labor sector, see Fabio Grobart, "The Cuban Working Class Movement from 1925 to 1933," *Science and Society* 34 (1975): 73–103.

26. Urrutia, "Racial Prejudice in Cuba," in *Negro Anthology, 1931–1933,* ed. Nancy Cunard (New York: Negro Universities Press, 1969), 473–78; Mercer Cook, "Urrutia," *Phylon* 4 (1943): 228.

27. Urrutia, "El nuevo negro," *Diario de la Marina,* August 27, 1932.

28. Keith Ellis, "Nicolás Guillén at Seventy," *Caribbean Quarterly* 19 (1973): 89–90; Ciro Bianchi Ross, "Conversación hacia los 70," *Cuba Internacional* 4 (June 1972): 18.

6

Marcus Garvey in Cuba

Urrutia, Cubans, and Black Nationalism

TOMÁS FERNÁNDEZ ROBAINA

I do not have the intention of interfering in the internal affairs of this country. I'm only trying to get the support of the Cuban Negroes . . . the problem of the American Negroes and the Cuban Negroes are essentially different although both have in common, the racial problem. . . . Our problem is exactly similar to that of Ireland. It is sometimes difficult to obtain the recognition of a right without fighting. The independence of Cuba is an example of this.
Marcus Garvey, March 1921

In March 1921 Marcus Garvey, the Jamaican-born black nationalist, disembarked in Cuba. He arrived aboard the *Yarmouth,* one of the ships in his infamous Black Star Line. His docking at Havana harbor was part of his tour of various Caribbean and Central American countries to meet with Universal Negro Improvement Association (UNIA) chapters and to collect funds for his primary enterprise, the founding of the Free State of Africa. His arrival in Cuba was highly anticipated and was covered in the black press of the time; for instance, it received front-page coverage on March 4 in the widely circulated *El Heraldo de Cuba.* The paper published portions of an interview conducted the day before in which Garvey mentioned the twenty-five UNIA chapters in Cuba and indicated his intention to visit those in Santiago de Cuba, Morón, and Nuevitas.[1]

During his stay in Cuba, Garvey's strategies and ideas were both warmly received and severely critiqued by various black communities on the island; however, most of the black Cuban press challenged the ideals he espoused. The weekly *La Antorcha* and the "Palpitaciones de la raza de color" column of the daily *La Prensa,* two papers popular during the decade before Garvey's arrival in Cuba, had long denounced race-based appeals.[2] As one Cuban writer explained, "Black nationalism was not likely to be adopted in a multi-racial country whose sons, independent of the colour of their skin, had forged the fatherland fighting . . . the Spanish colonial regime."[3] Yet, divergent opinions were expressed in the March 4 *El Heraldo de Cuba* stories. One observer spoke favorably of Garvey's public appearances: "There in the upper part of the stage was a man of the African race dressed in a wide red toga, adorned with green and black, which reached all the way down to his shoes. Marcus Garvey speaks with singular eloquence. One might say that he has mastered the art of the spoken word and that he exercises a strange fascination over his audience, which he makes laugh [and] cry out and generally excites at will."[4]

Less favorable comments came, however, from members of the newly founded and increasingly prestigious Club Atenas, a Havana-based black society. Most seemed to believe that Garvey had little to offer black Cubans. Even though the club held a reception for Garvey, its president, Miguel Angel Céspedes, disavowed Garvey's ideals of Pan-Africanism and his advocacy of a "back to Africa" movement. Céspedes is quoted as saying, "the black Cuban strove to create a republic where he could live in dignity and enjoy all the rights of a civilized and free man; he cannot imagine another homeland other than the Cuban homeland. He does not share in the Pan-African ideal because he has a cosmopolitan notion of the human spirit."[5]

Forced to defend himself in the Cuban press, Garvey argued that:

"It is a mistake to suppose that I want to take [all] Negroes to Africa. . . . Each negro can be a citizen of the nation in which he was born or that he has chosen but I see the building of a great state in Africa which, featuring in the concert of the great nations, will make the negro race as respectable as others . . . Cuban Negroes will be favored by the building of this African state because when this state exists they will be considered and respected as descendants of this powerful country which has enough strength to protect them."[6]

Notwithstanding the critiques, it is easy to understand why Marcus Garvey came to Cuba. He traveled throughout areas with high concentrations of blacks in North America, Latin American, the Caribbean, and Europe. And importantly, upon his arrival in Cuba, he found a rapidly growing black populace. Cuba's population, according to the 1919 census, had reached 2,048,980 inhabitants.[7] Eleven percent of these were listed as black, 16 percent as mulatto, 72 percent as white, and less than one percent as "yellow" (people of Asian origin). To indigenous blacks was added the ongoing influx of workers from Jamaica. In fact, there were possibly more than 50,000 Jamaicans resident on the island in March 1921. According to Juan Pérez de la Riva, a total of 99,212 Jamaican immigrants were in Cuba by the end of that year. These numbers, along with those for Haitian immigrants, continued to grow throughout the 1920s. The majority of the immigrants were located in the sugar-cane-growing areas of Camagüey and Oriente, but they also lived in Havana and in other provinces.[8]

It is with this population of Jamaican workers that Garvey became especially popular. As a super-exploited labor supply, the Jamaicans were resented by many black Cubans, who did not like being undercut by foreign workers, and by white Cubans, who feared a "blackening" of the island. In the words of Rupert Lewis, "as an economically exploited proletariat and as a minority cultural community, the West Indians were greatly attracted to the Garvey Movement."[9] In fact, according to UNIA member Alberto E. Pedro, "the growth of the association was seen in the meeting places that were scattered throughout our territory to carry out their propaganda. Generally, there was no lack of meeting places in the English speaking West Indian communities, as for example in the town of Buena Vista in the municipality of Marianao."[10] English and Spanish editions of *Negro World*, the UNIA newspaper, began to circulate throughout Cuba in the 1920s as numerous small UNIA chapters became active. Pedro noted that while most black Cubans refused to join the UNIA, many did read the paper and attend some meetings. However, by 1928 and 1929, both the *Negro World* and the UNIA were under attack in Cuba. They were deemed subversive under the Morúa Law, which forbade all openly race-based political organizations. And in 1930 the U.S.-backed president of Cuba, General Gerardo Machado (1925–33), also banned Garvey himself, stating that there was no racial problem in Cuba and "the propaganda of Garvey is prejudicial to society in Cuba."[11] Thus Garvey's only known visit to Cuba happened in 1921, and Cuba's UNIA chapters began to decline during the 1930s, as they did in the United States.[12]

Given that Garvey received so much attention during the 1920s, it is surprising that few Cubans today have even a vague idea of who he was and what he represented. This is despite the fact that books about him are available in the José Martí National Library and other libraries around Havana. In fact, when I started to investigate whether Cubans of the early 1920s ever considered abandoning the island for Africa or adopting the black nationalist ideals of Garvey, I found that Garvey was not very well known among Cuban writers or the general public.[13]

Scholarly neglect of Garvey's presence in Cuba is paralleled by a similar disregard for one of his contemporaries, Gustavo Urrutia (1881–1958).[14] Urrutia, although active earlier, did not become well known until April 1928, when a new column that he authored called "Ideales de una raza" (The Ideals of a Race) appeared in the Cuban newspaper *Diario de la Marina*. Urrutia's column grew to an entire page devoted to black topics that appeared in the Sunday edition for more than two years. Its eventual disappearance did not mean that Urrutia had ceased contributing to the dialogue concerning Cuban blacks. He continued to practice journalism and to advance the struggle and debate over the rights of Cuban blacks in another column called "Armonías" (Harmonies), which had emerged during the period when the "Ideals of a Race" Sunday page was published. The "Armonías" column appeared regularly until its author's death in 1958.

Urrutia became one of the most important black intellectuals of Cuba's republican period, and his campaign for black rights represents one of the richest periods in the social movement of black Cubans. Unfortunately, however, his contributions have not yet been compiled and published. This labor badly needs to be done so that all who are interested in Cuba's black history might have easy access to a valuable and until now infrequently consulted source of documents. Their importance resides in Urrutia's key role as a notable black Cuban thinker and a perceptive witness to important events of Cuban history.

This lack of attention reveals a shallow understanding of many black and white intellectuals of the period, as well as today. Most important, very few people are aware that Urrutia wrote about Marcus Garvey. An "Ideales" column written in January 1929 reveals his views on Garvey but also might be seen as a fair representation of enlightened black Cuban opinion, especially of those belonging to the colored societies of the time and in particular the members of the prestigious Club Atenas, of which Urrutia was a prominent member.

It was eight years after Garvey's visit that Urrutia published "El progreso de la raza negra y Mr. Garvey" in his "Ideales" column.[15] Why he chose to write about Garvey and what Garvey meant to Cubans we do not know with certainty. However, Machado's banning of the UNIA and of Garvey himself during the same period is an indication that the issue of black nationalism must have been part of the debates among Cuban blacks and Cubans in general. Also, given that thousands of sugar workers were being organized in the new unions at that time and that many such workers were Jamaican, one can only assume that heated discussion must have taken place in union meetings and in the UNIA meeting places called Liberty Halls. Also debated was the role immigrants should play and the role of blacks in general in the rising resistance to the U.S.-backed and much hated Machado. Debates must have been very hot indeed, for Urrutia's article reads as if he had been challenged to write it. He observed, "The ideology of Mr. Garvey has not had a warm reception among black Cubans. . . . Our rejection was well expressed years ago in the Atenas Club when the black leader visited us during a publicity trip and time has only confirmed it. . . . and it is that the black knows that to attain progress and extinction of the racial prejudices which mortify him, it is not necessary to break the brotherly links that link him to the white Cuban."[16]

I do not believe that Urrutia intended to condemn a specific remedy for the social, economic, and cultural problems of blacks. I think that the principles he advocated revealed the ongoing influence of José Martí[17] and of Antonio Maceo[18] on his thinking. Martí had very strongly argued for unity among Cubans of all races as necessary to win their independence; for Martí a Cuban was more than black, more than white, more than mulatto. Antonio Maceo expressed and put into practice similar ideas as a living role model. Maceo held that blacks in Cuba should ask for nothing based on race but rather on their condition of being Cuban. These ideas had won support among broad sectors of the population, and especially the lower-income groups where blacks were concentrated. Also significant was the Cuban public's knowledge of the situation of U.S. blacks under Jim Crow and segregation; there was fear that if blacks argued for separation, as some Cuban whites were doing, Cuba might come to resemble the United States. This warning was expressed by Nicolás Guillén only months after Urrutia's reflections on Garvey appeared:

> We seem to worry only about the way things look and we have a real terror of getting to the heart of the problem. . . . Foolishly we have been dividing into many sectors when we should be united and as time passes, that division will become so deep that there will be no room for the final embrace. That will be the day in which every Cuban town—it will happen in every one—will have its black neighborhood, like our neighbors to the North. And that is the road that all of us, those of us who are the same color as Martí along with those of us who are the same color as Maceo, should avoid.[19]

This does not mean that Urrutia and Guillén did not understand why African-Americans in the United States would consider black nationalism. Many understood, as Guillén did, that Garvey's "movement united the black masses of the United States to protest against the lynchings, the attacks by racists and discrimination in the social, political and economic spheres at the same time that he demanded an immediate cessation of racist practices around the world."[20] As O'Reilly indicates, "it was not surprising [to Cubans] that millions of blacks turned their backs on the hope of unity between blacks and whites and had no confidence in the possibility of a democratic change inside the United States. Their militancy itself was based on an armored wall of skepticism toward the prevailing power structure and a cynical attitude toward the capacity of the white man to free himself of racism."[21]

However, Cubans did not see Garvey's approach as applicable to themselves. Cuban blacks—at least those the press recorded as speaking with him in 1921, such as Céspedes, and later writers, such as Urrutia in the early 1930s—showed little interest in the Return to Africa program or in raising collective black consciousness about the racial question, as had been done in the United States. Yet the question was being raised: Had the demands for social justice and equal rights made by Cubans of African origin been met? While Machado argued yes and gave this reason for opposing Garvey, the majority of black Cubans knew the answer was no. Objectively, black Cubans were still very far from achieving the satisfaction of their material, spiritual, social, and political needs. In fact, it was difficult to ignore the indisputable fact that the Cuban homeland of that epoch was not the nation that Martí would have wished for all Cubans. It was also difficult to ignore the fact that while black Cubans had asked for nothing based on their blackness they also obtained nothing as blacks. Nonetheless there was no agreement that the solution could be found in the adoption of a Garvey-style approach.

Educated Cubans found a space propitious for the analysis of the racial question in Urrutia's *Diario de la Marina* column. There black and white intellectuals expounded their ideas, as inheritors and practitioners of the philosophy of Martí and Maceo. (Among these were Juan Marinello[22] and Nicolás Guillén.) And it was this vision, although still a dream deferred, that they strove to make real.

With the advantage of nearly seventy years' hindsight, we can ask ourselves: Were Céspedes' initial response to Marcus Garvey, and Urrutia's later one, positive ones? Did the position taken by Martí and Maceo on the racial question really contribute to the social and economic betterment of Cuban blacks? Has it proved to be true that the gradual passage of time and education can solve the racial problem?

When Fernando Ortíz was asked in 1959 about the racial problem in Cuba, he responded, "Cuba [is] where the gradual disappearance of the unfortunate forms of racism is more advanced than in other countries of America; in this nation it is less developed. That will be one of the most plausible social reforms that the present Revolutionary Government can make with firmness and tact."[23]

Ortíz's response acknowledges that the racial problem was still very much alive at the moment of the revolution's victory; while racism was less virulent in Cuba than elsewhere, it nevertheless existed. An ambitious enterprise such as the eradication of racism could not have been effected before 1959, despite well-intentioned efforts from many sectors, including legislators, journalists, workers, and intellectuals. The goodwill of only a few persons has always been insufficient to accomplish a task of this magnitude. Nor would it have been possible with only a favorable nod from the Cuban Revolution or from the most progressive sectors of Cuban society at the time.

In Cuba, rejection of the Garvey solution did not result in greater acceptance and understanding among the various racial groups. Because the majority of educated black Cubans accepted the philosophies of Martí and Maceo, fences were inexorably erected, fences that blocked a more realistic assessment of the racial question.

In the historical, political, and social context of the Cuban Revolution, the struggle to extirpate or at least greatly reduce racism and prejudice in Cuba has had a more favorable prognosis. The survival of the reproductive elements of racism is impeded as well. Part of this effort to eradicate racism is the need to understand the reaction of Cuban blacks to Garvey's visit and all that he represented as a consequence of their reading of Martí and Maceo. The theme of Garvey, particularly his 1921 visit to Cuba, has not yet been exhausted. Further research should explore his influences, implicit or explicit, on trends that emerged in the struggles of black Cubans during the decades from the 1930s through the 1950s. An invitation to seek out those influences is thus extended to the students of Garvey's work and to researchers of the social movement of Cuban blacks.

NOTES

Acknowledgment: This essay was translated by Francine Cronshaw.

1. "Marcus Garvey: Moisés de la raza negra," *El Heraldo de Cuba* (Havana), Mar. 4, 1921, pp. 1, 3.

2. *La Antorcha* (The Beacon) was a weekly paper that served as a platform for demands for black rights from 1917 to 1919. "Palpitaciones de la raza de color" (Issues of the Colored Race) was a column directed by Ramón Vasconcelos. Vasconcelos was an important Cuban journalist who wrote under the pseudonym "Tristán." This column was the most popular platform for airing the racial debate after 1912. It circulated in 1914 and 1915.

3. Alberto A. Pedro, "El nacionalismo negro," *Cultura* 64, no. 188 (June 1965), quoted in and trans. by Rupert Lewis, *Marcus Garvey, Anti-Colonial Champion* (Trenton, N.J.: Africa World Press, 1988), 103.

4. *El Heraldo de Cuba,* Mar. 4, 1921, 3.

5. From a speech by the president of the Club Atenas. *El Heraldo de Cuba* (Havana), Mar. 4, 1921, 3. The Club Atenas was the most exclusive of the social groups founded by black Cubans. In general only prosperous blacks of some intellectual distinction could belong to the organization.

6. *El Heraldo de Cuba* (Havana), Mar. 4, 1921, quoted in Lewis, *Marcus Garvey,* 109.

7. Republic of Cuba, *Censos de la República, 1919* (Havana: Arroyo y Caso, 1920).

8. Juan Pérez de la Riva, "Cuba y la inmigración antillana, 1930–1931," in *La república neocolonial,* ed. Juan Pérez de la Riva et al. (Havana: Editorial de Ciencias Sociales, 1979), 2:1–75.

9. Lewis, *Marcus Garvey,* 102–3.

10. Pedro, "El nacionalismo negro," quoted in Lewis, *Marcus Garvey,* 103.

11. Lewis, *Marcus Garvey,* 109.

12. Yet, according to Rupert Lewis, a skeletal UNIA existed in Cuba as late as 1965. The Jamaican-born Leonard Bryan, then quite old, served as its president, and a Cuban, Marcos Armenteros, who was only thirty years old, was its vice president (Alberto Pedro, interview with Rupert Lewis, Havana, 1978); see Lewis, *Marcus Garvey,* 108.

13. A foreign researcher once asked me about the possibility that as many as ten thousand blacks left Cuba for Africa in response to Garvey's slogans. To date research has not corroborated that hypothesis; on the contrary, it seems to indicate that blacks largely rejected Garvey's program. Nor are there indications that English-speaking immigrants might have left for Africa. See Pedro Pablo Rodríguez, "Marcus Garvey," *Anales de Caribe* (Havana), no. 7–8 (1987–88), and John Henrik Clarke, *Marcus Garvey and the Vision of Africa* (New York: Vintage Books, 1974).

14. Cuba's national poet, Nicolás Guillén (1902–86), stated at one point that he owed much of his own thinking to the work of Gustavo Urrutia. Urrutia was a major participant in the debate around the race question and the search for solutions to the problem of the black Cuban. Urrutia did not restrict himself to a purely sociological, economic, and political focus; he also analyzed culture, literature, music, and Afro-Cuban aesthetics. See

Tomás Fernández Robaina, "Aproximación al pensamiento y a la obra de Gustavo Urrutia," *Revista Unión* (Havana) no. 2 (1986).

15. Gustavo Urrutia, "El progreso de la raza negra y Mr. Garvey," *Diario de la Marina* (Havana), Jan. 13, 1929, 34.

16. Ibid.

17. José Martí (1853–95) is the father of Cuban independence and Cuba's national hero. He went to great lengths to promote the unity of all Cubans. To that end he wrote important articles seeking to persuade white Cubans to drop their fear of blacks, which the Spanish exploited to divert the movement for Cuban independence. Martí's writings need to be analyzed in their various contexts and according to the goals that he pursued. See, for example, his "Mi raza" in *Obras completas,* vol. 2 (Havana: Editorial Nacional de Cuba, 1963); and "Para las escenas," *Anuario de Estudios Martianos* (Havana), no. 1 (1978): 31–49.

18. Antonio Maceo y Grajales (1845–96) was the most outstanding figure of the Cuban wars for independence. Not only was he brave in combat but, as his correspondence reveals, he was a deep and penetrating thinker on a variety of topics as well.

19. Nicolás Guillén, "El camino de Harlem," *Diario de la Marina* (Havana), April 21, 1929, 4th sec., p. 11.

20. Ibid., p. 18.

21. Richard O'Reilly, *El pueblo negro de los Estados Unidos: Raíces históricas de su lucha actual* (Havana: Editorial Política, 1984), 187.

22. Juan Marinello (1898–1977) was an important Cuban intellectual of bourgeois origins who embraced the ideology of proletarianism. He contributed to the debate on the racial question with his party-oriented vision of society.

23. Fernando Ortíz Fernández (1881–1969) has been called the third discoverer of Cuba. He was the primary anthropologist who began to reevaluate African influences in Cuban culture in a scientific manner. He indicated in a concise fashion the importance that the arrival of black slaves had for Cuba in the economic, cultural, and spiritual realms. Fernando Ortíz, "Acerca de la cuestión racial," *Noticias de hoy* (Havana), April 7, 1959.

1. Frederick Douglass highlighted as cover story of *La Fraternidad,* February 21, 1889. This was Cuba's most important black newspaper in the late nineteenth century. Its editor was Juan Gualberto Gómez. *Courtesy of the José Martí National Library, Havana*

3. Cover of *Minerva Illustrated Universal Magazine: Sciences, Art, Literature and Sport: The Expression of the Colored Race*, January 1912.

2. Cover of *Minerva: Revista Quincenal Dedicada a la Mujer de Color*, 1888. *Photos this page courtesy of the Instituto de Literaturas y Lingüísticas, Havana*

4. Key section of *Minerva Illustrated Universal Magazine: Sciences, Art, Literature and Sport: The Expression of the Colored Race*, March 1912. This article is entitled "The Reason for a Protest."

5. Paulina Pedroso, Cuban revolutionary in Tampa's Ybor City, who along with her husband, Ruperto Pedroso, came to symbolize the very struggle for a *Cuba libre* during the 1890s. She was a friend and comrade of José Martí. As one of the supporters of La Unión Martí-Maceo in 1904, she was central to the turn-of-the-century Afro-Cuban community in Tampa and Ybor City. *Courtesy of Susan Greenbaum*

6. The first building of La Unión Martí-Maceo, at 1005 Sixth Avenue at Eleventh Street in Ybor City, in 1909. *Courtesy of Susan Greenbaum*

7. Cuban newspaper, *Heraldo de Cuba,* reporting on Marcus Garvey's visit to Cuba, March 21, 1921. *Courtesy of the José Martí National Library, Havana*

8. The black-centered column "Ideales de una Raza" (Ideals of a Race) was a major site of black Cuban debate in the late 1920s and early 1930s. It appeared in the widely circulated Havana newspaper *Diario de la Marina*. This example appeared in January 1929. *Courtesy of the José Martí National Library, Havana*

9. Nicolás Guillén and Langston Hughes. The photo was taken by Carl Van Vechten, perhaps in New York in 1949, when Guillén was known to have visited the city. *Courtesy of Robert Chrisman*

10. Signed photograph of a young Nicolás Guillén, given to Arturo Schomburg. *Courtesy of the Photographs and Prints Division, Schomburg Center for Research in Black Culture, the New York Public Library, Astor, Lenox and Tilden Foundations*

11. Regino Boti, Cuban writer and literary critic from the 1920s to the 1950s. *Courtesy of the Instituto de Literaturas y Lingüísticas, Havana*

12. Regino Pedroso, Cuban poet from the 1930s through the Revolution. *Courtesy of the Instituto de Literaturas y Lingüísticas, Havana*

13. The Cuban X Giants. They were the first U.S. black team to visit Cuba. While there in 1900, they played eighteen games, winning fifteen and losing three. They made a return visit in 1903, and the Cuban team won nine of the eleven games played in the series. *Photos this page courtesy of the National Baseball Library and Archive, Cooperstown, New York*

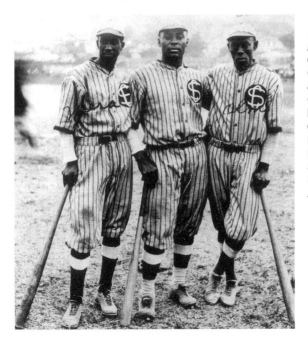

14. Oscar Charleston *(center)* is flanked by Pablo Mesa *(left)* and Alejandro Olms *(right)*. This trio from the Santa Clara 1923–24 championship team formed the greatest outfield in Cuban baseball. Both Mesa and Olms played in the Negro Leagues as well as with the East Coast–based Cuban Stars. Charleston first played in Cuba on the Indianapolis ABCs.

15. 1910 Stars of Cuba. This independent team, made up of Cubans, played on the black baseball circuit in the midwestern United States. Included are two of Cuba's most beloved and talented
early ballplayers, José Méndez *(middle row, third from left)* and Playo Chacón *(middle row, second from left)*. Courtesy of the Luis Muñoz Collection, Allentown, Pennsylvania

16. Bill Foster, who played for the 1927–28 Cienfuegos team of the Cuban Winter Leagues. Foster was considered one of the greatest left-handed pitchers in black baseball. He credits Cuban Luis Padrón with teaching him how to throw the "change up." They were teammates on the black Chicago American Giants, 1924–25. *Photos this page courtesy of the Luis Muñoz Collection, Allentown, Pennsylvania*

17. 1928 Cuban Stars (west) of the Negro National League.

18. 1945–46 All-Cubans team. This barnstorming unit was made up of players from the major Cuban teams and the New York Cubans of the Negro National League. Included are Silvio García *(back row, third from left)*, Luis Tiant *(back row, seventh from left)*, and Minnie Minoso *(front row, first on left)*. *Photos this page courtesy of the Luis Muñoz Collection, Allentown, Pennsylvania*

FABRICA DE CIGARROS

Clarck - Catcher

Bischoff - Catcher

Thomas - Outfielder

Westley - Infielder

Cooper - Pitcher

:·: HABANA :·:

A. Luque - Manager

V. González (Sirique)

Lloyd - Infielder

Levis - Pitcher

J. Calvo - Outfielder

B. Portuondo - Infielder

Compañía Cigarrera DIAZ
—S. A.—

19. Havana Baseball Club, Cuban Winter League, 1922–23. John Henry "Pop" Lloyd is at bottom, second from the left. Adolfo (Dolf) Luque, the famous team manager who played in both black baseball and the white majors in the 1920s, is center, to the right.

20. Cubans Frank Grillo "Machito," his sister Graciella, and their band performing at the Apollo, 1956. *Courtesy of the Gordon Anderson Collection, Schomburg Center for Research in Black Culture, the New York Public Library, Astor, Lenox and Tilden Foundations*

21. Machito and his Afro-Cuban band with Graciella at the Savoy Ballroom, Lenox and 140th Street, Harlem, 1940s. *Courtesy of Brown Brothers*

22. Chano Pozo, the famous Cuban percussionist who worked with Dizzy Gillespie in his development of cubop, in a white tuxedo. *Courtesy of Max Salazar*

23. Adam Clayton Powell and Fidel Castro in Havana soon after the triumph of the revolution, 1959. *From the Baltimore* Afro-American. *Photos this page copyright Afro-American Newspapers Archives and Research Center, Inc., 1991. Reprinted with permission.*

24. Fidel Castro with two local boys in a Washington, D.C., park. *From the Baltimore* Afro-American.

Amsterdam NEW YORK News

Harlem Has Big Stake In Cuba

By JOHN YOUNG, III

HAVANA—The people of Harlem now have a stake in Cuba. It came about in this manner: In the dark days of 1957, Rep. Adam Clayton Powell spoke out many times in the interest of Fidel Castro's fight to free the people of Cuba from the Batista yoke.

The Negro In Castro's Cuba

By JOHN YOUNG, III

HAVANA—The American Negro's strong interest Cuba today is but further proof of his ever-widening terest in the Third Front of freedom fighting: The ternational arena.

The People Demand Revenge

Why Castro Can't Stop Cuba's Mass Killings

By JOHN YOUNG III

Havana—There is an untold story concerning the hidden motive behind the mass executions in Cuba

It has remained untold because no Cuban official will admit it or even discuss it freely; mainly, however because only in retrospect do the pieces of the puzzle fall into perspective.

Amsterdam News In Cuba!

Adam Powell In Castro Spotlight

By M. A. LOCKHART

HAVANA, Cuba—Officials of the Fidel Castro Cuban government assured me here today that there will absolutely be no toleration of racial discrimination in Cuba at any level under Castro.

The assurance came at a jam-packed press conference called by Congressman Adam Clayton Powell whose championing

25. Collage of headlines from Cuba stories of January and February 1959 in the *Amsterdam News*. *Photos this page courtesy of the New York* Amsterdam News

Amsterdam NEW YORK News

No Tears For Africa?

26. Political cartoon by Melvin Tapley from the *Amsterdam News*, January 24, 1959. The cartoon contrasts U.S. politicians' sympathy for Batista's military men who were being sentenced to death in revolutionary people's courts (for committing atrocities) against their lack of concern for blacks being killed and tortured under apartheid in South Africa.

7

Nicolás Guillén and Langston Hughes

Convergences and Divergences

KEITH ELLIS

Siempre fuimos muy buenos amigos. (We were always very good friends.)
Nicolás Guillén, 1982

The Guillén-Hughes Encounter

As is likely to happen when one highly sensitive and deeply dedicated person meets another and they are both engaged in noble tasks that provoke strong reactions in their respective spheres, Nicolás Guillén (1902–89) and Langston Hughes (1902–67) took from their very first meeting impressions that would be lasting, respectful, and highly favorable about each other. North American literary critics and biographers in writing about the first encounter generally depict a meeting between a more senior, seasoned writer, Langston Hughes, and a less mature Nicolás Guillén. This picture is true on the evidence of their published poetic work at that time. The two had met for the first time in February 1930 on the second of Hughes's three visits to Havana. By then Hughes had become noticed in the United States with the publication of his poetry collections *The Weary Blues* (1926) and *Fine Clothes to the Jew* (1927), whereas Guillén had published only individual poems in certain Cuban literary journals, some not well known even on the island. The extensive body of poetry he had written between 1920 and 1929, which he had compiled under the title *Cerebro y corazón* (Brain and Heart), remained unpublished. That collection had not defined Guillén in the way that Hughes's already published books had represented the passions and the style of his lifelong poetic production.

Yet Guillén had already made the intellectual assessment of the world about him, particularly of Cuban society and culture, that would lead him inexorably to the artistic outlets he would come to adopt. The assessment is revealed in four combative journalistic pieces (discussed in detail below) that he wrote before he met Langston Hughes for "Ideales de una Raza," the page of the supplement of the newspaper *Diario de la Marina* devoted to cultural concerns of black Cubans. The pieces reflect Guillén's confidence in his diagnosis of Cuba's social and cultural ills and in his remedial prescriptions. Hughes himself might not have recognized this dimension in Guillén nor might he have had the opportunity to sort out from among Guillén's unpublished poems those that furthered his rectifying line of thinking about the condition of his people. Even with the passage of time, scholars in North America have had difficulty in perceiving the conceptual consistency of Guillén's writings; and this difficulty has impinged on the proper assessment of the Guillén-Hughes encounter.

In North America the relationship is usually discussed with the focus on the U.S. poet, on his dominant role; and among the most widely circulated versions of it is that found in Arnold Rampersad's monumental *The Life of Langston Hughes*.[1] His crucial lines dealing with Hughes's supposed early influence on Guillén are as follows:

> On one man certainly, Cuba's future national poet, (Hughes's) impact was immediate. Although Guillén had previously shown a strong sense of outrage against racism and economic imperialism, he had not yet done so in language inspired by native, Afro-Cuban speech, song, and dance; and he had been far more concerned with protesting racism than with affirming the power and beauty of Cuban blackness. Within a few days of Hughes's departure, however, Guillén created a furor in Havana ("un verdadero escándalo," he informed Hughes with delight) by publishing on the "Ideales de una Raza" page of April 20 what Gustavo Urrutia called exultantly "*eight formidable negro poems*" entitled *Motivos de son* (*Son Motifs*). For the first time, as Hughes had urged him to do, Guillén had used the *son* dance rhythms to capture the moods and features of the black Havana poor. To Langston, Urrutia identified the verse (which was dedicated to José Antonio Fernández de Castro) as "the exact equivalent of your 'blues'." Not long after, Urrutia reported that Guillén was suddenly writing "the best kind of negro poetry we ever had; indeed we had no negro poems at all" in Cuba until the new work. And when a local critic denied a re-

lationship between Hughes and Guillén's landmark poetry, Guillén refuted him at once in "Sones y soneros," an essay published in *El País* on
June 12 that year.

With such a result, Hughes's visit to Cuba had not been in vain.[2]

The opposite pole of opinion comes from the Cuban poet and literary
critic Regino E. Boti, who, writing in 1932, rejects the idea of Hughes's influence on Guillén:

> The tone of Nicolás Guillén's poetry being strange to Cuba, our re-
> searchers found it necessary to go abroad to provide him with an ances-
> tor. And they found what they were looking for in Langston Hughes;
> and now I answer—using the same question I was asked here in the vil-
> lage: What literary relationship exists between Hughes and Guillén? As
> far as what is essentially lyrical is concerned, none. Just as there is noth-
> ing in common between a Yankee and a Cuban as far as the particular
> qualities of each one are concerned. . . . The two poets are different, as
> are their songs. Hughes's muse waits. Guillén's makes demands.[3]

A basic step is made in sorting out such drastically opposed positions
and in elucidating the Hughes-Guillén relationship when we examine the
principal points Guillén made in the essays published in *Diario de la Marina* before Hughes's arrival in Cuba in February 1930.

In April 1929, Guillén published a piece titled "El camino de Harlem"
(The Road to Harlem).[4] He begins by quoting the charge issued by Lino Dou
(1871–1939) to Guillén's generation to carry on the struggle in Cuba for racial
equality. Guillén understood the charge to be a solemn, patriotic one because
he knew well the person from whom it came. With the death of Juan Gualberto Gómez,[5] Lino Dou became the highest-ranked black leader surviving
to Guillén's time who had figured among the great heroes of Cuba's nineteenth-century struggle for independence. Lino Dou had also served as a
member of the national House of Representatives during the same session in
which Guillén's father, Dou's good friend, had served (1909–12). Guillén held
him in the very highest regard, seeing him as embodying the heritage of Juan
Gualberto Gómez and Generals Antonio and José Maceo. All these patriots
had shown an unplumbable depth of commitment to a twin mission, as Guillén states in the essay, referring specifically to Juan Gualberto Gómez, who
"took upon his shoulders the double task of achieving his country's indepen-

dence, on the political side, and of raising the level of his race, of the black race, on the political and social side."[6]

Thus Guillén does not write lightly when in this essay he laments the continuing problem of racial discrimination in Cuba and asks that the people of his generation not be pessimistic, since pessimism inhibits action and the struggle that has to be waged against racism is of crucial importance and truly patriotic. There should be optimism, he says, so that the fight can be won; but one should never believe things to be better than they are because there is a great deal of hypocrisy in Cuba. This is evident in the cordial speeches the races make to each other even while citizens are being hurt by prejudice, discrimination, and even the kind of segregation one finds in certain Yankee regions. Guillén uses his own difficulties in finding employment for which he was eminently qualified to show just how implacably wicked the color line was in Cuba. There certain jobs—bank clerks, typists, rail and bus conductors—were the exclusive preserve of whites; and others, the most harrowing and physically stressful tasks—boiler room workers, for example—were for blacks. Blacks were even prohibited access to certain parts of Cuban cities. Guillén warns that the perpetuation of these practices will imperil the only sensible and healthy destiny for the Cuban population, that of being firmly integrated, and bound by what he called "the definitive embrace."[7] Cuba would then have opted for "the road to Harlem," for segregated communities of especially deprived and victimized black people.

In an essay published on May 5, 1929, entitled "La conquista del blanco" (The Conquest of the White Man),[8] Guillén attacks the trait of timidity that he finds in too many of his black compatriots. He counsels assertiveness in the face of the specious analysis of the racial situation prevailing in the country. Too many white Cubans were saying: "[t]he problem of the Cuban black is simply cultural."[9] Guillén points out that, of the whites and blacks who both enjoy a middling level of education and cultural development, the whites tend to enjoy an ease of living while blacks "everyday run into innumerable difficulties when they want to fulfill themselves, and they have to fight with annoying obstacles that originate from nothing more than skin color."[10] Blacks should insist on their rights and make their presence known. Their apathy is partly responsible for allowing whites to feel that they have the better parts of Cuban life all to themselves, so much so that whites come to be resentful when blacks encroach—as those whites perceive it—on their spaces. Guillén concludes this essay, as he does the previous one, with a negative model provided by the United States: Cuban blacks have the responsibility to insist on the exercise of their full rights within their country, which they should not allow to take on the character of a southern cotton plantation. It should be said too that Guillén's prescription of assertiveness coincides with the message of one of his poems of this pre-1930 period, "Palabras fundamentales" (1928) (Fundamental Words).[11] This essay also prefigures, particularly in the heightening of the message and tone of its last three lines, "Llegada" (Arrival),[12] the powerful opening poem of the book *Sóngoro cosongo* (1931); and as Guillén made clear in his essay "Sones y soneros" (1930),[13] he conceived of *Motivos de son* (1930) and *Sóngoro cosongo* (the latter title is taken from a poem in the former book) as one single project.

Guillén returns to the goal of the meeting of the two races and imputes blame to those whites who would retard the process in his essay entitled "El blanco: he ahí el problema" (The white man: there is where the problem is),[14] also published in *Diario de la Marina* on June 9, 1929. The following quotation encapsulates his argument:

> Mientras el blanco no se disponga a reconocer que en igualdad de condiciones debemos disfrutar de idénticos derechos, no se habrá dado un solo paso en firme en el acercamiento de los dos grandes núcleos que integran la población cubana.[15]

> (As long as the whites are not disposed to recognize that under equal conditions we ought to enjoy identical rights, there will not be a single firm step taken toward bringing together the two great nuclei that make up the Cuban population.)

In the last of these essays, entitled "Rosendo Ruiz" (*Diario de la Marina,* January 26, 1930),[16] Guillén combines his arguments about racial harmony with the question of Cuban cultural expression. He decries the tendency of Cubans to accept what is loudly advertised and to suppress values that are natural and authentic to Cuba:

> Nada que no haya venido de París, o por lo menos de Nueva York, de donde, desdichadamente, nos viene todo, desde los zapatos hasta el frío, tiene para nosotros interés.[17]

> (Nothing that hasn't come from Paris, or at least from New York,

from where, unhappily, everything comes to us, from shoes to cold weather, holds any interest for us.)

And he adds, "we reject the vernacular with an ingenuousness that is really touching."[18] In this essay it is once more the turn of blacks to be the object of his faultfinding, particularly those who, with their imitative gaze on European and North American models, disparage their full heritage. "The black Cuban," he writes, "is alienated from his own beauty. It seems that there is a fear of being black."[19] They are scandalized when aspects of their culture are presented as significant cultural offerings, such as Eliseo Grenet had recently done in a Havana theater. (Grenet was an acclaimed Cuban composer, pianist, and orchestra leader who drew on popular Cuban motifs in his compositions and who was later to put *Motivos de son* and other Guillén poems to music.) Guillén counsels his fellow blacks not to flee from their cultural heritage in order to embrace the Euro-American, thereby ceding all prestige to the latter, since to do so would polarize and falsify Cuban culture. Always alert to the patriotic goal of unifying and strengthening the nation, he urges them instead, as he would urge whites, "to mix together in your spirit both currents, in an embrace of oceans, as in the fracture of an internal isthmus."[20]

All this is introductory to his interview of Rosendo Ruiz, who, in Guillén's view, was at that time the great artist of popular Cuban music, an artist who had been neglected and never before interviewed despite being for more than twenty years the composer of some of the most popular *sones, guarachas,* and *boleros.* The *son* is the featured genre in the interview.[21] It is mentioned some eight times; it is the subject of two paragraphs; and its natural, authentic sound and its profound impact on Guillén are apparent in the essay's climactic close. He had earlier prepared the mood of this climax by revealing his reaction when Ruiz mentioned one of his compositions, "Rosina y Virginia." Guillén writes lyrically of his attachment to this song at different stages of his youth, which he revisits, swept by the emotion of being in the composer's presence: "My heart leapt back to my brief past."[22] He returns from his sentimental association of his youth with Ruiz's music to hear the musician's latest composition, "Te veré" (I'll catch up with you), a *son* with a "Lucumi" (West African) motif, with Ruiz smiling ecstatically as he sings:

Acuérdate bien, chaleco,
que te conocí sin mangas,
en casa de Lupizamba,

cuando bailaba el muñeco.
Tú te va a degraciá
si te pone a jugá
con Bembé. . . .[23]

(Remember this, Mr. Waistcoat,
that I met you as a sleeveless shirt,
in Lupizamba's house,
dancing the muñeco.
You'll catch hell
if you go messing
with Bembé. . . .)

Moved by the music of the *son* as well as its lyrics—in the course of which popular speech comes to predominate and which he takes pains to quote—Guillén writes of its mesmerizing quality. Because it is such a hallmark of his poetic thinking with regard to Cuban society, we should note here too the music's centripetal effect: "The African rhythm wraps us in its warm, wide, life force that encircles just like a boa."[24] In this state of heightened passion and reason he reaches this conclusion about the *son:* "That is our music and that is our soul."[25] There can be little doubt that the *son,* so defined, is being recognized by Guillén as a consummate poetic vehicle. It is therefore not surprising that within three months of writing this article he should make the *son* his means of poetic expression in *Motivos de son.*

There are important conclusions to be drawn from the four essays I have been discussing with regard to Guillén's thinking about art and society in Cuba up to January 1930. He understood his position with regard to the racial situation in Cuba to be in the patriotic tradition of black national heroes such as Antonio Maceo, Juan Gualberto Gómez, and Lino Dou and of white national heroes such as Carlos Manuel de Céspedes and José Martí. All of these saw the struggles for independence and against slavery and racial discrimination to be inextricably bound together. In their will to win they were implacable. By the late 1920s, in Guillén's view, the targets to be attacked had evolved from colonialism to neocolonialism and imperialism, and from slavery to racial discrimination. He saw it as his patriotic duty to promote Cuban values, to make Cuban popular culture a pillar in the quest for full sovereignty, and to use his literary talent to foster the equality and unity of the Cuban population. Although he placed the greater part of the blame for racial prejudice on whites, he also put blame on the blacks for insufficiently valuing their own talents and efforts and for failing to assert themselves.

Guillén found a unifying medium in popular cultural expression, particularly in the music created by popular composers such as Rosendo Ruiz, who had been ignored by the media while for decades his *sones* and other compositions reflected the spirit of the people. Embedded in these essays are several images and concepts that were soon to reappear in poetic form, thus confirming a tight bond between his literary journalism and his poetry already at this early stage. In addition to my earlier observation about the link between the essay "La conquista del blanco" and "Llegada," "Llegada" is the opening poem of *Sóngoro cosongo,* a strong link also exists between "La canción del bongó" (The Song of the Bongo),[26] the second poem of this book, and the essay "Rosendo Ruiz." In the essay, the personified bongo is the voice of experience that makes large-scale social demands—"the profound requirement of the bongo, with its serious grandfather's voice"—prefiguring the authoritative bongo of the poem that tells mulatto truths to a society of descendants of whites and blacks.[27]

Perhaps the most consequential of the seeds planted in the essays that will later grow into poetry is one garnered from Ruiz's *son* "Te veré." Guillén's quotation of this *son,* which he found to be so moving and exemplary, ended with the lines "si te pone a jugá [jugar] con Bembé" (if you go messing with Bembé). Guillén was later to explain how he came to write *Motivos de son,* how the sound of the words "negro bembón" reverberated in his mind as he went to sleep and on the following morning he wrote the *son* "Negro bembón" followed by the other seven *sones* that make up the original book. In the first lines of Guillén's initial *son,* "¿Por qué te pone tan bravo / cuando te disen negro bembón . . . ?" (Why do you get so mad / when they call you thick-lipped black man), Ruiz's "te pone" is repeated and "bembón" is phonically and rhythmically close to reproducing the name Bembé. There is a suggestion here that the seed sown in the journalistic encounter with Rosendo Ruiz, which itself was motivated by Guillén's by then well-formulated and clearly demonstrated sociocultural national interests, had germinated, sprouted, and flourished in his first book of *sones.*

In view of all this, Hughes's impact on Guillén's formation would seem to have been greatly overestimated in Rampersad's earlier quoted appraisal. Guillén wrote his first book of *sones* in a single day; but his orientation toward the *son* as literary expression was not a process achieved in a few days. It was a part of his effort to improve the lot of blacks, which was in turn an effort to continue the struggle of patriots to strengthen the national culture and the national life. In dedicating *Motivos de son* to José Antonio Fernández de Castro, he demonstrated his confidence in his bond with a progressive white Cuban who shared his values.[28] On the other hand, Hughes, with the apparent impossibility of any foreseeable reconciliation of whites and blacks and no strong tradition of heroes of both races who were genuinely dedicated to and had fought together for equality, expressed a passion for the welfare of blacks, for consoling them in their separate misery. Thus while Guillén urged Cuba to avoid "the road to Harlem," to the setting up of isolated and deprived black communities, Hughes embraced Harlem. This distinction nevertheless left the two writers considerable common ground and parallel perceptions. Because of this and their personal congeniality, their happy meeting in Havana marked the beginning of a lifelong friendship that was strengthened by convergences while it endured divergences.

Common Ground and Parallel Perceptions

Foremost among their parallel perceptions at the time of their meeting was the aesthetic value of their respective peoples' musical heritage: Hughes's demonstrated view that popular black American musical rhythms, the blues and jazz, were fitting formal means for his poetry; and Guillén's belief that the Cuban *son*, the product of the blending of African and Spanish instruments that was popular among the masses, was the soul of Cuba and a natural basis for his unifying project. It can be assumed that they were mutually encouraging, but only peripherally; and in that sense Boti seems not to have erred in rejecting any essential Hughes impact on Guillén. At the same time it is incredible that, as Rampersad reports, Hughes suggested to Guillén that he use the *son* rhythms in his poetry and that Guillén was startled at the suggestion. There is no evidence of this.[29] Nor is it accurate to say, as Rampersad does (apparently although not declaredly following Edward Mullen),[30] that "when a local critic denied a relationship between Hughes and Guillén's landmark poetry, Guillén refuted him at once in 'Sones y soneros.' " Guillén in this article responds to Ramón Vasconcelos's accusation that he is lowering the standards of his own poetry and of Cuban poetry by writing *sones*. He defends his practice by elaborating on arguments he had already advanced in his article on Rosendo Ruiz, including his promotion of Cuban cultural expression that truly reflects lived Cuban reality. He does not make mention of Hughes in the essay.

Since Rampersad evidently believes that Hughes on his brief visit gave Guillén the advice that transformed him into the poet of *Motivos de son,* it is not surprising that he uses the adjective "cheeky" and its synonyms to characterize Guillén's attitude to Hughes in "Conversación con Langston Hughes," his interview of March 2, 1930,[31] and in some of his subsequent comments. The tone of the interview reflects the Cuban's self-assurance, ample grounds for which lay in the scope and acuity of his analysis of his nation's condition. So that, far from regarding the American as a mentor or master, which would have contradicted his complaints about other Cubans who were susceptible to North American guidance, he was respectful and not wide-eyed, treating Hughes on equal terms. (Even with the disadvantage of speaking in Spanish, Hughes could well express the subtleties of his thinking.) The so-called "cheeky" words are used by Guillén in his physical description of Hughes. Having expected an older man on the first encounter, Guillén is surprised to find "un jovencito" (a really young man) who looks like "un 'mulatico' cubano" (a light brown [i.e., relatively privileged] Cuban). But Guillén hastens to distinguish between such a Cuban, sometimes even a university graduate who too often wastes his time organizing weekend parties, and Hughes, who is nobly and passionately interested in matters that affect the majority of black people in Africa and in this hemisphere. He quotes Hughes speaking eloquently for himself in the interview:

> vivo entre los míos; los amo; me duelen en la entraña los golpes que reciben y canto sus dolores, traduzco sus tristezas, echo a volar sus ansias. Y eso lo hago a la manera del pueblo, con la misma sencillez con que el pueblo lo hace.[32]

> (I live among my people; I love them; the blows they get hurt me to the core and I sing their sorrows, I express their sadness, I put their anxieties to flight. And I do all this the people's way, with the same simplicity with which the people do it.)

Hughes is so keen on demonstrating his faithful, natural way of "feeling" and representing blacks that he declares that he has never written a sonnet, thus emphasizing his allegiance to forms derived from black American culture.[33] Guillén is impressed by Hughes's devotion. By taking him to cultural centers where blacks meet, he can see the intensity of his guest's commitment, comparing it no doubt with his own broader focus that included also the national situation. The interview ends with Hughes's declaration: "I should like to be black. Really black. Truly black!" Considering that Hughes made this declaration in March 1930, readers of Guillén's poem "Pequeña oda a un negro boxeador cubano" (Little Ode to a Black Cuban Boxer),[34] who know this poem as part of the book *Sóngoro cosongo* of 1931, and who recall the last lines of that poem—"and in the face of the whites' envy / speak truly black"—will be tempted to see in the words "negro de verdad" (truly black) a specific example of Hughes's influence on Guillén. But it must be remembered that the poem first appeared in *Diario de la Marina* on December 29, 1929, under the title "Pequeña oda a Kid Chocolate."[35] Besides, it is almost certain that Guillén brought this early version of the poem to Hughes's attention, since it contained the lines directed at the boxer:

De seguro que a ti
no te preocupa Waldo Frank,
ni Langston Hughes
(el de "I, too, Sing America").[36]

(Doubtless you
are not concerning yourself with Waldo Frank,
nor Langston Hughes
[he of "I, too, Sing America"].)

It seems that Hughes's declaration in the interview is a case of Guillén quoting Hughes quoting Guillén.

This is not the only kind of interchange that suggests closeness of identity between the two poets. Each one practices a form of projection onto the other's identity or experience. For example, when Guillén in "Conversación con Langston Hughes" calls him "un jovencito de veintisiete años" (a young man of twenty-seven years) and says he looks just like "un 'mulatico' cubano," both of these descriptions apply precisely to Guillén himself. Both writers were born in 1902, and a better definition of *mulatico* in this context could hardly be found than Guillén's ironic self-description in his essay "El camino de Harlem" a year earlier: in it he calls himself "a light-skinned black with 'good' hair."[37] It is this playful mirroring rather than cheekiness that is the remarkable feature of this and some subsequent Guillén descriptions or characterizations of Hughes. A particularly useful example of Hughes's resort to projection is found in his offer of advice to

Guillén in a letter of July 17, 1930.[38] This is perhaps the best-known letter of their correspondence. In it Hughes acknowledges and reacts to Guillén's *Motivos de son* with high praise for the uniform high quality of the poems. He writes: "Man! Your *Motivos de son* are stupendous! They are both very Cuban and very good. . . . I don't know which one I like best. I like them all." Despite his enthusiasm, Hughes adds:

> And be careful not to write new "Motivos" too hastily. Give them time to grow inside your heart. Let *Social* and all the other magazines wait until the poems are really ready. Sometimes success is dangerous, because everyone wants a repeat, and then the poet writes more quickly than he should, in detriment to his art. I expect you will not . . . ; forgive me for the advice. You are a wise man. . . . But they are so good, the first "Motivos," that all the ones that follow will have to be as good, or better. And poems are not written because the public wants them, but because the poet is ready to sing.[39]

It seems somewhat strange that in commenting on a collection he regarded as superb, a collection that was written in one day, Hughes should devote so much of his commentary to warning his able contemporary against hasty and premature writing, that he should be so preoccupied with this question. The explanation lies in the phenomenon of projection. Hughes's trip to Cuba and thence to Haiti had been financed by his patron of this period, a wealthy New Yorker named Charlotte Mason whom he called "Godmother." Upon his return to the United States, needing to absorb his experiences—his meeting in Cuba not only with Guillén but with most of the literary circle of Fernández de Castro, the influential editor of the literary section of *Diario de la Marina,* and his meeting with Jacques Roumain and his literary circle in Haiti, and his deeper understanding of Cuban and Haitian realities—he could not simply continue writing as his patron impatiently urged him to do. A tense and humiliating situation developed for the badgered Hughes, who had scarce financial prospects, when Mason withdrew her patronage. But rather than oblige her with work that he would judge to be premature, hasty, or inauthentic, he finally stood on the principle of defending his poetic integrity. At the time of writing his first letter to Guillén and still stinging from the repercussions of his decision both financially (he mentions in the letter that he lacked the funds to send Guillén a telegram) and emotionally (he tried in other ways, perhaps too hard, to keep the relationship with Mason alive), Hughes is so conscious both of the pressure of success on artistic integrity and of the importance of this principle to his consolation and vindication that he communicated his advice to his friend and colleague without having any real evidence that it was needed.

The friendship between the two poets was further strengthened with Hughes's next and final visit to Cuba in 1931. A gesture from Hughes that contributed greatly to their deepening friendship was Hughes's writing in Havana. In his characteristic combination of realistic forms, direct language, and lucid analysis, he wrote his anti-imperialist poem "To the Little Fort San Lázaro":

> Watch tower once for pirates
> That sailed the sun-bright seas—
> Red pirates, great romantics,
> > Drake
> > De Plan
> > El Grillo
> Against such as these
> Years and years ago
> You served quite well—
> When time and ships were slow.
> > But now,
> Against a pirate called
> THE NATIONAL CITY BANK
> What can you do alone?
> Would it not be
> Just as well you tumbled down,
> Stone by helpless stone?[40]

Guillén was thrilled to see coming from a U.S. poet views on the victimization of Cuba that coincided with those he himself had expressed in the same 1929 poem in which Hughes had been mentioned, "Pequeña oda a Kid Chocolate":

> ese mismo Broadway,
> es el que estira su hocico como un enorme puente
> > húmedo,

para lamer glotonamente/
toda la sangre de nuestro cañaveral[41]

(that same Broadway,
is the one that stretches its snout with an enormous
    humid extension,
to lick up gluttonously
all the blood of our canefield)

and in his "Caña" (Cane), first published in June 1930:

El negro
junto al cañaveral.

El yanqui
sobre el cañaveral.

La tierra
bajo el cañaveral.

—Sangre
que se nos va![42]

(The black man
next to the canefield.

The Yankee
over the canefield.

The land
under the canefield.

Blood
that goes out from us!)[43]

In Guillén's poems, more so than in Hughes's on this subject, imperialism characteristically provokes a great sense of urgency, a marked tendency to be combative.

Imperialist intervention in Cuba was also in part responsible for retarding the improvement in race relations for which Guillén and his comrades were militating. Hughes himself directly encountered racial discrimination in Cuba. He was brought before the courts for attempting to go to
an American-controlled, whites-only beach. He was quick to notice, since
something even harsher had plagued his own experience, the color line that
applied generally in Cuba, and about which Guillén had written earlier.
Hughes saw that the color line spawned the pathos of those who futilely
insisted that they were white. And one such was the subject of Guillén's
poem "El abuelo" (The Grandfather).[44]

Underlying their problem, of which this kind of distorted preoccupation was symptomatic, Hughes could feel the pernicious and pervasive
influence of what Guillén called the "the white man who makes of whiteness his anthem and flag."[45] Guillén had confronted two of these in the
persons of a "Dr. Martínez" and Gastón Mora in his 1929 essay "El
blanco: he ahí el problema"; and he would be even more keenly combative against another, Ramiro Cabrera, in his essay "Racismo y cubanidad"
(Racism and Cubanness), published on June 15, 1937, in *Mediodía,* a
journal by then edited by Guillén.[46] Cabrera had published in the newspaper *El Siglo* an article whose title, "Africanismo e hispanismo," was certain to grab Guillén's attention; for him these were the elements that *together* constituted the national identity. But the sociologist Cabrera,
representing a current in Cuban intellectual life of those times—one that
is being desperately stirred now outside Cuba by some opponents of the
Cuban government[47]—weighs in on behalf of the idea of segregation,
targeting the education system. He claims that blacks are impeding the
progress of whites; and not content with the de facto segregation already
in force in the materially privileged Catholic schools, he advocates a thor-
oughgoing separation of whites from blacks in the entire school system.[48]
Guillén debunks the pretensions of science on which the sociologist bases
his arguments and places them in the context of the Hitlerian fomenting
of fascism. He cites the achievements of blacks in Cuba, even during the
days of nineteenth-century slavery when they had no benefit of instruction, and points out that, despite their disadvantaged social and economic situation in the 1930s, the achievements continued. The racial
panorama that Guillén saw and reacted to was easily recognizable to
Hughes, for whose society systematic segregation was not merely a proposal but was institutionalized and legal.

The Spanish Civil War

Guillén's "Racismo y cubanidad" was published four days before he left for Mexico, on June 19, 1937, on an extended trip that ended in Spain and France, where he renewed his personal contact with Hughes. Both had been invited to the sessions of the International Congress of Writers for the Defense of Culture to be held in several Spanish cities and Paris. Both poets had written poems about the Spanish Civil War before they arrived in Spain. Hughes in his "Song of Spain" beseeches workers to withhold their labor from the fascists and their allies who are destroying Spain.[49] Guillén in his more developed and elaborate *España: Poema en cuatro angustias y una esperanza* (Spain. Poem in Four Anguishes and a Hope), displays the firm Marxist ideology that had evolved out of his early antiracist, anticolonialist, anti-imperialist outlook and his belief in the unifying power of popular culture.[50] He urges a victory of workers and those who share their perspective in the struggle, and identifies himself:

Yo,
hijo de América,
hijo de ti y de Africa,
esclavo ayer de mayorales blancos dueños de látigos
     coléricos;
hoy esclavo de rojos yanquis azucareros y voraces;
yo chapoteando en la oscura sangre en que se mojan mis
     Antillas;
ahogado en el humo agriverde de los cañaverales;
sepultado en el fango de todas las cárceles;
cercado día y noche por insaciables bayonetas;
perdido en las florestas ululantes de las islas
     crucificadas en la cruz del Trópico;
Yo, hijo de América,
corro hacia ti, muero por ti.[51]

(I,
a son of the Americas,
a son of Spain and Africa,
a slave yesterday of white overseers and their choleric
     whips;

today a slave of red, sugary, voracious Yankees;
I, splashing about in the dark blood in which my West Indies are
    soaked;
drowned in the bittergreen smoke of the canefields;
buried in the mire of all the prisons;
encircled day and night by insatiable bayonets;
lost in the howling woodlands of the islands crucified on the cross of
    the Tropics;
I a son of the Americas,
run to you, I die for you.)

Guillén arrived in Spain in time to attend the Madrid session of the
Congress and spoke there on July 6, 1937. Hughes and Guillén met at the
Paris session, where Guillén spoke on July 16 and Hughes, according to
Rampersad, spoke three days later. Guillén, in this speech, refers to his
Madrid speech, stressing his Cuban perspective on the Spanish Civil War.[52]
The reader will see how the following paragraph from his Paris speech
brings together the essence of Guillén's thinking as we have been observing
it from his first essay of 1929 to the essay published four days before he left
Cuba on the journey that would take him to Spain. The paragraph also reflects the principal currents of his poetry from the "Oda a Kid Chocolate"
of 1929 to *España: Poema en cuatro angustias y una esperanza,* which preceded the speech by two months. In a steady succession of first-rate
books—*Motivos de son* (1930), *Sóngoro cosongo* (1931), *West Indies Ltd.*
(1934), *Cantos para soldados y sones para turistas* (1937) (Songs for Soldiers
and "Sones" for Tourists)[53]—that reveal the exceptional artistic ingenuity
that is a feature of his whole work, he had cultivated the themes of antiracism, anticolonialism, and anti-imperialism, and saw promise in the co-
hesive powers of popular culture. All of this was consistent with his patriotic effort to unify his country and secure its sovereignty as well as with the
solidarity he felt with those suffering similar fates. The paragraph reads:

Decía yo, además, y ahora quiero ratificar aquella afirmación, que el
negro cubano es, junto con el blanco, un componente insuprimible
en la elaboración histórica de Cuba, hasta el punto de que tratar de
separarlo, como querría el fascismo, sería sumergir el país en un caos
criminal. El negro, por último, forma la mayoría de las clases traba-
jadoras, esclavizadas, de Cuba, y está ligado por tanto, dolorosa-

mente, a todo el sombrío proceso económico de aquella sociedad semicolonial, saqueada por el imperialismo norteamericano. ¿Cómo no va a sentir en lo más hondo de su tragedia la tragedia del pueblo español? La siente, y comparte con el blanco del pueblo los mismos ardores de liberación y lucha que conmueven a todos los hombres oprimidos del mundo, sin más raza que la humana.[54]

(I was saying, besides, and now I want to affirm that statement, that the black Cuban is together with the white Cuban, an unsuppressible component in the historical development of Cuba, to the extent that to try to segregate blacks, as fascism would like to do, would be to submerge the country in criminal chaos. Blacks, after all, form the majority of the working, slaving classes of Cuba, and they are therefore linked, painfully, to the whole shady economic process of that semicolonial society, sacked by U.S. imperialism. How could they not feel in the depth of their own tragedy the tragedy of the Spanish people? They feel it, and they share with the white masses the same eagerness for liberation and struggle that touches deeply all the oppressed people of the earth, of no other race than the human race.)

Hughes's late arrival in Europe was due to his reluctance to accept several invitations to the Congress, having committed himself in early 1937 to lead a travel tour to Europe that summer.[55] When the tour was canceled, he arrived in time for the Paris session; and there he spoke forthrightly, beginning his speech that has come to be known by the title "Too Much of Race" as follows:

Members of the Second International Writers Congress, comrades, and people of Paris: I come from a land whose democracy from the very beginning has been tainted with race prejudice born of slavery, and whose richness has been poured through the narrow channels of greed into the hands of the few. I come to the Second International Writers Congress representing my country, America, but most especially the Negro peoples of America, and the poor peoples of America—because I am both a Negro and poor. And that combination of color and of poverty gives me the right then to speak for the most oppressed group in America, that group that has known so little of American democracy, the fifteen million Negroes who dwell within our borders.[56]

He ends his speech by blaming "the reactionary and Fascist forces of the world" for keeping writers like him and Guillén from reaching out "their hands in friendship and brotherhood to all the white races of the earth."[57] His black identity and his focus on blacks, as subjects and as reading public, pervade his writings on the Civil War for *The Afro-American, The Volunteer for Liberty,* and other journals, as well as his autobiographical *I Wonder as I Wander.* And his concern for his physical safety, contrasted with Guillén's calm (as Hughes himself describes it) when they were under Fascist air bombardment in a Barcelona hotel, indicates that he was not ready to make Spain his final cause, even while he saw the ramifications the war and fascism held for blacks.[58]

Hughes had traveled widely before he went to Spain, sometimes as a seaman in the merchant marine, at other times specifically to further his development as a writer and to pursue his sociopolitical interests. His extensive travels in the Soviet Union would have been useful experience politically and journalistically for his 1937 visit to Spain. In contrast, Guillén's visit to Spain was an extension of his first trip outside Cuba. Yet his political and literary maturity, his knowledge of Spanish history and culture, and his sense of discipline as a member of the Communist Party of Cuba (he joined it formally while he was in Spain, but had collaborated with it for several years previously) made him helpful to Hughes in large and small ways until the American left Spain in December 1937. Guillén remained there through the more perilous times that would ensue, returning to Cuba in mid-1938. As was the case for so many who shared the experience of defending the Spanish Republic, and perhaps for Guillén and Hughes more intensely than most, the experience heightened their mutual appreciation and deepened their friendship. It would happen that in the 1950s and 1960s their approach to international affairs diverged in important ways. This had a great deal to do with how they fared against hostile domestic forces.

Race and the Social Poet

The reactions of both Hughes and Guillén to the harshly adverse conditions of their respective societies for a long time created similarities in their poetry and strengthened the bonds between the two men. In the 1930s Hughes began to write hard-hitting poems, with militant expression of social awareness resonating in insistent cadences. He condemned the use of the judicial system to slaughter blacks, as in "Christ in Alabama"

(1931)[59] and other poems dedicated to the Scottsboro case. He deprecated the exploitation of black workers in "Air Raid over Harlem" (1935).[60] His earlier-mentioned, anti-imperialist "To the Little Fort, San Lázaro" (1931)[61] had been preceded, in December 1930, by the scathing "Merry Christmas,"[62] in which bellicose imperialism is shown to be casually wreaking destruction on a succession of nonwhite countries. In "Roar China!" (1937) he celebrated the measures China had taken to free its people from the monstrous imperialist indignities and dictates they had suffered. And in the face of social injustice, he went further than other poets who in our time have desperately linked social and Christian themes—for instance, the Ernesto Cardenal of the "Salmos" (Psalms)[63]—by offering poems such as "A Christian Country" (1931)[64] and "Goodbye, Christ" (1932),[65] in which deities are not only questioned but accused of collusion.

Writing in 1947 about "My Adventures as a Social Poet,"[66] Hughes begins:

> Poets who write mostly about love, roses and moonlight, sunset and snow, must lead a very quiet life. Seldom, I imagine, does their poetry get them into difficulties. . . . Unfortunately, having been born poor— and also colored—in Missouri, I was stuck in the mud from the beginning. Try as I might to float off into the clouds, poverty and Jim Crow would grab me by the heels, and right back on earth I would land.[67]

His difficulties were legion and his responses varied greatly. He had noticed from the start of his career that the hostility of a sector of readers was a natural concomitant of social poetry. His declaration of 1926, "The Negro Artist and the Racial Mountain," was his first response, a resolute one, to those in the mainstream for whom poetry dealing with the real life of blacks was a double affront: socially, because it raised a subject they found to be inconvenient; and aesthetically, because it went against the grain of both avant-garde playfulness and classical sobriety.

For parallel reasons Guillén's poetic representations of the issues that his essays of 1929 had shown to be troubling him evoked similar reactions. The constitutional proscription of racial discrimination in Cuba had not prevented its affliction of institutions that were as widely distributed throughout the country as banks or as theoretically exemplary as the Roman Catholic Church; and the prestige of the Cuban literary journal *Revista de Avance* (1927–30) ensured the predominance of the art-for-art's-sake wave and an implied acquiescence in the social status quo. Guillén therefore had good cause for writing, "No ignoro, desde luego, que estos versos les repugnan a muchas personas, porque ellos tratan asuntos de los negros y del pueblo. No me importa. O mejor dicho: me alegra."[68] (I realize, of course, that these verses disgust many people, because they deal with blacks and the masses. I don't care. Or better: it makes me glad.)

Hughes too had had good cause to write in "The Negro Artist and the Racial Mountain":

> We younger Negro artists who create now intend to express our individual dark-skinned selves without fear or shame. If white people are pleased we are glad. If they are not, it doesn't matter. We know we are beautiful. And ugly too. The tom-tom cries and the tom-tom laughs. If colored people are pleased we are glad. If they are not, their displeasure doesn't matter either. We build our temples for tomorrow, strong as we know how, and we stand on top of the mountain, free within ourselves.[69]

The subsequent dialectical course of Guillén's poetry, his responses to the obstacles to social progress as they became identifiable, led naturally to the view of poetry expressed in the poems "Guitarra"[70] of 1942 and "Arte poética"[71] of 1958. The latter, especially, bears some resemblance to Hughes's 1947 statement[72] with regard to the two poets' greater attraction to society than to nature.[73] Of deeper significance is the main difference between the two: whereas Hughes emphasizes the writer's difficulties as a consequence of the social conditions affecting his production, Guillén does not mention his own troubles, notwithstanding his poems dealing with the pain of exile that follow "Arte poética" in the book *La paloma de vuelo popular: Elegías* (1958) and the various penalties, including imprisonment, meted out to him by the Batista regime. In fact exile is so subtly and even obliquely treated in some of his poems that they are misread as poems in praise of nature by one Guillén critic.[74] And even when an "I" in such poems seems to reflect the poet's personal troubled situation, that "I" is readily convertible into "we," a recognizable group of comrades or class allies who are working together to achieve concrete goals, goals that have evolved from those set by ideological ancestors who made a deep historical mark. So that Guillén's troubles were always mitigated by a sense of stable comradeship that Hughes did not enjoy.

The Cuban poet acted assertively and always with a firm and clear concept of the national good. He considered his literary project to include an effort to unite the population and was confident that this aim was based on unassailable good sense and human values. He could count on staunch allies like Regino Pedroso, of African and Chinese ancestry, and white writers such as Juan Marinello, Angel Augier, Carlos Rafael Rodríguez, José Antonio Portuondo, Mirta Aguirre, Pablo de la Torriente Brau, and José Antonio Fernández de Castro to face and accept the full consequences of striving for and realizing this aim. Hughes had noticed how Fernández de Castro, his first host in Cuba and the person he got to know best of that group, was genuinely involved in his whole society and how familiar and naturally at ease he was with the black sector. Hughes regarded him with esteem and affection, called him a "person extraordinary of this or any other world."[75] He carried out a more extensive correspondence with him even than with Guillén, and in one of his letters to Guillén (October 28, 1948) indicated that he had gone to meet with Fernández de Castro on one of the latter's trips from Cuba to Panama.

Despite the fact that Hughes had a forebear who fought alongside John Brown and others who fought against slavery and for equality, the past could not provide him with a sufficient basis for a quest for racial harmony. "America never was America to me" is the dispiriting refrain of the poem "Let America Be America Again,"[76] and for him there is no solace in the past, as his poem "History" of the same book (*A New Song*) indicates:

> The past has been
> A mint of blood and sorrow—
> That must not be
> True of tomorrow.[77]

Hughes's allegiance to blacks in general resulted in loose personal ties with other black writers and with black social and political organizations. He did complain about the conservative formation of blacks in some of their educational and religious institutions, but his "feel" for the sorrows of blacks did not allow him to distinguish between those blacks who would be allied with him in the pursuit of progress and those who would not. He did not probe critically the dispositions that produce the contrast we may notice between a William Monroe Trotter and a Booker T. Washington, a Nelson Mandela and a Mangosuthu Buthelezi, a José Eduardo dos Santos and a Jonas Savimbi, an agnostic who believed in the social good, as Hughes himself was, and, like Léopold Sédar Senghor, a loyal follower of an imperial religious denomination. Whereas in financial matters Guillén threw in his lot with his comrades and subsisted or suffered with them, Hughes tended to chance individual relationships with sponsors or patrons.[78] We have already seen that Charlotte Mason wished to exercise considerable control over him, leading to his agonizing rift with her. A few years later Noel Sullivan became his benefactor, providing him with lodging, financial support, and some sumptuous banquets; but Hughes found that along with dinner he had to swallow conversation in which fellow guests praised Mussolini and damned Eleanor Roosevelt, and he felt the pressure to alter his production. Critics have written cheekily about Hughes in this regard.[79] But he might thus have explained himself to his primary audience, U.S. blacks: "Beautiful and wonderfully creative people that you are, you are suffering the travails and humiliations of racial discrimination and have always done so. I see no way out. I feel for you. I love you. I unmask and detest the structures—economic, social, religious—that have wounded and are wounding you. At the same time I live from my writing in this system; and knowing of its punitive spirit, I must tread carefully, sometimes to the extent of renouncing some of my poems."

Guillén's reflections on Hughes's difficulties and his own unwavering credo with regard to art and society are summed up in a piece he wrote in Spain in 1937, shortly after Hughes had left that country. The article is important for our purposes because he provides his view of his own practice and of Hughes's in the context of the origin and development of the black vogue in the arts in the early decades of this century. Indeed, if to the following quoted passage we add Guillén's comments on negritude made in my interview with him in 1973, we will get his view of the full range of what might be called black poetry in his lifetime.[80] Guillén writes in his essay entitled "Cuba, negros, poesía"[81] (Cuba, Blacks, Poetry):

> Ya se sabe, por lo demás, que el encanto científico que despertaron los estudios realizados por Frobenius y otros etnólogos en las selvas africanas, generó en seguida una corriente literaria. Morand, Cendrars y muchos más, buscaron en el continente oscuro aliento para su producción, y bien pronto devino tal experiencia una aventura plena de fresco, perturbador interés. Moda. Turismo circunstancial que no caló hondo en la tragedia humana de la raza. . . .
>
> Pero de la periferia arrancó la marcha hacia la entraña. Por lo pronto, señalemos el hecho de que el movimiento negro fue dando a cada atmósfera social una temperatura lírica diversa: mientras en cier-

tas latitudes, como el Sur yanqui, penetra hasta el hueso en el dolor
algodonero del paria oscuro (Langston Hughes) y se mantiene aislado
en cierto modo, obedeciendo a imperativos sociales y económicos
bien conocidos, en otros tiende a fundirse—se funde—con los ele-
mentos de criollismo blanco, en busca de una sola voz nacional. Así
en Cuba. De manera que al llegar hasta la Isla aquella onda exótica,
no fue una novedad sorprendente: antes bien, abrió de un solo
golpe el camino propio, permitiendo comprender que por la
expresión de lo negro era posible llegar a la expresión de lo cubano;
de lo cubano y sin matiz epidérmico, ni negro ni blanco, pero
integrado por la atracción simpática de esas dos fuerzas fundamentales en la composición social isleña. Por eso dista mucho de ser
fortuito que de inmediato fuera la sabiduría popular la más rica
mina de explotación artística, ni que en ella hundiera su mano la
poesía para encontrar rápidamente sustancias primarias, vírgenes,
que no hacía falta inventar o exportar, como ha ocurrido en otras
literaturas, donde la *moda* languideció hasta extinguirse. No el
guajiro de Vélez Herrera, cuya dimensión social es limitada; ni el
indio de Fornaris, cuya vida es un fantasma, iban a dar contenido a
una poesía de proyección nacional, sino el negro en carne viva,
desollado por el látigo; el negro fundido con el blanco; el autóctono
sustituto del indio, y el hombre que lo esclavizó. Drama
afroespañol: toda la imborrable mulatez de la Isla.[82]

(Besides, it is already well known that the scientific enchantment awakened by the studies of Frobenius and other ethnologists in the African
jungle immediately generated a literary current. Morand, Cendrars and
many others sought in the dark continent inspiration for their production, and very soon that experience evolved into a veritable adventure of
fresh, disturbing interest; into a fashion; into circumstantial tourism
that did not fathom the human tragedy of the race. . . .

But there was a movement from the periphery inward. For now, let
me point out that the black movement gave to each social climate a different lyrical temperature. While in certain areas, such as the Yankee
south, the movement penetrates to the bone in the cottonfield pain of
the black pariah (Langston Hughes) and remains in a certain sense isolated, obeying well-known social and economic imperatives, in others it

tends to merge—it is merged—with the elements of white criollism in search of one single national voice. That's how it is in Cuba. So that when that exotic wave reached the Island, it wasn't a surprising novelty: rather it opened up with one stroke our own path, allowing an understanding of the fact that through black expression it was possible to arrive at a Cuban expression; Cuban without regard to skin shade, neither black nor white, but integrated by the friendly attraction of those two fundamental forces in the social composition of the island. Because of that it is hardly fortuitous that immediately popular knowledge was the richest mine of artistic development, or that poetry should dig into it to rapidly find primary, virginal substances that didn't have to be invented or exported, as has happened in other literatures, where the *fashion* languished until it expired. Neither the peasant as portrayed by Vélez Herrera, whose social dimension is limited; nor the Indian of Fornaris's works, who exists only as a ghost, were going to provide the content of a poetry that would have national scope. But the blacks would in their full reality, flayed by the whip; the blacks fused with the whites; the autochthonous substitutes of the Indians, and those who enslaved them. They formed an Afro-Spanish drama: the whole unerasable mulatto condition of the Island.)

The fact that Guillén is writing this from Civil War Spain reminds us of the international concerns and involvement that are evident in *West Indies Ltd.* (1934), which initiates his intense focus on imperialism and, consequently, on the United States. The concern for the plight of blacks in the American South that he had shown in his essays of 1929 was to take powerful poetic form in his "Elegía a Emmett Till" (1956) (Elegy to Emmett Till), which expressed keen repugnance at the torture and murder of the fourteen-year-old black boy.[83] Later, responding to a vacuous statement about the assassination of Martin Luther King Jr. by the then-socialist poet Evgeny Yevtushenko ("His skin was black but his soul as pure as white snow"), Guillén mocks the Soviet poet in a paean to King, exalting his blackness in the poem "¿Qué color?" (What Color?).[84]

Another event that will have provoked Guillén's indignation was the summoning of his friend Langston before Senator Joseph McCarthy's Permanent Subcommittee on Investigations of the Committee on Government Operations in March 1953. In a declaration to the committee, a summary of which he published under the title "Langston Hughes Speaks," the U.S. poet reveals his acute discomfort.[85] On one hand, he places himself in the tradition of his abolitionist forebears: his grandmother's first husband, who died with John Brown at Harper's Ferry, having already served with his wife as a conductor on the Underground Railroad; the grandfather who went to jail for preventing the recapture of fugitive slaves; and his great-uncle, who was an outstanding abolitionist, legislator, and academic. On the other hand, he distances himself from many of his poems of the 1930s—and not just the poem "Goodbye, Christ," which had been troubling him for some years,[86] but poems that for the most part would have strengthened his bonds with Guillén, calling them "out-dated examples of my work."[87] His behavior, scrutinized by the authorities and overeagerly invigilated by the press, subsequently became so acceptable that he was sent on official tours of African countries.[88] Guillén was no doubt understanding of his friend's plight, and his indignation was directed at Hughes's accusers. He particularly targeted Hughes's main accuser, aiming at him his caustic and emphatic poem "Pequeña letanía grotesca en la muerte del senador McCarthy" (1958) (Little grotesque litany on the death of Senator McCarthy);[89] and he continued his attack on McCarthyism five years later in the poem "Crecen altas las flores" (The flowers grow tall):[90]

Murió McCarthy, dicen. (Yo mismo dije: "Es cierto,
murió McCarthy . . .") Pero lo cierto es que no ha muerto.[91]

(McCarthy is dead, they say. [I myself said: "It is true,
McCarthy is dead . . ."] But the truth is that he is not dead.)

As we shall soon see, Guillén would ultimately demonstrate in his prose writings that his trust in Hughes's basic allegiance to the causes they had both shared superseded any reproachful feelings divergence might have caused.

Conclusion

Guillén and Hughes saw each other for the last time in 1949, when the former attended a peace conference in New York. Guillén writes cordially of the U.S. poet in his *Páginas vueltas: Memorias* (1982, 105–8) (Turned Pages: Memoirs), discussing this visit and his entire relationship with Hughes—their first meeting in Havana in 1930 (when he knew only one of Hughes's poems, "I Too Sing America"), the common experiences and shared outlooks that sealed their friendship in Spain in 1937, their correspondence. Nowhere in this valuable book, however—either in the pages on Hughes, where he recalls the American's enjoyment of a particular cabaret performance of the *son,* or in the pages where he describes in considerable detail the genesis and publication of *Motivos de son*—does he point to any influence Hughes might have had on his own poetry.[92] What he certainly stresses is their close friendship. He ends his recollection of Hughes by saying: "Siempre fuimos muy buenos amigos. Intercambiábamos regalos y postales, sobre todo por Pascuas. De veras que sentí mucho su muerte" (108).[93] (We were always very good friends. We used to exchange gifts and cards, mostly at Christmas. His death touched me very deeply.)

The Cuban poet's immediate response to the news of Hughes's death had been his concise, comprehensive, moving article "Recuerdo de Langston Hughes" (Remembering Langston Hughes),[94] which was published in the *Revista de Granma* on June 3, 1967, some twelve days after the death of the U.S. poet. Guillén, expressing surprise that one who had always seemed so youthful to him should have passed on, reviews Hughes's Cuban relations and the development of their friendship. He sums up Hughes's literary contribution: "[desde] su primer libro, *The Weary Blues* . . . toda la obra de este gran poeta ha estado dedicado a luchar por la libertad del negro en el llamado mundo libre norteamericano" ([from] his first book, *The Weary Blues* . . . the whole work of this great poet has been dedicated to fighting for the freedom of blacks in the so-called free world of the United States). He considers Hughes to have achieved glory through this work, having eschewed the intimate styles of a Marcel Proust or a James Joyce to give voice to his people in a style that was formed at a time when blacks in his country's South were being roasted alive. Guillén ends his essay:

> Por supuesto que la valoración definitiva de la obra de Langston Hughes vendrá en su día. Lo tenemos ahora demasiado cerca para juzgarlo en todas sus dimensiones. Nos duele su muerte tanto como nos apasionó su vida. La presión imperialista lo lastimó más de una vez, le inhibió lamentablemente otras. Con todo, su figura literaria es bien simpática, y el ardor, la sinceridad, y constancia con que ayudó al progreso y liberación de los negros norteamericanos merece el más profundo respeto. Yo personalmente he perdido un amigo generoso, de cuya inteligente bondad guardo un recuerdo fresco, juvenil; un claro recuerdo que no envejece.[95]

(Of course, the definitive appraisal of Langston Hughes's work will come in due time. We are too close to it now to judge it in all its dimensions. His death hurts us as much as his life excited us. Imperialist pressure injured him more than once, and lamentably inhibited him at other times. Nevertheless, his literary character is very attractive, and the zeal, sincerity and constancy with which he furthered the progress and freedom of U.S. blacks deserves the most profound respect. I personally have lost a generous friend of whose intelligent kindness I have a fresh, youthful memory; a clear recollection that never grows old.)

Guillén would have been disappointed to know of the deprived conditions of Hughes's fatal hospital stay.[96] Hughes had battled hard and long in a tough environment; and by the 1960s, his final decade, this sensitive man, obviously joyful and pathetically free in his creativity, was battered, bruised, and unfulfilled. In his case the limited variations of tone reflect conditions that do not change and the absence of real belief that there will be change. If his first book is *The Weary Blues* (1926), that title could also encapsulate the poetry of his middle years, represented well by the weary refrain "America never was America to me" (1935). His last poem, "Flotsam" (1968), published posthumously in *The Crisis*—the journal that had marked the beginning of his adult poetic career—is also a weary blues, the poet's homeland not affording him the anchor he has desperately sought over the four decades of his writing:

On the shoals of Nowhere,
Cast up—my boat,
Bow all broken
No longer afloat.

On the shoals of Nowhere,
Wasted my song—
Yet taken by the sea wind
And blown along.[97]

Guillén insisted that Cuba be Cuba for the Cuban people, for those with or without work, with or without land, and that this comprehensive vision necessitated what he called in his "Arte poética" of 1958 "el múltiple trino"[98] (the multiple trill). In his poems of 1930 the contrast between the attractive music of the *son* and the discordant frustrations that typify the experiences of the characters in their dramatic encounters makes of the music a model of harmony to which people may aspire in their social relations. This contrapuntal function gives way to harmony between happy music and the new achievements and possibilities in the period of the triumph of the revolution. Guillén now applies the title of Rosendo Ruiz's composition "Te veré" to a *son* that celebrates the agrarian reform in a time of reckoning for the small group of foreigners and natives who, protected by the security apparatus of successive regimes, had come to consider land owernship to be their exclusive privilege:

> Vivo sin tierra en mi tierra
> sin tierra siempre viví
> no tengo un metro de tierra
> donde sentarme a morir.
> Te veré.
>
> Con Fidel que me acompaña
> con Fidel verde y florido
> vengo a cortarte la mano,
> vengo a coger lo que es mío,
> Te veré.[99]
>
> (I live landless in my land
> and landless I've always lived,
> I have not a meter of land
> where I can sit down to die.
> I'll catch up with you.
>
> With Fidel besides me,
> with Fidel green and flowery,
> I come to cut your hand,
> I come to take what is mine,
> I'll catch up with you.)

This poem appeared in his book *Tengo* (I Have) (1960), its title suggesting a sense of satisfaction that was denied to Hughes. Guillén quoted the final lines of the title poem in 1985, during the last of our conversations in his office as president of the Union of Writers and Artists of Cuba, a position he occupied from its founding in 1961 until his death in 1989:

> Tengo, vamos a ver,
> tengo lo que tenía que tener.[100]

> (I have, let's see,
> I have what I had to have.)

In *Tengo* too there is a seven-stanza poem titled and beginning "Vine en un barco negrero. Me trajeron" (I came in a slave ship. They brought me),[101] in which eight- and four-syllable lines alternate, all of them with intensifying assonance in e-o, the four-syllable lines reminding us, although now in a solemn, emphatic tone, of the reaffirming tetrasyllables of the *son*. In this poem he traces Cuba's history through heroic black figures like José Antonio Aponte, the leader of a spirited slave rebellion. Antonio Maceo, the anticolonial and antislavery fighter, and Jesús Menéndez, the assassinated leader of the national sugar workers' trade union in the Batista era; and, after alluding to the patriotic and unifying mission he had declared in "El camino de Harlem," he ends the poem with the lines:

> ¡Oh Cuba! Mi voz entrego.
> En ti creo.
> Mía la tierra que beso.
> Mío el cielo.

> Libre estoy, vine de lejos.
> Soy un negro.[102]

> (Oh Cuba! I give you my voice.
> I believe in you.
> Mine is the land I kiss.
> Mine is the sky.

> I am free, I came from afar.
> I am black.)

NOTES

Acknowledgment: Parts of this essay that were originally in Spanish have been translated by the author unless otherwise indicated.

1. Arnold Rampersad, *The Life of Langston Hughes,* vol. 1, *1902–1941: I Too Sing America* (New York: Oxford University Press, 1986). Among others who express the idea of Hughes's decisive influence on Guillén are Edward Mullen, "The Literary Reputation of Langston Hughes in the Hispanic World and in Haiti," *Langston Hughes in the Hispanic World and in Haiti,* ed. Edward Mullen (Hamden, Conn.: Archon Books, 1977), 15–46; Faith Berry, *Langston Hughes: Before and Beyond Harlem* (Westport, Conn: Lawrence Hill and Co., 1983), 121; Richard L. Jackson, "The Shared Vision of Langston Hughes and Black Hispanic Writers," *Black American Literature Forum* 5, no. 3 (Fall 1981): 90; and "Langston Hughes and the African Diaspora in South America," *Langston Hughes Review* 5, no. 1 (1986): 33.

2. Rampersad, *The Life of Langston Hughes,* 1:81.

3. Regino E. Boti, "La poesía cubana de Nicolás Guillén," *Revista Bimestre Cubana* 29 (May–June 1932): 352.

4. *Prosa de prisa,* 3 vols. (Havana: Editorial Arte y Literatura, 1975–76), 1:3–6. Referred to as *P.P.* in subsequent notes.

5. Juan Gualberto Gómez (1854–1933) was born free to parents who were slaves. Having sought out every possible opportunity to become well educated in Cuba and in France, he led an active life as a journalist, founder of journals, novelist, teacher, independence fighter, and politician. A close associate of José Martí and Antonio Maceo, he was banished from Cuba and imprisoned several times by the Spanish authorities—once because he joined in the protest of Baraguá led by Antonio Maceo against the insurgents' signing the Pact of Zanjón, which halted the Ten Years War (1868–78), the initial war for independence. He founded in 1892 the Directorate of the Societies of Color with the aim of furthering the intellectual progress of Cuban blacks and of combating racial discrimination. He was also the leader of the group of Cubans who protested the imposition of the Platt Amendment on the First Republic. The new international airport in Varadero is named for him. "Baraguá" has become for Cubans a symbol of the uncompromising pursuit of sovereignty and justice. See Guillén's essay "Don Juan" (*P.P.,* 2:150–57), in which he considers Juan Gualberto Gómez along with José Martí as a forger of Cuban nationality.

6. All translations from the Spanish are mine, except where indicated.

7. *P.P.,* 1:6.

8. *P.P.,* 1:7–9.

9. *P.P.,* 1:7.

10. *P.P.,* 1:8.

11. *Obra poética,* 2 vols. (vol. 1, 1920–58; vol. 2, 1958–72), ed. Angel Augier (Havana: Instituto Cubano del Libro, 1972), 1:102. This text will be referred to as *O.P.* in subsequent notes.

12. *O.P.,* 1:177–78.

13. *P.P.*, 1:20–22.
14. *P.P.*, 1:10–11.
15. *P.P.*, 1:11.
16. *P.P.*, 1:12–15.
17. *P.P.*, 1:12.
18. Ibid.
19. Ibid.
20. Ibid.
21. The *son* can be described as a musical form of contagious and provocative rhythm that is composed of two parts: the *motivo* or *letra* sung by the *sonero* (the principal voice), sometimes in harmony with a second voice; and the *coro* (which may also be called the *estribillo*, the *sonsonete*, or the *bordón*), in which the voices of the instrumental players reply to or second the *motivo.* The subject matter embraces the vast material of Cuban popular culture, from *pregones*, or vendors' street cries, to flamboyant personalities, to the musicians and their instruments. The basic instruments are the guitar; its relative the *tres*, which has three pairs of strings and initiates the rhythm; the bongo drums; the bass; the *claves*, two cigar-shaped, sonorous hardwood sticks that are struck together to keep the beat; and the maracas. The trumpet and other wind instruments were added later. See Keith Ellis, *Cuba's Nicolás Guillén: Poetry and Ideology* (Toronto: University of Toronto Press, 1985), pp. 65 and 231. For jazz in Hughes's poetry see Jean Wagner, *Black Poets of the United States* (Urbana: University of Illinois Press, 1973), pp. 400–415 and 461–75; and James de Jongh, "The Legendary Capital: The 1920s and 1930s: City of Refuge," *Vicious Modernism: Black Harlem and the Literary Imagination* (Cambridge: Cambridge University Press, 1990): 15–32.
22. *P.P.*, 1:14.
23. *P.P.*, 1:15.
24. Ibid.
25. Ibid.
26. *O.P.*, 1:178–79.
27. For two studies that show how Hughes's and Guillén's treatment of race are guided by their national milieu, see Enrique Noble's "Aspectos étnicos y sociales de la poesía mulata latinoamericana," *Revista Bimestre Cubana* 40 (January–June 1958): 166–79, and his "Nicolás Guillén y Langston Hughes," *Nueva Revista Cubana* (Havana), (1962): 41–85. A more detailed exploration of this fruitful approach is David Arthur McMurray's "Dos negros en el Nuevo Mundo: Notas sobre el 'Americanismo' de Langston Hughes y la Cubanía de Nicolás Guillén," *Casa de las Américas* 14 (January-February 1974): 122–28. For Hughes's treatment of the mulatto, see the study by Arthur P. Davis, "The Tragic Mulatto Theme in Six Works of Langston Hughes," *Phylon* 16, no. 2 (1955): 195–204, and Wagner, *Black Poets of the United States*, 454–57.
28. Guillén could discern well who would and who would not be his allies in the Herculean struggle. Fernández de Castro was clearly in the first category. Typical of a compatriot in the second category was Jorge Mañach, who had made a point of telling Urrutia that even

though he admired Guillén's fight against racial discrimination, he could not easily abide the poet's presence in his house. Guillén, *Páginas vueltas: Memorias* (Havana: Unión de Escritores y Artistas de Cuba, 1982), 88. This text will be referred to as *P.V.* in subsequent notes.

29. Neither in Hughes, "Langston Hughes: Six Letters to Nicolás Guillén," trans. Carmen Alegría, *Black Scholar,* July–August 1987, 55–62, nor in the Guillén-Hughes epistolary that will appear in the *Revista de Literatura Cubana,* nos. 24–25, nor in any of Guillén's or Hughes's writings can anything be found to substantiate Rampersad's claim.

30. Mullen, *Langton Hughes in the Hispanic World,* 30.

31. *P.P.,* 1:16–19.

32. Ibid., 1:18.

33. There is hyperbole in this declaration by Hughes. He had in fact, though infrequently, written sonnets. Guillén at this time had written numerous sonnets, and he would write many more. He maintained in several interviews throughout his career that the discipline and inventiveness involved in writing sonnets and other fixed forms was salutary for poets. See Nancy Morejón, ed., *Recopilación de textos sobre Nicolás Guillén* (Havana: Casa de las Américas, 1974).

34. *O.P.,* 1:180–81.

35. Ibid., 1:485.

36. Ibid. Guillén will no doubt have known Hughes's poem from José Antonio Fernández de Castro's translation of it published in the Havana journal *Social.* Edward Mullen informs us that this was the first translation of a Hughes poem into Spanish ("The Literary Reputation of Langston Hughes," 25). Speaking of these lines, Richard Jackson has said, "After Hughes left Cuba, Guillén respectfully deleted an unfavorable reference he had made about Hughes in the 1929 version of his 'Pequeña oda a un negro boxeador cubano' where he accused Hughes of being unconcerned about the black boxer" (in "The Shared Vision of Langston Hughes and Black Hispanic Writers," 90). The lines do not seem to support this interpretation. It seems rather that the young boxer, busy with his training, cannot be preoccupied with these two exceptional U.S. writers, Hughes and Waldo Frank, who wrote sympathetically about blacks. (In addition to Guillén's "Conversación con Langston Hughes," see also his "Conversación con Waldo Frank," in *P.P.,* 1:73–79.) It is more likely that Guillén dropped the lines because it was too obvious that the boxer would not be concerned about two authors who at that time were known in Cuba only to a few intellectuals. Guillén himself, since he did not read English at that time, knew no other text by Hughes than the above-mentioned translated poem; see *P.V.,* 105.

37. *P.P.,* 1:5.

38. Hughes, "Langston Hughes: Six Letters.to Nicolás Guillén," trans. Carmen Alegría, *The Black Scholar* (July–August 1985): 56.

39. There is more potential for irony than Rampersad seems to intend when he follows the long paragraph I have quoted (in which he claims that Hughes influenced Guillén decisively) with the brief paragraph: "With such a result, Hughes's visit to Cuba had not been in vain. But what about his own future? With Godmother to guide him, Langston looked forward to the coming year of work" (Rampersad, *Life of Langston Hughes,* 1:181).

In addition to the fact that the year of work in which Hughes was to be guided by Charlotte Mason would not happen, as Rampersad well knew when he wrote the sentence, the contradiction between the images of Hughes as dominant guide of Guillén, which Rampersad believed to be true, and Hughes as continuing to be guided by Mason would have been ironic, if both were true.

40. Hughes, *Good Morning Revolution: Uncollected Social Protest Writings by Langston Hughes*, ed. Faith Berry (Westport, Conn.: Lawrence Hill and Co., 1973), 25–26. This text will be referred to as *GMR* in subsequent notes.

41. *O.P.*, 1:80 and 1:485.

42. *O.P.*, 1:188.

43. In Hughes's translation of this poem in *GMR*, pp. 37–138, he renders "El yanqui" as "White man" (*GMR*, 138), suggesting a black-white issue and removing the imperialist, externally exploitative factor that is clearly indicated by Guillén's use of "yanqui." In general, though, his translations into the language of much of his own art are excellent.

44. *O.P.*, 1:204–5.

45. *P.P.*, 1:10.

46. Ibid., 1:65–67.

47. This, I believe, is the true meaning of the word "controversial," which appears on the back cover of Vera M. Kutzinski's *Sugar's Secrets: Race and the Erotic of Nationalism* (Charlottesville, Va.: University Press of Virginia, 1993). The book is a natural progression of her distorted reading of Guillén's poetry in an earlier book, where she fabricates a secret hostility of the black Guillén for the white Fidel. Her concern for maintaining the separateness of black culture in Cuba has of course its obvious corollary in separating white culture. Such separateness would not be new to Cuba; it found his highest expression in slavery, and Langston Hughes's brush with the law in Cuba was part of that heritage.

48. See, for example, Fidel Castro and Frei Betto, *Fidel y la religión: Conversaciones con Frei Betto* (Havana: Oficina de Publicaciones de Consejo de Estado, 1985), 136–41, where the Cuban president describes the deprivation he felt when, in contrast to his earlier experience at home and in Santiago (where he had an especially inspiring black primary-school teacher), he was faced (at about the time of Cabrera's essay) with a Jesuit-run high school whose students and teachers were all "supuestamente blancos" (supposedly white), p. 139.

49. Langston Hughes, *A New Song* (New York: International Workers Order, 1938), 21–23.

50. *O.P.*, 1:251–62.

51. Ibid., 1:259.

52. *P.P.*, 1:85.

53. *O.P.*, 1:165–250.

54. *P.P.*, 1:85.

55. Rampersad, *Life of Langston Hughes*, 1:337–39. To say, as Jean Wagner does (*Black Poets of the United States*, 392), that Guillén accompanied Hughes to Spain is to imply for Guillén the diminished role in the relationship that is too frequently assumed by U.S.-based

critics. In fact, we learn from Guillén's *Páginas vueltas: Memorias* (p. 108) that Guillén was really instructing Hughes on the significance of the Spanish conflict in the context of Spanish history.

56. *GMR,* 97.

57. Ibid., 99.

58. Hughes describes his own trembling and other physical discomforts in reaction to the explosions and depicts Guillén, in contrast, "sitting calmly like Buddha on a settee under a potted palm. He said, 'Ay, chico, eso es!' (Well, old boy, this is it!) which was of little comfort." See Rampersad, *Life of Langston Hughes,* 1:346. Guillén had expressed his full commitment to Spain in the poem *España: Poema en cuatro angustias y una esperanza,* quoted above: "Yo, hijo de América, / corro hacia ti, muero por ti" (I, a son of the Americas, / run to you, I die for you).

59. Berry, *Langston Hughes,* 136.

60. *GMR,* 28–31.

61. Ibid., 25–26.

62. Ibid., 26–27.

63. Ernesto Cardenal, *Antología* (Managua: Editorial Nueva Nicaragua, 1983), 112–23.

64. *GMR,* 36.

65. Ibid., 36–37.

66. Ibid., 135–43.

67. Ibid., 135.

68. *O.P.,* 1:175.

69. Hughes, "The Negro Artist and the Racial Mountain," *The Nation,* June 23, 1926, 694.

70. *O.P.,* 1:265–66.

71. Ibid., 2:9–10.

72. *GMR,* 135–53.

73. My faith in my argument that resemblance does not necessarily indicate influence, which is developed in my article "Concerning the Question of Influence," makes me unable to accept the view of Richard L. Jackson that these statements by the two writers amount to an instance of Hughes's influence on Guillén. See Ellis, "Concerning the Question of Influence," *Hispania* 55, no. 2 (May 1972): 340–42. Besides, Guillén's words, taken from the prologue to *Sóngoro cosongo* (1931), reflect what had really happened in the public reaction to his *Motivos de son* (1930), the poems of which were reappearing in the 1931 publication.

74. See Luis Iñigo Madrigal's comments in Madrigal, ed., *Nicolas Guillén, Summa poética* (Madrid: Ediciones Cátedra, 1976), 34.

75. Rampersad, 1:177.

76. Hughes, *A New Song,* 9–11.

77. Ibid., 19.

78. There is a suggestion in Hughes's extensive correspondence with José Antonio Fernández de Castro, the most with any Cuban, that he valued this kind of relationship—that

is, with a white man for whom skin color did not matter. He felt, however, that such relationships were not available to him in the United States except in rare cases, such as that of Maxim Lieber, his longtime friend and literary agent until Lieber had to flee to Mexico under the pressure of McCarthyism.

79. Houston A. Baker Jr. writes harshly of Hughes's "pinched and nomadic wandering" and adds, "If we call before the bench Langston Hughes, we find him starting out as a college student, a bohemian poet who turned out funky stanzas to the tune of a Park Avenue patron." See Baker's *Afro-American Poetics: Revision of Harlem and the Black Aesthetic* (Madison: University of Wisconsin Press, 1988), pp. 56 and 59. At every turn Hughes faced forms of censorship to which he was largely vulnerable because of his precarious financial condition, which frequently took him to the edge of destitution—apparently even while he was enjoying success as a poet and Broadway playwright. For instance, when *Esquire* magazine offered immediate payment and proposed that he suppress the ending of the poem "Let America be America Again"—in particular the final two stanzas (as it appears in *The New Song*), which contained what Hughes called "the dialectic solution" or the assertive power of the people—Hughes was obliged to accept (Rampersad, *Life of Langston Hughes*, 1:320).

80. Published in Ellis, "Conversation with Nicolás Guillén," *Jamaica Journal* 7, no. 102 (1973): 77–79, and subsequently in Keith Ellis, *Cuba's Nicolás Guillén: Poetry and Ideology*, 226–27.

81. *P.P.*, 1:94–101.

82. Ibid., 1:99–100.

83. *O.P.*, 1:409–12.

84. Ibid., 2:239–40.

85. *GMR*, 143–45.

86. Ibid., 36–37.

87. Ibid., 144.

88. Arnold Rampersad, *Life of Langston Hughes*, vol. 2, *1941–1967: I Dream a World* (New York: Oxford University Press, 1988), 322–23. Hughes had to deny, for example, false reports in the *New York Times* and the New York *Post* that he had dined with Fidel Castro during the Cuban leader's stay at the Hotel Teresa in Harlem in 1960. He denied another fabricated report in *Time* magazine that he had met with Dr. Castro.

89. *O.P.*, 2:25–26.

90. Ibid., 2:70–74.

91. Ibid., 2:71.

92. *P.V.*, 77–94.

93. I am told besides, by Guillén's good friend and biographer, Angel Augier, that in his last years, in health and in sickness, Guillén often referred warmly to Hughes in his conversation.

94. *P.P.*, 3:314–16.

95. Ibid., 3:316.

96. See Berry, *Langston Hughes: Before and Beyond Harlem*, 328–29. Having already

pointed out the tendency of critics based in the United States to hasten to the presumption that Hughes was the dominant figure in the Hughes-Guillén relationship, I must now point to another evident susceptibility in them: namely, to an accommodative sensitivity to the political climate in which they write. It is a troubling trait because it has a distorting effect on their presentation and interpretation of Hughes's biography and his texts. For example, Mullen's dedicatory in his edition of Hughes's writings reads: "To the memory of Langston Hughes (1902–1967), who wanted America to be America again." The dedicatory evokes the poem "Let America Be America Again." But the title, reiterated in the poem, cannot be said to demonstrate that Hughes believed that there had been a desirable or model America sometime in the past. The other, more personal refrain in the poem, "America never was America to me," attests to that. Rampersad (*Life of Langston Hughes,* 2:420–23) seems to go to lengths that show considerable faith in New York's health-care system in his attempt to deny Berry's account of poor medical care given to an apparently indigent Hughes before he died.

Berry herself, writing in the introduction to the 1973 edition of *Good Morning Revolution,* points out how, under the threat and reality of political pressure, Hughes became wary of the part of his work that might be characterized as radical. She added that her decision to publish those writings in 1973 was coincidental to and not influenced by a period of "amicable overtures by Washington to the U.S.S.R. and the People's Republic of China" (xx). She continues, "The collection was not prepared to follow in the footsteps of official political policy, a pattern often obvious in American cultural and artistic endeavors" (xxi). And yet Berry in her 1992 "Preface to the Revised Edition" shows real deference to the temper of those new times. She is no doubt mindful of the high standing then-Soviet president Mikhail Gorbachev enjoyed in the West, a standing befitting the most conspicuous dismantler of the Soviet system. She quotes with apparent approval Gorbachev's description of Lenin that downplays the idea of class struggle and treats Lenin's goal of a classless society as if it were his view of immediate reality. She then speaks in a similar vein of Hughes, doing to him the equivalent of what Gorbachev does to Lenin, by suggesting that the optimism of the dream in Hughes's lyric "I Dream a World,"

A world I dream where black or white,
Whatever race you be,
Will *share* the bounties of the earth
And every man is free

which she uses to open both editions of *Good Morning Revolution,* is more characteristic of his message than his perception of racial and class oppression and his call for solidarity and struggle. (See Hughes, *Good Morning Revolution: Uncollected Writings of Social Protest by Langston Hughes,* ed. Faith Berry, rev. ed. [New York: Citadel Press, 1992].) Fortunately her more serene 1973 "Introduction" remains as a part of the 1992 edition.

Berry gives evidence of further academic accommodation to the political zeitgeist in discussing her decision to omit from her collection Hughes's poem "One More S in the U.S.A." The title is repeated in the refrain of the poem:

> Put one more S in the U.S.A.
>   To make it Soviet.
> One more S in the U.S.A.
>   Oh, we'll live to see it yet.
> When the land belongs to the farmers
>   And the factories belong to the working-men—
> The U.S.A. when we take control
>   Will be the U.S.S.A. then. (Wagner, *Black Poets of the United States*, 435–36)

She points out the inconsistency of Jean Wagner, who, having called the poem at an earlier time "inept," "grotesque," and "Communist propaganda," now criticized her in his review of *Good Morning Revolution* for omitting the poem he claimed to be "the only really revolutionary poem which Langston Hughes ever wrote" (quoted by Berry in *GMR,* 1992, xv). Berry shows a similar inconsistency when she rejects the poem as "agitprop" while suggesting that Wagner's condemnation of it as propaganda is in error because it is the judgment of one of those "academicians [for whom] Hughes wrote the poem 'Letter to the Academy'" whose works fail to address the realities of poverty and prejudice (*GMR,* 1992, xv–xvi).

The fact is that Berry fails to justify the omission of the poem from her collection. Perhaps she was influenced by Hughes's willingness to sacrifice such poems to right-wing pressure in the 1950s and 1960s. Or perhaps she felt intimidated by critics like Wagner, who, in addition to what is quoted above, wrote that there was something about the poem that was "irredeemably false," adding that "as Charles I. Glicksberg has pertinently remarked . . . the Negro is deeply rooted in the American tradition, and he desires above all else to see the promises of democracy extended to include him. Besides what the Negro especially suffers from is White America, not capitalist America" (Wagner, *Black Poets of the United States,* 436).

In such ways, the constraint we first noticed in its censorious effects on Hughes as anthologist or critic of his own work is in turn felt and extended by the critics. Thus comes to be imposed on a whole people the censorship of those who claim to know the permissible limits of these people's feelings and of their constitutional rights.

97. Hughes, "Flotsam," *The Crisis,* June–July 1968, 94. In introducing the text of this poem, Berry writes of Hughes, "Few knew him better than he knew himself. In the end, he was uncertain what he had accomplished by his work, despite all he had tried to do. His last poem in *The Crisis* seemed to say so" (*Langston Hughes,* 328). Nancy Morejón in "América de Langston Hughes," a chapter in her book *Fundación de la imagen,* assesses his aim as a unifying one in which blacks would be able to realize their full potential in a country with a unified population. See Morejón, *Fundación de la imagen* (Havana: Editorial Letras Cubanas, 1988), 268. Alice Walker considers him to have possessed an exquisite sense of justice (see Walker, *In Search of Our Mothers' Gardens* [New York: Harcourt Brace Jo-

vanovich, 1983], 176]). The assessments taken together seem to confirm Berry's portrait of an ultimately deeply disappointed Langston Hughes.

98. This term, which bears an allusion to the great Nicaraguan poet Rubén Darío, is from Guillén's poem "Arte poética," *La paloma de vuelo popular.* It indicates the wide range of opportune music resulting from his use of the whole gamut of Hispanic verse forms supplemented by his many innovations.

99. *O.P.,* 2:103.

100. Ibid., 2:70.

101. Ibid., 2:91–92.

102. Ibid., 2:92.

8

Not Just Black

African-Americans, Cubans, and Baseball

LISA BROCK AND BIJAN BAYNE

When they first come over here Cubans didn't want to be . . . recognized as
black—and you couldn't blame them. Because in their hometown they were
Cubans; . . . You didn't read in the paper about no black Cubans, no colored
Cubans. They was all Cubans.
Lorenzo Piper Davis, Birmingham Black Barons

When I came to the United States, I was surprised and a bit amused to hear some
black ballplayers tell me that I didn't understand prejudice and discrimination
because I was Cuban, not black. What nonsense! . . . I told these players to look
at me and then they tell me I am not black. Cuba was not the racial paradise
some might want them to believe. Just as in the United States, there were many
sections of Cuba, and many neighborhoods, where you only saw white people.
And here in this country, the signs in restaurants and buses prohibiting blacks
applied as much to me as it did to them.
Minnie Minoso, New York Cubans

When the first National Negro League (NNL) was formed in 1920 and its
rival, the Eastern Colored League (ECL), was organized in 1923, African-
Americans and Cubans already had nearly forty years of intimacy through
baseball. Alessandro (Alex) Pómpez, a Cuban, was among the original owner-
founders of the ECL; while José Méndez, Havana's "crack pitcher"[1] with the
"smooth delivery" and "quick release,"[2] took the Kansas City Monarchs to
the 1924 colored world series as the team's first player-manager.[3] Similarly,
dozens of independent black teams had been barnstorming in Cuba at least
since 1900, and individual black players had begun relocating to join Cuban
teams by 1907. By 1910 John Henry Lloyd, known for his fielding of balls,
had been nicknamed "El Cuchara" ("Scoop") by his Cuban fans.[4] No more

poignant example exists of this "brotherhood of the glove" than the name chosen by the first North American black team to rise to prominence: the Cuban Giants, founded in 1885 in Long Island, New York.

To Cubans and African-Americans, baseball was never solely for sport or entertainment. It emerged during a half century when the hopes and dreams of emancipated slaves and Cuban nationalists had soared, only to be dashed by malevolent racism and a slippery but vicious U.S. imperialism. By 1910 Jim Crow practices had drawn a color line through much of American life and U.S. elites had hijacked Cuban independence. Thus, as baseball became America's national pastime, it settled in African-American and Cuban communities as a natural site in which racism and imperialism could be mediated. Baseball directly confronted the thinly veiled myths of black male "unmanliness"[5] and became a "metaphor for nation"[6] for both Cubans and African-Americans. By the time of Jackie Robinson's "integration"[7] of baseball in 1947, hundreds of rural and working-class players and tens of thousands of African-American and Cuban fans had come to know each other through baseball. A study of the role of baseball and their interactions through it reveals much about each group's identity and the paradoxes one finds when two groups of color live on the border of race and empire.

Baseball Fever

"Baseball fever"[8] swept through North America and Cuba like a moving train during the post–Civil War years. Requiring only a bat, ball, and something weighty to serve as bases, "nines" (teams) popped up in U.S. and Caribbean cities and in small rural towns. Workers and employers, neighborhood groups, social clubs, churches, and temples organized teams and drew fans. Metropolitan, state, and regional formations emerged; leagues and associations rose and fell. By 1876 the National League of Professional Base Ball Clubs was established, after numerous false starts. Its eventual rival, the American League, was created in 1903. These two national organizations, which still exist today, were made up of professionals—men who made their living playing ball—and became known as organized baseball's major leagues. Between 1876 and 1895, an estimated fifty-five to seventy-eight players of color[9]—including Fleet Walker, George Stovey, and Frank Grant—distinguished themselves in emerging major league clubs.[10] There was brief hope by black communities and some white scouts that baseball would be integrated. They were disappointed. By 1898 no known black players remained. A consensus had coalesced among a majority of white commissioners, owners, players, and fans that only all-white teams would be permitted to compete against each other in the majors.[11]

African-Americans and Cubans, however, had joined in the baseball fever long before the majors were formed, and they continued to do so after the Jim Crow decision was taken. By 1900 the two peoples had fielded hundreds of nines in their respective communities. Baseball clearly and decisively captured both people's imaginations and developed parallel to the game in white North America. That it took root so quickly must have been due to its perceived openness to all social classes and its communal character, which encouraged women, as well as men, to become participant observers. These features were new in American sporting life, which had been a masculine sphere largely controlled by the rich; it was not seen as something of great benefit to women or community. Baseball, in fact, had begun among the elite; yet with expanding industries, advances in transportation and communication, new trends in commerce and consumerism, and an expanding middle class, baseball quickly became accessible to more diverse groups of people. Even as the owners of major league teams became business magnates concerned with profits and returns on investment, the game itself remained open to a diverse set of skilled men and some women. Moreover, baseball offered lower-class men, if they could secure a position on an economically viable team, the possibility of employment and upward social mobility.

Athletic philosophy was being recast by midcentury to accommodate baseball. Colleges, which had begun to establish intercollegiate teams, regarded sport as a character-building endeavor aimed at taming "male biological outburst" while still encouraging "manly" prowess.[12] An 1869 article in the *New Orleans Picayune* summed up a general, if somewhat classist, opinion on the benefits of baseball for the working classes: "no parent will object to his son taking up bat and ball in preference to the dice, the cards or the glass . . . better to be on the playing field than at a gambling table or at other assemblages more seductive yet more vicious, and more dangerous to the impressionable minds of the rising generation than ever a trial of manly muscle in the open air can be."[13] Mark Twain saw baseball as the "symbol, the outward and visible expression of the drive and push and struggle of the raging, tearing, booming nineteenth century."[14]

Such a public discourse was not lost on African-Americans or Cubans. For a very brief moment, baseball was a cultural symbol of progress and modernity and "catered to the desire of blacks [and Cubans] to belong."[15] Af-

ter all, it gained in popularity during the 1860s, a decade of rising black ex-
pectation. Reconstruction was soon underway in the South, and Cuba's Ten
Years War (1868–78) was being fought not just to win independence from
Spain but also to end Cuban slavery. Yet baseball very quickly took on deeper
meaning. By 1878 the Republican government of Rutherford B. Hayes had
abandoned Reconstruction and pulled federal troops out of the South. Southern blacks were left vulnerable to state governments bent on the reinstitution
of white supremacy and to organized white terrorists determined to protect
racial privilege.

Similarly, Cuba's Ten Years War ended abruptly with neither independence from Spain nor an end to slavery having been achieved. The war ended
not because of a decisive Spanish victory but because of a split in the Cuban
anticolonial forces. The creole political leadership, largely composed of white
conservative elites, signed the Treaty of Zanjón with Spain on February 7,
1878, against the wishes of nationalist military leaders, who were largely black
and progressive. In fact, the generals and soldiers in the field had felt they were
in a good position to win the war. However, creole elites, realizing that they
could not achieve independence without ultimately abolishing slavery, wished
to retain their wealth and privilege in any new government. If generals Antonio Maceo and Máximo Gómez and the black, mulatto, and white *mambises*
(integrated units) triumphed, elites knew that would not be the case. Progressives envisioned the immediate abolition of slavery and massive social reforms. In pursuit of these objectives, their soldiers had already freed slaves as
they liberated territory, set fire to tobacco and sugar estates, and disrupted
commercial activity. Their desire "to break the back of the enemy by destroying its economic base caused great trepidation among elites."[16] Racist elites
preferred to remain under the yoke of Spain rather than have their privilege
and wealth circumscribed. Maceo, Flor Combret, and five hundred soldiers
refused to sign the Treaty of Zanjón in their famous "Protest of Baraguá" and
continued what is now known as *la guerra chiquita* (the little war) for another
year. Lacking financial support, it too came to an end in 1879.

Early baseball in Cuba and in black North American communities reflects this late nineteenth-century tumult. Philadelphia's Pynthian Base Ball
Club is a good case in point. Organized in 1866 by activists and educators,
the club articulated objectives like those of most black voluntary associations: "to expand social relationships, promote [important] causes of [the
day]"[17] and encourage business transactions. In less than a year, the club
had organized four teams, which competed against local black teams. By

the end of the year, club members were hosting visiting teams from Albany, Washington, D.C., and Baltimore, and Pynthian teams were traveling as far west as Chicago. Visiting teams normally stayed for a few days in the host city, where they were provided with safe and clean lodging and treated to banquets, dances, and picnics. By 1878 the Pynthians had become a club to be reckoned with, a high-society coterie with social networks throughout the South, East, and Midwest. Its teams had hundreds of fans, and they often rented the bigger white ball fields to accommodate them. There were also white spectators, especially during off seasons in the white leagues, and Pynthian teams often played and defeated local white teams. The Pynthians were clearly an example of a successful black middle-class sports and social club that used sport as a way into the American mainstream.

Even these members of Philadelphia's "colored aristocracy,"[18] however, were unable to escape prejudice, controversy, and racial violence. For example, in the fall of 1867, when the club sought admission into the Pennsylvania State Convention of Baseball Players, the largely white group refused even to vote on its petition. Interestingly, because segregation in baseball was not yet official, the club was allowed to send a delegate, R. S. Bun, to the convention. However, when Bun presented the Pynthians' request to be included in the new statewide organization, the club was asked to withdraw its application to avoid the embarrassment of a rejection. Bun was not embarrassed but angry and initially refused to do so. Under pressure from white delegates who, while individually supportive, were unwilling to stand up for the Pynthians' inclusion, the only "colored" applicant withdrew its request.[19]

To such indignities were added incidents of racial violence. Team members often had to cross Bambridge Street, Philadelphia's own Mason-Dixon line, in order to find a pasture large enough for practice. According to Pynthian records keeper William Carl Bolivar, they were often attacked by white, usually Irish, mobs, either along the way or after they had reached the practice area. This was the reason, according to another source, that the men from all four teams always crossed Bambridge Street together. In most cases they must have given as much as they got since there is little in the records to indicate that any member was seriously hurt.[20]

A few years later, however, a founder of the club was fatally attacked under different circumstances. On October 10, 1871, educator and activist Octavius Catto was on his way to the scene of a riot that had broken out as whites attempted to stop blacks from voting. He apparently carried a gun, although lore has it that the gun was not loaded. One Frank Kelly, a white man, passed Catto on the street, saw him and his gun, and shot him dead. After a ten-day trial held six years later, Kelly was acquitted.[21]

Many baseball historians recall this story, but none of them, to our knowledge, elaborate on a couple of telling points. First, Catto was like many Pynthian members: he had many interests and multiple memberships. In fact, the group's members were often involved in a variety of social, political, and educational organizations. The Pynthian Club, while primarily focused on baseball, served a somewhat coalitionist function in bringing members with various other interests together.[22] Second, Catto was an officer of a Philadelphia black brigade. He, along with other members of his brigade, had been summoned by their commander, a General Wagner,[23] to defend the black community, which was at that moment under attack. His role, at least on that day, was to defend the right of the black community to vote. That such brigades existed among Philadelphia's colored middle classes is evidence both of the precarious situation of all blacks, regardless of class, and of the level of militancy that existed among some of them. While many agitated for equality within America's emerging (and largely white) middle class, they also developed a racial struggle defined by, and for, the black race only. They had no choice; they saw both as necessary.

The Pynthians were inevitably caught in the double consciousness of being American and being black yet to be theorized by W.E.B. Du Bois.[24] This duality and conflicts among competing interests are evident in an interaction between two Pythian members. In 1869, member William Still, a civil rights activist, coal dealer, and a clerk in an antislavery society had fallen behind in his membership dues. Asked to pay up, he wrote, "Our kin in the South famishing for knowledge, have claims so great and pressing that I feel bound to give of my means in this direction to the extent of my abilities, in preference to giving for frivolous amusements."[25] Pynthian secretary J. C. White tersely replied that "neither the acquisition nor disposition of your means is a matter of interest to us as an organization."[26] Either White was indifferent to his "kin" just coming out of slavery in the South or he saw no connection between their fate and the timely payment of club dues. While White's vision for the baseball club is not clear in his response, Still's is implied in his letter. He obviously viewed the club as "frivolous" in the context of the larger black struggle. One wonders if Still had always judged the club so sternly or if its role in his life had changed. Whatever the case, Still ended, as did others, in questioning the place of baseball in the black community.

In Cuba baseball and the independence movement evolved concomitantly, giving baseball a stronger ideological character than it had in the United States. Louis Pérez Jr. argues that baseball was not only a sign of modernity for mid–nineteenth century Cubans but that it became an anti-Spanish symbol at a critical moment in the formation of Cuban national identity. Initially introduced to the island by students, immigrants, and sailors who had lived in the United States, "baseball sharpened the distinctions between Cubans and Spaniards when those distinctions were increasingly assuming political implications."[27] Importantly, "baseball [culture] offered the possibility of national integration" (in ways that bullfights, for example, could not) by being open to "all Cubans of all classes, black and white, young and old, men and women."[28] And as Cubans fought three anticolonial wars—the final independence war coming in the years 1895–98—and sent thousands of political exiles, students, workers, and war refugees abroad, baseball became "[their] sport, [their] state of mind and [their] statement."[29] Between the late 1870s and early 1890s more than two hundred baseball teams were organized across the island; and as nationalist revolutionary clubs were established in Tampa, New Orleans, New York, and Philadelphia, they too organized baseball clubs.

Only this juncture of nationalism and baseball can explain the early and lasting position of the sport in Cuban culture and the centrality of Cubans to baseball in general. Cuba became "Caribbean baseball's first epicenter"[30] and its players the game's "apostles."[31] It is common knowledge that it was Cuban exiles and immigrants who stoked the fires of baseball in the Dominican Republic, Puerto Rico, and Mexico.[32] Cubans, in fact, gained a reputation as great ballplayers even before the turn of the century. Interestingly, Pérez points out that, given what the United States came to mean to Cuba, the Cuban appropriation of baseball "may at first appear improbable . . . even slightly unseemly."[33] In fact, José Martí and others had warned Cubans against allowing culture from the North to penetrate so deeply.[34] But among Cubans baseball had come to stay, as it had among African-Americans. It offered too much in the way of recreation, physical stimulation, individual and group self-esteem, male pride and bonding, social and communal cohesion, and as a means of making a living for it to be discarded. And it was something at which Cubans excelled. To reject it because of its origins would have been tantamount to throwing out the baby with the bathwater.

There is little discussion in Pérez's article (or others, for that matter) on the impact of racism on early Cuban baseball. While there is mention of the fact that teams were created by Afro-Cuban societies in the nineteenth century—societies that were comparable to voluntary organizations in the United States—there is little on the role of baseball clubs specifically among Afro-Cubans.[35] Did these early clubs serve multiple interests, or face racist challenges, as the Pynthians did? Did contradictions arise among them? Since segregation was rarely as rigid in Cuba as in the United States, how did integrated revolutionary ball clubs accommodate or mediate race?

What is clear is that African-Americans perceived Cuban baseball through a racial prism; in fact, by the turn of the century they longed to be identified with it. Strikingly, among the names of emergent black ball clubs, the words "Cuban" or "Havana" are second only to "Giants," a reference to the white New York Giants. In addition to the first Long Island Cuban Giants, there were the Trenton, New Jersey, Cuban Giants, the York Cuban Giants, the Ansonia Cuban Giants, the Cuban X-Giants, the Genuine Cuban Giants, the Famous Cuban Giants, and the Havana Red Sox, among other variations.[36] Why African-Americans had such a strong wish to be identified with Cuban baseball has yet to be fully explored. Most baseball historians have problematically argued that they hoped to be perceived as Cuban and thereby receive a more positive reception in baseball and possible entrance into the white leagues. Many writers have said that black ballplayers spoke in "gibberish," hoping that whites might take them for native Spanish speakers. This story has been so accepted in baseball legend that it was depicted in the classic black baseball film *Bingo Long's Traveling All-Stars and the Motor Kings*. In this film, Richard Pryor, in the character of a ballplayer, slicks his hair back, speaks English with Spanish inflections, and pretends to be Cuban. In the long run his hopes are disappointed.

But this explanation, wedged deep in black baseball lore, raises two knotty issues: one, that African-Americans believed other ethnic groups of color and foreign-born blacks to be the recipients of better treatment from North American whites than they themselves were; and, two, that there existed a less rigid racial system in Cuba. That African-Americans might have attempted to manipulate a different social construction of race to their own advantage is possible, and perhaps even likely. Yet to believe that intelligent ballplayers actually thought anyone might believe them to be anything other than who they were, especially over time, is highly improbable.

What is more likely, especially during the era that the "Cuban" team title was under its greatest contestation (that is, the 1870s until about 1920), is that African-American ballplayers had recognized the Cubans' passion and ability in baseball and sought to identify their own teams with Cuba for reasons of racial pride and politics. Consider that similar pride had led a New Orleans team to call itself the Pinchbacks, after P.B.S. Pinchback,[37] who was elected lieutenant governor of Louisiana during Reconstruction and served as governor of that state for an interim period of forty-three days in 1875. Two Philadelphia teams incorporated the words Liberty and L'Ouverture into their names,[38] honoring the great ideal and the eighteenth-century Haitian revolutionary leader. One Baltimore team called itself the "Monrovians" after the Liberian capital established by African-Americans in 1822, and another called itself the "Lord Hannibals" after the ancient African leader who invaded Europe on elephant back.[39] For these names to have been selected by the teams and accepted by their fans points to their social currency. And such currency points in turn, at least in some measure, to a racial consciousness among nineteenth-century blacks that was both historical and international.[40]

The missing piece in most black baseball histories, then, is what Cuba specifically meant to African-Americans by the turn of the century. It is clear that African-Americans had long been aware of black Cuban resistance to slavery, of the integrated *mambí* army, and of the black military leadership of Antonio Maceo. Cuba's integrated national independence movements captured the imagination and the solidarity of a North American people who were allowed only belatedly and under great hardship to fight in segregated and despised Civil War units. Frederick Douglass had urged African-Americans to join their brethren in the antiracist Ten Years War, and Henry Highland Garnet, along with other black American leaders, founded a Cuban anti-slavery society. Early black writers such as Martin Delaney had long followed Cuban slave revolts, and black newspapers reported on all of Cuba's wars. The name Maceo, in fact, became popular among blacks in North America toward the end of the century.[41] In the 1880s, and surely by the 1890s, black baseball clubs were probably playing Cuban revolutionary clubs in New Orleans, New York, Key West, Tampa, and Philadelphia, since both were there and racism affected all those living in the United States who were phenotypically black.[42]

Cuba, then, existed in the ideological universe of black Americans and served as one among the many political statements one finds in black baseball. Cuba's place in that universe grew more significant during the independence struggle that resumed in 1895. With nearly half of the senior army ranks "made up of people of color, African-Americans recognized it as a black man's war."[43] This reinforced a belief seeded during the Ten Years War, that Cuba was a place where integration was possible. "African-Americans own deteriorating status made them particularly prone" to such an idea.[44] The expanding African-American press wrote often about Cuba and was steadfast in supporting its right to self-determination. When the United States intervened in the war, ostensibly on the side of Cubans, and recruited African-American men to go fight, many went. This was the first extraterritorial war in which African-American men would fight as free men, and the entire black community watched. Black soldiers sent letters to the press, many confirming better race relations among Cubans than among North Americans. Not surprisingly, Cuba joined Liberia, Africa generally, and Haiti as a touted site for black emigration. While some Cuban and African-American voices always opposed U.S. involvement in Cuba, it was not until 1902, when the Platt Amendment to the Cuban constitution was signed, that both communities came to critically understand U.S. penetration. This amendment paved the way for a more complete U.S. hegemony over Cuba.

First Contact

It is fitting that the first professional black American team known to travel and play ball in Cuba was the Cuban X-Giants. According to Dixon and Hannigan's *The Negro Baseball Leagues: A Photographic History,* they visited in 1900 and played eighteen games. They returned to Cuba in 1903 to play eleven more games and continued to go there regularly during the first decade of the century.[45] The first team of professional Cubans known to play on the black circuit in the United States were the All-Cubans in 1904.[46] According to Robert Peterson, there were most likely two or more Cuban teams touring the United States every year after that.[47] Little is known about these early encounters except that Cuban teams were integrated, Cuba soon became a regular stop on the "Negro circuit," and the teams quickly recognized each other's talent.

Because ballplayers at this time were usually independent agents, it was not uncommon for players to hop from club to club. Teams would often be constructed for a special series or exhibition games. Thus, it is highly likely that from very early on, Cuban and black American ballplayers were living and playing ball for short stints in each other's communities. A report from the *Indianapolis Freeman* seems to confirm this: "The Cubans are very clever ball players when it comes down to squeeze playing. . . . I will also tell you why it is so hard to defeat these Cuban Clubs . . . because [many] of their teams consist of American Negro star ball players such as a Lloyd and [catcher Bruce] Petway."[48] There is a picture of John Henry (Pop) Lloyd in Cuba dated the "early 1900s," and we know that José Méndez pitched for a Havana team in

1908, winning a three-game-to-none victory over the (white) Brooklyn Royal Giants. It is also quite likely that Andrew (Rub) Foster, who went on to become the major force behind the Negro National League in 1920, traveled to Cuba with the Cuban X-Giants in 1903.

The prehistory of the Cuban X-Giants is telling of early black baseball and the image of Cuba in it. Established in 1896 in Brooklyn, New York, by manager-owner E. B. Lamar, it was made up of many members of the original Cuban Giants team, which had been founded in 1885 by Frank Thompson, the headwaiter at the Argyle Hotel in Babylon, New York. The Argyle was a large summer resort on Long Island that catered to members of the East Coast establishment. It was built in 1882 by Austin Corbin, president of the Long Island Railroad. During their first year the Cuban Giants competed with local teams as entertainment for the hotel's guests.[49] The team was made up of the black wait staff at the hotel, although it is clear that Thompson hired known ballplayers as waiters in order to build his team.[50]

There had developed a practice of black participation in sports that were considered particularly grueling while another tradition encouraged black sportsmen to engage in minstrel-like performances. Both traditions continue today (black professional boxers and the Harlem Globetrotters being prominent examples). It was largely in keeping with the first tradition that slaves and then free blacks became the first American boxers and jockeys. (The latter were called on to do hard and dangerous long-distance riding when the sport of horse racing first began.)[51] Some of the emerging black baseball clubs were in line with the second practice. Nonetheless, Thompson's team continued to hone their skills by playing better teams during the hotel's off season. Within a year they had established such a reputation that most of the players left to become professionals. The majority went to New Jersey to become Trenton's Cuban Giants (taking their name with them). In Trenton they became the premier, unbeatable black team of the day. A white promoter, J. M. Bright, established the team and became its manager. Thompson's hotel-based team came to an end. However, *Sporting News* wrote in 1888, "This club with its strongest players in the field, would play a favorable game against such clubs as the New Yorks or Chicagos [of the white leagues]."[52]

J. M. Bright, like many promoters of the day, was largely interested in the money to be made in black baseball. Cuban Giant team members and others viewed him as "extremely selfish in his financial dealings."[53] He was also careless of his players' well-being. As Sol White has noted, Bright was known for entering a ballpark packed with paying customers and refusing to play until local promoters agreed to boost the guarantee.[54] The ploy often worked, but players were always concerned; they were the ones at risk from the wrath of angry spectators, many of whom were white. By 1890 most of the Cuban Giants had grown tired of Bright's antics and went to play for the Monarchs of York, Pennsylvania, and in 1896 many settled in Brooklyn with Lamar.

Player mobility was the norm in early black baseball. Lacking protections, professional players were vulnerable to all manner of unscrupulous activity; many moved around in search of a decent (if rarely a good) deal. Similarly, hundreds of teams and tens of colored leagues formed, only to fail because of inadequate financial backing. Early black ball was, in fact, characterized more by individual talent and reputation than by team loyalties with large fan followings. That the Cuban Giants—among them Clarence Williams, George Williams, George Stovey, William T. White, and George Parago[55]—worked hard to stay together and to keep the team name intact is important. It illustrates that they were a winning combination and enjoyed a reputation as the Cuban Giants. Their various manager-promoters always billed them as members of the original Cuban Giants, even though Bright angrily continued his Trenton team under some version of the same name for several years. Bright's most notable team was the Famous Cuban Giants. When Lamar picked up many of the players and chose the name Cuban X-Giants, he obviously was challenged by someone, maybe Bright, because he was quoted in *Sporting Life* as saying, "We are informed legally that the name of Cuban X-Giants is not incorporated and that we have a perfect right to the use of the same."[56] Interestingly, a Cuban club that toured the circuit during the first decade of the century made it clear that they were real Cubans by calling themselves the "All Cubans." Even though the Cuban Giants did not possess a single Cuban player, the fact that the first professional black ball club of recognized talent was called Cuban linked Cuba with high-quality baseball in the minds of many African-Americans[57] and served to create a welcome place for Cubans in black baseball even before many were touring the United States. This reputation reinforced by real Cuban talent made all-Cuban teams the hottest clubs drawing the largest audiences in black baseball from 1910 onward.[58]

Paradoxically, one wonders if black ballplayers felt any guilt at using the good Cuban name. After all, African-Americans might have been offended had the shoe been on the other foot. But chances are they did not. During this era of racist violence and U.S. expansion, rural and working-class blacks largely focused on their own domestic situation, while more prominent blacks "voic[ed] their aspirations to the middle class"[59] by arguing that they, having lived in the great United States, would be good agents of progress among the world's colored people. Interestingly, while overt imperialism was hotly debated among North American blacks and opposed by most, the Western "civilizing mission" aimed at "primitive" peoples was not. More than likely, a good number of black ballplayers and journalists did hold paternalistic views of the Caribbean and Latin America. In fact, the *Indianapolis Freeman* article mentioned above, after noting that North American blacks were playing on Cuban teams, went on to report that the Cubans were improving *because* African-Americans had been teaching them the fine art of baseball.[60]

How Cubans felt about the appropriation of their name we cannot be sure, but there is evidence that some did not like it. A *Philadelphia Tribune* article reports that Cubans had sent a message to the Spanish minister in Washington, D.C., asking him "to use his best efforts to stop the team from using Cuba's good name to fool the American public."[61] The Cuban X-Giants did change their roster to include five Cubans, who appeared in the lineup for the 1906 season.[62] Could they have done this to appease the critics? We do not know, and in the long run it did not matter. As all-Cuban teams began to compete regularly in black baseball, the Cuban X-Giants and even J. M. Bright's renamed Famous Cuban Giants faded away.

More research is needed on the early sentiments of Cubans about U.S. blacks as they might have been formed through early baseball. Interactions initially involved U.S. sailors and soldiers to the island; blacks were numbered among those in the military.[63] From the 1880s, we know that "crews aboard United States merchant vessels, often idle at Cuban ports for weeks, . . . organized themselves to play local Cuban Clubs. Cuban rivalry became a common aspect" of these exchanges.[64] It is likely that black men were also among these crews. Moreover, with the large provincial ports of Matanzas, Cárdenas, and Santiago de Cuba "being filled with U.S. ships"[65] during the sugar harvest, it is probable that it was Afro-Cubans who played against these ship teams. Afro-Cubans were both highly represented in the populations of these provinces and predominated as dock workers in all the ports of Cuba.[66] Thus, Afro-Cubans and black Americans probably came into considerable contact through baseball in the process of U.S. economic penetration.

One wonders if conflict arose in these exchanges. If resentment was expressed through baseball, it would surely have occurred during the U.S. occupation of 1898–1902.[67] By that time North American army posts were organizing baseball competitions between Cuban and U.S. soldiers and with local Cuban clubs. Some of the known matches were between the U.S. Seventh Cavalry and the Cubanos, U.S. Troop L and Matanzas, U.S. Battery K and Fin de Siglo,[68] and others. The all-black 25th Infantry was also there. While we do not possess evidence that this team specifically played in Cuba during the occupation, it is highly likely that it did. Formed in 1894, this unit became well known for playing baseball during the U.S. occupations of Hawaii and the Philippines. By 1914 they had become one of the premier military teams, beating most of their white compatriots.[69] As Pérez aptly wrote, "it can only be imagined what values and meanings were assigned to the outcome of games pitting the occupied against the occupiers,"[70] especially when both were black. On June 29, 1902, the Cuban "Committee of Veterans and Societies of the Colored Race" held a historic meeting at the Albizu Hotel in Havana to protest both the Platt Amendment and the rapid pace of Cuban and North American racism in the new republic.[71] A key organizer of the meeting, Juan Gualberto Gómez, had suggested some years earlier that baseball might "carry Cuba to . . . social and political development."[72] One wonders what he thought after 1902.

Blackness and Whiteness

Objective conditions and common interests, not paternalism or resentment, shaped the ensuing history of black American and Cuban interactions through baseball. According to baseball historian Donn Rogosin, African-Americans and Cubans both found themselves operating largely within a "black context."[73] Because of Cuba's demography and history, blacks, whites, and players of mixed racial backgrounds made up most Cuban professional teams. These integrated teams would then be designated as "black" in the polarized racial paradigm of the United States; the one-drop rule applied not just to individual players but to entire clubs. Thus, racially mixed Cuban teams were made to play on the black circuit.[74]

Most professional Cuban players played on one of Cuba's five big professional teams—Almendares, Santa Clara, Cienfuegos, Marianao, or Havana. Some players re-formed as the All-Cubans, Cuban Stars, Havana Stars, or Havana Red Sox to tour the summer black baseball circuit in the United States. Beginning in about 1910 at least two, and often three, Cuban teams regularly played in black American baseball; one toured the Midwest circuit, another played the East Coast, and one was often on tour in the South.[75] At times intact Cuban teams would also book tours. For example, Almendares came quite a few times and, like black American teams, played an array of city and regional black and white company-based clubs as well as ad hoc teams organized by small towns in need of entertainment and city promoters hoping to make fast money from ticket sales. They also played minor league, semiprofessional, and at times, major league franchises.[76] Short-lived clubs also emerged in North American cities to play in black city leagues, as well as in regional and even national associations.[77]

In 1917 a team called the Havana Cubans joined the black Chicago city league and was headquartered in the heart of the thriving black community known as Bronzeville. Its booking agent was the famous pitcher and Negro League founder, Rube Foster.[78] A *Chicago Defender* article applauded the fact that the famous players Juan Luis Padrón, Cristóbal Torriente, and José Méndez were on the team. Similarly, a Cuban Stars team was based in Cincinnati for the 1921 summer season. The team was made up of well-known players like Bienvenido "Hooks" Jiménez and H. "Pastor" Parda, and its games with black ball clubs were enthusiastically followed throughout that summer by the *Cincinnati Enquirer,* the city's major daily newspaper.[79] According to baseball organizer Willis Cumberland (Cum) Posey, "when the Cubans Stars . . . of Cincinnati . . . did not return to the United States the next year, fans of the west were deprived of the privilege of seeing one of the most colorful clubs, and one of the strongest baseball clubs ever assembled in any league."[80] Most of the Cuban Stars players continued competing in black baseball, either on all-Cuban teams or in largely black American clubs.

During the 1920s, Cubans had a team in the Midwest-based Negro National League called the Cuban Stars–West and one in the Eastern Colored League called the Cubans Stars–East. The two leagues organized four black world championship series (1924–1927), which, with expanding black urban communities, drew thousands of spectators in northern and southern cities. When these black leagues collapsed during the Depression, Cuban teams struggled to survive, just as the American teams did, and a few were always included in fluctuating new league structures. There was a short-lived East-West League in 1931–32 and a second National Negro League operated between 1933 and 1937. It was during this era that big East-West All Star games were inaugurated, and Cuban players such as Martín Dihigo, Luis Tiant Sr., Silvio García, and Orestes Arrieta Armas (Minnie) Minoso always appeared in All Star lineups. "The All-Star game became an annual classic and proved to be the biggest single event in black baseball each season."[81]

In 1937 a new realignment again organized the black teams into two groups: the new Negro American League (NNL) comprised teams from the Midwest and the South, and another Negro National League encompassed those of the East. For twelve years these two leagues held vigorous competitions and organized seven Negro World Series. Importantly, the Cuban Stars–East, who won the early Eastern Colored League pennant, went on to become Negro World Series champions in 1947. Cubans remained in organized black baseball until its final collapse in the 1950s. As Rogosin put it, "In every decade there were Cuban stars in black baseball and there was always . . . all-Cuban team[s].[82]

The integration of Cuban teams into American black baseball was thorough. Major black newspapers reported on Cuban players and their teams as regularly as they did any team of North American blacks. Havana was often a stop on the black circuit. Cuban clubs endured the grueling tour schedule that all black teams did, moving from one black urban cluster to another, often playing up to five games at each stop. For instance, the NNL schedule for the 1929 season, as reported in the *Chicago Defender,* had the Cuban Stars–West in Memphis on April 26, in Birmingham on April 29, back in Memphis on May 3, in Nashville on May 11, in St. Louis on May 18, in Chicago on May 25, back in Nashville on May 30, in Detroit on June 8, and in Kansas City on June 22.[83] However, the discomforts of constant travel were offset by the open arms and effusive enthusiasm that increasingly greeted all black teams in burgeoning black urban centers.

These communities were usually made up of first-generation immigrants from the rural South who joined a population that was rapidly expanding between the world wars. Black areas in Harlem, Detroit, Pittsburgh, Chicago, and Newark grew by nearly 250 percent between 1920 and 1950.[84] It was in this context that home teams, and not just the individual players, became "rallying points" and "unifying elements" for black communities involved in massive transition and socioeconomic development.[85] Indeed, comments Donn Rogosin, "[a] city without [at least one] Negro League team was almost by definition a second rate city."[86] Skilled players became heroes for a race in need of heroes; their teams became symbols for rapidly changing cities in need of new identities. Cubans such as Martín Dihigo joined this class of heroes and were followed by the press and by fans just as other black celebrities were.[87] Much like today, prominent ballplayers moved among black entertainers, politicians, and businessmen.[88] During the best of times for big black baseball clubs, players frequented the hottest night clubs and, while on the road, stayed in the best hotels black communities had to offer.[89]

Still, as young Cuban men—black, mixed race, and white—ventured into American baseball, they shared not only in the black community's pride but also in its struggle against the indignities of racism and segregation. During the regular season, teams played hotly contested games before large welcoming black city crowds; but in the off season they supplemented their incomes by playing in small, usually white, towns craving for any kind of baseball. Indeed, a majority of their games were barnstorming exhibitions held "wherever a profitable afternoon beckoned."[90] Cuban players, then, had two distinct experiences in the United States. In large black enclaves they associated with black celebrities, and fans clamored for autographs; but in segregated towns like Peoria, Little Rock, and Greensboro, they slept on cramped buses, ate crackers and sardines, were often forbidden to use bath and toilet facilities, and might be threatened or attacked if they happened to beat the local white team.[91]

The paradoxical life of black baseball is reflected in the divergent views of Cubans Luis Tiant Sr. and Minnie Minoso. When Luis Tiant Jr. wanted to play ball and asked his father, pitcher Luis Tiant Sr., about life in the Negro leagues, his father warned against it. Life on the road was brutal and American racism was harsh, he advised.[92] Refusing to be swayed, the son went on to become a talented and loved player. Minnie Minoso, on the other hand, always dreamed of a good life in the Negro leagues, and not just because he saw them as a stepping stone into the majors. He had seen the way Cubans adored Martín Dihigo and other "black context" players.[93] Blacks could make money, become famous, and be loved in the Negro leagues.[94]

Interestingly, a few phenotypically white Cubans were plucked from "black" teams to play in the white majors.[95] Their experiences are telling of a certain homologous racial identity that the United States applied equally to Cubans and to American blacks within its national borders. In many ways, all Cubans, no matter how white, were "black" in the eyes of most Americans. The 1911 controversy involving Rafael Almeida and Armando Marsans is a good example. Looking for cheaper players and long interested in the talented black player pool, Cincinnati Reds president Garry Hermann thought that securing white Cubans might be a solution. However, he and his manager, Clark Griffith, were concerned that Almeida and Marsans, who had toured the Negro circuit on Cuban teams, be able to "pass" as white among their fellow white players and in front of white fans.

Víctor Muñoz, a trusted scout in Cuba, was contacted about this concern. Muñoz vouched for the players' whiteness, assuring Hermann in a letter that he personally knew the parents of both players and "none of them have other but pure Caucasian blood in their veins, their claim to be members of the white race is as good as yours and mine."[96]

Local Cincinnati sportswriters were nevertheless skeptical and turned up the heat on the Reds management. According to baseball historians Lonnie Wheeler and John Baskin, Hermann was so nervous when he went to the train station to pick up his new players that he nearly had a heart attack when he mistook two Pullman porters for Almeida and Marsans.[97] The two Cubans proved to be suitably white, however, and when their pictures appeared in the paper, one reporter wrote: "Ladies and gentlemen, we have in our midst two descendants of a noble Spanish race, with no ignoble African blood to place a blot or spot on their escutcheons. Permit me to introduce two of the purest bars of Castillian soap that ever floated to these shores, senors Alameda [sic] and Marsans."[98] Perhaps there is justice in the fact that the two proved to be players of average talent and only played in Cincinnati for a season or two.

A few other Cubans passed the whiteness test and continued to play for years in the white major leagues. Strikingly, though, many found themselves, like their black brothers, the targets of taunts and racial slurs. According to eighteen-season major leaguer Ossie Bluege, "In those days, all Cuban ball players were called niggers."[99] This happened even to players of exceptional talent and those who were apparently white. Such was the case of Adolfo "Red" Luque, who after a brief stint with the Boston Braves[100] joined the Cincinnati Reds in 1918. Luque, "the Pride of Havana," was a star pitcher, and like his two predecessors, played with Negro league teams before joining the majors. While credited with taking the Reds to the World Series in both 1919 and 1923,[101] and known as the first Latin American to pitch in the white World Series,[102] he is often remembered in baseball lore as a "hot-headed" Cuban. He earned this reputation in August 1923, when the Reds were playing the New York Giants to an overflow crowd of nearly six thousand in Cincinnati's Redland Field. Throughout the game, Giants players directed a steady stream of racial epithets and insults toward Luque.[103] At a certain point, Luque, probably remembering his years with Boston, where he was often called nigger,[104] had had enough. He charged the Giants bench, and punched out Giants player Charles Dillon (Casey) Stengel; several people were required to pull him off Stengel.

After getting some water and apparently settling down, Luque grabbed a bat and calmly walked back to the Giants bench, ready to go at it again. This time he was thrown out of the game. Interestingly, the *Cincinnati Enquirer* reported sympathetically on Luque's actions.[105] Ossie Bluege had a similar view of the incident. When speaking of Luque, he said "those guys had their sense of national honor."[106]

Nonetheless, such name-calling was common. During the years (1935–49) when Cuban Roberto Estalella "integrated" the major leagues by playing with the Washington Senators, he was described as having the "retarding Negroid features of a Bantu tribesman" and called "a Freckled-faced, red-headed jig."[107] When another Cuban, Preston Gómez, joined him with the Senators in 1944, the white press made jokes about the "conga line in Washington's dug out,"[108] and Red Smith, the sportswriter, wrote that "there was a Senegambian somewhere in the Cuban batpile."[109] A teammate recalls that an opposing player once told Gómez, "you may be Cuban, but you're a nigger sonuvabitch to me."[110] In general, this "Latin era" in Washington stimulated a more narrowly constructed stereotype of Cubans and others from Spanish-speaking countries. Thus, layered on top of the antiblack diatribes were jibes about their "unusual" way of speaking English and their "hotheadedness." One player said, "I couldn't tell if he was cussing me out or not."[111] After all, he "jabbers away in their lingo."[112]

As these examples show, there was a definite connection between "black" and "Cuban" in the American popular psyche. This link was probably forged during the Cuban-Spanish-American War, as two currents in racial nationalism combined. One was defensive and domestically directed against blacks as "the perpetual foreigner" within, and the other was aggressive and externally directed at Indians, Hawaiians, Filipinos, mestizos, and "niggers" abroad. During the war, government statements, journalistic reports, war-inspired fiction, and even political cartoons "remapp[ed] the political coordinates" of Cuba's long revolutionary struggle.[113] Familiar racist stereotypes were trotted out to frame Cuba as "black" and thereby delegitimize its right to nationhood in the minds of white America. Then, Cuba's "inability" (because of U.S. occupation) to establish responsible government became a rationalization for continued white domination. Blacks, in this paradigm, could not be trusted with equality anywhere in the world. In fact, from 1900 to 1930, the Caribbean and Latin America as a whole were largely cast as "black" and "female" as justification for U.S. penetration and domination: They were too Indian, too mestizo, too black, too female, and too childlike to join the world of white masculine nations.[114] Amy Kaplan, in her careful analysis of Teddy Roosevelt's Rough Riders, illustrates the importance of the Cuban-Spanish-American War to the construction of racial identity. With Reconstruction firmly toppled and Jim Crow enshrined in law,

> external and internal fronts met to pose the question of the position of African Americans in relation both to the [United States] reconfigured by the Spanish American War and to the newly colonized subjects acquired by that war. Would these subjects be assimilated into a post-Reconstruction model of race relations at home and would the empire abroad facilitate the subjugation of blacks as colonized subjects at home?[115]

The answer to Kaplan's musings is a resounding yes.

Black Americans, like their white counterparts, also understood Cubans to be "black" in the U.S. racial context. As Nell Painter has argued, "for anyone living [during the early part of the century] the parallel between white supremacy at home and imperialism abroad was obvious.[116] This consciousness was displayed during the forays of Almeida, Marsans, Luque, Estalella, and every other Cuban who joined the majors. According to Donn Rogosin, the black press followed Cubans in the majors more than they did white players.[117] The reason was that the introduction of "white" Cubans into the majors was seen as the first step toward the integration of native-born black players. A September 1911 New York Age article made this vision explicit: "Now that the first shock is over, it would not be surprising to see a Cuban a few shades darker than Almeida and Marsans breaking into the professional ranks, with a coal-black Cuban on the order of the crack pitcher Mendez making his debut later on. . . . With the admission of Cubans of a darker hue in the two big leagues it would then be easy for [U.S.] colored players" to join their ranks.[118] There were rumors over the years that darker Cubans were in fact being considered for admission to the white majors. While José Méndez was clearly the best Cuban pitcher during the early part of the century, and all would have loved for the honor to have been his, his time slipped away in the teens. Cristóbal Torriente, a 1920s hard-hitter who was very fast and had a lifetime batting average of .339, was considered, supposedly because of his light skin. However, "his hair gave him away."[119] Martín Dihigo, widely considered the best all-around player in the 1920s, was just too dark, while Silvio García was told by Leo Durocher, some years later when Durocher managed the Brooklyn Dodgers, that he would surely sign him up "if [only] he could ... do ... something about that skin color."[120]

The reality was this: phenotypically black Cubans did not integrate the major leagues before black Americans did. They were all just too black. Some black American ballplayers resented those white Cubans who did secure positions on white major-league teams. Many of those players continued to play on integrated Cuban teams during the winter, which always had a good smattering of black Americans. Blacks thus had to play with whites who could live in two worlds and attain a salary and status forbidden to them. Black players also knew, because they played them regularly, that there were many among their own ranks more talented than the Cubans who broke into the majors; and they often commented on that and on white players' abilities in general.[121] To the white Cubans' credit, most recognized black talent and worked hard to maintain their friendships with blacks. After playing with and against racists in the majors during the regular season, playing in a black context must have been a welcome change for these men. Most probably deeply desired to maintain these baseball ties in Cuba. Some, in fact, continued to work for the best of the Negro leagues and maintained long-term friendships.

One example was Dolf Luque. After joining the majors, he managed the Havana, Almendares, and Marianao teams in Cuba. As manager, he employed many Negro league players and served as a scout in Cuba for various Negro league teams. He is also fondly remembered in baseball lore for praising the great José Méndez. This incident supposedly occurred in 1923, during a huge Havana parade honoring Luque for his role in Cincinnati's World Series win that year. According to Juanelo Mirabal, as he moved through the streets in a brand-new car that had been a gift of the Cuban people, Luque spotted an aging and sick (with tuberculosis) Méndez sitting on the sidelines. He stopped the procession and went over said, "You should have gotten this car, you're a better pitcher than I am. This parade should have been for you.[122]

The "blackness" and "in-betweenness" of white Cubans in the majors complicated notions of race in North American baseball. On one hand, some black Americans viewed these Cubans as "passing" and were outraged by that. For many, one was either black or white, and "passing" was viewed as denying one's heritage. This sensibility was heightened after World War I, which initiated a new era of discourse on racial pride and civil rights. The growth of black baseball, in fact, paralleled the rise of Marcus Garvey, the Harlem Renaissance, and the NAACP, the founding of the Brotherhood of Sleeping Car Porters,[123] the establishment of the Congress of Industrial

Organizations (CIO), the Scottsboro case, and the "don't buy where you can't work" campaigns. Thus, rumors were always afloat in black baseball circles about the black mothers of various white Cubans, which was seen as evidence of their passing. Black American players such as Chino Smith were known for resenting Cuban whites who played in the majors.[124]

Yet there were blacks as well as whites who sought to take advantage of a perceived softness of the "Cuban" color line. That same 1911 *New York Age* article had, in fact, encouraged U.S. blacks to "keep their mouths shut" so that they might "pass for Cubans." There are also many stories about white talent scouts desiring black players and musing about the possibility of black players' passing. Quincy Troupe wrote that in the late 1920s a white scout approached him after a game to ask if he was interested in playing in the big leagues. He suggested that Troupe go to a Latin American country, learn to speak Spanish, become acculturated, and then return and try out for the majors.[125] There is a much older "passing" story about Charlie Grant, who in this instance was encouraged to pass as an Indian. In 1901 John McGraw, then manager for the Baltimore Orioles, tried to sign Grant as a Cherokee named Chief Tokohama. As "Tokohama" practiced with the team during spring training, his true heritage was supposedly discovered and he was not signed.[126]

Otherness along the Color Line

Belief in a softness in the color line for Cubans and Indians is interesting. While it did lead to thorny, and sometimes erroneous, perceptions about the supposed advantages of being Cuban or Indian in North American baseball, the notion does provoke questions about U.S. hegemony over all peoples of color. Were blacks, Cubans, and Indians treated differently, and if so, in what ways? Was one group considered more of a threat than the others? How were perceived enemies constructed in U.S. racial discourse? And what impact did the "enemy," once constructed, have on relations between the racist culture and "its" people of color and among peoples of color themselves?

While it is beyond the reach of this essay to explore such questions, it seems important to touch upon them, for many Negro league players and blacks in general truly believed the color line to be more relaxed for Cubans, Indians, and other non-native blacks in the United States than for themselves. For instance, a cartoon appeared in a 1910 *Chicago Defender* daily edition depicting an Uncle Sam figure standing at a table to serve a New Year's dinner.

Portions of justice, opportunity, and good treatment are being dished out to five "Negroid" children who are labeled the Philippines, Hawaii, Puerto Rico, Cuba, and American Negroes. All the children have some of these "foods" in their bowls except the child representing the American Negro. On the front wall of the dining room is a sign that reads "Sweet Land of Liberty"; on the back wall a second sign reads "Land of the Free and Home of Race Riots." Under the entire scene a caption reads "Meone [My Own] Overlooked—As Usual."[127] A similar opinion was expressed in 1924 by DeHart Hubbard, a track and field star who was an owner of Negro league teams. He wrote, "A Cuban can play organized baseball, a Mexican is good enough to play, but never a man of [pure] African descent."[128] While the signs in the *Chicago Defender* cartoon articulate the contradictions embedded in American notions of freedom, with its denial of black Americans, history has shown that U.S. imperialism always took more than it gave to any of its semicolonial possessions. Similarly, Hubbard makes a sloppy analogy between Mexicans and Cubans inasmuch as most African-Americans knew that many Cubans, and possibly some Mexicans, were of obvious African descent.

Still, as has been shown, there were minor differences in white baseball's treatment of native-born blacks and other peoples of color. A few Caribbean, Latin American, and Native American players did penetrate the segregated majors when by all appearances blacks could not. In the analogy John Seymour suggests in his *House of Baseball,* Indians were in the basement of the white house of baseball, in the company of white derelicts and prisoners, while the blacks were in a separate outhouse structure.[129] But Indians were only permitted in the basement of the "main house" because they fulfilled criteria that most blacks could not, none of which were any less racist. In the minds of most twentieth-century whites, Indians were a "de-voiced," debilitated, and decreasing minority who had not been viewed as a threat since the late nineteenth century. Most had been killed through genocidal practices. Moreover, in the racist discourse of the day, Indians seem to suffer more from a "lack" of civilization and not from "bad" civilization, as blacks did; thus they might benefit from being "civilized" through baseball.[130] Finally, and very importantly, there were more Indians who, like Cubans, could pass the phenotypically white test than there were black Americans who could, even though one can count on one's hand the numbers of Indians who are known to have done so.

Cubans, like Indians, presented little threat inside the United States, even though the island itself remained ideologically untrustworthy because of its more relaxed attitudes toward racial mixing. (U.S. policy makers worked to circumscribe these with some success.) For most North Americans, Cubans were feminized colonial subjects, and as long as the island remained tightly under U.S. control and their "racial mixing" was contained there, white Americans felt little to fear from an occasional Cuban playing on a white team. In fact, Havana came to seem "exotic" in the white cultural schema largely *because* it was racially mixed and afforded a racially charged atmosphere. Middle-class white tourists traveled to Cuba to be temporarily absorbed in its "dusky" culture of Afro-Cuban music, dance, and religion without fear of a demise of white cultural hegemony. As long as "home" remained under tight white control, Cuba was a wonderful playground.[131]

Native-born blacks, however, were an integral part of that home, and so was white privilege. Whiteness and the power that came with it had to be defended against the push for black rights. In the minds of many whites, freedom and slavery, humanism and brutality, power and submission, and desire and disdain were rigidly constructed racial pendulums that swung in direct counterbalance to each other. If blacks were truly free, whites could never hope to be; if blacks had social and economic mobility, it must be because whites had lost theirs; if black culture attained respectability, Western civilization would be torn asunder. Thus, the specter of black equality on the baseball field, as in American life, caused psychic disorientation for many whites before the modern civil rights movement.[132] Only this level of psychic distress can explain the violent outrage of white fans, players, and owners at the sight of a "nigger on the field."[133] Open competition with blacks represented, for many whites, a challenge to their superior status and self-perceptions. It was this fear that led the commissioner of baseball, Kenesaw Landis, to ban white major league teams from competing against nonwhite clubs in 1923. Until that time, white major league clubs often held practice games with teams outside the majors during the winter months in Cuba. On more than a few occasions they were soundly defeated by Negro league and Cuban teams.

There were many ironies in segregated baseball, all of which point to—despite a nasty and virulent racism—the socially constructed and nonessentialist nature of race in sport. For instance, even though white fans, players, and owners were determined to preserve white privilege in sport, as in society, many nonetheless recognized, and thoroughly enjoyed watching, black talent. As we have pointed out, some whites enjoyed watching blacks compete against each other, especially in boxing and in horse racing; in fact, this was the reason behind the founding of the first black professional baseball team, the

Cuban Giants. There were always white fans who regularly attended the Negro league games in northern and southern cities. Moreover, there were also those white players who wanted to pit their skills against blacks. In fact, even after Landis's 1923 ban, which forbade intact major league clubs from competing against nonwhite organizations, there continued to be individual major leaguers who joined ad hoc formations during the off seasons and played teams of color in Cuba. Many local and regional white teams also played Negro league clubs. Of course, black teams were often treated poorly in the small towns in which they played, and they risked violence if they happened to beat local or regional favorites. Yet it is nonetheless interesting that a white promoter (usually) had invited them, a white team had agreed to play them, a landowner had offered a field for the game, and there were usually white fans ready to watch the contest. Obviously, competitive baseball was more important, at least at certain times (even if whites desperately hoped to defeat blacks), than maintaining the color line.

In addition, there were always white clubs who wanted to recruit black talent for the majors. While many baseball historians mention this yearning, most admit that it was nearly impossible to pass off black Americans as Cubans, let alone as white. Not only would scouts have to match talent with very light skin color, they would also have to find black players willing to forgo their families and their culture to pretend to be persons they were not in order to live in a world that was hostile to who they really were—just for the money. Most of course were not prepared to make such a sacrifice. However, according to Janet Bruce, there were more than a few black players who did pass. In fact, Bruce provocatively argues that skin color and not genealogy were the primary determinants in recruitment of players for white baseball.[134] Yet it is difficult to ascertain how many passed since doing so required one to live a public lie.

Nonetheless, the notion that white baseball was prepared to socially reconstruct a person's race, as was done in Hollywood, for the sake of building a winning (and therefore profitable) team is very telling. Baseball owners desirous of maintaining whiteness while securing black talent could only do so by forcing black players to become "white." That Cubans became a gauge for how black a "white" player could be in early baseball is also interesting. Many scouts and owners, wanting Cuban talent, used Cuba's more racially flexible paradigm to argue that some Cubans were really just "darker whites." Indeed, Cubans were given slightly more latitude by the owners. Yet, as was shown earlier, many fans and sports writers rejected such arguments, pointing to

Cubans' Spanish language and Afro-Latino culture as well as their color. Those Cubans who passed the whiteness tests continued to be questionable "whites" in what was nevertheless considered white baseball.

Manipulation of the color line was tolerated in white baseball as long as it could be proven to benefit the club. What was not negotiable was white cultural dominance and elite economic control of baseball as a whole. For this reason, the number of dark "white" Cubans and "previously black" players remained small among the major league rosters. The vast majority of black, Cuban, and other players of color continued to play within an expanding and increasingly joyful Negro league structure until the 1950s. Integration began to be considered only after the Negro leagues had gained in stature and economic clout. During the early 1940s, black teams were drawing tens of thousands of fans to their contests; their capital base and organizational capabilities were growing as well. Black entertainers such as Louis Armstrong and Lena Horne were beginning to invest in teams, and strong black players were beginning to make enough money during the regular season to live on. It was at this time that the white majors began to approach the Negro leagues, which had been calling for integration since the 1930s. What Negro league owners and their friends had sought was an integration of an intact Negro league structure, or at least whole teams that would remain under black ownership. Effa Manley, the only woman owner of a Negro league team (the Newark Eagles), was steadfast on this position. The major league owners and scouts, however, had another agenda. As always, they were interested in attracting black talent to their own teams while preserving their own dominance.

They began to work behind the scenes to identify players who were talented and, very importantly, had the "right attitude" to be the first openly black players on white major league teams. The "right attitude" meant a willingness to tolerate racism and to accept white domination of baseball in general. Not surprisingly, owners first thought of hiring a Cuban. According to baseball lore, Branch Rickey of the Brooklyn Dodgers first approached Silvio García, the dark Cuban infielder who played with the New York Cubans in the Negro leagues. Rickey posed a series of questions to test García's tolerance for racism and his general attitudes about race. He asked, "What would you do if a fan called you a nigger and spit on you?" Supposedly, García responded by saying, "I would take my knife out and cut him." This, of course, was not the right answer and Rickey continued his search. He found Jackie Robinson, who had also played in the Negro leagues but was prepared to tolerate knee-jerk racism and more for the sake of integration. In fact, Robinson's evolving political attitudes could not have served white baseball better. After joining the Brooklyn Dodgers, he went on to attack the Negro leagues and to support conservative agendas. While he led the way toward the integration of baseball, which most Americans began to see as a good thing, such a process was only possible with the demise of the Negro leagues and the maintenance of white domination in baseball. The fact that the Negro leagues continued functioning for over ten years alongside the integrated majors illustrates the determination of some owners, players, and loyal fans to keep them going. But once the white majors began to offer lucrative salaries to openly black and Cuban players, the Negro leagues could not compete. Black and Cuban baseball players were integrated into the major league structures with neither black nor Cuban owners among them.

NOTES

Acknowledgment: Parts of this essay that were originally in Spanish have been translated by the author unless otherwise indicated.

1. Information about Méndez comes from a baseball poster announcing the September 24–26, 1916, barnstorming series between the Indianapolis ABC's and the All-Nations, which Méndez pitched for. Poster displayed in Richard Bok's *Turkey Stearnes and the Detroit Stars: The Negro Leagues in Detroit, 1919–1933* (Detroit: Wayne State University Press, 1994), 54. For further discussion of Méndez's pitching skills, see "The Cuban Stars Baseball Team," *Half-Century Magazine,* vol. 7, no. 4 (October 1919): 8; John B. Holway, *Voices from the Great Black Baseball Leagues* (New York: DaCapo Press, 1992), 3–4; Bruce Chadwick, *When the Game was Black and White: The Illustrated History of Baseball's Negro Leagues* (New York: Abbeville Press, 1992), 33–34.

2. James A. Riley, *The Biographical Encyclopedia of the Negro Baseball Leagues* (New York: Carroll and Graf, 1994), 545; and John Holway, *Black Ball Stars: Negro League Pioneers* (Westport, Conn.: Meckler Books, 1988), 50–59.

3. This is not surprising given that Cubans had been part of earlier attempts to start black leagues in the United States in 1906 and in 1908. Both attempts failed, as did many attempts even by white players and owners. The NNL and ECL were the first national black leagues to succeed over time. For more information on pre-1920 attempts, see *Sol White's History of Colored Baseball, With Other Documents on the Early Black Game, 1886–1936,* comp. Jerry Malloy (Lincoln: University of Nebraska Press, 1995), 119–20; Donn Rogosin, *Invisible Men: Life in Baseball's Negro Leagues* (New York: Kodansha International, 1995), 11; Janet Bruce, *The Kansas City Monarchs: Champions of Black Baseball* (Lawrence: University of Kansas Press, 1985), 56–57.

4. Phil Dixon and Patrick J. Hannigan, *The Negro Baseball Leagues: A Photographic History* (Mattituck, N.Y.: Ameren House, 1992), 103; and Holway, *Black Ball Stars,* 38.

5. For a good discussion of how middle-class constructions of manliness during the latter nineteenth century emphasized self-restraint and the control of masculine passions—a goal that black men, because of their biologically determined "brutishness," could not achieve—see Gail Bederman, "Civilization, the Decline of Middle-Class Manliness, and Ida B. Wells's Antilynching Campaign (1892–94)," in *We Specialize in the Wholly Impossible: A Reader in Black Women's History,* ed. Darlene Clark Hine, Wilma King, and Linda Reed (New York: Carleson, 1995), 407–29. For a good analysis of the impact of manliness and race during the Cuban-Spanish-American War, see Amy Kaplan, "Black and Blue on San Juan Hill," in *Cultures of United States Imperialism,* ed. Donald E. Pease and Amy Kaplan (Durham, N.C.: Duke University Press, 1993).

6. Louis Pérez Jr., "Between Baseball and Bullfighting: The Quest for Nationality in Cuba, 1868–1898," *Journal of American History* 81 (Sept. 1994): 494.

7. Baseball had been integrated in the mid nineteenth century with players like Fleet Walker and George Stovey, among others. They were driven out of white major league play by the late 1880s. During the years of segregation, there were Cuban players of "dubious" racial background, such as Adolfo Luque, who played in the white majors.

8. Harold Seymour, *Baseball: The People's Game* (New York: Oxford University Press, 1990), 534.

9. Harold Seymour says about fifty-five black players played in integrated organized ball before the color line was drawn, while Sol White listed about seventy-eight in his registry (*Baseball: The People's Game,* 162–68; *Sol White's History,* 162–68).

10. Seymour, *Baseball: The People's Game,* 456.

11. There is a very good discussion of this process in David W. Zang, *Fleet Walker's Divided Heart: The Life of Baseball's First Black Major Leaguer* (Lincoln: University of Nebraska Press, 1995), pp. 38–39, 42–44, 54–56. Zang examines how Walker and other early black players were haunted by the changing political climate and increasingly overt racism in baseball. He details the role of Adrian "Cap" Anson, the player-manager of the Chicago White Stockings in the early 1880s, who made the ouster of blacks from baseball his "calling." Anson was the most consistent and vocal crusader demanding the ouster of blacks from the major leagues. Zang points out that remarks by Anson and other whites in baseball reveal that the ouster of blacks had much to do with white fear of defeat by blacks in sport and what that would mean for white power. For another good discussion see William M. Kimok, "Black Baseball in New York State's Capital District, 1907–1950," *Afro-Americans in New York Life and History,* October 1, 1992, vol. 15–18, pp. 42–43.

12. Zang, *Fleet Walker's Divided Heart,* 19.

13. Dale Somers, *The Rise of Sports in New Orleans, 1850–1900* (Baton Rouge: Louisiana State University Press, 1972), 117.

14. Twain is quoted in Somers, *The Rise of Sports,* 115.

15. Seymour, *Baseball: The People's Game,* 534.

16. Lisa Brock, "Back to the Future: African-Americans and Cubans in the Time(s) of Race," *Contributions in Black Studies* 12 (1993): 18

17. J. Thomas Jable, "Sport in Philadelphia's African-American Community, 1865–1900," in *Ethnicity and Sport in North American History and Culture,* ed. George Eisen and David K. Wiggins (Westport, Conn.: Praeger, 1995), 159.

18. This is a term used by Willard B. Gatewood to describe northern black elites such as these; see his *Aristocrats of Color: The Black Elite, 1880–1920* (Bloomington: Indiana University Press, 1990). Jable also confirms that a majority were indeed light skinned, which supports Gatewood's position that there was a color preference among blacks of some income ("Sport in Philadelphia's African-American Community," 159). Zang mentions this issue as well (*Fleet Walker's Divided Heart,* 81).

19. For a discussion of this incident, see Mark Ribowsky, *A Complete History of the Negro Leagues, 1884–1955* (New York: Birch Lane Press, 1995), 13–15; Seymour, *Baseball: The People's Game,* 537–38; Jable, "Sport in Philadelphia's African-American Community," 162–64.

20. Pynthian records and minutes of meetings, which were often signed, are examined in Seymour, *Baseball: The People's Game,* 537–38; and Jable, "Sport in Philadelphia's African-American Community," 162–64. This incident as well as others are discussed in these sources.

21. See Seymour, *Baseball: The People's Game,* 537–38, and Jable, "Sport in Philadelphia's African-American Community," 162–64.

22. Numerous members are mentioned in the literature on the club, which indicates that they engaged in a variety of activities. The multifunctional nature of black clubs was to continue in black baseball.

23. Seymour, *Baseball: The People's Game,* 537; Jable, "Sport in Philadelphia's African-American Community," 164–65.

24. David K. Wiggins has in fact analyzed the inevitable double consciousness involved in black participation in American sport, in which there has always been little room "to deviate from accepted white standards of performance and forge any notion of racial consciousness." Despite this, he notes, "black athletes devised an assortment of responses . . . that served both as a palliative and a source of liberation." See David Wiggins, "The Notion of Double Consciousness and the Involvement of Black Athletes in American Sport," in Eisen and Wiggins, *Ethnicity and Sport,* 134.

25. Seymour, *Baseball: The People's Game,* 536.

26. Ibid., 537.

27. Pérez, "Between Baseball and Bullfighting," 506.

28. Ibid.

29. Ibid., 493.

30. Paula J. Pettavino and Geralyn Pye, *Sport in Cuba: The Diamond in the Rough* (Pittsburgh: University of Pittsburgh Press, 1994), 40–41.

31. Rob Ruck, "Baseball in the Caribbean," in *Total Baseball,* ed. John Thorn and Pete Palmer (New York: HarperPerennial, 1989), 533.

32. Many scholars confirm this role of Cuban baseball players. For more discussion see Alan M. Klein, *Sugarball: The American Game, the Dominican Dream* (New Haven: Yale University Press, 1991), pp. 16–17, 32; and Gilbert M. Joseph, "Forging the Regional Pas-

time: Baseball and Class in Yucatán," in *Sport and Society in Latin America: Diffusion, Dependency, and the Rise of Mass Culture* (New York: Greenwood Press, 1988), pp. 30–31, 33–34.

33. Pérez, "Between Baseball and Bullfighting," 494.

34. Ibid., 513.

35. Pérez does mention what appears to be a chapter of an edited book written in the early part of the century. The chapter is "El baseball y la raza de color" (Baseball and the colored race) in *El base ball en Cuba y América,* ed. Rámon S. Mendoza, José María Herrero, and Manuel F. Calcines (Havana, 1908).

36. Information on team names was collected from many baseball books, including *Sol White's History of Colored Baseball;* Dick Clark and Larry Lester, eds., *The Negro Leagues Book* (Cleveland: Sabir Press, 1994); and Seymour's *Baseball: The People's Game.*

37. Somers, *The Rise of Sports in New Orleans,* pp. 120, 126.

38. Jable, "Sport in Philadelphia's African-American Community," 175.

39. Dixon and Hannigan, *The Negro Baseball Leagues,* 32; and Seymour, *Baseball: The People's Game,* 539.

40. Interestingly, Cuban ball clubs were doing exactly the same thing at the same time. A team called Yara was formed in 1876 in Matanzas, a region particularly known for slave revolts during the nineteenth century. The "Grito de Yara" proclaimed the rebellion that signaled the Ten Years War. Another team selected Anacaona as their name "after the Taína Indian princess who perished resisting the Spanish conquest." Pérez, "Between Baseball and Bullfighting," 511.

41. Naming in general was one of the many ingenious methods used by blacks to subvert white power and assert their humanity during and after slavery. It was, in fact, a highly contested terrain, an area of psychic privacy that was consistently violated by whites. Whites could call blacks literally anything. Most common was what Kevin Gaines has called "the first name address" for blacks of any age by whites of any age. Use of "Mister," "Missus," or "Miss" was rare, even by a young white person addressing an older black. Of course, whites could and often did call blacks "boy" or "girl." Blacks, however, were forced to show whites "respect" by using the proper honorific in combination with the last name for adults and the first name for children—Mrs. Smith, Mr. Jim. It was not uncommon for black parents to name their children President, General, Queen, or even Mister and Miss as a way to compel some semblance of social respect from whites. For discussion see Kevin Gaines, *Uplifting the Race: Black Leadership, Politics, and Culture in the Twentieth Century* (Chapel Hill: University of North Carolina Press, 1996), 55–56. For additional mention of the popularity of Maceo's name in the United States, see Philip Foner, *Antonio Maceo: "The Bronze Titan" of Cuba's Struggle for Independence* (New York: Monthly Review Press, 1977), 267–68; and José Yglesias, "Martí in Ybor City," in *José Martí in the United States: The Florida Experience,* ed. Louis A. Pérez Jr. (Tempe: Arizona State University, Center for Latin American Studies, 1995), 108.

42. There is much evidence placing both Cuban and black teams in these cities at exactly the same time. In addition to Louis Pérez Jr. and Seymour, see Mark Ribowsky, *The*

Negro Leagues, 20–21; Gerald E. Poyo, "The Cuban Experience in the United States, 1865–1940: Migration, Community and Identity," *Cuban Studies* 21 (1991): 19–36.

43. Brock, "Back to the Future," 19.

44. Ibid.

45. Robert Peterson, *Only the Ball Was White: A History of Legendary Black Players and All-Black Professional Teams* (New York: Oxford University Press, 1970), 60; Rogosin, *Invisible Men,* 153; Dixon and Hannigan, *The Negro Baseball Leagues,* pp. 42, 102.

46. "The Cuban Stars Baseball Team," *Half-Century Magazine,* vol. 7, no. 4 (Oct. 1919): 8; *Sol White's History,* 46; Clark and Lester, *Negro Leagues Book,* 57.

47. Peterson, *Only the Ball Was White,* 60–61; and Rogosin, *Invisible Men,* 61–62.

48. The *Indianapolis Freeman* is quoted in Dixon and Hannigan, *The Negro Baseball Leagues,* 43, but with no date. We might assume that the piece appeared sometime during 1909 or 1910 because it was in those years that both Petway and Lloyd played on the famous Havana Reds, a team that defeated the white American League's Detroit Tigers in numerous games. For discussion, see Holway, *Black Ball Stars,* 36–41, among other sources.

49. Mark Ribowsky, *The Negro Leagues,* 21–22; Julius Tygiel, "Black Ball," in Thorn and Palmer, *Total Baseball,* 488.

50. Riley, *Biographical Encyclopedia,* 202–3.

51. For discussion of both these issues, see Wiggins, "The Notion of Double-Consciousness," 133–56. Sol White, Donn Rogosin, and others remark on the development of performance in black baseball. White audiences often had difficulty viewing blacks as highly skilled players, and encouraging them to "act out" reduced whites' uneasiness with black talent. Blacks quickly learned that beating a local white team while barnstorming could provoke problems. Thus they too might deliberately "ham it up" and, given the situation, purposefully lose rather than risk the anger of white racism. For a good discussion of how blacks used "performance" to make a living while subverting white expectations, see Kimok, "Black Baseball in New York State's Capital District," 41–74.

52. Quoted in *Sol White's History,* xxv.

53. Ibid., xxxvi.

54. Ibid.

55. Ibid., xxxix–xl.

56. *Sporting Life,* April 11, 1896, quoted in ibid., xxxv.

57. Rogosin, *Invisible Men,* 61.

58. Articles from the *Cincinnati Enquirer,* May 10, 1911, and the *Chicago Defender,* July 10, 1915, say as much, but so do many baseball scholars of this era. For broad discussion on the appeal of Cuban ballplayers, see Charles E. Whitehead, *A Man and His Diamonds: A Story of Andrew "Rube" Foster and His Famous American Giants* (New York: Vantage Press, 1980), pp. 26, 46, 50, 71.

59. See Kevin Gaines, "Black Americans' Racial Uplift Ideology as 'Civilizing Mission': Pauline E. Hopkins on Race and Imperialism," in Pease and Kaplan, *Cultures of United States Imperialism,* 437.

60. White also says this (*Sol White's History,* 89–91).

61. *Philadelphia Tribune,* June 1, 1912.

62. Clark and Lester, *Negro Leagues Book,* 57–59; *Sol White's History,* 32.

63. Willard B. Gatewood Jr., *Smoked Yankees and the Struggle for Empire: Letters from Negro Soldiers, 1898–1902* (Urbana: University of Illinois Press, 1971), 6–8. Bruce, *Kansas City Monarchs,* 20–21. Many players on the first (1920) Kansas City Monarchs Team were from the 25th Infantry, so many that the Monarchs were sometimes known as the "army team."

64. Pérez, "Between Baseball and Bullfighting," 504.

65. Ibid.

66. The first known Cuban labor union was formed in 1812 by dockworkers in the town of Regla near Havana. It was organized by Afro-Cubans who were largely members of black Cuba's *cabildos* (black societies) and practitioners of Abakua, a religion with African origins. The union and Abakua spread to Cárdenas and Matanzas very early. By 1900 these Afro-Cubans are said to have had a virtual monopoly over dockworkers.

67. Pérez, "Between Baseball and Bullfighting," 515.

68. Ibid., 516.

69. Dixon and Hannigan, *The Negro Baseball Leagues,* 79.

70. Pérez, "Between Baseball and Bullfighting," 516.

71. Tomás Fernández Robaina discusses this historic meeting in "The 20th Century Black Question," in *Afro-Cuban: An Anthology of Cuban Writing on Race, Politics and Culture,* ed. Pedro Pérez Sarduy and Jean Stubbs (Melbourne, Australia: Ocean Press, 1993), 93.

72. Pérez, "Between Baseball and Bullfighting," 513.

73. Rogosin, *Invisible Men,* 153. Many writers examine this black context of baseball. See Peter C. Bjarkman, *Baseball with a Latin Beat* (Jefferson, N.C.: McFarland Publishers, 1994), 171–82; Orestes (Minnie) Minoso, with Fernando Fernández and Bob Kleinfelder, *Extra Innings: My Life in Baseball* (Chicago: Regbery Gateway, 1983), 132; Peterson, *Only the Ball Was White,* 61.

74. The one-drop rule was clearly evident in the placement of a team called the All Nations in black baseball. Led by J. L. (Wilkie) Wilkinson, the All Nations was composed of Cubans, black Americans, Hawaiians, Mexicans, Asians, whites, and one women known as Carrie Nation, who played second base. The team was known as a "black" team and played on the black circuit between 1912 and 1918. Bruce, *Kansas City Monarchs,* 15–17.

75. In 1929 a team called the Havana Red Sox toured the South—Shreveport, Atlanta, and other cities (*Chicago Defender,* March 16, 1929). In 1940 the Cuban Stars–East played a series of games against the Newark Eagles: in Savannah, Georgia, on April 20, in Augusta, Georgia, on April 21, and in Savannah again on April 24. The two teams moved throughout Georgia and North Carolina, playing twelve games in total by May 2 (*Pittsburgh Courier,* April 20, 1940). Minoso also discusses playing in the South (see his *Extra Innings,* 33–35; and Brock, Cunningham, and Baez, Minnie Minoso interview, Chicago, Dec. 11, 1996).

76. In the summer of 1915, Almendares toured the United States. On August 6 the team beat New York's Empire City in New York 9 to 4, and on August 20 they beat Cam-

den City 10 to 6. On August 6, 1915, the black Lincoln Giants beat the Havana Stars 8 to 4 at Olympia Field in New York City (*Chicago Defender,* August 7, 1915, and *Chicago Defender,* August 21, 1915).

77. There was a Cuban team in New Jersey called the "Long Branch Cubans," who played not only on the black circuit but also the white majors; some sources indicate that this was largely a white team. On August 6, 1915, the Long Branch Cubans beat the New York Yankees 2 to 1 (*Chicago Defender,* August 7, 1915). On September 1, 1917, the Long Branch Cubans beat the New York–based Cuban Stars 3 to 1 (*Chicago Defender,* September 2, 1916.

78. Chicago *Defender,* March 31, 1917). The Chicago City League is also mentioned in Dixon and Hannigan, *The Negro Baseball Leagues,* 104, and Ribowsky, *Negro Leagues,* 68–69.

79. *Cincinnati Enquirer,* July 21, 1921.

80. Willis Cumberland (Cum) Posey was an average black ballplayer who became well known as the owner-manager of the Pittsburgh Homestead Greys. He became a member of the new National Negro League of the 1930s and was a sports columnist for the *Pittsburgh Courier.* Cum Posey, "Posey's Points," *Pittsburgh Courier,* April 20, 1940.

81. James Overmeyer, *Effa Manley and the Newark Eagles* (Metuchen, N.J.: Scarecrow Press, 1993), 31–32. For more discussion of the importance of All-Star games, see Riley, *Biographical Encyclopedia,* xviii; Dixon and Hannigan, *The Negro Baseball Leagues,* 161–67; Ribowsky, *Negro Leagues,* pp. 171, 176–77. Minoso stated that he had never before seen so many blacks in one place as he did at these All Stars games (Brock, Cunningham, and Baez, Minnie Minoso interview, Chicago, Dec. 11, 1996.

82. Rogosin, *Invisible Men,* 61–62.

83. *Chicago Defender,* April 6, 1929. The Cuban Stars–East also made the circuit during the 1920s playing Pennsylvania's Hilldale team, the Atlantic City, N.J., Bachrach Giants, the Baltimore Black Sox, the Brooklyn Royal Giants, and the New York–based Lincoln Giants. *Amsterdam News,* June 17, 1923.

84. According to Richard Bok, Philadelphia's population climbed from 84,000 in 1910 to 134,000 in 1920; in the same period Chicago's rose from 44,000 to 109,000, and Detroit's went from 6,000 to 41,000 (Bok, *Turkey Stearnes and the Detroit Stars,* 36). According to Rob Ruck, Pittsburgh's black population rose from 20,000 in 1900 and to approximately 50,000 in 1930 (Rob Ruck, *Sandlot Seasons: Sport in Black Pittsburgh* [Urbana: University of Illinois Press, 1993], 9–10). According to Erma Watkins-Owen, the black population of New York City went from 60,000 in 1900 to 338,000 in 1930; it has the highest concentration of Caribbean-born immigrants in the United States. See Watkins-Owen, *Blood Relations: Caribbean Immigrants in the Harlem Community, 1900–1930* (Bloomington: Indiana University Press, 1996), 4.

85. Rogosin, *Invisible Men,* 93–95.

86. Ibid., 93.

87. Bjarkman, *Baseball with a Latin Beat* (219–22), and Holway, *Black Ball Stars* (244), talk about the famed Dihigo and other Cubans in the black communities.

88. For another rich discussion of black urban life and baseball in the mid-twentieth

century, see Amiri Baraka, *The Autobiography of LeRoi Jones* (New York: Freundlich Books, 1984). Joe Louis, Bill "Bojangles" Robinson, and Louis Armstrong became intimately involved in black ball clubs as owners, entertainers, and even players. At series openings Lena Horne and dozens of other celebrities threw out the first ball or paraded before, during, or after big games. Some black ballplayers married entertainers; for instance, Frank Duncan of the Monarchs married jazz recording artist Julia Coles. See Dixon and Hannigan, *The Negro Baseball Leagues,* 105. Minnie Minoso confirmed the "star" ties when he said that Sarah Vaughn and Nat "King" Cole were good friends of his (Brock, Cunningham and Baez, Minnie Minoso interview, Chicago, Dec. 11, 1996).

89. Interestingly, Rogosin lists the Hotel Nacional in Havana among such hotels. Others included the Theresa and Woodside in Harlem, the Vincennes and Grand in Chicago, the Gotham in Detroit, the Dunbar in Los Angeles, the Grand on Market Street in Newark, the Street Hotel at Eighteenth and Paseo in Kansas City, and the Rush Hotel on Fourteenth Street in Birmingham (Rogosin, *Invisible Men,* 101).

90. Ibid., 118.

91. Theodore Rosengarten, "Reading the Hops: Recollections of Lorenzo Piper Davis and the Negro Baseball Leagues," *Southern Exposure* 5, nos. 2–3 (1977): 67; and Kimok, "Black Baseball in New York State's Capital District," pp. 41, 44.

92. Holway, "Will the Real Luis Tiant Stand Up," *Baseball Digest,* Jan. 2, 1976, 74–78.

93. Brock, Cunningham, and Baez, Minnie Minoso interview, December 11, 1996; Minoso, *Extra Innings,* pp. 12, 13, 31, 32; Minnie Minoso with Herb Fagan, *Just Call Me Minnie: My Six Decades in Baseball* (Champaign, Ill.: Sagamore Publications, 1994), 23; Bjarkman, *Baseball with a Latin Beat,* 223.

94. No individual represents the centrality of Cubans in black baseball better than Alessandro (Alex) Pómpez. He was the prime mover behind Cuban teams operating in the United States. He rose, like Sam Greenlee and Effa Manley, to be synonymous with organized baseball in the black community. Like them, he entered organized baseball with a capital base accrued as a banker in Harlem's prolific numbers racket. It appears he was born in Tampa of Cuban parents. Even though Pómpez may have been considered mulatto in a Latin American racial context, he clearly operated in Harlem's black social life. He was the owner, manager, and promoter of the Cuban Stars during the second decade of the century and brought them into the Eastern Colored League in 1923. In 1935 he reorganized his team as the New York Cubans and based them in a stadium that he leased in upper Harlem (around 240th Street) called the Dyckman Oval. In 1941 his New York Cubans were in the Negro National League championship playoff, and in 1947 his team won the NNL flag and the Negro World Series.

95. White owner desire to secure black players was discussed as early as 1919 in a periodical *The Half Century Magazine* (vol. 7, no. 4 [Oct. 1919]). Also see Bjarkman, *Baseball with a Latin Beat,* 198.

96. Victor Muñoz to Garry Hermann, June 17, 1911, Hermann Papers, National Baseball League, quoted in Robert F. Burk, *Never Just a Game: Players, Owners and American Baseball to 1920* (Chapel Hill: University of North Carolina Press, 1994), 181–82.

97. Lonnie Wheeler and John Baskin, *The Cincinnati Game* (Wilmington, Ohio: Orange Frazier Press, 1988), 174–75; also see Lee Allen, *The Cincinnati Reds* (New York: Putman, 1948), 96.

98. Burk, *Never Just a Game,* 182.

99. Robert Heuer interviews the veteran ballplayer Ossie Bluege in an essay about Minnie Minoso, "Chicago's First Black Ball Player Came via the Cuban Connection," *Chicago Reader,* May 5, 1987, 18.

100. Daniel C. Frio and Marc Onigman, "'Good Field, No Hit': The Image of Latin American Baseball Players in the American Press, 1871–1946," *Revista/Review Interamericana,* Summer 1979, 203.

101. Riley, *Encyclopedia of the Negro Leagues,* 498.

102. Bjarkman, *Baseball with a Latin Beat,* 26.

103. *Cincinnati Enquirer,* August 8, 1923, 26.

104. Frio and Onigman, "'Good Field, No Hit,'" 203.

105. The *Cincinnati Enquirer* of August 8, 1923, carried a cartoon serial on the entire Luque incident, treating it as if it were a boxing match. The paper's tone indicated that even they thought Luque was not wrong for defending his pride.

106. Heuer, "Chicago's First Black Ball Player," 18.

107. Ibid., 19–20.

108. Ibid., 20.

109. Jules Tygiel, *Baseball's Great Experiment: Jackie Robinson and His Legacy* (New York: Oxford University Press, 1983), 25–26. The *Pittsburgh Courier* followed the treatment of Cubans in Washington; see issues dated Nov. 3, 1945, and May 25, 1940.

110. Heuer, "Chicago's First Black Ball Player," 20.

111. *Washington Post,* March 14, 1944, 14.

112. *Washington Post,* March 21, 1945, 15.

113. Amy Kaplan, "Black and Blue on San Juan Hill," 222.

114. For good discussion of this see John Johnson, *Latin America in Caricature,* (Austin: University of Texas Press, 1993), 17.

115. Kaplan, "Black and Blue on San Juan Hill," 220.

116. Nell Irvin Painter's comment from *Standing at Armageddon: The United States, 1877–1919* (New York: Norton, 1987), 161, is quoted in Gaines, "Black Americans' Racial Uplift," 436.

117. William Donn Rogosin, "Black Baseball: The Life in the Negro Leagues" (Ph.D. diss., University of Texas at Austin, May 1981), 61.

118. *New York Age,* Sept. 28, 1911.

119. Holway, *Black Ball Stars,* 126.

120. Rogosin, *Invisible Men,* 182.

121. Dolf "Red" Luque competed in the Cuban Winter League for thirty-four years, from 1912 to 1946. For the Negro leaguers, both the Afro-Americans and Cubans, he was a consistent measure of their skills against white major league players. Dolf's name—as a

player, coach, and manager—appears more than any other name in black baseball literature of the day.

122. Holway, *Black Ball Stars,* 59.

123. Until the mid 1920s, Cuban teams, like all black clubs, traveled by train and were attended to by Pullman sleeping car porters, who in the 1920s had formed the powerful Brotherhood of Sleeping Car Porters union. A relationship developed between these two sets of traveling blacks, so much so that John Henry (Pop) Lloyd, the black player that Babe Ruth called the best player of their era (1900–1920), is said to have worked with A. Philip Randolph, popular founder of the Porter's union.

124. Bjarkman, *Baseball with a Latin Beat,* 199–204.

125. Quincy Troupe, *Twenty Years Too Soon* (Los Angeles: S & S Enterprises, 1977), 42.

126. Bruce, *Kansas City Monarchs,* 288; Peterson, *Only the Ball Was White,* 54–57; *Sol White's History,* 78–79; Dixon and Hannigan, *The Negro Baseball Leagues,* 92, Ribowsky, *Negro Leagues,* 53–54.

127. "The New Year Dinner," *Chicago Defender,* January 1, 1910.

128. Hubbard is quoted in Dixon and Hannigan, *The Negro Baseball Leagues,* 248.

129. See Seymour's chapter on Indians (*Baseball: The People's Game,* 379–95).

130. For a good discussion of the social construction of "the Indian," see Robert Berkhofer Jr., *The White Man's Indian: Images of the American Indian from Columbus to the Present* (New York: Random House, 1978).

131. During the era of colonialism in Africa, the Portuguese-controlled city of Lourenço Marques (now Maputo) in Mozambique provided a very similar "exotic" atmosphere for the racially rigid South Africans. Later key bantustans inside South Africa were set up to provide highly controlled but integrated zones for entertainment purposes, such as in the famous Sun City in Bophuthatswana. Yet integration of the sort seen in Cuba or in Lourenço Marques was not possible inside the United States or South Africa, where white control had to be strictly maintained. In the United States, the closest examples were "tourist" pockets such as the Cotton Club in Harlem, in which all the customers were white and the entertainment was black. While technically integrated, whites and blacks for the most part did not mix. However, New York's Savoy Ballroom was a direct challenge to this exoticization of black culture. For a time the majority of the Savoy's customers were black and Latino, and whites were a minority; all engaged in mixed dancing. Interestingly, it became such a site of "equality" that Mayor La Guardia temporarily closed it down in 1943. For a good discussion of the Savoy see Russell Gold, "Guilty of Syncopation, Joy, and Animation: The Closing of Harlem's Savoy Ballroom," *Studies in Dance History* 5, no. 1 (Spring 1994): 5–64. Also see Bruce M. Tyler, *From Harlem to Hollywood: The Struggle for Racial and Cultural Democracy, 1920–1943* (New York: Garland Publishers, 1995), 223–40.

There has also been considerable discussion on gender and tourism. Linda Carty's "Women in Caribbean Tourism: The 'Unlabeled' Commodities" offers a good theoretical understanding (paper presented for the Fifth Conference of North American and Cuban

Philosophers, June 18–July 3, 1993, Havana). "Dusky" was a term commonly used in the press between about 1900 and 1950 to describe Cubans.

132. Such relations between the oppressor and the oppressed group are not atypical, though: they exist between Spanish and mestizo Creoles and Indians in Guatemala, the French and Algerians in France, and even the Anglos and Chicanos and Indians in the southwestern part of the United States.

133. This comment was so common that Art Russ Jr. used it for the title of his book. See *Get that Nigger off the Field* (New York: Tiger Publishing, 1984).

134. Bruce, *The Kansas City Monarchs*, 5.

9

Cuban Social Poetry and the Struggle against Two Racisms

CARMEN GÓMEZ GARCÍA

The Middle Passage
and the plantation economy
after centuries of sweat and anaemia
turned our West Indies
into an eternally indestructible outcrop of solidarity.
Pedro Pérez Sarduy, "Cumbite"

Poets should not be seen as removed from everyday life, as people whose literary production is disconnected from the social reality that surrounds them. Rather, the reverse should be true: poets are rooted in a given society, and their work can be read as a more or less lyrical rendering of it. When a poet's work is of a high artistic caliber and the poet identifies with the concerns of the people, the poet can contribute to the transformation of his or her society. The poet's impact increases with the depth and breadth of his or her vision and his or her ability to reflect with vitality and veracity and harmony and beauty the concerns of the time.

Few poets in early Cuban history are known to be of African descent, yet slavery became a common social theme from very early on. This is seen more clearly in the nineteenth century, when poets of color added their perspective on what was increasingly seen as Cuba's principal social ill. A key difference between Cuba and the United States with respect to race is that black people were rarely seen as tangential to Cuban society. Unlike in the United States, their numbers were quite large—50 or 60 percent of the population at times—and their presence and participation in society as a whole could not be ignored. It is therefore not surprising that the hero of Cuba's first known poem, the "Espejo de paciencia" (Mirror of Patience) by

Silvestre de Balboa (1608), was black. The protagonist's name was Salvador Golomón, and he was famous in Cuban lore for having killed the pirate Gilberto Girón in fierce combat in order to free the kidnapped bishop Juan de las Cabezas Altamirano.

During the nineteenth century, the abolition of slavery and the rise of Cuban nationalism appeared as themes in Cuban poetry. Touched by their society's dreams and desires, many poets envisioned a unified nation free of slavery. After independence, poets of color continued to speak in verse of continuing racial indignities and to call for a republic free of all forms of racism. To these concerns was added the omnipresent United States imperialism. Cuban social poets, both black and white but especially those of color, captured with energy and clarity, as well as passion and depth, Cuba's deepening hostility to U.S. domination and its particular forms of racism and capitalism. Nationalism, antiracism, and socialism all infused Cuban's growing sense of *cubanidad* (national spirit) and their poetry.

Slavery and Nationalism

The introduction of the steam engine (1819), the vacuum boiler (1840), and the first centrifuge led to a crisis of the slave-holding economy. New labor-saving technology was making the use of slave labor less profitable. In response, the more progressive sectors of the Cuban land-holding and slave-owning bourgeoisie began to contemplate the national future. Initially, they considered eliminating the infamous black slave trade, and this raised the possibility of abolishing slavery itself. Some even began to call for an end to Spanish colonialism. These sentiments were reflected in the verses of many of Cuba's most notable nineteenth-century poets. Interestingly, many of the early nationalist poets saw slavery not simply as a problem for blacks but as a morally bankrupt system that corrupted all those around it. In his "Hymn of the Exile" José María Heredia, Cuba's leading poet of the early independence era, addresses the moral malaise that slavery engendered in Cuban society:

> Dulce Cuba en tu seno se miran,
> en el grado más alto y profundo,
> las bellezas del físico mundo,
> los horrores del mundo moral.
> Te hizo el cielo la flor de la tierra;

mas tu fuerza y destino ignoras,
y de España en el déspota adoras
al demonio sangriento del mal.

¿Ya que importa que al cielo te tiendas
de verdura perenne vestida
y la frente de palmas ceñida
a los besos ofrezcas del mar,
si el clamor del tirano insolente,
del esclavo el gemir lastimoso
y el crujir del azote horroroso
se oye solo en tus campos sonar?[1]

(Sweet Cuba in your breast one sees,
to the highest and deepest degree,
the beauties of the natural world,
the horrors of the moral world.
Heaven made you the flower of the earth
but your strength and fate you ignore
and of despotic Spain you adore
the bloody demon of evil.

What does it matter that to heaven you show off
dressed in perennial green
and the front of palm trees pressed
to the kisses you offer from the sea,
if the clamor of the insolent tyrant,
the painful moaning of the slave
and the cracking of the horrible whip
resound throughout the countryside?)

Blacks, of course, did not wait for the bourgeoisie to comment on slavery, but must have done so themselves in their songs and verses from the time of their first arrival in Cuba. Yet we have few of their poems written in Spanish from the early centuries. Despite this fact, Ramón Guirao in his *Orbita de la poesía afrocubana* (1938) managed to collect a series of anonymous poems inspired by black slaves and free blacks in the late eighteenth and early nineteenth centuries. These poems illustrate that blacks were less concerned with the moral implications of slavery than with the poverty and indignity it brought to their lives. Mirta Aguirre also reproduced some of that anonymous poetry from the nineteenth century in an essay she wrote entitled "Poesía and cubanía." One of the poems appears below.

Mayorá su messé
que cosa bamo jassé
Yo tumbo la caña,
yo yena carreta
y lleva trapiche
que jora comé?[2]

(Foreman your grace
what ever are we going to do
I cut down the cane,
I fill the cart
and take it to the sugar mill
what is there to eat now?)

By the mid nineteenth century, Cuba's free population of color had expanded. Especially vocal about racial discrimination, it added its particular vision and strength to the growing abolitionist and nationalist movements. In fact, as Cuba grew rife with political agitation, anti-Spanish conspiracies, and slave rebellions, so did its poetry. Free black and mulatto poets began to attain prominence. Juan Francisco Manzano, representative of the former, and Gabriel de la Concepción Valdés, a mulatto known as Plácido, became particularly notable. Plácido is probably the best known, although historians and critics have questioned the quality of his poetry as well as his political loyalties. José Antonio Fernández de Castro argues in an interesting essay that "it is indisputable that Plácido possessed lyric qualities, but he made poor use of them. . . . Roundelays and odes in his hands became instruments of adulation. Too often the rich and powerful saw themselves portrayed in the most flattering terms in his poems"[3] and that is why they liked him. Nonetheless, Plácido was an abolitionist and became implicated in the so-called "staircase conspiracy" of 1844, which the Spanish characterized as the broadest and most sweeping abolition conspiracy of the day. He, along with other abolitionists, was tried, found guilty, and condemned to death. It is said that one of the arguments used against him was his sonnet "El juramento" (The Oath), which reflects a deep-seated spirit of rebellion against oppression, as evidenced below:

A la sombra de un árbol empinado
que está de un ancho valle a la salida
ha un pequeño arroyo que convida
a beber de su líquido argentado.

Allí fui yo por mi deber llamado
y haciendo altar la tierra endurecida
ante el sagrado código de vida
extendidas mis manos he jurado.

Ser enemigo eterno del tirano
manchar si me es posible mis vestidos
con su execrable sangre, por mis manos

derramarla con golpes repetidos,
y morir a las manos del verdugo
si es necesario por romper el yugo.[4]

(In the shadow of a tall tree
at the entrance to a wide valley
there is a tiny stream which invites
one to drink of its silvery liquid.

I went there out of duty
and making an altar of hardened earth
before the sacred code of life
with outstretched hands, I swore.

To forever be the enemy of the tyrant
to stain my clothing if at all possible
with his abominable blood, by my own hand

to spill his blood with repeated blows,
and die at the hands of the executioner
if it is necessary to cast off the yoke.)

Although Plácido became a martyr in the growing struggle against Spain, Fernández de Castro believes him to have been a mediocre poet. In fact, de Castro asserts that Plácido's unjustified death by firing squad was the only reason for his later fame. The tale of his death magnified his fame and that of the verses attributed to him. "La plegaria," the best known, is vastly superior to the rest of his work.[5]

Juan Francisco Manzano, unlike Plácido, was born into slavery. He gained his freedom when, impressed with his talents, a group of white Cuban intellectuals headed by Domingo Del Monte pooled their money to purchase his freedom. Manzano largely imitated the style, language, and themes of white poets of the day, and many of his poems never made direct reference to slavery. Given the social cost paid by Plácido, Manzano may have preferred caution. Still, in the following poem, one cannot help but read slavery into his discussion.

> Cuando miro el espacio que he corrido
> desde la cuna hasta el presente día,
> tiemblo y saludo a la fortuna mía
> mas de terror que de atención movido
>
> Sorpréndeme la lucha que he podido
> sostener contra suerte tan impía
> si tal puede llamarse la porfía
> de mi infelice ser, al mal nacido.
>
> Treinta años ha que conocí la tierra;
> treinta años ha que en gemidor estado
> triste infortunio por doquier me asalta
>
> Mas nada es para mí la cruda guerra
> que en vano suspirar he soportado,
> si la comparo ¡Oh Dios! con lo que falta.[6]
>
> (When I look at the ground that I
>   have covered
> from the cradle until the present day
> I tremble and thank my good fortune
> More out of terror than complacency

It is surprising the struggle that I have
been able to sustain against such ungodly luck
if luck has anything to do with the persistence
of my unhappy self, to the accursed born.

For thirty years I have known the world;
thirty years in a state of lamentation
Sad misfortune assaults me from every side.

The worst war is nothing to me
which in vain I sigh to have to tolerate,
if I compare it—O God!—with what is still left.)

Given Spain's tyranny, many patriotic nationalists and abolitionists expressed themselves through a more or less veiled language. Identifying with Cuba's Indian heritage was one way to do that since no native societies remained by the nineteenth century. Writing about the struggles of Cuba's aboriginal peoples against the invading Caribe tribe stirred up patriotic sentiment without directly referring to Spain or slavery. A case in point is José Fornaris in his "Cantos del siboney" and Juan Cristóbal Nápoles Fajardo (nicknamed "el Cucalambé") with his "Rumores del hórmigo."[7] It is impossible not to hear in Cristóbal Nápoles's verses—sung to a Guajiran melody out in the jungle and by patriots in exile—an open and stirring call to arms in the struggle for independence, masked in pre-Columbian allegory:

Yo soy Hatuey, indio libre
sobre su tierra bendita,
como el caguayo que habita
debajo del ajenjibre.
Deja que de nuevo vibre
mi voz allá entre mi grey,
que resuene en mi batey
el dulce son de mi guamo
y acudan a mi reclamo
y sepan que aun vive Hatuey.

¡Oh Gaurina! . . . Guerra, guerra
contra esa perversa raza

que hoy incendiar amenaza
mi fértil y virgen tierra
en el llano y en la sierra,
en los montes y sabanas,
esas huestes caribanas
sepan, al quedar deshechas
lo que valen nuestras flechas,
lo que son nuestras macanas.[8]

(I am Hatuey, free Indian
on his blessed soil,
like the lizard who lives
underneath the ginger plant.
Let my voice again rise
over there among my people,
let resonate in my village
the sweet sound of my conch horn
and may they respond to my call
and know that Hatuey still lives.

Oh Guarina! . . . War, war
against that perverse race
who today threaten to burn
my fertile virgin land
on the plains and in the mountains
in the jungles and savannahs,
those Caribe hordes
will know, when they are undone
what our arrows are worth,
what our macanas are.)

No poet during the nineteenth century captured the imagination and hearts of Cuban society as did José Martí. More so than other nationalist leaders, Martí urged all Cubans, despite their social class or race, to work together for independence. He did this as a political leader and as a poet. He reflected most vehemently on the horror produced by slavery, and like Heredia focused on its destructive role in dividing the Cuban nation. In his *Versos sencillos* (Simple Poetry) Martí voiced indignant protest against slavery:

El rayo surca sangriento
el lóbrego nubarrón:
echa el barco, ciento a ciento,
los negros por el portón.

El viento, fiero, quebraba
los almácigos cepudos,
andaba la hilera andaba
de los esclavos desnudos.

El temporal sacudía
los barracones henchidos:
una madre con su cría
pasaba, dando alaridos.

Rojo, como el desierto,
salió el sol al horizonte:
y alumbró a un esclavo muerto,
colgado a un ceibo del monte.

Un niño lo vió: tembló
de pasión por los que gimen.
¡Y al pie del muerto juró
lavar con su vida el crimen!9

(Blood-red lightning cleaves through
the melancholy storm cloud; a ship
Disgorges blacks by the hundreds
Through the hatches.

The threatening wind swept
the full-leafed mastic trees,
And rows of naked slaves
Walked onward, onward.

The storm shook
the quarters filled with slaves;
a mother with her children
passed by, crying aloud.

Red as a desert sun
the sun rose at the horizon
and illuminated a dead slave
hanging from a ceiba in the forest.

A child saw him: he trembled
with passion for those who moan with pain
And at the foot of the corpse he vowed
to cleanse the crime with his life!)

Anti-Imperialism and Proletarian Verses

As Spanish dominion over Cuba ended in 1898, a new stage in the nation's economic, political, and cultural development began. It was the era
of North American hegemony and new, somewhat different nationalist
stirrings. Old desires for independence were complicated by increasing
U.S. domination. While it took many Cubans some time to comprehend
the new situation, a few agitators and poets were immediately frustrated
with the lack of real autonomy. Most notable was a poet from Matazanas,
Bonifacio Byrne, known by some as "the poet of the war." He wrote the
widely known poem "Mi bandera."

Al volver de distante ribera
con el alma enlutada y sombría
afanoso busqué mi bandera
y otra he visto además de la mía

¿Dónde está mi bandera cubana,
la bandera más bella que existe?
¡Desde el buque la ví esta mañana,
y no he visto una cosa más triste!

Con la fe de las almas austeras,
hoy sostengo con honda energía
que no deben flotar dos banderas
donde basta con una la mía.[10]

(Returning from the distant shore
with mournful and melancholy soul
I eagerly sought my flag
and saw another flying alongside my own

Where is my Cuban flag
the most beautiful flag that exists?
I saw it from the ship this morning
and have never seen anything so sad!

With the faith of austere souls
today I maintain with deep energy
that two flags should not be flown
where one is enough, my own.)

During the first years of the neocolonial republic, few poets wrote as Byrne did. Poetry reflected society's uneasiness at what the future held, its apathy. Also, because a few blacks were represented in the new party structures, many argued that racism was no longer a problem. Deep-seated social protest, which had stirred social poets of the past, was necessary to revitalize the social poetic tradition after 1898. It began to occur in the third decade of the twentieth century, when deteriorating economic and social conditions reflected the increasing submission of the Cuban economy and polity to North American interests. These conditions were exacerbated by a growing argicultural working class as well as hunger and poverty in the cities. A tiny group of foreigners were growing rich as increasing numbers of Cubans got poorer and poorer. Thus social injustice and political corruption engendered unrest. In 1923, Martínez Villena wrote the "Mensaje lírico civil," and it began to set the new stage for anti-imperialist poetry. In that poem the poet claims that independence was still an unfinished process, despite the sacrifices made by Cuba's revolutionary heroes:

Hace falta una carga para matar bribones
para acabar la obra de las revoluciones;

para vengar los muertos que padecen ultraje
para limpiar la costra tenaz del coloniaje;

para poder un día con prestigio y razón
extirpar el Apéndice a la Constitución.[11]

(We need an attack on rascals and idlers
to finish the work of the revolutions;

In order to avenge the deaths which suffer insult
to clean off the sticky crust of colonialism;

To be able one day with prestige and rightness
extirpate the appendix to the Constitution.)

Francisco Javier Pichardo was perhaps the best known of the republican poets to dramatize what foreign domination meant to Cuba's rural folk. In his verses, romantic themes of the peasantry often appeared. In "La canción del labriego" (The Song of the Laborer) he cries out:

Yo sé querer la tierra: de mis callosas manos
las rústicas caricias hacen dorar los granos,
Yo crujo en las encinas, yo tiemblo en el arbusto,

Y aguardo en la cosecha mi única alegría
Yo sé querer la tierra. Señor: Vos que sois justo
decidme si la tierra no debe de ser mía[12]

(I know how to love the land: from my calloused hands
the rough caresses make the grains golden,
I rustle in the oaks, I tremble in the bush,

And I store in the harvest my only happiness
I know how to love the land. Lord: you who are just
decide for me if the land should not be mine)

And in *El precepto* (The Commandment) Pichardo's complaint sounds even more revolutionary:

La vida es redención: con el trabajo
a diario hay que ganarla, tajo a tajo.
Es pecado vivir unos de otros;

Nos redime el trabajo y no la guerra.
Para comer el pan que es de nosotros
todos tenemos que labrar la tierra.[13]

(Life is deliverance: one must earn it
day by day, task by task
It is a sin for some to live off
    others;

Work redeems us and not war.
To eat the bread which is ours
All of us need to work the land.)

Such poems, written in the 1920s, ushered in a new wave of Cuban social protest poetry focused on national problems and the U.S. economic presence in the Cuban economy, although anti-imperialism itself was not always expressed so forthrightly or courageously. Among the poets participating in literary social protest in the 1920s was Agustín Acosta, author of the widely known poem "La zafra" (The Sugar Harvest). In another poem about sugar entitled "Las carretas en la noche" he alludes to the economic dependency of Cuba's major industry on the United States:

Por las guardarrayas y las serventías
forman las carretas largas teorías.

Vadean arroyos . . . cruzan las montañas
llevando la suerte de Cuba en las cañas

Van hacia el coloso de hierro cercano:
van hacia el ingenio norteamericano,

Y como quejándose cuando a él se avecinan
cargadas, pesadas, repletas,

¡con cuantas cubanas razones, rechinan
las viejas carretas. . . !14

(Along the pathways and the roads
the carts form long theories.

They cross streams . . . they cross mountains
taking the destiny of Cuba in the sugar cane

They go towards the iron colossus nearby:
they go to the North American sugar refinery,

And as if complaining when they approach it
loaded, heavy, filled up

with how many Cuban motives, the old carts
creak along. . . !)

Interestingly, sugar production and the condition of the rising agricultural proletariat became, like sugar and slavery before it, the primary
social ill and corrupting force in Cuban society. This time, however, the
proletariat was not all black and the foreign tyrant was not Spain. Increasing numbers of whites found themselves in poverty, and the United
States now dominated the economy. Pichardo Moya continued this
theme that others began, denouncing in his 1926 "El poema de los cañaverales" (Poem of the Cane Fields) political corruption along with Yankee
economic penetration:

Máquinas. Trapiches que vienen del Norte
Los nombres antiguos sepulta el olvido
Rubios ingenieros de atlético porte
y raras palabras dañando el oído

. . . .
El fiero machete que brilló en la guerra
en farsas políticas su acero corroe

y en tanto, acechando la inexperta tierra
afila sus garras de acero Monroe.[15]

(Machines. Sugar mills which come from the North
Oblivion buries the old names
Blond engineers with athletic build
and strange sounding words which disturb one's hearing
. . . .
The ferocious machete which shone in the war
has its steel corroded by political farces
and meanwhile, lurking over the inexperienced land
Monroe sharpens his talons of steel.)

It was also during the 1920s that one began to see socialist sensibilities more expressly integrated into the nationalist patriotic fabric. As in many places in the world, poetry in Cuba registered the defeat of the czarist regime in Russia and the ascendancy of the working class under Lenin's leadership. Interestingly, it was Regino Pedroso (who was black) who initiated the movement toward proletarian poetry when, on October 30, 1927 (the tenth anniversary of the October Revolution), his poem "Fraternal Greetings to the Mechanics Shop" appeared in the literary supplement to the most popular Havana newspaper, *Diario de la Marina*. Perhaps because he was black, he did not forget to address the issue of race in his poem, which concludes with a sharp and emotional challenge to the Soviet Union not to let people like himself down. He reveals that he has such great hope in the U.S.S.R. that it frightens him because he also knows the contradictions that are latent in all societies.

Yo te saludo en grito de igual angustia humana

¿Fundirán tus crisoles los nuevos postulados?
¿Eres sólo un vocablo de lo industrial: La fábrica?
¿O también eres templo
de amor, de fe, de intensos anhelos ideológicos
de comunión de razas?
. . . .
Yo dudo a veces, y otras
palpito, y tiemblo, y vibro con tu inmensa esperanza;

y oigo en mi carne la honda VERDAD de tus apóstoles:
¡que eres la entraña cósmica que incubas la mañana![16]

I greet you with a similar cry of human pain

(Will you cast your crucibles with the new principles?
Are you only a word in the vocabulary of industry: the factory?
Or are you also a temple
of love, of faith, of fervent ideological goals
and communion between the races?
. . . .
I sometimes doubt, and at other times
I quiver, and I tremble and I shake with your immense hope;
and I hear in my flesh the deep TRUTH spoken by your apostles:
that you are the cosmic womb which holds the future!)

Pedroso was to become the leading exponent of what is known as pro-letarian poetry, which was integrated with the growing anti-imperialist po-etry. One is able to discern the skilled working of antiracist, anti-imperialist, and socialist threads in his collection of proletarian poetry entitled *Nosotros*. Two such poems, entitled "Los conquistadores" and "Habrá guerra de nuevo" (There Will Be War Again), were particularly heralded. Cuba's proletarian poetry was interesting because it was not romantic but often satirical and realistic. It encouraged people to think about what it meant to be socialist by warning against those who would call themselves socialists but live off the backs of the Cuban poor. Such a theme is found in José Zacarías Tallet's "El equilibrista" (The Tightrope Walker) and "Simpatizantes" (The Sympathizers). The following paired verses are from the latter poem:

Siempre tiene en la boca el anti-imperialismo,
Marx, Lenin, la dialéctica, la URSS, el comunismo,

el amor libre, el arte de masas, la visión
del mundo socialista y la revolución.

Pero no deja un día de cenar a manteles
para abrir al obrero sus teóricos joyeles;

ni sacrifica el precio de un libro o una pijama
para que coma un preso o salga una proclama.

(Para servir la causa con efectividad
necesita instruirse, y con comodidad).[17]

(He always speaks of anti-imperialism,
Marx, Lenin, dialectics, the USSR, communism,

Free love, the art of the masses, the vision
of a socialist world and the revolution.

But not a day goes by that he fails to dine on a tablecloth
in order to share his theoretical treasures with a worker;

Nor does he sacrifice the price of a book or pair of pajamas
so that a prisoner may eat or a proclamation may appear.

[To serve the cause effectively
one needs to educate oneself, and in comfort.])

The proletarian movement would also be present to a greater or lesser extent in the poetry of Manuel Navarro Luna, María Villar Buceta, and Mirta Aguirre, to cite only a few of those beginning their literary careers at that time.

Black Transitions

While the Afro-Cuban appeared as a literary theme early in Cuban poetry, it was not until the late 1920s that the theme experienced an unparalleled boom, when it became part of, and helped inform, new definitions of *cubanidad.* Interestingly, around 1926 the recognition of a black cultural reservoir (the *afronegrista* literary current) began to develop among non-black intellectuals. This interest emerged with the coming together of two trajectories. One came from Europe, where it was propelled by Leo Frobenius, who had carried out ethnological research on black African culture and published *Black Decameron* in 1914. His influence was felt by the leading devotees of painting, sculpture, music, dance, and European literature;

Cuban artists were clearly influenced by these movements. The other trajectory came from African culture in the Americas. In the West Indies, the black presence continued to leave a deep impression on the general population and on cultural production as a whole. Black artistic expression that had grown roots in the Americas now found an audience. Referring to this fusion in the Cuban case, Ramón Guirao correctly noted, "The black African trend did not develop in Cuba as it did in Europe, bereft of tradition and unrelated to the larger human experience. The bilingual lyricism of Spanish and African dialects has its own historical background and an as yet undefined future. It could, paired to the creole sensibility, form a great vernacular poetry."[18]

The Puerto Rican poet Luis Palés Matos, with his "Danza negra," is considered the leader of the new trend in Hispanic America. Some years earlier, however, the Cuban poet José Manuel Poveda produced the poem that became the song "El grito abuelo" (The Grandparent Cry), considered by most critics to be the precursor of *negrismo* (negritude) in Cuba.

Melodiousness, sensuality, and picturesqueness are features of what became known as *negrista* poetry, especially in its early manifestations. Problematically, though, *negrismo* relies on flashy descriptions and emphasizes the sensorial and perceived erotic nature of people of African origin. Numerous writers then and later have criticized such nonblack visions of "the black." Not surprisingly, Regino Pedroso was one of the first Cuban poets to object to certain *negrista* poetry for exoticizing the black Cuban. In his particularly skillful way, though, he integrates a critique of elites (both Cuban and foreign) and their use of the black Cuban for their own longings with a reproach to black Cubans who participate in the satisfying of those problematic and narrow desires. The following two poems are particularly poignant:

> Para sus goces
> el rico hace de ti un juguete
> y en Paris, y en New York, y en Madrid y en La Habana,
> igual que bibelots
> se fabrican negros de paja para la exportación;
> hay hombres que te pagan con hambre la risa:
> trafican con tu sudor,
> comercian con tu dolor,
> y tú ríes, te entregas y danzas.[19]

(For his pleasures
The rich man makes a toy of you
and in Paris, and in New York, and in Madrid and in Havana,
just like souvenir toys
they make black people out of straw for export;
there are men who pay you with a hungry belly for
    your smile:
they traffic in your sweat,
they trade in your pain,
and you laugh, you give in and you dance.)

Negro, hermano negro,
enluta un poco tu bongó.

¿No somos más que negro?
¿No somos más que jácara?
¿No somos más que rumba, lujurias negras y comparsas?
¿No somos más que mueva y color
mueva y color?[20]

(Black man, black brother,
tone down your bongo drum a bit.

Are we not more than black?
Are we not more than revelers?
Are we not more than rumba, black libido and comparsas?
Are we not more than movement and color
movement and color?)

Still, the *negrista* movement, with all of its contradictions, did serve to reinforce the black presence in Cuban culture and to encourage an appreciation of African contributions to the society as a whole. From that point onward, many nonblack Cubans extolled the importance of Afro-Cubans to the very definition of what it meant to be Cuban. The black presence would be incorporated into Cuban culture and enter into a productive partnership with Hispanic poetic models to produce an authentic and distinctive expression that was a truly Cuban poetry.

Nicolás Guillén

No poet represented the synthesis of these revolutioary currents in Cuba as did the poet of color Nicolás Guillén. He made the best of *negrista* trends and incorporated in a more subtle way the confrontational poetics of Pedroso to become the first widely recognized poet to capture the character of black Cuban culture. We know he appreciated Pedroso because upon publication of Pedroso's *Nosotros* he wrote, "[This work] opens the way to politically sensitive poetry or Cuban social protest poetry. The first attempts to write political poetry—was it Pichardo or Tejera?—[are] overshadowed by and are a far cry from the ringing clarity of the metallic strophes of [these] poems. They strike a new and unusual note."[21] But it was to be Guillén, in my opinion, who achieved the highest aesthetic quality in social poetry. In 1930 he published a handful of poems in the literary supplement of *Diario de la Marina.* They in fact appeared on the "Ideales de una raza" page directed by the leading black intellectual Gustavo E. Urrutia. The same group of poems was later published in a pamphlet entitled *Motivos de son.* The date of this signal event? April 20, 1930.

As Roberto Fernández Retamar wrote of Guillén and *Motivos de son,* "Black poetry was not a style but rather a way of life."[22] Guillén refines it in a stylistic sense and charges its content with social significance, "which turns it into lovely poetry with lower class roots as well as social protest poetry, the highest manifestation of any genre."[23] Mirta Aguirre offers the following assessment of the publication of *Motivos de son* as a landmark event in Cuba's cultural history:

> simply, without any ostentation, as if he had always known it, one day he offered the correct solution to the question of Cuban intellectuals influenced by European reflective styles in their attempts to treat the insertion of the black into Cuban literature. What he offered was neither forced onomatopoetics, nor pastiche essays on purely African topics, but rather in a direct and simple way, the natural reality of mulatto Cuba: the *son.*[24]

Guillén's poetry had broad repercussions on the international scene as well as in Cuba itself, where most poets and writers showed their admiration for Guillén's poetry more or less spontaneously. What they most appreciated was the emergence of a new voice that seemed to capture the soul of the Cuban people. It should be noted that Nicolás Guillén's poetry was not just concerned with negritude; it also reflected a broad social consciousness. More and more, his verses were committed to the most progressive and revolutionary stances of the Cuban people and armed with the proletarian ideology of Marxism-Leninism.

Nicolás Guillén's poetic production was marvelously rich. After *Motivos de son* he published *Sóngoro cosongo* (1931), in which poems reflecting a high degree of political consciousness appear as veritable monuments to the Cuban masses, such as "Velorio de Papá Montero" (Burial of Papa Montero), "Secuestro de la mujer de Antonio" (The Abduction of Antonio's Woman), or "Quirino." Among the political verses, a tiny jewel of a poem entitled "Caña" (Sugarcane) synthesizes in a masterful way all the poverty and exploitation suffered by the Cuban people at the hands of U.S. imperialism:

El negro
junto al cañaveral

El yanqui
sobre el cañaveral

La tierra
bajo el cañaveral

¡Sangre
que nos va!25

(The black man
next to the canefield

The Yankee
over the canefield

The earth
under the canefield

Blood
that is draining away from us!)

ARCIA

226 CARMEN GOMEZ GARCIA

In 1937 Guillén published *West Indies Ltd.*, in which the social content of his poetry became more pronounced and his anti-imperialism more sharply defined. "Cantos para soldados y sones para turistas" (Songs for Soldiers and Ballads for Tourists) appeared in 1937, with two well-defined themes indicated by the title. In the songs for soldiers, poems such as "No sé por qué piensas tú" (Why, Soldier, Does It Seem to You) and "Elegía a un soldado vivo" (Elegy to a Living Soldier) are notable. Guillén challenges the soldier to realize that he forms part of the people he is hired by the foreign oppressors to mistreat and subjugate.

In the "Sones para turistas" Guillén gave life to a character deeply ensconced in folk culture who also represented a well-defined anti-imperialist position. Named José Ramón Cantaliso, this character "sang straightforwardly, very plainly," so that the tourists from the United States "might understand him well." Cantaliso sang in proud tones:

¿Quién los llamó?
Gasten su plata
beban su alcohol,
cómprense un güiro,
pero a mi no,
pero a mi no,
pero a mi no.[26]

(Who invited you?
Spend your money
Drink your alcohol
Buy yourself a gourd,
But not me,
but not me
but not me.)

Guillén recognized that a basic problem was one of social class and not just different nationalities. He sent poor people in that distant land—his equals—a warm and fraternal message:

Cuando regresen a Nueva York,
mándenme pobres
como soy yo,

como soy yo,
como soy yo.

A ellos les daré la mano
y con ellos cantaré
porque el canto que ellos saben
es el canto que yo sé.[27]

(When you return to New York,
Send back your poor people
just like me,
just like me,
just like me.

To them I will give my hand
and I'll sing with them
because the song they know
is the same song I know.)

At the same time the above poems appeared, Guillén joined the Cuban Communist Party, and from that point on his poetry became increasingly partisan in tone. It never became strident or pamphleteering, however; he knew how to combine form and content without letting one overpower the other. His verses are emotional and moving as much for what they say as for the way in which they say it. As René Depestre would say, "the work of this great sovereign poet is admirable testimony to the possibility of fusing pure poetry with politics."[28]

Cuban Social Poets and U.S. Racism

Guillén's rise to influence was part and parcel of heightened revolutionary activies in Cuba during the 1930s. Cuba was politically oppressed by a dictatorial regime in the service of U.S. economic interests, and writers increasingly reacted to both dictatorship and the American economic presence by expressing anti-imperialist sentiments. What is most surprising and probably little known is that many Cuban writers began to take an interest in the situation of blacks in the United States, and the poetry of many writers contained violent denunciations of the racism that blacks were subjected to in the United

States. Thus, to their deepening anti-imperialism and socialism was added a greater awareness of how U.S. racism worked.

In 1931 a horrifying event in the tiny town of Scottsboro, Alabama, captured the world's attention. Nine black youths ranging from thirteen to twenty years of age, and subsequently known as the Scottsboro Boys, were accused of the rape of two white women and of beating white youths. The incident was alleged to have occurred while all were traveling in the same train car. Despite lack of evidence of sexual violence and initial statements by the women indicating that they had not been the victims of rape, the youths were put on trial and the women were pressured to counter their previous statements. Their perjured testimony, coupled with race hatred, provided the rationale for guilty verdicts for all and death sentences for eight of the young men. The ninth was sentenced to life in prison. Due to a mass movement in support of the Scottsboro Boys led by the Commmunist Party of the United States, none of the youths were executed, but they did serve prison sentences ranging from six to nineteen years despite their innocence.[29]

The event stirred deep international indignation, and in Cuba particularly the trial had a great impact. A Cuban journalist named Manuel Marsal published a book entitled *El negro en los Estados Unidos de América: El caso Scottsboro* in 1932. In it he comments:

> In the packed courtroom one noted a strange sense in the air, a sense of satisfaction when the judge and public prosecutor spoke without any great distinction, after listening to the hesitant statements of the two girls, apparently tutored for several days beforehand. Without any doubt, it was certain that the court reporter had not bothered to even take statements from the accused. [In any case] what of importance could those poor unfortunates say, if one way or the other their execution was imminent?[30]

More than one Cuban poet reflected in verse the indignation of the Cuban people over the infamous event. Regino Pedroso's poem "Hermano negro" (Black Brother), which originally appeared in his book *The Tumultuous Days,* a collection of poems written between 1934 and 1936, denounced the U.S. society that had once again sunk its fierce fangs into black flesh:

Negro, hermano negro,
silencia un poco tus maracas.

Y aprende aquí,
y mira allí,
y escucha allá en Scottsboro, en Scottsboro,
entre un clamor de angustia esclava
ansias de hombre,
iras de hombre,
dolor y anhelo humanos de hombre sin raza.[31]

(Black man, black brother,
Silence your maracas a while.
And learn here,
and watch there,
and listen yonder in Scottsboro, in Scottsboro,
among the lamentation of slave distress
longings of man,
rage of man,
human pain and yearnings of a man without race.)

Poet Marcelino Arozarena in "Evohé" also lifts his cry in protest, with verses reminiscent of Pedroso's writings, and calls on his race brothers and sisters to stop dancing and partying long enough to contemplate the terrible situation suffered by blacks in Cuba and other countries, and most especially in the United States, where events like Scottsboro can occur:

¡Evohé!

 suelta el bongó,

no seas risa de turistas en rumbática
 secuencia:
tu indigencia
tus hermanos
piensa un poco en Scottsboro y no en Oggún[32]

(Evohé!

 drop the bongo drum,

don't be the butt of smiles of tourists in showy sequence:
your indigency
your brothers
think a little more about Scottsboro and less about Oggun)

Even the poet Mirta Aguirre, who generally ignored the black theme in her work despite an otherwise markedly proletarian focus, was moved by the Scottsboro affair. In a piece entitled "Scottsboro" written in 1935, she openly attacked the treatment of blacks in the United States:

Scottsboro en Alabama,
Scottsboro en Yanquilandia.
Es un hierro puesto al fuego
y elevado en las entrañas de una raza.
Nueve negros casi niños, sin trabajo
Dos mujeres, prostitutas.
Ley de Lynch, capitalismo, burguesía,
las tres K del turbia historia
Y a los pies del monstruo enorme de mil garras,
nueve negros casi niños.
Scottsboro en Alabama,
en la tierra imperialista: Yanquilandia
es un manto de martirio y es un manto de vergüenza
que cobija las dos razas.[33]

(Scottsboro in Alabama,
Scottsboro in Yankeeland.
It is an iron put to the fire
and lifted into the belly of a race.
Nine blacks almost children, out of work
Two women prostitutes.
Lynch law, capitalism, bourgeoisie,
the three Ks of shady history
And at the feet of the enormous monster with a
    thousand claws,
nine blacks almost children.
Scottsboro in Alabama,
in imperialist territory: Yankeeland

is a cloak of martyrdom and a cloak of shame
which covers the two races.)

Two years before, in 1933, Aguirre had written a poem with the same title as Pedroso's "Hermano negro" (Black Brother). In it she also displayed angry pain and a sense of shame over racial discrimination, while at the same
time that she emphasized how the system operated among the neighbors to
the north:

¿Cómo puedes no odiarme siendo blanca?
Hermano negro, ¿sabes cuantas vidas arranca
a tu raza la mía
en la Federación
de Estados Norteamericanos cada año?

Si yo fuera tú, odiaría
sin tasa
a todos los miembros de esa raza
que te hacen injustamente tanto daño.
Tú sabes quien fue el juez de Lynch, no ignoras
que te hallas
en peligro de muerte a todas horas
por culpa de tu hermano,
y en vez de maldecirlo, callas.

Yo soy blanca, tú negro, ¡y me tiendas la mano!
Hermano negro, hermano negro,
igual que Magdalena Paz, la comunista
yo te pido perdón
por todos los dolores que el prejuicio racista
vertió en tu corazón.[34]

(How can you not hate me for being white?
Black brother, do you know how many lives
    are taken
from your race by mine
in the Federation
of North American States every year?

If I were you I would hate
without measure
all members of that race
that unfairly causes you so much harm.
You know who was the lynch judge, don't forget
that you are
in danger of death at all times
because of your brother,
and instead of cursing him, you are silent.

I am white, you black, and you offer your hand!
Black brother, black brother,
the same as Magdalena Paz, the communist
I beg your forgiveness
for all the pain that racist prejudice
has emptied into your heart.)

But it was undoubtedly Nicolás Guillén who most frequently and to greatest lyrical effect attacked racial discrimination in the United States in his poetry. If one reviewed Guillén's vast poetic output between the early 1930s and his death in the 1980s, one would frequently find blunt and caustic denunciations of segregation and discrimination in the United States, along with reference to their best-known symbols, such as Jim Crow, lynch law, and the hateful Ku Klux Klan. At times his criticism is directed toward the phenomenon of racism in general, but generally he speaks to specific violent events that moved broad sectors of world opinion with their cruelty and sadism. Guillén, who became the most notable Cuban poet of all times, uses his skills to denounce Yankee imperialism and its discriminatory excesses. His verses, imbued with deep lyrical beauty, are strong, vigorous, and sometimes heavy with satirical meaning.

An example of Guillén's use of racial symbols is the ten-line stanza entitled "USA," published in January 1949 and appearing in the "Sátira política" section of his *Obra poética:*

Ir donde un negro y sacarlo
de su casa en forma dura,
sin contemplación quemarlo.
Escupirlo, pisotearlo,

y, al fin, en turbio montón
seres que salvajes son
celebrar aquella gracia
¡ese es yanquidemocracia
con fascistilustración!³⁵

(To go where the black is and to pull him
out of his home in a rough way,
without hesitation to burn him.
To spit on him, to step on him,
and, finally, in murky crowds
of beings who are savages
to celebrate that happy event
This is Yankeedemocracy
with fascistenlightenment!)

Another example can be found in one of the *décimas* (ten-line stanzas) of the poem "El soldado Miguel Paz y el sargento José Inés," written in 1952. The poem says:

No conozco otra nación
donde el negro sufra tanto;
en mares de sangre y llanto
navega su corazón.
La piel oscura es baldón
que allá inspira odio profundo
¡y de ese cáncer inmundo
que al propio blanco envilece,
quisiera el yanqui, parece,
ver enfermo a todo el mundo!³⁶

(I know no other nation
where the black person suffers so much;
in oceans of blood and moans
his heart must navigate.
Dark skin is an affront
which inspires deep hatred there
and from that filthy cancer

which vilifies the white himself,
the Yankee appears to wish
to see the whole world through sick eyes!)

Guillén did not write in generalities when he wrote of racism but focused on specific indignities with which each human spirit could identify. The "Elegía a Jesús Menéndez," in addition to stanzas that allude to the horrors of the Ku Klux Klan, Jim Crow, and lynching, also refers to the Martinsville Seven in a fragment of beautiful and poetic prose. The Martinsville (Virginia) Seven were seven young black men who were accused in 1949 of raping a white woman. After a very public trial, they were convicted and sentenced to death. Unlike the Scottsboro case, these young men were indeed executed in the first week of January 1951.[37]

Siete voces negras en Martinsville llaman siete veces a Jesús por su nombre y le piden en siete gritos de rabia, como siete lanzas, le piden en Martinsville, en siete golpes de azufre, come siete piedras volcánicas, le piden siete veces venganza.

(Seven black voices in Martinsville call seven times to Jesus by name and they ask in seven cries of rage, like seven lances, they ask in Martinsville, in seven strikes of sulphur, like seven volcanic rocks, they ask seven times for revenge.)[38]

When in 1952 the eminent actress Josephine Baker, born in the United States but naturalized as a French citizen, was refused service in an American night club, Guillén dedicated a poem to her. "Brindis" is a strong condemnation of U.S. claims to democracy:

La democracia Josefina
no anda en el Norte bien.
En el Sur Jim Crow y Lynch pasean
    del brazo,
se sientan juntos a comer,
en el Este, qué diablos
en el Este también
ser negro es un problema
de los que no se pueden resolver.

En el Oeste un negro tiene
menos de lo que un perro puede tener
En fin que allá la Rosa de los Vientos
hay que mandarla a componer[39]

(Democracy, Josephine,
is not doing well in the North.
In the South Jim Crow and Lynch walk arm in arm,
they sit down together to eat,
in the East, what the devil
in the East also
being black is a problem
of the kind with no solution.

In the West a black has
less than that which a dog might have
Which means that there the Rosa de los Vientos
needs to be sent to be fixed.)

Guillén continues later in an ironic tone:

¡Albricias (mientras tanto) buena suerte!
¡Alza tu vaso, vamos a beber!
¡Bien pudieran lincharte, Josefina,
y apenas si te niegan la entrada a un cabaret![40]

(Congratulations [meanwhile] good luck!
Lift your glass, let's toast!
They could have lynched you, Josephine,
but they only denied you entrance to a nightclub!)

In 1956 Guillén wrote what is, at least for me, the loveliest of his poems against racial discrimination in the United States, entitled "Elegy to Emmett Till." It originated in a brief news story published the year before in the magazine *The Crisis,* which, despite its brevity, filled Guillén with horror: "The mutilated body of Emmett Till, 14 years old, of Chicago, Illinois, was pulled out of the Tallahatchie River, near Greenwood, on August 31, three days after having been abducted by a group of whites armed with guns."[41] The original news clip in translation served as an introduction to the poem, which opens with great beauty and narrative force:

> En Norteamérica
> la Rosa de los Vientos
> tiene el pétalo sur rojo de sangre.[42]

> (In North America
> the Rosa de los Vientos
> has its southern petal red with blood.)

The poem goes on to describe the horrifying scenes that the great river of the south, the Mississippi, the "old brother river of the blacks," as Guillén says, contemplates impotently from its banks:

> árboles silenciosos
> de donde cuelgan gritos ya maduros
> . . . .
> cruces de fuego amenazante
> . . . .
> y hombres de muerte y alarido
> . . . .
> y la nocturna hoguera
> con un eterno negro ardiendo
> un negro sujetándose
> envuelto en humo el vientre desprendido,
> los intestinos húmedos
> el perseguido sexo,
> allá en el Sur alcohólico,
> allá en el Sur de afrenta y látigo,
> el Mississippi cuando pasa.[43]

> (silent trees
> from which hang already ripe screams
> . . . .
> burning crosses threatening
> . . . .
> and men of death and screams

. . . .
and the nocturnal bonfire
with an eternal black burning
a black submitting himself
enveloped in smoke the belly falling out
the intestines moist
the sex organ persecuted,
there in the alcoholic South,
there in the South of insult and whip,
the Mississippi [sees] as it passes.)

What the river contemplates as it passes by is all the brutality and the animosity that the racists take out against the black man, whom they hang from a tree or set alight in a bonfire for the "crime" of having a dark skin.

In his poem Guillén stresses that in the case of Emmett Till, the incident seems even more cruel when one realizes that the victim was not an adult but barely more than a child:

ahora un niño frágil
pequeña flor de tus riberas
no raíz todavía de tus árboles
no tronco de tus bosques,
no piedra de tu lecho
no caimán de tus aguas:
un niño apenas,
un niño muerto, asesinado y solo
negro.[44]

(now a fragile child
small flower of your banks
not yet a root of your trees
not a trunk in your forests
not a stone in your bed
not an alligator in your
    waters:
barely a child
a dead child, killed and only
black.)

The description Guillén offers of Emmett Till is moving and tender; he could have been any child in the United States if it were not for the color of his skin:

Un niño con su trompo
con sus amigos, con su barrio
con su camisa de domingo
con su billete para el cine,
con su pupitre y su pizarra,
con su pomo de tinta,
con su guante de béisbol,
con su programa de boxeo
con su retrato de Lincoln
con su bandera norteamericana,
negro.[45]

(A child with his spinning top
with his friends, with his
   neighborhood
with his Sunday best shirt
with his ticket for the movies,
with his school desk and slate,
with his bottle of ink,
with his baseball glove,
with his boxing program
with his portrait of
   Lincoln
with his American flag,
black.)

Naturally, Guillén does not fail to note, in simple and poetic fashion, the "horrible crime" committed by that adolescent who was brutally taken from his house in the night to be savagely murdered and his body thrown into the waters of the great river:

Un niño negro asesinado y solo
que una rosa de amor
arrojó al paso de una niña blanca.[46]

(A black child murdered and just
because of a rose of love
he threw in the path of a white girl.)

He explains how, in the United States, the union of a young black man
with a white woman is an intolerable offense. It was not even permissible,
as in this case, for a young black man to whistle in admiration at a young
white woman. There was no rape, no insults or gross remarks, only a whistle of admiration, a simple wolf whistle. That was sufficient motive for a
child of fourteen years to be subjected to violent torture, to be murdered
and thrown into the Mississippi River. It is to the river that Guillén ex-
presses his anger, demanding justice that he knows for the moment to be
illusory:

¡Oh viejo Mississippi,
oh rey, oh río de profundo manto!
detén aquí tu procesión de espumas,
tu azul carroza de tracción oceánica,
mira este cuerpo leve,
angel adolescente que llevaba
no bien cerradas todavía
las cicatrices en los hombros
donde tuvo las alas;
mira este rostro de perfil ausente,
deshecho a piedra y piedra,
a plomo y piedra,
a insulto y piedra,
mira este abierto pecho
la sangre antigua ya de duro coágulo.
Ven y en la noche iluminada
por una luna de catástrofe,
la lenta noche de los negros
con sus fosforescencias subterráneas
ven, y en la noche iluminada
dime tú, Mississippi
si podrás contemplar con ojos de agua ciega
y brazos de titán indiferente,
este luto, este crimen,

este mínimo muerto sin venganza,
este cadáver colosal y puro:
ven y en la noche iluminada,
tú, cargado de puños y de pájaros,
de sueños y metales.
Ven y en la noche iluminada
Oh viejo río hermano de los negros,
ven y en la noche iluminada,
ven y en la noche iluminada,
dime tú, Mississippi . . .[47]

(Oh old Mississippi,
Oh king, oh river of deep cloak!
Hold back your procession of foam
your blue float of oceanic traction,
look at this light body,
adolescent angel who bore
not fully healed yet
the scars on his shoulders
where he had his wings;
look at this face without a profile,
destroyed by stone after stone,
with bullet and stone,
with insult and stone,
look at this open breast
the old blood already coagulated hard.
Come and in the night illuminated
by a moon of catastrophe,
the slow moon of the blacks
with its underground phosphorescence
come, and in the illuminated night
tell me, Mississippi
if you can see with blind watery eyes
and the arms of an indifferent giant,
this mourning, this crime,
this minimal death without hope of revenge,
this colossal and pure corpse:
come and in the illuminated night,

you, loaded with fists and with birds,
with dreams and metal.
Come and in the illuminated night
Oh old brother river of the blacks,
come and in the illuminated night,
come and in the illuminated night,
tell me, Mississippi . . .)

Toward the end of the decade of the 1950s another racial incident renewed the opprobrium of world opinion. The landmark 1954 Supreme Court decision, *Brown v. Board of Education,* set aside the practice of racial segregation in public schools. Many black children made use of the court ruling to seek entry into schools that previously had admitted only whites. In response, more or less violent demonstrations took place in many cities, particularly in the South. White supremacist resistance to school integration culminated in September 1957 in Little Rock, Arkansas, when governor Orval E. Faubus unleashed a violent campaign against nine black students who sought to attend Central High School.

Guillén responded to the events of 1957 with a poem entitled "Little Rock," which was included in his book *La paloma del vuelo popular.* In that book, the poet used the last name of the hateful governor as an adjective that concentrated all the injustice and inhumanity of American racism. It read:

En aquel mundo faubus
bajo aquel duro cielo faubus
   de gangrena,
los niños negros pueden
no ir junto a los blancos a la escuela.[48]

(In that Faubus world
under that hard Faubus sky of gangrene,
the black children can
not attend school together with whites.)

Guillén ends the poem by calling the attention of minority populations to how horrible it would be if the U.S. practices of discrimination were generalized across the globe:

y bien ahora,
señoras y señores, señoritas,
ahora niños,
ahora viejos peludos y pelados,
ahora indios, mulatos, negros,
    zambos,
ahora pensad lo que sería
el mundo todo Sur
el mundo todo sangre y todo látigo,
el mundo todo escuelas de blancos para
    blancos,
el mundo todo Rock y todo Little,
el mundo todo yanqui, todo faubus

Pensad por un momento
imaginadlo un solo instante.[49]

(And well, now,
ladies and gentlemen, young ladies,
now children,
now bald old people and those with hair,
now Indians, mulattos, blacks, zambos,
now think what it might be like if
the whole world were all South
the whole world all blood and all lash,
the whole world white schools for whites,
the whole world all Rock and all Little,
the whole world all Yankee, all Faubus

Think of it for a moment
imagine it for a single instant.)

Even after the dawn of the Cuban Revolution on January 1, 1959, Guillén continued to rail against the ferocious racism of the United States. His "El gran zoo" (The Great Zoo) a work of great irony published in 1972, contains two drawings that characterize the monstrous creations of U.S. racism: lynching and the Ku Klux Klan. His irony is caustic when describing "Lynch" (the lynch law):

Lynch de Alabama
Rabo en forma de látigo
y pezuñas terciarias.
Suele manifestarse
con una gran cruz en llamas.
Se alimenta de negros, sogas,
fuego, sangre, clavos
alquitrán.
    Capturado
junto a una horca. Macho.
Castrado.[50]

(Lynch of Alabama
Tail in the shape of a whip
and tertiary hooves.
It usually appears
with a large flaming cross.
It feeds on blacks, ropes,
fire, blood, nails,
tar.
    Captured
at a hanging. Male.
Castrated.)

Guillén is no less caustic in his description of the beastly KKK:

Este cuadrúpedo procede
de Joplin, Misurí,
Carnicero.
Aulla largamente en la noche
sin su dieta de negro asado.

Acabará por sucumbir
Un problema (insoluble) alimentarlo.[51]

(This quadruped originates
in Joplin, Missouri,
Carnivorous.

It howls long into the night
without its usual diet of roasted negro.

It will eventually succumb.
Feeding it is a[n insoluble] problem.)

President John F. Kennedy, in a vain attempt to counteract the example of the Cuban Revolution among other nations of the Third World, and especially the rest of Latin America, created the Alliance for Progress in 1961. Guillén's response was a poem entitled "Crecen altas las flores" (The Flowers Grow Tall). In that poem Guillén mentioned the horrors of segregation and racism that characterized U.S. race relations and threatened to spread to its economic vassals and dependencies in the Caribbean:

Adelante Jim Crow; no te detengas; lanza
tu grito de victoria. Un ¡hurra! por la Alianza

Lynch, adelante, corre, busca tus feotes. Eso
eso es lo que urge. . . ¡Hurra por el Progreso!

Así de día en día (aliados progresando
bajo la voz de Washington, que es una voz de mando)

hacer de nuestras tierras el naziparaíso:
ni un indio, ni un mal blanco, ni un negro, ni
    un mestizo.[52]

(Hurry on, Jim Crow; don't hold back; raise
your cry of victory. A "hurrah" for the Alliance

Lynch, hurry on, run, look for your whips. That
is what is urgent. Hurrah for Progress!

Thus from day to day [allies progressing
under the voice of Washington, which is a commanding voice]

make a Nazi paradise of our lands:
not a single Indian, bad white, black, or mestizo.)

One of Guillén's most significant poems of the post-revolutionary period written about American racial discrimination was "Está bien" (It Is All Very Well), which appeared in October 1963 in *Bohemia* magazine. Two other brief poems also appeared in that issue, entitled "Gobernador" (Governor) and "Escolares" (School Children). The first poem was motivated by the nonviolent resistance movement that gained popularity in the 1950s and 1960s as a tactic for fighting against segregation in the United States. While Guillén recognized that nonviolent civil disobedience in response to racism was "all very well," he also called on U.S. blacks to consider the possibility of combating violence with armed struggle. Interestingly, with this poem Guillén entered into the heated debate then taking place in the United States between the traditional (nonviolent) civil rights movement and black-power advocates concerning which strategy was most effective.

Bien tus sermones en los templos dinamitados,
bien tu insistencia heroica
en estar junto a los blancos,
porque la ley—¿la ley?—proclama
la igualdad de todos los americanos.

Bien
está muy bien
Requetebien,

hermano negro del Sur crucificado.
Pero acuérdate de John Brown,
que no era negro y te defendió con un fusil en las manos.

Fusil: arma de fuego portátil
(es lo que dice el diccionario)
con que disparan los soldados
Hay que agregar: Fusil (en inglés "gun")
arma también con que responden
los esclavos.[53]

(All very well your sermons in dynamited churches,
well your heroic insistence on
being together with the whites,

because the law—the law?—proclaims
the equality of all Americans.

Well
it is all well
it is all very well,

black brother of the crucified South.
But don't forget John Brown,
who was not black and who defended you *fusil* in hand.

Fusil: a portable firearm
[that's what the dictionary says]
with which soldiers shoot.
One should add: *Fusil* [in English "gun"]
also a weapon
with which slaves respond.)

In summary Guillén was the Cuban poet who most energetically combated racial discrimination wherever it might occur, most especially in
Cuba and the United States. Yet there would not have been a Guillén had
Pedroso and Manzano and Plácido not preceded him. In their poetry blacks
sing in their own voices, the ancestral voice, and with a rhythm that originated on African shores but forged a home in a nationalist, socialist Cuba.

NOTES

Acknowledgment: This essay was translated by Francine Cronshaw.

1. José María Heredia, "Himno del desterrado," in *Poesía social cubana,* ed. Mirta
Aguirre et al. (Havana: Editorial Arte y Literatura, 1985), 33.

2. Mirta Aguirre, "Poesía y cubanía," in *Estudios literarios,* ed. Mirta Aguirre (Havana:
Editorial Letras Cubanas, n.d.), 60.

3. José Antonio Fernández de Castro, *Tema negro en la literatura cubana* (Havana: El
Mirador, 1943), 31.

4. Gabriel de la Concepción Valdés, "El juramento," in Aguirre et al., *Poesía social
cubana,* 37.

5. Fernández de Castro, *Tema negro,* 33.

6. Juan Francisco Manzano, "Mis treinta años," in Aguirre et al., *Poesía social
cubana,* 36.

7. Both José Fornaris and Juan Cristóbal Nápoles Fajardo and their works are mentioned in Mirta Aguirre, "Poesía y cubanía," *Estudios literarios,* 52.

8. Juan Cristóbal Nápoles Fajardo, cited by Mirta Aguirre, "Poesía y cubanía," 57.

9. José Martí, *Obra completas* (Havana: Editorial de Ciencias Sociales, 1975), 16:106–7.

10. Bonifacio Byrne, "Mi bandera," in Aguirre et al., *Poesía social cubana,* 40.

11. Rubén Martínez Villena, "Mensaje lírico civil," in Aguirre et al., *Poesía social cubana,* 192. Villena is referring to the Platt Amendment of 1902, which gave the U.S. government the right to intervene on Cuban soil and established U.S. economic and political hegemony over Cuba.

12. Francisco Javier Pichardo, "La canción del labriego," in Aguirre et al., *Poesía social cubana,* 147.

13. Francisco Javier Pichardo, "El precepto," in Aguirre et al., *Poesía social cubana,* 148.

14. Agustín Acosta, "Las carretas en la noche," in *Cincuenta años de poesía cubana (1902–1952),* ed. Cintio Vitier (Havana: Dirección de Cultura del Ministerio de Educación, 1952), 86–87.

15. Felipe Pichardo Moya, "El poema de los cañaverales," in Aguirre et al., *Poesía social cubana,* 166.

16. Regino Pedroso, "Salutación fraternal al taller mecánico," in *Regino Pedroso, Poemas* (Havana: Bolsilibros Unión, 1966), 48.

17. José Zacarías Tallet, *Poesía y prosa* (Havana: Editorial Letras Cubanas, 1979), 95.

18. Ramón Guirao, *Orbita de la poesía afrocubana* (Havana: Antología, 1938), xx.

19. Regino Pedroso, "Negro, hermano negro," in *Regino Pedroso, Poemas,* 99.

20. Ibid., 100.

21. Nicolás Guillén, "Prólogo," in *Regino Pedroso, Poemas,* 7.

22. Roberto Fernández Retamar, *El son del vuelo popular* (Havana: UNEAC, Contemporáneos, 1972), 15.

23. Ibid.

24. Mirta Aguirre, "Guillén, maestro de poesía y decoro ciudadanos," in *Ayer y hoy* (Havana: Bolsilibros Unión, 1980), 81.

25. Nicolás Guillén, *Obra poética,* 2 vols. (Havana: Editorial Arte y Literatura, 1972), 1:129.

26. Ibid., 200–201.

27. Ibid., 201.

28. René Depestre, "Orfeo negro," in *Recopilación de textos sobre Nicolás Guillén,* ed. Nancy Morejón (Havana: Casa de las Américas, 1974), 88.

29. See Dan T. Carter, *Scottsboro: A Tragedy of the American South* (London: Oxford University Press, 1971).

30. Manuel Marsal, *El negro en los Estados Unidos de América: El caso Scottsboro,* 2d ed. (Havana: Editorial Hermes, 1932), 72.

31. This poem is included as "Hermano negro" in *Regino Pedroso, Poemas,* 100.

32. Marcelino Arozarena, "Evohé," *Canción negra sin color* (Havana: UNEAC Contemporáneos, 1983), 39. Oggun is an orisha (patron saint, god) in the Afro-Cuban religion Santeria.

33. Mirta Aguirre, "Scottsboro," in *Obra poética de Mirta Aguirre: Dinámica de una tradición lírica,* ed. Susana A. Montero (Havana: Academia, 1987), 121.

34. Aguirre, "Hermano negro," 125.

35. Guillén, "USA," *Obra poética,* 1:273.

36. Guillén, "El soldado Miguel Paz y el sargento José Inés," *Obra poética,* 1:378.

37. For more information on the Martinsville Seven, see Eric Rise, *The Martinsville Seven: Race, Rape, and Capital Punishment* (Charlottesville and London: University Press of Virginia, 1995).

38. Guillén, "Elegía a Jesús Menéndez," *Obra poética,* 1:433.

39. Guillén, "Brindis," *Obra poética,* 2:277–78.

40. Ibid., 278.

41. Guillén, "Elegía a Emmett Till," *Obra poética,* 1:400.

42. Ibid., pp. 400–401.

43. Ibid.

44. Ibid., 401.

45. Ibid., 401–2.

46. Ibid., 402.

47. Ibid., 402–3.

48. Guillén, "Little Rock," *Obra poética,* 2:23.

49. Ibid., 24.

50. Guillén, "El gran zoo," *Obra poética,* 2:237.

51. Ibid., 239.

52. Guillén, "Crecen altas las flores," *Obra poética,* 2:85.

53. Guillén, "Está bien," *Obra poética,* 2:109.

10

CuBop!

Afro-Cuban Music and Mid-Twentieth-Century American Culture

GEOFFREY JACQUES

I already had been listening to [recordings of] Dizzy's collaboration with Chano Pozo, and I'd always had an underlying interest in his style, but it wasn't until I put my foot on Cuban soil that I could really understand what it was all about.
Roy Hargrove, Crisol

My father was the piano player and bandleader of the Tropicana orchestra, and when I was a child, I would sit with him in the rehearsals, and that's where I got my love of jazz music. I would hear Roy Haynes, Nat "King" Cole, Stan Getz, Zoot Sims, Cab Calloway—all the American stars came to play in Havana.
Chucho Valdez, Irekere

The African-American poet Langston Hughes visited Cuba in 1930 looking for a partner to help him write an opera. Hughes was looking (at the behest of a rich white patron) for primitivism. He never found his partner, but he did find friends, including Nicolás Guillén, who became the twentieth century's most important Cuban poet.[1]

What Hughes also found was the rumba, the Cuban dance that was on its way to becoming one of the most popular ballroom dances of all time. He described the music he found in the cafés of Havana as "essentially hip-shaking music—of Afro-Cuban folk derivation, which means a bit of Spain, therefore Arab-Moorish, mixed in." Hughes was full of enthusiasm for this music, in part because he saw it as a working class expression. "In Cuba, in 1930, the rumba was not a respectable dance among persons of good breeding." He was also not above a certain hyperbolic exoticism when conveying his love of the rhythms he heard. These sounds, he said, "speak of the earth, life bursting warm from the earth, and earth and sun moving in the steady rhythms of procreation and joy."[2]

The music Hughes heard in Havana probably did not sound like the softly pulsating dance-band music that brought a musician like Xavier Cugat to world fame, with its sweet trumpet solos and lush violins. It was likely that what he heard was a heavily percussive music, its main instruments being sticks and drums accompanying a lone singer. It was much closer to original jazz and blues than it was to the evolved rumba that made its way to the top of the charts in Hollywood and New York a few years later.

Perhaps if Hughes had found a collaborator for his opera, the relationship between African-American and Cuban music might have evolved differently. But Cuban music was, in relationship to U.S. popular music in general and to African-American music in particular during most of the first half of this century, a source of decadence as well as creativity. This all changed, paradoxically, after World War II, as postwar jazz revolutionaries found a way to use Cuba as a reservoir of aesthetic inspiration and, implicitly, sociopolitical agitation; and as demographic and cultural changes on the mainland helped create conditions for another Cuban musical style to become vastly popular throughout the United States.

African-American musicians and others working in Afro-American idioms were always aware of the musical potential of Cuba. Eubie Blake cites at least one ragtime-era composition, the "Cubanola Glide" of 1909, that seems to have had that island as inspiration.[3] During the early part of the twentieth century, Cuban and African-American musical styles traveled along parallel, if different, tracks. Musicians in both countries used brass bands extensively, mainly for outdoor concerts. Many of the most famous post-Emancipation New Orleans bands, for example, were brass bands; and during the late nineteenth century, the modern Cuban dance band (the *danzón* orchestra), often consisting of tuba, trombone, clarinet, two violins, and two tympany drums, was created as an alternative to the overpowering presence brass bands had in indoor dances.[4]

The modern Cuban dance band developed at the same time that jazz was moving away from its brass-band stage. The development of a ballroom (that is, indoor) dance music in New Orleans and New York in the early twentieth century was also accompanied by a change in musical instrumentation from a strictly brass-band format to one using reed and string instruments and by the introduction, in about 1905, of the modern drum set.[5]

Historians have argued for years about specific "Spanish" influences on jazz.[6] But direct evidence for the source of such influences is sketchy. And yet New Orleans musicians early on showed some overt influences from Spanish-influenced music. Some of this influence came from Mexico (whose styles had often been said to have been influenced by Cuba). At least one prominent family of New Orleans musicians, the Tio brothers, Lorenzo Sr. and Luis, came from that country. These two, together with Lorenzo Tio Jr., are considered the most important of early New Orleans clarinet players.[7]

However, perhaps the most significant early example of direct contact between African-American musicians and Cuba occurred during the late nineteenth century, when the New Orleans–based Onward Brass Band enlisted in the Spanish-American War, where they performed as the Ninth Immunes Regimental Band.[8] The Onward was one of the most influential brass bands in New Orleans, and one of the longest lived. Between 1889 and 1931, scores of important New Orleans musicians were members of this band, including Joseph "King" Oliver and Lorenzo Tio. After 1903 its leader was New Orleans–born cornetist and cigar maker Manuel Pérez.[9] Whether the Onward Brass Band carried any Cuban musical influences back to New Orleans is unknown. It is possible to speculate, however, that the "Spanish tinge" habanera rhythm used by some New Orleans musicians in their music (for example, by Ferdinand "Jelly Roll" Morton in "New Orleans Joys") resulted as much from the contacts and associations cited above as it did from the Spanish culture that existed in New Orleans itself.

Yet these influences were submerged in jazz for several decades, and when they did find overt expression, it was often in novelties and in music that was more overtly related to Mexico than to Cuba, such as Louis Armstrong's 1930 recording "The Peanut Vendor" and his 1935 recording "La Cucaracha."[10] This recording was made in the early days of the popular large dance orchestra in the United States. Known as the "big band," this orchestra would dominate popular music throughout the Americas and Europe for the next twenty years. Its usual composition was a percussion section made up of a piano and trap drum set; a string section, based on a string bass and guitar, and sometimes augmented by violins; a horn section divided almost equally between reed instruments (clarinet and tenor, alto, and sometimes baritone saxophones) and brass instruments (trumpets and trombones); and vocalists. The purer jazz bands, like Armstrong's, usually played without violins, and featured, to varying degrees, improvising soloists on various instruments.

Both commercial and pure jazz bands shared this instrumentation. The difference between the two was largely in the quality of their solo horn and piano interludes and the extent to which they exhibited the rhythmic quality known as swing. Despite these variances, however, both jazz and more commercially popular dance bands shared the radio airwaves and, often, the same dance halls.

It was within this environment that the first truly popular Cuban orchestra in United States arose. This was the orchestra led by violinist Xavier Cugat, which made its first commercial recordings in 1933. Cugat, a Spaniard by birth who was raised in Cuba, was a child musical prodigy. He moved to the United States permanently in the late 1920s, and was playing the newly opened Waldorf Astoria in New York in 1932.

Cugat's orchestra was one of the most popular dance orchestras of its time. The music it played ranged from the lightly swinging and sentimentalized "sweet" dance music favored by other popular, commercial, white-led bands to rumbas, tangos, boleros, and other Latin American styles. Though some of his songs featured brief, improvised passages, most of the songs were highly arranged, and the rhythms were discreet and unobtrusive, which appealed to a broad white American audience.[11]

This band's first big hits came at the same time as the appearance of the Benny Goodman Orchestra, which became the most popular of the white big bands of the 1930s. The huge commercial successes of these bands also marked the beginning of a change in the development of jazz music as an art form. In this light, Cugat's orchestra can be seen as an example of the contradictions (for example, commercial success acompanied by artistic decadence and decline) that led to the modern jazz revolution of the World War II years.

The popularity of Cugat's band was mirrored in the World War II era by that of a band led by Desi Arnaz, a singer once in Cugat's employ. Playing much of the same repertoire as his one-time employer, Arnaz enjoyed immense popularity by war's end with hits like "Babalu" and "Cuban Pete." Like Cugat, Arnaz was deeply admired by a wide public as well as by many Cubans recently arrived in the United States. Gustavo Pérez Firmat discusses at length the impact of Arnaz's popularity on the emergent Cuban-American identity.[12] The records he made in the late 1940s for RCA existed in a wide commercial space—that nexus of U.S. culture where the big band met Hollywood.[13] But this apex of popularity for Arnaz, whose performance emphasized humor, gags, and ethnically self-deprecating novelty, was also a symptom of what by then was ailing big-band dance music as a whole. Comments LeRoi Jones (Amiri Baraka), "Big band jazz, for all practical purposes, had passed completely into the mainstream and served now, in its performance, simply as a stylized reflection of a culturally feeble environment. Spontaneous impulse had been replaced by the arranger, and the human element of the music (which was central to black jazz and blues) was confined to whatever difficulties individual performers might have reading a score."[14]

This may seem an unfair characterization of popular Latin jazz of the 1940s, but this music was similar to much other dance music of its day. Whatever drive had been introduced by swinging dance orchestras of the 1930s, such as those of William "Count" Basie and James Melvin "Jimmie" Lunceford, had been largely replaced by a resurgence of the "sweet" commercialism that dominated popular dance orchestras of the 1920s. Other groups, most notably Frank "Machito" Grillo's group, the Afro-Cubans, were attempting a fusion of jazz and Cuban music. That fusion made significant headway during the early 1940s, but Afro-Cuban music did not really become Afro-Cuban *jazz* until musicians found a way to create a Cuban influenced, jazz-dominant musical form.

That they found that way in the wake of the modern jazz revolution of the 1940s should not be surprising, given the social dimensions of that revolution. In contrast to earlier black American musical developments, bebop carried with it a conscious social component. It was seen as an artistic movement in rebellion against racial oppression; it was, as well, a movement of cultural and social rebellion. Jones explains, "The term bebop, which began merely as an onomatopoeic way of characterizing a rhythmic element of the music, came to denote some kind of social nonconformity attributable to the *general* American scene, and not merely to the Negro."[15] This was reflected in many ways, not least of which was a certain conscious internationalism that found its reflection as an aesthetic concern within the music itself. Bebop, though originated by African-American musicians, was the first American musical style in which both black and white musicians shared in creating some of its original public statements.[16] This internationalism was also reflected in the search by modern jazz musicians for ways to use other musical styles and elements in a way that was different from the highly arranged commercial big bands to expand the jazz vocabulary. The use of Cuban music, then, had both an aesthetic and social function in the 1940s jazz revolution.

The strain of jazz that goes by the name Afro-Cuban is a product of tremendous demographic and cultural changes in the United States in the 1940s. Until then, the Cuban population in the United States was relatively small. But the population jumped from 18,000 in 1940 to 79,000 in 1960.[17] This accelerated immigration, which included many musicians, introduced a more diversified Cuban culture. Much of Cuban musical culture was already part of the mainstream, thanks in part to the popularity of band leaders like Cugat and Arnaz. So the influx of the World War II years and after provided avenues through which the diversity of U.S. culture, kept under the official cover of white supremacy since the Civil War, could more speedily emerge as the country's mass culture. These developments were spurred by demographic shifts, including increased immigration from the Caribbean, the rise of the black population in U.S. cities, and the general rise in the U.S. urban population; and by the increased attention by Hollywood and other media to the Caribbean and Central and South America as a byproduct of the U.S. need to strengthen its domestic security in wartime. Another factor was the growth of mass-entertainment media over the first half of the twentieth century, through which many artists of color—particularly jazz instrumentalists like Louis Armstrong and popular vocalists like Ethel Waters—became widely admired national figures. All this had the effect of softening racist attitudes among portions of the white population. This is reflected, first of all, in the growing popularity of Latin American culture during the 1940s, as seen in both motion pictures and in popular music;[18] and, secondly, in the development of a jazz style that recognized a fusion of Cuban and African-American cultures.

Scholars and musicians generally agree that trumpeter Mario Bauza is the pioneer of Afro-Cuban music. Machito's Afro-Cubans' recording in 1943 of Bauza's "Tanga" is generally identified as the beginning of the style.[19] Bauza, as a respected member of several jazz bands of the period and bandmate of John "Dizzy" Gillespie in the orchestra led by Cabell "Cab" Calloway, was the first prominent Cuban-American jazz composer.[20] Machito's musical apprenticeship was served in several Cuban dance bands both in Havana and in the United States. When he started his own band in New York in 1940, it was a largely Cuban band playing a Cuban version of North American jazz. "I became inspired when I heard Duke Ellington," Machito later said, "But we quickly went into our own style." Ellington himself recorded several Latin-influenced compositions, including "Caravan," written by the Puerto Rican–born trombonist Juan Tizol, and "The Flaming Sword."[21] Bauza added, "Our idea was to bring Latin music up to the standard of the American orchestras."[22]

This last sentiment does not simply reflect an inferiority complex. Dance orchestras all over the world in the 1930s wanted to sound like the Chick Webb, Duke Ellington, or Jimmie Lunceford bands. But the statement also suggests an absence, the sense of something missing. The missing piece would be supplied, for serious jazz practitioners, several years later.

On September 29, 1947, Dizzy Gillespie premiered his new orchestra at Carnegie Hall. The program closed with Ella Fitzgerald singing "How High the Moon" and other songs. It opened with orchestra performances of several of Gillespie's revolutionary bebop classics, including Gillespie and Tadd Dameron's composition "Cool Breeze," Charlie Parker's "Relaxin' at Cammarillo," Gillespie's "One Bass Hit," a Tadd Dameron composition, "Nearness," and Gillespie's "Salt Peanuts." The Gillespie–Charlie Parker Quintet performed bebop standards including Gillespie's "Dizzy Atmosphere" and "Groovin' High," and Parker's "Confirmation" and "Ko-Ko."[23]

But the concert's historic significance came after the intermission, when the orchestra performed the "Afro-Cuban Drum Suite" and two collaborative compositions by Gillespie and George Russell, "Cubano-Be," and "Cubano-Bop." Here is where the marriage between Cuban-American dance music and African-American jazz was consummated. It was one thing for a Cuban band, even one led by a veteran jazz musician, to play a jazz-influenced Cuban music. But that music was not yet truly a jazz form. In Machito's music, for example, the drums dominate in a way that they rarely do in jazz. Even the advanced harmonies in the introduction to Machito's "Tanga" often led to a set of horn improvisations that felt constricted by the heavy rhythmic overlay provided by the drums. In jazz, each section of a band or orchestra balances and supports the other, creating a truly collective musical expression. In this context, drumming, though essential, rarely dominates a jazz performance. In the Gillespie performances, for example, the drums, though certainly present, do not dominate but provide a backdrop for the melodic and harmonic explorations of the leading voices, the horns.[24]

This is true in the commercially recorded, studio version of "Cubano-Be" and "Cubano-Bop."[25] Here the Cuban influence is exhibited in the expanded (for a jazz orchestra) rhythm section and also, perhaps most strikingly, by the horns, which play a complicated set of figures that go far beyond the melodically arranged assortment of riffs (relatively simple, repeated figures) that were the hallmark of much of the music played by the majority of both Cuban and jazz orchestras of the day.

On the stage that night was one of the greatest Cuban percussionists, Luciano "Chano" Pozo. He is generally credited with providing the hands-on training and inspiration that allowed the Gillespie orchestra to turn a Cuban-influenced jazz style into an organic Afro-Cuban jazz style.

"Cubano-Be" and "Cubano-Bop" were the epitome of Afro-Cuban jazz as an experimental form. But the really popular song in this style was "Manteca," which became one of Gillespie's biggest hits.[26] This was the song that introduced Afro-Cuban jazz to the wider public, and here is where the distinctive jazz character of the Afro-Cuban style can be heard to greatest advantage.

"Manteca" starts with Pozo's conga drumming and a percussive orchestral riff playing in unison, which soon gives way to a rapid-fire introduction by Gillespie, which is preceded by a shout (presumably by Gillespie) of the song's name. The riffs that provide the song's main theme are similar to the riff-based Afro-Cuban music played by Machito and similar bands. But what Gillespie added to Pozo's set of riffs is what sets "Manteca" apart.

"Chano wasn't too hip about American music," Gillespie remembered. "If I'd let it go like he wanted it, it would've been strictly Afro-Cuban, all the way. There wouldn't have been a bridge. I wrote the bridge."[27] The sixteen-bar bridge turned "Manteca" into North American music, jazz music, by providing a 4/4 rhythmic base on which to conduct bebop-style improvisation. The jazz rhythm also changed the balance between soloist and percussionists; though still essential, the drummers remained in the background, allowing each soloist's statement to stand out in the foreground. (As is often the case in purer Afro-Cuban compositions, such as Bauza's "Tanga," the soloist appears to compete on an equal footing with the percussionist.) The compositions "Manteca," "Cubano-Be," and "Cubano-Bop" featured Cuban percussion heavily, especially the congo drum, but the overall compositions were dominated by the harmonic advances propelled by the bebop players.

Another striking characteristic about the development of Afro-Cuban *jazz* (as distinct from the jazz-influenced Afro-Cuban music practiced by Machito) is the use the beboppers made of Cuban music to make a larger aesthetic and even social point: Afro-Cuban music provided African-Americans with the first mass-based arena since the end of the Garvey movement in the 1920s in which to project Africa and African culture as the base of black American culture. And it provided jazz with a way of affirming Africa that was removed from the self-deprecating connotations sometimes associated with Ellington's "jungle music" of the late 1920s–early 1930s period.[28]

This use starts with the legend of Chano Pozo himself. Numerous musicians who knew Pozo sometimes elided his Cuban nationality when referring to him. "He was really African, you know," said Gillespie. "Chano

wasn't a writer, but stone African. He knew rhythm—rhythm from Africa."
George Russell, the co-composer of "Cubano-Be" and "Cubano-Bop,"
with Pozo and Gillespie, said, "Chano's concept came from Africa."[29]

Of course, the Cubans themselves more openly proclaimed the African
roots of their music, and this made it easier for American jazz musicians to
appropriate the identification with Africa for their own purposes. The references to Pozo's Africanness, while taking full account of the drummer's
relationship to the African religious survivals in Cuba,[30] also helped black
American musicians use Cuban culture to expand the African-American
cultural palette and identity. Unlike the Harlem Renaissance, where the
image of a vague, mythical Africa dominated, Pozo, as both fact and legend, allowed the beboppers who collaborated with him a way of specifying
an African dimension in jazz. Perhaps no better example of this exists than
in descriptions of his performances with the Gillespie orchestra in
1947–48. "When [Pozo] came out front," writes Dan Morgenstern, describing one such performance at the Apollo Theater, "—a powerfully built
black man stripped to the waist, bathed in purple light—lit up his oil lamp
and began to heat the skins of his congas, it was a tableau that created
tremendous anticipation. And when he had finished his beautifully timed,
unhurried, stately and dramatic preparations and began to play and chant,
he gave everything the prelude had promised, and more."[31]

The appropriation of authentic African aesthetic devices into African-
American music—even if the importation came, as it were, second hand, by
way of Cuba—was of deep artistic significance. Afro-Cuban rhythms were
welcomed as a way of reintroducing polyrhythms into the music decades after New Orleans–style jazz faded as a progressive force in jazz. And in this new
environment, the new rhythmical approach allowed more harmonic and
melodic freedom for the soloist. This fact is only hinted at in the early Afro-
Cuban jazz classics; it is more developed in a series of recordings made by
Charlie Parker a few years after the Gillespie recordings. These records serve
as a useful contrast to the Gillespie recordings, if for no other reason than the
fact that they are the first major instance in which major jazz soloists are performing on recordings of Cuban music directed by Cuban musicians.

For one thing, these records return the discourse between African-
American and Cuban musicians to the terrain of experimentalism that was
the hallmark of Chano Pozo's work with Gillespie. While the operative motif throughout this music remains the Cuban riff, the presence of Parker especially changes the relationship between the instrumental soloist and the

repeated percussive and other musical figures played by the orchestra. In part, this change is a result of Parker's extraordinary musical abilities. Nevertheless, the difference between Parker's playing and that of many other musicians (Gillespie excepted) who improvised to Cuban rhythms lies in the fact that Parker, like Gillespie, played against the rhythms, instead of allowing himself to be dominated by the music's rhythmical structure.

That was how Parker was able to take a composition like "No Noise" (performed by Machito and his orchestra) and turn it into his own personal expression. This record, originally released as two sides of a 78-rpm record, stands as a nearly laboratory example of how Parker's approach to Latin sounds was revolutionary.[32] The first side features a solo by tenor saxophonist "Flip" Phillips (Joseph Fillipelli). Phillips, whose saxophone work with Woody Herman's orchestra made him a famous jazz musician, sounds hemmed in by the rhythms in Machito's orchestra. His attempts to negotiate the rhythms sound forced and cumbersome. He pulls off a decent solo, which would be a credit to just about any musician.

But the music only comes alive when Parker arrives, playing against both the complex rhythms laid down by the four-person percussion section (maracas, bongos, congas, and timbales) and the simple, but virtually melodyless, riff played by the orchestra. This is by no means to imply that Parker paid no attention to the rhythmical idiom in which he way playing. In fact, he did just the opposite. Instead of trying to apply conventional concepts of melody to the sea of rhythm in which he found himself, Parker sounds as though he is assuming the identity of the drummers; the best way to describe his improvisation is to visualize Parker using his saxophone as if it were a drum. A comparison of each solo shows up the attempt by Phillips to attach a melody where none seems appropriate as a demonstration of the profound challenge posed by the introduction of Cuban rhythms into jazz.

Perhaps an even more intriguing section of "No Noise" than Parker's solo is the orchestral arrangement by René Hernández. Though the song itself is not a mambo (the recording's program notes call it a *montuno,* and a section of Chico O'Farrell's "Afro Cuban Suite" is titled "Mambo"), it shares with some of the most famous mambo records the disassociated sensibility denoted by musical figures, riffs, whose relationship to each other is, to say the least, unconventional. This is most evident in the second part of "No Noise," between Parker's two solos. Here is a precursor of the really revolutionary development that was just then being proposed by Cuban music: the "new" music of mambo.

One of the distinguishing characteristics of jazz has always been its use of noise as a musical element. Sometimes, the noise element was a consequence of certain instrumentation: washboards, for example. (To some ears, early recorded blues and jazz seems little more than pure noise.) Other times, noise and nonsense were used as experimental tropes—for example, in Louis Armstrong's 1928 recording "Heebie Jeebies," in which nonsense syllables were introduced in what is most assuredly the first purely jazz vocal recording.

This "noise" element was a feature of the bebop revolution. The cacophony apparent in some of the early modern jazz records must have sounded noiselike to people who were used to the more straightforward sounds of, say, Harry James; songs like "Anthropology," "Ko Ko," or "Klaunstance" probably sounded like nonsense to such fans. One contribution of bebop to modern American musical culture was the fact that it uprooted the formalist tendencies that had taken hold in U.S. popular music by the mid-1940s, reintroducing experimentalism into the more artistically inclined branches of popular music. As I have been suggesting, aspects of this experimentalism included the rise of Afro-Cuban jazz and the Cuban-American musical collaborations of the mid-1940s. But there is one more important site of this experimentalist impulse, one that produced what was probably the most popular experimental musical form of the twentieth century.

Arguments abound concerning the precise origins of the Cuban-based musical form called mambo.[33] But as far as North American music is concerned, one personality stands out: pianist, vocalist, and bandleader Dámaso Pérez-Prado, known professionally as Pérez-Prado. Pérez-Prado's records of 1949–50 are considered the main starting point of the wildly popular mambo musical and dance craze that animated U.S. popular culture during the first half of the 1950s.

Pérez-Prado created some of the most original music ever recorded on this continent; and part of its uniqueness lies in its extreme hybridity. More than any other Cuban-born musician of the midcentury, Pérez-Prado created a musical form that was a true amalgam: jazz riffs, musical figures drawn from popular music, big band–style brass music combined with airtight arrangement and stripped-down Cuban percussion, and a rare gift for the telling, dramatic musical moment were all a part of this style.

The most striking thing about Pérez-Prado's mambo is its relentless experimentalism. It is a dissonant, discordant music in which traditional melody and rhythm are subverted to a cacophony of sounds loosely arranged around a (more or less) steady rhythm characterized by a vamp figure (what Cuban musicians call the *guejeo*) most often played by the piano. It is a music with abrupt changes in voicing between the band's saxophone and trumpet sections, a music whose improvisational passages appear to have little connection to the snatches of song that introduce them. Indeed, sometimes an improvised passage may seem to come from another musical genre altogether.

"Mambo No. 5," one of Pérez-Prado's biggest hits, fits the above description. A saxophone-section riff is followed by a vocal grunt, which introduces an orchestral fanfare that is followed by another vocal sound, which is itself followed by a few bars of the rhythm section, dominated by a tambourine playing the beat. This is followed by another vocal: male voices twice shouting, "Hey!" Another grunt reintroduces the orchestral fanfare. Then an organ solo (which sounds like a 1960s rhythm and blues solo) is itself punctuated by grunts. Two notes, played by the saxophone section, are played twice. They are then joined by the trumpets, turning the two notes into a second fanfare. The earlier fanfare then is repeated, ending the song.

It is hard to call any part of "Mambo No. 5" a melody. The whole thing sounds like musical fragments united by a tambourine playing the beat and punctuated by vocal grunts. The grunts are Pérez-Prado's trademark, and they helped propel him to fame.

This whole assemblage of musical effects is described by Pérez Firmat (writing about another of Pérez-Prado's compositions, "Que rico el mambo") as "a brief, brash outburst of sound, complex in its internal harmonies and dissonances, but disquietingly uniform in texture." He describes the vocals in a typical Pérez-Prado mambo as "minimalist to the point of absurdity." When words and music meet, Pérez Firmat adds, "the result is often logoclassia, the disarticulation or fragmentation of language." The mambo "exploits language for its onomatopoeic or phonic qualities, not for its meaning-bearing capacity. Words are valued for their sound, not their sense."[34] All this was played with a rhythm that was unlike that played by traditional Afro-Cuban dance bands, either in Cuba or in North America. Pérez-Prado had a rhythmic sense that was more syncopated and had a more developed hybrid of Cuban and U.S. urban rhythm. This rhythm, stemming from the mixed influences of American jazz and traditional Cuban dance music, allowed for a freer melodic expression by the orchestra's horn sections.

The mambo created by Pérez-Prado is a direct descendent of bebop.[35] Bebop also relied on complex harmonies and dissonances; and even though many bebop compositions were reworked versions of popular songs, they subverted previously held notions of melody, so that often the songs sounded like a collection of melodic fragments and flourishes. The elevation of scat singing from the novelty status it had held since Armstrong's "Heebie Jeebies" to an honored place within the bebop pantheon also reintroduced language fragmentation into American popular art music. Like the beboppers, Pérez-Prado was influenced by all forms of modern music. For example, the influence of Stravinsky (Pérez-Prado's favorite composer, says Pérez Firmat) is evident in Pérez-Prado's penchants for abruptly terminated fanfares, polyphonic voicing, and churning, almost autonomous rhythm. And all this unfolds within the tight framework of the three-minute 78-rpm record!

Within Pérez-Prado's orchestras, noise sometimes played as big a role as nonsense. I have already alluded to the grunts and shouts that pepper his music. But there are other instances where musical growls and groans of a sound quality unheard elsewhere in the popular song–based art music of the day are dominant in mambo. In a recording of the standard "Tabu" by Peréz-Prado, the dominant trumpet solo growls in a style reminiscent of James "Bubber" Miley, the famous Ellington orchestra trumpeter.

Unlike bebop, which—though widely noted and acknowledged as an art form—achieved only fleeting popularity outside a limited (though still surprisingly large) audience for serious jazz, mambo was one of the earliest manifestations of post–World War II U.S. popular music. As much an American as a Cuban product, mambo generated an extremely popular culture craze in the early 1950s. Between 1951, the year of Peréz-Prado's first U.S. national tour, and 1954, mambo became a dominant theme in the popular culture. It was the subject of articles in major magazines on the mambo "craze," while mambo dances were taught to middle- and upper-class teens at Arthur Murray's dance academy in Manhattan.

The popularity of mambo can best be seen in the influence it had on other forms of popular music, particularly on the emergent form of rock and roll. A list of mid-1950s popular song titles containing the word "mambo" would have to include songs by Ruth Brown, The Charmers, The Crows, The Diablos, The Enchanters, Slim Gaillard (with "Mishugana Mambo"), Bill Haley and the Comets, Wynonie Harris, and Johnny Rae and the Robins (with their 1954 "Loop de Loop Mambo").[36]

To be sure, these songs were not mambos in the Pérez-Prado sense; but they do indicate something of the license given U.S. popular music by mambo. The very "weirdness" of mambo helped open the door for another strange music, and rock and roll owes something of its origins to Peréz-Prado.

The legacy of mambo can also be seen in another unlikely place. Mid-

1950s experimental jazz owes something to Pérez-Prado. This is especially true of artists like Sun Ra, who created music that was very close in structure and spirit to the 1949 hits of Pérez-Prado.[37] The Chicago bandleader's experiments with polyphony, dissonance, and syncopation and vamping, and his quest to create, within the context of a traditional jazz orchestra, a music signifying "weirdness" ("other worlds" is a favorite Sun Ra trope), are evidence that Peréz-Prado's experiments found a sympathetic ear among musicians whose explorations in the 1960s were to take jazz beyond bebop.

This is the way Afro-Cuban music entered both the mainstream of American popular culture and the mainstream of American experimental artistic culture—through mambo, this "haven for the heterogeneous,"[38] and specifically through Peréz-Prado.

Cuban music continues to be an influence on North American music as a whole, but the most famous Cuban musicians—Machito, Mario Bauza, and their disciples—are identified with a musical form that adheres to traditional Cuban forms. Peréz-Prado, on the other hand, created an experimental music that easily became a part of the mix of an emerging set of multicultural U.S. musical arts. It is in that mix that Cuban music exerts its most profound influence on U.S. music.

NOTES

1. Langston Hughes, *I Wonder as I Wander: An Autobiographical Journey* (New York: Thunder's Mouth Press, 1986), 8; Arnold Rampersad, *The Life of Langston Hughes* (New York: Oxford University Press, 1986), 1:176–81.

2. Hughes, *I Wonder as I Wander,* 8.

3. Al Rose, *Eubie Blake* (New York: Shirmer, 1979), 47.

4. Max Salazar, "Two Centuries of Charanga," *Latin Beat* (August 1994): 12–13.

5. The origins of the mode drum set are somewhat obscure and controversial, but some historians trace it to New York in 1905, and to the work of the percussionist in James Reese Europe's Society Orchestra, Buddy Gilmore, "the first jazz drummer in the modern sense of the word." See James Weldon Johnson, *Black Manhattan* (New York: Athenaeum, 1968), 122, and Samuel B. Charters and Leonard Kunstadt, *Jazz: A History of the New York Scene* (New York: Da Capo, 1962), 38.

6. For a discussion of this issue, see Gunther Schuller, *Early Jazz* (New York: Oxford University Press, 1968), 57–62.

7. Samuel B. Charters. *Jazz New Orleans, 1885–1963* (New York: Oak, 1963), 9.

8. Charters, *Jazz New Orleans,* 14–15; Charters and Kunstadt, *Jazz: A History of the New York Scene,* 53–54.

9. Charters, *Jazz New Orleans,* 43–46.

10. Louis Armstrong, "The Peanut Vendor," on *From the Original OKeh's,* vol. 4, King Jazz CD KJ149FS (recorded Dec. 23, 1930). "La Cucaracha" on Louis Armstrong, *Back in New York* (recorded October 3, 1935), MCA-1304, 1980.

11. Cugat's 1930s records are available on a number of compact disk releases. *Adios Muchachos* (Pro-Arte CDD 3406, 1992) contains several of the band's earliest hits, including "Sibony," "Babalu," "My Shawl," and "Yours," with a vocal by Dinah Shore.

12. Gustavo Pérez Firmat, *Life on the Hyphen: The Cuban-American Way* (Austin: University of Texas Press, 1994), 23–78.

13. Many of these records are collected on CD: Desi Arnaz and His Orchestra, *Babalu,* RCA 0-7863-66865-2 (recorded 1946–49).

14. LeRoi Jones (Amiri Baraka), *Blues People: Negro Music in White America* (New York: William Morrow, 1963), 180.

15. Jones, *Blues People,* 190.

16. In this regard, the number of white musicians who played on some of the earliest recordings by both Charlie Parker and John "Dizzy" Gillespie is striking: pianists Dodo Marmarosa and Al Haig, drummer Stan Levy, and guitarists Chuck Wayne and Bill DeArango are just some examples.

17. A. J. Jaffe, Ruth M. Cullen, and Thomas D. Boswell, *The Changing Demography of Spanish Americans* (New York: Academic Press, 1980), 247–48.

18. Cuba was especially suited, says Pérez Firmat, to be the source for mainstream U.S. culture's Latin tinge. "As an unofficial, (and at times official) protectorate of the United States during most of the first half of this century, Cuba was not a mysterious country. In the popular mind it was an accessible paradise, foreign and familiar at the same time." Nowhere is this mainstreaming of a type of Cuban image more eloquently demonstrated than in the film and television career of Desi Arnaz. *Life on the Hyphen,* 61–62; chaps. 1–2.

19. Max Salazar, "Afro-Cubop History," *Latin Beat,* March 1992, 20.

20. Bauza, born in 1911 in Havana, lived in New York beginning in 1931 and played with orchestra leaders Noble Sissle and Sam Wooding before joining Chick Webb's orchestra in 1933. He joined Don Redman in 1938 and Cab Calloway in 1939 before forming his own orchestra. See John Chilton, *Who's Who of Jazz: Storyville to Swing Street* (New York: Time-Life, 1978), 25.

21. An excellent description of "Caravan" (recorded in May 1937 for Columbia) is contained in Gunther Schuller, *The Swing Era: The Development of Jazz, 1930–1945* (New York: Oxford University Press, 1989), 87–88. "The Flaming Sword" was recorded October 17, 1940, for RCA Victor, and can be heard on Duke Ellington, *In a Mellotone,* RCA Victor CD RCA 0786351364-2.

22. Jordi Pujal, liner notes, Machito and His Afro-Cubans, *Cubop City,* Tambao Cuban Classics, TCD-012, 1992 (recorded 1949–50).

23. "Dizzy Gillespie's Carnegie Program," *New York Amsterdam News,* September 27, 1947, 21.

24. This concert was recorded and has been issued on a variety of labels. See Dizzy Gillespie with Al Fraser, *To BE, or not . . . to BOP* (New York: Doubleday, 1979), 509.

25. Dizzy Gillespie, *The Greatest of Dizzy Gillespie,* RCA Victor LPM-2398 (recorded December 22, 1947).

26. One poignant bit of bebop legend has it that Chano Pozo, just moments before his murder in a Harlem bar, played this song on the bar's jukebox. See Max Salazar, "Chano Pozo," *Latin Beat* (Los Angeles) parts 1–3, April–June 1993. "Manteca" was originally recorded by Gillespie's orchestra for RCA Victor on December 30, 1947.

27. Gillespie and Fraser, *To BE, or not . . . to BOP*, 321.

28. Ellington himself discusses this much-heralded aspect of his career in an alarmingly off-hand way. "During one period at the Cotton Club," he wrote in the autobiography originally published the year before he died, "much attention was paid to acts with an African setting, and to accompany these we developed what was termed 'jungle-style' jazz. (As a student of Negro history I had, in any case, a natural inclination in this direction.)" This is a far cry from the degree of self-conscious pro-African sentiment pronounced by the beboppers. Duke Ellington, *Music is My Mistress* (New York: Da Capo, 1980), 419.

29. Gillespie and Fraser, *To BE, or not . . . to BOP, 319–24.*

30. Pozo was a widely known Cuban percussionist and composer by the time he joined Gillespie's orchestra in 1947; his composition "Blen, Blen, Blen" was widely performed by Cuban orchestras, including Cugat's band. Max Salazar, in the most extensive biographical essay on Pozo available in English, refers to his membership in the African-influenced Abakwa religion. See Salazar, "Chano Pozo."

31. Dan Morgenstern, jacket notes, *The Dizzy Gillespie Orchestra at the Salle Pleyel: Paris, France,* Prestige 7818. The February 28, 1948, recording that these notes accompany gives some idea of the drama Pozo brought to the orchestra, especially in the band's rendition of the "Afro Cuban Suite."

32. "No Noise" does not appear on the CD issue of the Parker-Machito recordings, *The Original Mambo Kings.* It can be found on the Verve compilation *Afro-Cuban Jazz* (Verve VE-2-2522). "No Noise" was recorded either in December 1948 or January 1949.

33. One summary of this controversy is found in Max Salazar, "Who Invented Mambo," *Latin Beat Magazine,* October 1992, 9–12, and November 1992, 9–12.

34. Pérez Firmat, *Life on the Hyphen,* 87.

35. This is both aesthetically and chronologically true. Though Pérez-Prado had experimented in Cuba with transforming the original mambo—which early in the century had emerged from religious music to become a constituent of traditional Cuban dance music—into an autonomous form, the modern mambo did not take shape until Pérez-Prado's 1946 visit to the United States. There, it is said, U.S. bands playing modern jazz impressed him (Stan Kenton is often mentioned). The first Pérez-Prado mambos were recorded in March 1949. See Salazar, "Who Invented the Mambo," part 1 (October 1992), p. 12, and Pérez Firmat, *Life on the Hyphen,* 85.

36. Vernon Boggs, "Rhythm 'n' Blues, American Pop and Salsa: Musical Transculturation," *Latin Beat Magazine,* February 1992, 19.

37. See especially "Between Two Worlds" and "Angels and Demons at Play," from Sun Ra, *Angels and Demons at Play,* Chicago: Saturn 407 (recorded 1955–58).

38. Pérez Firmat, *Life on the Hyphen,* 80.

11

The African-American Press Greets the Cuban Revolution

VAN GOSSE

Every white man who cuffs, beats, deprives and abuses even the lowest colored person, simply because he is white and the other colored, should have seared upon his consciousness the fact that it is possible for the tables to be turned. Castro has proved it in our time.
Ralph Matthews, Baltimore *Afro-American*, 1959

The American white man claims to be upset by the latest developments in Cuba. Only the fool can expect to exploit and oppress peoples over an extended period of time without provoking animosity and resistance.
Robert F. Williams, *The Crusader*, 1959

In the nearly four decades since the victory of the 26th of July movement on January 1, 1959, black North Americans have been the only consistent source of U.S. solidarity with the Cuban Revolution. African-American politicians such as Mervyn Dymally and Jesse Jackson have not shrunk from the metaphoric or real embrace of Fidel Castro, a tradition that extends back in time to the grandfather of modern black urban politics, Representative Adam Clayton Powell Jr. As recently as December 1992, the widespread extent of this sympathy was put on display when Bill Clinton nominated Spelman College president Johnetta Cole to his postelection transition team. Cole had played a leading role throughout the 1970s and 1980s in the Venceremos Brigade, which tried to bridge the U.S. blockade on trade and travel with Cuba using delegations of ordinary citizens. Although conservatives seized upon this personal history to derail Cole's nomination, the episode highlighted the sympathies with Cuba that extended into the mainstream of black academic and institutional life.

Black America's solidarity was reinforced by the material support the Cuban government gave to black liberation struggles in Africa, starting in the early 1960s and reaching a climax during the late Cold War years. Neoconservative U.S. strategists dismissed the thousands of Cuban troops in southern Africa in the 1980s as "Soviet proxies," but the confrontation with the South African army in Angola was seen by many with a personal stake in opposing white supremacy as an exemplary instance of internationalism. African National Congress leader Nelson Mandela underlined this with his 1991 trip to the island, in the face of Cuba's international isolation following the Soviet Union's demise.

What is often forgotten now is that black American solidarity with Cuba began during the revolution's earliest days, before it dubbed itself "socialist" or "communist." One incident, of course, is still remembered with fondness or horror, depending on the source: Fidel Castro's weeklong stay in Harlem's Hotel Theresa during September 1960, when he bearded white America with a smiling ferocity, greeting its enemies, from Nikita Khrushchev to Malcolm X, as if he were the potentate at home in his domain and they the visitors.

The famous Harlem visit did not take place in a vacuum, however. It built upon a preceding wave of black interest and sympathy, largely journalistic, that began during the revolution's earliest days in power in 1959. At a point when the struggle to fulfill the amorphous promises of *Brown v. Board of Education* was at its most bitter, and Southern politics had been taken over by the White Citizens Council in most states, the sudden triumph in Cuba appeared to much of the black press as a metaphor for what needed to be done at home. This chapter examines the nuances of the black media's discovery of Castro and Cuba, both in terms of what it augured and what it tells us about black politics in the age of Eisenhower.

Despite or perhaps because of the heavy, highly favorable coverage of Castro's guerrilla struggle in the white press during 1957–58 (including the *New York Times, Time* and *Life, Look,* and even the ultraconservative *Chicago Tribune*), the major black papers ignored the issue. At most it was treated as a human-interest story, but one presumed to be of interest to black readers only to the extent that African-Americans were personally involved. Thus the only coverage of the Cuban rebellion in New York's *Amsterdam News* was two stories on black servicemen in the large group of GI's and U.S. businessmen kidnapped by Raúl Castro's rebel column in July 1958.[1] Indeed, there was considerably more coverage of Haiti than of Cuba during 1958, as the new regime of François Duvalier consolidated its hold on power.

The indifference disappeared after Fulgencio Batista's abrupt fall from power on January 1, 1959. Several of the most important black newspapers suddenly discovered Cuba via trips underwritten by the provisional government, part of its "Operation Truth" whereby hundreds of international journalists and observers were brought to the island in January 1959. The result was a flood of coverage with four recurrent themes, all with long-term implications for black America's attitude toward the Cuban Revolution:

1. the interracial character of Castro's 26th of July Revolutionary Movement, reflected in the integration of ordinary combatants and the very visible black figures in the leadership;
2. the ostentatious presence of Adam Clayton Powell Jr. in Cuba, arm-in-arm with Castro;
3. Castro's public attacks on discrimination, both in Cuba and in the United States, and his explicit calls for immediate racial equality;
4. the hypocrisy of U.S. politicians in denouncing the executions of Batista's worst henchmen as a "bloodbath," given the longterm U.S. support for the dictator, repeatedly compared by black editorialists to official tolerance for white-supremacist violence at home and abroad.

Each of these points will be explored in a chronological examination of the various kinds of black newspaper coverage. At the outset, however, it is worth underlining that what resounds most forcefully is the theme of white hypocrisy. Responses to the executions in Cuba cast in a sharp light how black America was beginning to break with the viewpoint of white liberalism at the end of the 1950s. The acceptance, in certain cases even applause, for Cuba's firing squads contrasts forcefully with the deep distaste felt by white Americans who had hailed Castro in 1957–58, but could not stomach the public shooting of war criminals, no matter what their crimes.

Unlike white America, black reporters and editorialists put the Cuban experience, including the executions, in an international context. They found a host of ready frames of reference, from "massive resistance" in Dixie to the rapidly quickening struggle in South Africa and other parts of that continent still under colonialism. The particular frame that many articulate African-Americans put upon the Cuban experience can be seen most vividly in an editorial-page cartoon from the *Amsterdam News*. Over the caption "No Tears for Africa?" a balding, Adlai Stevenson–type white liberal is shown crying buckets of tears as he stares at a newspaper headline reading "Castro to Execute 400." Behind him, unseen and ignored, looms a shirtless black man, hugging a woman and child, arm raised in remonstrance and perhaps supplication, while a whip curls around his shoulders. The hand holding the whip is labeled "South Africa," and in the background are mountains of black bodies.[2]

Not all of the black papers joined in this sudden intensive interest in Cuba and Castro. Some, including the *Atlanta Daily World,* the *Pittsburgh Courier,* and the *Philadelphia Tribune,* were content to run an occasional story and wire-service photos.[3] This choice may have reflected a more conservative politics (or location), or simply an assessment of their readers' concerns. Among the most prominent newspapers, the *Chicago Defender* exemplified a moderate response to the revolution: it did not send a reporter to Cuba, but it featured many dramatic photos and ran a January 1959 editorial with the ironic title "Triumph of a 'Lost Cause'":

> We laughed at Castro's efforts to liberate his people from a despot who had an insatiable thirst for power. The rebels' victory shows once more that right can triumph over wrong, and that tyrants possess no special immortality.
>
> Our experts, not long ago, had written off Castro's cause as a hopeless venture. He was discounted and derided as a dreamy idealist while American guns and American money extended the life of Cuba's oppressive dictatorship.
>
> We have no right to rejoice with the liberators in their ecstatic hour of glory. It is a privilege reserved to those who believe in the cause of freedom everywhere. Instead we should bow our heads in shame, drop to our knees and repent. An open admission of our sins may be the beginning of our conversion to the fundamental creed of enlightened democracy.[4]

Most clearly pro-Castro among the black newspapers and magazines were the Baltimore-based *Afro-American* (with four regional editions the largest-circulation black newspaper in the country), the already mentioned *Amsterdam News,* and the weekly magazine *Jet.*

The *Afro-American*'s first response to the Cuban revolutionary triumph was to highlight the plight of a group of black Virginia teachers trapped in Havana when Batista fell and chaos descended.[5] Its tone soon changed. By the next week, the *Afro* was pointing out that "but a short while ago" Batista had been hailed as a liberator by black or mulatto Cubans, and had "inspired the same type of interest throughout the darker world that the emergence of Christophe must have caused when he smashed the armies of Napoleon." Noting that now Castro was appealing to Cuba's nonwhite population, whose interests Batista had betrayed (a common theme), the *Afro* editorialist suggested that, "From where we sit it looks like the colored folk are coming into their own again." Then, after quoting Che Guevara's bitter comments on the U.S. government's having supplied Batista with bombs he used against his own citizenry, the writer concluded, "Oops! Looks like we picked the wrong side again."[6]

His interest clearly whetted by the stateside controversy over whether this was a revolution worth supporting, *Afro-American* editor Clifford Mackay flew to Cuba to sample the revolutionary intoxication first-hand, initiating a series of *cinéma vérité*–style travelogues that continued until late February. Mackay himself played a starring role as a stand-in for his black Yankee readers. Indeed, the January 24 issue focused simply on the fact that he had gone to Cuba, with a front-page photo of the intrepid editor standing in the island sun and grinning. Then, on January 31, Mackay wrote as if from Adam Clayton Powell's side, describing in considerable detail the peripatetic congressman's statements and doings in Cuba, and showing him in intimate conference with Fidel during their joint appearance before a Havana crowd estimated at one million. Citing Powell's baiting on the floor of Congress by the conservative Republicans Gordon Scherer of Ohio and William Springer of Illinois, Mackay also described the widespread scorn among Cubans for U.S. politicians who denounced Castro's executions but showed little concern for white terror at home.

That Mackay was genuinely affected by his experience is best indicated by one headline in that January 31 issue: "FANTASTIC! Inside Cuba—'Will Eliminate Discrimination'" (a quote from Castro himself). Indeed, a sense of euphoria runs through his writing as he speaks of the thousands of "bearded dark-skinned Cubans" in the 26th of July movement, striving "shoulder to shoulder with their lighter brothers," and admiringly quotes Castro's pledge of a "real democracy, not the synthetic kind." Mackay found nothing objectionable about the most notorious of the war-crimes trials, when Major Jesús Sosa Blanco was tried in a huge stadium under bright lights (provoking horror in much of the U.S. press and in Congress), since Sosa was being shot for the "bloody slaughter of nine members of colored Castillo family," as a photo caption put it.[7]

The *Afro*'s coverage climaxed with its February 7 issue, much of which was devoted to happenings great and small on the island. A full-page photo spread focused on Havana vividly emphasized Cuba's blackness and especially the legacy of Antonio Maceo. The issue also featured Mackay's detailed account of everything from local prices for toothpaste, liquor, and cars to the visual qualities of Cuban women. An accompanying article in that week's *Afro Magazine* profiled "Castro's Right Hand Man," a black Cuban politician named Gabino Ulacia who suggested that the notorious segregationist and Arkansas governor Orval Faubus come to Cuba: "He get good example of democracy. Maybe he stop making war on children." Equally noteworthy in political terms, moreover, was that week's musings by the *Afro*'s featured political columnist, Ralph Matthews. Noting his "relish" at the "rather gory accounts" of the executions, Matthews made explicit the relevance of Cuba for North American Negroes who had suffered too long in silence: "Every white man who cuffs, beats, deprives and abuses even the lowest colored person, simply because he is white and the other colored, should have seared upon his consciousness the fact that it is possible for the tables to be turned. Castro has proved it in our time." For him, Castro was succeeding where the victors in the American Civil War had signally failed:

Not one traitor was strung up and the whole nation has been made a laughing stock because the descendants of these scalawags have never laid down their arms, observed the rules of the country, admitted defeat or ceased to prosecute the rebellion at any time.

. . . What a price we have paid for this folly! A divided nation, a breeding ground for men like Faubus, Almond, Eastland and their ilk who make a shamble of constitutional law and mockery of democracy.

A few good tomb stones distributed on a states rights basis would have spared us all this.[8]

One might expect that Matthews was an exceptional voice, noteworthy only by comparison with the absence of any equivalent white enthusiasm for executions. However, a look at several other key black publications reveals a strikingly similar tone concerning not only the 26th of July's firing squads but other features of the revolution as well.

Like the *Afro-American,* New York's *Amsterdam News* at first responded to the revolutionary victory quizzically, focusing mainly on the local connection: in this case, Congressman Powell of Harlem, whom the *News* generally did not favor. Various stories in January 1959 noted Powell's claim to have provided key support to the rebels with House of Representatives floor speeches in March 1958 that exposed and led to a cutoff of military aid to Batista by the Eisenhower administration. History bears out the importance of Powell's role in this case, though the *News* reported rather nastily in a front-page news article that Powell was "Attempting to take some part of the credit of the Castro overthrow of the Batista government."[9]

The rapid shift to all-out fervor and blanket coverage came, as elsewhere, when black journalists went to see for themselves; a subhead on the front page of the January 24, 1959, issue announced: "Amsterdam News in Cuba!" In this case, not one but two *News*-men went to the island: M. A. Lockhart, the paper's publicity director, and John Young III. The former set the new, "you are there" tone with the portentous lead of his first article: "Officials of the Fidel Castro Cuban government assured me here today that there will absolutely be no toleration of racial discrimination in Cuba at any level under Castro."[10]

John Young's sensational pieces in the next three issues of the *News* overshadowed Lockhart's rather stately style. Even now, the photo on the top left edge of the January 31, 1959, front page remains shocking: in terrible close-up, a handsome, mustachioed young Cuban, eyes closed, swings at the end of a thick rope. The caption beneath blares a three-word message, "WHY CASTRO KILLS." This almost pornographic image, its meaning for this audience made specially piquant by the dead man's evident whiteness, was in fact a "teaser" for the featured story by Young just below, "Why Castro Can't Stop Cuba's Mass Killings." An even more brutal montage of photos depicting Batista's repression followed on an inside page: corpses hog-tied by the roadside; one of Batista's soldiers grinning, "torch in hand, while a dead prisoner burns"; the living displaying their ghastly stigmata; another head-shot of a corpse, with marks of torture stitched across face and neck. Young's point was in fact neither terribly original nor at all outlandish. He suggested that the executions, "when viewed with this background of atrocities," were strictly necessary in Cuban terms: "The Revolutionary Army and the whole population of Cuba, without speaking a word to each other, have decided that Batista and his leaders must never again rise to power. They believe that death—and only death— of the leaders and potential leaders can make this certain, certain, at least, in their time." Young then suggested that "We Americans, including the people of Harlem, must bear some of Castro's responsibility" for the mass shootings since "we allowed our Government to aid Batista"; he added that "the U.S. Government has no excuse . . . it could have stopped these atrocities years ago." He concluded this piece with the hope that the "violent remedy for a sick Cuba" does "not kill the patient."[11]

By the next week any such equivocation was dispelled. Like Mackay, Young sharpened his focus on "The Negro in Castro's Cuba," and in the guise of front-line reporting, promulgated what amounted to a manifesto for internationalizing the civil rights struggle. Asserting at the outset that "The American Negro's strong interest in Cuba today is but further proof of his ever-widening interest in the Third Front of freedom fighting," he went on to announce that

It is a mark of his destiny that in the present world struggle between Russia and the United States for friendship of Colored Peoples, the mantle of leadership has fallen upon the shoulders of the American Negro. This leadership has made him increasingly sensitive to injustice wherever it may occur in the world.

It logically follows, therefore, that Cuba, with a great Negro population, should draw the active interest that has been manifested in Harlem during the present crisis.

Then, too, the Batista injustices of lynching and police state are so remindful of the identical practices now prevalent against the Negro in the South.

Young then quoted Castro's declaration on January 22, before a large group of international journalists, that "As Revolutionaries and idealists, we are against discrimination in any form." Young commented, "One look at the army men guarding Castro gave the impression that he really meant what he said. Probably no army on earth is as integrated as that of Cuba's Revolutionary Army."

In all of this Young was largely repeating in a more politically articulate fashion the observations made at this same time by others, already cited here. But at the end of this article, he returned to the theme of his title ("The Negro in Castro's Cuba") and made explicit the peculiar sense that many American blacks seemed to have that Castroism was going to settle some long unbalanced accounts, in Cuba first, and vicariously for many others as well. Predicting that "the future looks bright" for people of color on the island, he gave the bluntest reason for optimism available then or later (and perhaps the most accurate): "Because most of the trained men who ran all the key jobs in Cuba are either executed, in jail or in exile."[12]

Positive as the coverage by the *Amsterdam News* was to this point, its solidarity became even more direct in the issue of February 14, 1959. Under the headline "Castro's Cuba Needs U.S. Help," John Young III assayed the significance of the "wide and sympathetic coverage given to the Cuban revolution by the Negro newspapers and magazines," detailing what he saw as the immediate, mainly economic needs of Castro's provisional government. He climaxed this final article written from Havana with what amounted to a premature call for a solidarity organization, much like what emerged a year later as the Fair Play for Cuba Committee:

> Today, there is an air of freedom about in Havana, that is heady atmosphere [*sic*] for those who detest oppression.
>
> That is why our press and other media ought to voluntarily make a contribution to Cuba's future, by urging tourists to go there now. This would constitute a sort of lend-lease goodwill towards a neighbor that needs our help and encouragement.
>
> We citizens of the U.S. can help Cuba. At this time, there is an opportunity for some of our most responsible and courageous citizens to set up a new committee for Cuban-American friendship. . . .
>
> Those Americans who now hesitate to embrace Castro and his new Cuba because of the executions might do well to recall that it was our own Thomas Jefferson who wrote:
>
> "The tree of liberty must be refreshed from time to time with the blood of patriots and tyrants!"[13]

There is little question that Young was not exaggerating when he described "wide and sympathetic coverage" in the American black press, even if not all of the major black papers went as far as the *Amsterdam News* or the *Afro-American*. *Jet*, the weekly news-and-entertainment magazine of black life, echoed the themes already made familiar. Between human-interest stories (it put a smiling black woman officer in the rebel army, Gladys Trava, on its February 19, 1959, cover), it reported the exciting prospects for black Cubans under the new regime:

> During the days of rugged guerrilla fighting between the forces of Cuban Dictator Fulgencio Batista and the makeshift army of Fidel Castro, a new type of Democracy had been born. The age-old practice of discrimination had fallen in the wake of necessity, and the Castro forces had been completely integrated both in race, creed and color.
>
> Last week, hosting 372 reporters for Operation Truth, Castro declared that his new Cuba would follow the same non-discrimination practice. Cubans had good reason to believe him.

Interestingly, this piece went on to devote most of its space to discussing which of the *batistianos* facing imprisonment or death were black, and how Batista had "gained some sympathy among Negro intellectuals because his mother was colored, and because he once opened the National Hotel to house Haiti's ex-President Paul Magloire." It pointed out that, nonetheless, "the workers (most of Cuba's estimated three million Negroes fall into that category) were chiefly among victims of the Batista regime," citing Gabino Ulacia (here his name was spelled "Bagino") as a prime example, and concluding that "there was a hope among Negroes that indeed, the new order of integration would prevail, and that the hard-won Castro victory would bring them new status and a new way of life in strife-torn Cuba." A striking example of the race consciousness of black journalism at this time is the sidebar feature, titled "Black Bravery," that ran right under the above-quoted story; a sequence of four photos showed the execution by firing squad of black lieutenant Enrique Despaigne, who had been found guilty of killing fifty-three Cuban civilians. Like Mackay, Lockhart, Young, and others, Simeon Booker of *Jet*, author of all these pieces, visited Cuba as part of Operation Truth.[14] As late as April 1959, *Jet* provided a rundown of how "Negro Cubans Benefit From Sweeping Castro Reforms," citing Castro's economic plans to benefit the very poor and his declaration that there was no such thing as a "pure Caucasian" and speaking with scorn of those who feared Castro's "radicalism."[15] The reader, having noted the intensity of the coverage described in the preceding pages, may be surprised to discover that after the first two months of 1959, the flood of interest in the U.S. black press slowed to a trickle. Despite the continued controversy over Cuba, very few stories appeared until January 1960, when a group of African-Americans returned from a Christmas and New Year's Eve junket sponsored by the Cuban government.

Why this sudden fall-off in coverage? After all, there is no reason to think that black America suddenly lost interest in Cuba's revolution. One must look instead to the episodic character of any foreign reportage in the black press; lacking the space and resources for comprehensive attention to foreign matters, it had largely taken advantage of the Cubans' largesse. Even more important, however, were the many competing demands for space—the profusion of newsworthy crises affecting black citizens of the United States during that year.

Always central in terms of political news, of course, was the frustrating effort to make any progress in desegregating the southern states, against the Dixiecrats' unyielding determination to protect white privilege. One good example of how the fight below the Mason-Dixon line could easily push Cuban news to the side is the absence of black newspaper coverage of Fidel Castro's triumphal visit to the States in late April 1959. At first glance, this absence seemed to signal real political estrangement. Some black papers did run a syndicated story on how "Castro Dodged Color Questions" during his trip, focusing on the arrest of Gabino Ulacia, the same "top Negro political leader" earlier profiled in the *Afro-American*.[16] But Castro's visit coincided with the killing of Mack Charles Parker in Poplarville, Mississippi, perhaps the last of the old-style lynchings whereby a black prisoner was simply taken from jail during the night and murdered; and it seems clear that the Cuban leader's visit simply paled by contrast with this horrifying event. In any case, Fidel made no special effort to reach out to black America on this particular visit. He spoke to students at Harvard and Princeton but not at Howard or some other historically black college campus, and his trip uptown to Harlem would wait for another eighteen months, during which U.S.-Cuban relations drastically worsened.

Starting in September 1959, following Castro's attempt that spring to influence mainstream American public opinion by personal suasion, the Cuban Tourist Commission developed a new strategy for appealing to black America, which they evidently regarded as their best potential base of support in the United States. Late in the year M. A. Lockhart left the *Amsterdam News* and joined a public-relations firm that included former heavyweight boxing champion Joe Louis as a partner and spokesman. Working through their prior relationship with Lockhart, the Cubans contracted with this firm to have Louis promote a major campaign of black tourism in Cuba. The first stage of this campaign, at the end of 1959, was a huge, all-expenses-paid Christmas trip to Cuba by a delegation of prominent black Americans. Louis and Lockhart were asked to focus on signing up other African-American sports celebrities, including Jackie Robinson,

Roy Campanella, and Willie Mays. In the end, none of these famous athletes went to Cuba that Christmas other than Louis, but seventy-two other black U.S. citizens did, and prominent among them were the publishers of several black newspapers, including the *Chicago Defender,* the *Cleveland Call and Post,* and the *Philadelphia Tribune.*

As the counsel of the Senate Internal Security Subcommittee put it, interrogating one of Lockhart's partners eighteen months later, this "was an outstanding public relations stroke." This impressive group was photographed and televised in the United States, and shown enjoying a lavish New Year's Eve at the Havana Hilton with Fidel, with Joe Louis at the center. (*Jet* ran a photograph of Fidel looking deferentially at a smiling Louis with the caption "Two Strong Men.")[17] Upon their return, the newspaper owners filled their papers with eyewitness reports, such as those that ran in every issue of the twice-weekly *Philadelphia Tribune* between January 2 and 16, 1960.

Some may see this final junket as evidence that the interest of black journalists in Cuba was essentially opportunistic, and proof that they possessed little ideological consistency and were easily swayed by free trips and the "insider" treatment rarely if ever available in the United States. There may be an element of truth in this suspicion. Only a few black reporters, such as John Young III and later William Worthy (affiliated with the *Afro-American*), seemed to have a strong perspective on the possible relevance of Cuba's revolutionary process outside of Cuba. (Worthy was prosecuted by the Kennedy administration for his illegal trips to the island after the January 1961 travel ban was imposed.) Most of the others were simply attracted to Castro's iconoclastic celebrity and the egalitarian tone of the 26th of July movement.

But if the appeal of Castro to black journalists transcended formal politics, if he was to them as much a cultural as a political hero, then these writers (and their editors and publishers) were only responding to grassroots pro-Castro sentiments in urban black communities across the United States. This is the real import of the favorable coverage of the Cuban Revolution in the North American black press during 1959, and ever since. The desire to represent the Cubans' point of view, implicitly challenging the perspective of the white press, reflected an impulse toward Third World solidarity that in 1959, at the height of the decolonization drive in Africa and elsewhere, ran deep in black America. Cuba and Castro brought that impulse much closer to home, and in so doing indicated the ways in which the nascent anti-imperialism of African-Americans would surface powerfully a few years later, during the era of "Black Power," the Black Panther Party, and the multiracial movement against the war in Vietnam.

NOTES

1. See "Marine Reveals How Cubans Kidnapped Him," *Amsterdam News,* August 2, 1958, 1, concerning Private First Class Joseph Anderson. This article did highlight Anderson's comment that "Those rebels got a lot of heart. They are not fighting for money," a common theme in all of the American press coverage of this hostage taking. See also the follow-up story on August 9, 1958, about another black New Yorker, Navy Seabee Albert Matthews.

2. *Amsterdam News,* January 24, 1959. The accompanying editorial was titled "Inconsistent," and began thus: "We think that United States officials should keep their hands off, and their mouths shut on the activities of Fidel Castro in Cuba. We don't know all the facts about Castro and Batista (and no one else in the United States does either, for that matter). But if facts are worth official notice, they are worthy of consistency. And when United States officials criticize Castro for shooting down enemies of his government, it is not being consistent with its past attitude on such things." The editorial then went on to compare congressional outrage regarding Cuba to U.S. silence regarding the fact that "thirty leaders of the African National Congress were to go on trial for their lives Monday, January 19, for 'treason.'"

3. See "Powell Demands U.S. Recognize Castro's Regime," *Pittsburgh Courier,* January 10, 1959, as well as a photo with the caption "Scenes from Castro Triumph," January 17, 1959; and "Dictator Batista, Part Negro, Despised Dark-Skinned Cubans," *Philadelphia Tribune,* January 6, 1959. (Editor John A. Saunder recalled an earlier junket to the island and concluded that "Fidel Castro, the new Cuban strong man, has to be better than Batista was, as far as dark-skinned Cubans are concerned. For if he is any worse, the darker peoples of Cuba will be in for partial serfdom and slavery all over again, and Castro may find himself where Batista is now."). Also see the *Atlanta Daily World,* January 3 and 4, 1959, with wire-service photos and stories on the front page, including a dramatic snap of Che Guevara resting among his troops.

4. *Chicago Defender,* January 17, 1959. Also see the January 31 issue for a large closeup photo of Castro and Powell talking.

5. See front-page story, "'Bombing, Gunfire All Around Us,'" *Afro-American,* January 10, 1959.

6. *Afro-American,* January 17, 1959.

7. Ibid., January 31, 1959.

8. Matthews quotes from the *Afro-American,* February 7, 1959. For the rest of the month, Mackay continued to file his "Inside Castro's Cuba" reports, mixing photos and mini-biographies of black members at all levels of the 26th of July movement with comments on roomservice prices in the February 14 issue; more of the same appeared on February 21. After March, however, the *Afro's* coverage dropped off very sharply, as is discussed below.

9. *Amsterdam News,* January 10, 1959. Also see a January 17, 1959, article titled "Powell Aide Was Castro Fighter," focusing on Arnold Johnson, a Cuban-born insurance underwriter in Harlem who was a longtime associate of the minister-politician. (See Van Gosse, *Where the Boys Are: Cuba, Cold War America and the Making of a New Left* [London: Verso, 1993], 78–79, for a longer discussion of Powell and Johnson, and the latter's reported ties to American Communists.)

10. *Amsterdam News,* January 24, 1959. Lockhart may have been imitating the style of the famous *New York Times* correspondent Herbert L. Matthews in his 1957–58 pieces from rebel Cuba, which had helped make Fidel Castro one of the most famous fugitives in the world. The rest of this first-person article focused on the arrival of Powell and his tumultuous press conference defending Castro to the U.S. and world press, as well as Lockhart's own opinions and interactions with Cuban officials and others. The unstated subtext, of course, was that here was one front-burner story where black journalists and politicians were not relegated to the sidelines but given pride of place. As Lockhart repeatedly reminded his readers, "this reporter has been given a front row seat" at the upcoming trials, the ostensible reason why he and Mackay, along with nearly four hundred other international journalists, had accepted the provisional government's offer of an expense-paid trip to the island.

11. All quotations from the *Amsterdam News,* January 31, 1959.

12. All quotations from the *Amsterdam News,* February 7, 1959. Reinforcing Young's point, in this same issue M. A. Lockhart published his own conclusions as "Observation in Cuba." After describing in pedantic detail his personal schedule, including an airline flight to Venezuela with Castro ("served elegantly by two pretty stewardesses, one a Negro girl and I wonder whether she would qualify for a job with an American airline"), Lockhart declared that, "There is one thing of which I am sure, the Citizens of Cuba feel a new freedom that they have not felt before and are behind the new government of Senor Castro." He then stressed that "I personally experienced no discrimination whatsoever and was told by an official of the hotel, by the new tourists' commissioner and others that the American Negro would be welcomed to Cuba both as a tourist and a businessman." This latter statement may seem like a throwaway, but at a time when Miami was strictly segregated, it was a more radical declaration than any of Fidel's grand statements about brotherhood.

13. *Amsterdam News,* February 14, 1959.

14. See *Jet,* February 5, 1959, "Integration the New Order Declares Cuba's Fidel Castro"; also the editorial "Governor Bans Jim Crow in Cuban Province," February 12, 1959.

15. *Jet,* April 16, 1959.

16. See *Amsterdam News,* May 9, 1959. Otherwise the *News* ran a curious little boxed story on its May 2 front page on how Castro and Adam Clayton Powell Jr. had "missed" each other, letting its readers surmise why these two former friends had not met while Castro was in New York. Just above was a snapshot of Fidel at a huge rally in Central Park, with "Harlem businessman" Arnold Johnson peering over his shoulder. The *Afro-American* ran a photo on its April 25, 1959, front page of Castro kneeling and talking to two black children in Washington, D.C.'s Meridien Hill Park; one of them is tugging on the Cuban pre-

mier's beard. On May 6, 1959, the *Afro's* UN correspondent Charles P. Howard contributed a favorable report on Castro's appearance before the United Nations Correspondents Association. Compared to the voluminous and detailed reports in the white press of Castro's every move, this is very scant coverage.

17. *Jet,* January 21, 1960; also see Gosse, *Where the Boys Are.*

Epilogue

DIGNA CASTAÑEDA FUERTES

When I was young, my father played *la bolita*. Poverty in the psuedo-republic caused everyone to play the *bolita* in the hope of getting a bit more money to take care of the family. My father, like Lisa Brock's grandmother, did win at times. And on one occasion he won pretty big, but that was a long time before the revolution and he is now passed. What is interesting, though, is that I had not thought about this activity in the context of my father until Brock and I began talking about the linkages between African-Americans and Cubans. In fact, although my work has long focused on slavery in the Caribbean, I had not really thought about race and pan-African ties after slavery until I chaired a panel at which Brock presented a paper critiquing Carlos Moore's book *Castro, the Blacks, and Africa*.[1] Moore attacked the Cuban revolution for being starkly racist, and Brock challenged his style and the method by which he reached his conclusions. While Brock and I agreed that Moore's work appeared disingenuous and unscholarly, Brock pointed out that African-Americans had long supported Cuba, and Moore's book might have a negative impact on that support. She also criticized Cuban revolutionary scholars for not having written more on race, leaving someone like Moore such an open arena. While all of this interested me, I did not completely agree for I felt that the revolution had done tremendous things for black Cubans; and I was not quite sure what Brock wanted us to do. Cuban scholars are proud of our African heritage and many of us are in fact working on the African contributions to Cuba.

I was somewhat taken aback, but pleased, when Brock asked if I would co-edit this book and solicit essays from Cuban scholars. She felt it needed scholars with Cuban perspectives able to draw upon Cuban-based documents, archives, and sensibilities. It became clear that we did not want an anthology that simply put black Cuban and black North American histories side by side but rather one in which each chapter addressed a nexus of interchange. The topic was fresh, and my hope was that it would contribute to better relations between North Americans and Cubans and encourage a deeper understanding of racism and its different manifestations.

As the authors of this book began submitting their essays, and I began to read them, my memory was jogged in ways that I never expected. My memories about the U.S. presence in Cuba before 1959 and my view of race in general grew sharper with this project. For instance, I remember a scene from the documentary *Ahora* (Now) by the filmmaker Santiago Alvarez, which portrayed the brutality suffered by American civil rights activists in the southern United States in the 1950s and 1960s. I was a young women, and I remember being completely astonished by it. I also recalled one day in the 1950s when I happened to be walking on a Havana street; suddenly, and seemingly out of nowhere, a group of U.S. Marines appeared, marching down the street. It was scary enough for a young black Cuban women to see this foreign force, but I was also startled to see that they were totally racially divided; black troops marched on one side and whites on the other. I had never seen Cuban people so starkly separated like that. In fact, I spent my childhood and adolescence among whites and blacks on a rural farm, and I never perceived racial segregation in that way.

This does not mean that racism did not exist in Cuba, but during that time segregation was more in evidence at the higher levels of the government and among the elite, who liked to imitate the racial norms of North Americans. As a result, they developed white neighborhoods and limited the access of blacks to higher education and employment. They denied jobs to us in banks, department stores, universities, public offices, public transportation, and also even in some low-wage jobs such as domestic work. (There were enough poor white Cubans to fill the demand for domestics.) As a result of economic discrimination, blacks were also discriminated against socially. There were social clubs and private recreation societies exclusively for upper-class whites. And even though working class and poor whites were not necessarily residentially segregated, many were socially segregated. Blacks and mulattos developed their own organizations: some were social and cultural, some were religious, and some were mutual-aid societies.

Racism remained substantially unchanged during the first fifty-seven years of the republic, in spite of antiracist demands by Cuban blacks and progressives. From the triumph of the revolution in 1959, we began to eliminate the obstacles limiting the mobility of the stigmatized sectors. The revolution began to implement measures that favored all members of the society without distinction of class, sex, race, or religion. In the process the children of illiterates became literate. Later, a plan was created for all to continue their secondary education. The schools were nationalized, and from that moment all education was free. In addition, children were given free meals, books, and uniforms. Similarly, university education was free, and new employment opportunities were created especially for women and blacks. Similarly, newly literate women and blacks were able to attend night schools to pursue primary, secondary, and university educations. The university offered courses for workers in order that they could finish their study and still work. In this way, Cuba became a gigantic school for children, youths, and adults, and all studied together in the same schools without the distinction of race. Opportunities for jobs and economic security were open to all. I myself am a product of that time of hope and prosperity.

In spite of great progress at the institutional level, some Cubans continue to harbor racial prejudices; yet it has been difficult for them to establish a power base in revolutionary Cuban. However, since the fall of the socialist countries in eastern Europe, Cubans have found themselves in a tremendous crisis, and this crisis constitutes a threat to the achievements of the Cuban social project. Cuba's need to become part of the international economic system has worked against the established social achievements, bringing such unwelcome effects as increased racism around tourism and foreign-owned industry and a promotion of individualism, all creating new challenges that we must face.

In this historical moment, we hope that this book, by looking into our common past, will help us negotiate a common future. The largely white counterrevolutionary Cuban population in Miami (who have hostile relations with blacks in that city), the U.S. blockade and propaganda campaign against our nation, and our people's inability to focus on much else other than our crisis has led many in both communities to forget and neglect our history of fraternal ties. Yet in this era of greater globalization of multinational corporate ownership and production, we need knowledge of those ties even more. It seems essential that a body of scholarship be generated away from its customary national context and toward a more crosscultual and transnational frame.

Our book, of course, is only a humble beginning. *Between Race and Empire* in fact stimulates more questions than it answers, and we are aware of its weaknesses and its limitations. More work is clearly needed in the areas of women, gender, and sexual orientation, and we hope others will take this anthology as a challenge. Yet there is a rich history of hitherto unknown linkages wonderfully examined and analyzed throughout the essays included in this collection. That most of the authors found themselves unable to write about relations without applying some level of comparative analysis of race, identity, class, nationality, and gender is also telling. It shows that any examination of African-American and Cuban ties demands a critical theoretical eye, further emphasizing the multiple reasons for doing what Lisa Brock has called "international history from below."[2] What can studying relations across cultures and beyond national borders tell us about blackness, whiteness, working-class status, and gender? What do we discover about each set of people as distinct from, and similar to, the other as we begin to unravel such ties? Do we develop paradigms along the way that are then applicable to the study of other peoples, places, and times?

Our answer to this final question is that we surely hope so. But we also desire something else—that our collaboration might be an example. It became clear that, while difficult, international collaboration was an important part of the entire project. We did what we were studying; we engaged in relations as we evoked them. This gave the book a sense of wholeness that is hard to put into words. Although ours is a different time and a different political setting, co-editing this book made us feel issues that must have come up in past relations, such as language and cultural conflicts, economic differences, unequal levels of infrastucture development, and so forth. Yet that small link between my father, Lisa's grandmother, and *la bolita* proves how similar people's lives actually were, a fact that no doubt fostered the kinds of relations examined in these essays. That both family members played the numbers also illustrates how two sets of people not in state power employed similar survival and empowerment strategies. They disrupted elite hegemony over the totality of their economic lives, and created their own buoyant underground economy within their own communities. Moreover, while numbers bankers, sometimes employing thousands of people, could become individually rich, the *bolita* and the numbers were open to a wide range of people, allowing thousands to play. Risking only a nickel or dime, players might win anywhere from ten or twenty dollars to a few hundred dollars many times in their lives. Winners would pay some bills, help a friend or family member, or save for some long-term project. My education funds were begun from *la bolita,* just as Lisa's were from the numbers. I would not have thought this important had I not pursued this work. Interestingly, it is exactly this kind of site, where oppressed people empower themselves, that Melina Pappademos argues should be the focus of comparative work in the African diaspora.[3] In doing that, she argues, we shift the paradigm from comparative race relations from the top down to comparative antiracist struggles from the people up.

NOTES

1. Carlos Moore, *Castro, the Blacks, and Africa* (Los Angeles: Center for African Studies, UCLA Press, 1988).

2. Lisa Brock, "Questioning the Diaspora: Hegemony, Black Intellectuals, and Doing International History from Below," *Issue: A Journal of Opinion* 24, no. 2 (1996): 9–12.

3. Melina Pappademos, "Romancing the Stone: Academe's Elusive Template for African Diaspora Studies," in ibid., 38–49.

ABOUT THE EDITORS AND CONTRIBUTORS

Editors

Lisa Brock is associate professor of African history and diaspora studies at the School of the Art Institute of Chicago. She is on the editorial collective of the journal *Radical History Review* and is the Latin American liaison of the Pan African Caucus of the African Studies Association. Her articles on African-Americans and Cubans have appeared in *Cuban Studies, Contributions in Black Studies, Issue: A Journal of Opinion,* and *Temas: Cultura, Ideología, Sociedad.* Her book on comparative black struggle in U.S. and Cuban history is forthcoming.

Digna Castañeda Fuertes is professor of Caribbean studies in the Department of History and Philosophy at the University of Havana. Her book *The Haitian Revolution: 1794–1804* was published in 1992, and her numerous articles on slavery and women have appeared in *Bohemia, Journal of Caribbean Studies,* and *Casa de las Américas.*

Contributors

Bijan Bayne is a freelance sports historian, journalist, and cultural critic who resides in Washington, D.C. His articles on baseball, basketball, and black popular culture have appeared in the *Metro Chronicle, Washingtonian,* and *Common Boundary.* He is currently working on a book entitled "Baseball Spoken Here," which examines Latin American and Caribbean baseball players in the United States.

Jualynne E. Dodson is associate professor in the Departments of Ethnic Studies and Religious Studies at the University of Colorado at Boulder. Her articles have appeared in *The Encyclopedia of African American Culture and History* and *Women and Religion in History.*

Keith Ellis is a professor in the Department of Spanish and Portuguese at the University of Toronto. He is a member of the editorial boards of the

Revista Canadiense de Estudios Hispánicos and the University of Toronto Romance series. He has published four books on Nicolás Guillén and is a fellow of the Royal Society of Canada and an honorary member of the Union of Writers and Artists of Cuba.

Tomás Fernández Robaina is a senior researcher at the José Martí National Library in Havana, Cuba, and lectures at the University of Havana. He has published extensively on the subject of Afro-Cubans and is considered the primary bibliographer of sources about blacks in Cuba. One of his most recent books is *El negro en Cuba, 1902–1958* (1993).

Carmen Gómez García is the senior director of Cuba's National Archive in Havana. She is also a professor at the University of Havana in the Department of History and Philosophy. Her articles on socialism, intellectuals, and race have appeared in the *Revista Cubana de Ciencias Sociales* and *Granma*. Her book *Carlos Baliño, el primer pensador marxista cubano* was published in 1985.

Van Gosse is currently co-chair of the editorial collective of the *Radical History Review* and has taught at Rutgers University, George Mason University, and Wellesley College. His articles have appeared in the *Radical History Review* and elsewhere. His most recent book is *Where the Boys Are: Cuba, Cold War America and the Making of a New Left* (1993).

David J. Hellwig is a professor in the Department of History at Saint Cloud State University. He has published numerous works on the African-American press and its relationship with black peoples in the Americas. He is the editor of *African-American Reflections on Brazil's Racial Paradise* (1992).

Geoffrey Jacques is a culture critic, journalist, essayist, and editor who resides in New York City. He has worked as an organizer for the American Federation of Musicians Local 802, and his articles on art and culture have appeared in *Freedomways, NKA: Journal of Contemporary African Art,* and *Race and Reason.* His two books are *Hunger and Other Poems* and *The African-American Experience.*

Nancy Raquel Mirabal is an assistant professor in the Department of La Raza Studies at San Francisco State University. She has published widely on

Cubans in the United States. Her most recent work, "Más Que Negro: José Martí and the Politics of Unity," appeared in *José Martí in the United States: The Florida Experience,* edited by Louis Pérez Jr. (1995).

Carmen Montejo Arrechea was a senior researcher at the Centro de Investigadores de la Cultura Cubana in Havana, Cuba. In 1992 her study of educational and recreational societies of free persons of color in colonial Cuba won the prestigious Premio Internacional de Ensayo Gonzalo Aguirre Beltrán (Veracruz, Mexico) for the best original manuscript in the Americas that year.

Rosalie Schwartz taught Latin American history at several southern California universities. She retired in 1996 and now devotes herself to research and writing. Her latest book is *Pleasure Island: Tourism and Temptation in Cuba* (1997). Other books include *Across the Rio to Freedom* (1975) and *Lawless Liberators: Political Banditry and Cuban Independence* (1989).

INDEX

Note: all photographs (following page 128) referenced below appear as italicized numbers.